CISSP

6th Edition

by Lawrence C. Miller and Peter H. Gregory

for **dummies**®

A Wiley Brand

CISSP For Dummies®, 6th Edition

Published by: **John Wiley & Sons, Inc.**, 111 River Street, Hoboken, NJ 07030-5774, www.wiley.com

Copyright © 2018 by John Wiley & Sons, Inc., Hoboken, New Jersey

Published simultaneously in Canada

No part of this publication may be reproduced, stored in a retrieval system or transmitted in any form or by any means, electronic, mechanical, photocopying, recording, scanning or otherwise, except as permitted under Sections 107 or 108 of the 1976 United States Copyright Act, without the prior written permission of the Publisher. Requests to the Publisher for permission should be addressed to the Permissions Department, John Wiley & Sons, Inc., 111 River Street, Hoboken, NJ 07030, (201) 748-6011, fax (201) 748-6008, or online at http://www.wiley.com/go/permissions.

Trademarks: Wiley, For Dummies, the Dummies Man logo, Dummies.com, Making Everything Easier, and related trade dress are trademarks or registered trademarks of John Wiley & Sons, Inc. and may not be used without written permission. CISSP is a registered certification mark of (ISC)², Inc. All other trademarks are the property of their respective owners. John Wiley & Sons, Inc. is not associated with any product or vendor mentioned in this book.

For general information on our other products and services, please contact our Customer Care Department within the U.S. at 877-762-2974, outside the U.S. at 317-572-3993, or fax 317-572-4002. For technical support, please visit https://hub.wiley.com/community/support/dummies.

Wiley publishes in a variety of print and electronic formats and by print-on-demand. Some material included with standard print versions of this book may not be included in e-books or in print-on-demand. If this book refers to media such as a CD or DVD that is not included in the version you purchased, you may download this material at http://booksupport.wiley.com. For more information about Wiley products, visit www.wiley.com.

Library of Congress Control Number: 2018941678

ISBN 978-1-119-50581-5 (pbk); ISBN 978-1-119-50610-2 (ebk); ISBN 978-1-119-50609-6 (ebk)

Manufactured in the United States of America

V089446_051518

Contents at a Glance

Table of Contents

Introduction

Since 1994, security practitioners around the world have been pursuing a well-known and highly regarded professional credential: the Certified Information Systems Security Professional (CISSP) certification. And since 2001, *CISSP For Dummies* has been helping security practitioners enhance their security knowledge and earn the coveted CISSP certification.

Today, there are more than 120,000 CISSPs worldwide. Ironically, some certification skeptics might argue that the CISSP certification is becoming less relevant because so many people have earned the certification. However, the CISSP certification isn't less relevant because more people are attaining it — more people are attaining it because it's now more relevant than ever. Information security is far more important than at any time in the past, with extremely large-scale data security breaches and highly sophisticated cyberattacks becoming all too frequent occurrences in our modern era.

There are many excellent and reputable information security training and education programs available. In addition to technical and industry certifications, there are also many fully accredited postsecondary degree, certificate and apprenticeship programs available for information security practitioners. And there are certainly plenty of self-taught, highly skilled individuals working in the information security field who have a strong understanding of core security concepts, techniques and technologies.

But inevitably, there are also far too many charlatans who are all too willing to overstate their security qualifications and prey on the obliviousness of business and other leaders — who think "wiping" a server, for example, means "like, with a cloth or something" — in order to pursue a fulfilling career in the information security field, or perhaps for other more dubious purposes.

The CISSP certification is widely held as *the* professional standard for information security professionals. It enables security professionals to distinguish themselves from others in the information security field by validating *both* their knowledge and experience. Likewise, it enables businesses and other organizations to identify qualified information security professionals and verify the knowledge and experience of candidates for critical information security roles in their respective organizations. Thus, the CISSP certification is more relevant and important than ever before.

About This Book

Some say that the Certified Information Systems Security Professional (CISSP) candidate requires a breadth of knowledge many miles across but only a few inches deep. To embellish on this statement, we believe that the CISSP candidate is more like the Great Wall of China, with a knowledge base extending over 3,500 miles — maybe a few holes here and there, stronger in some areas than others, but nonetheless one of the Seven Wonders of the Modern World.

The problem with lots of currently available CISSP preparation materials is in defining how high (or deep) the Great Wall actually is: Some material overwhelms and intimidates CISSP candidates, leading them to believe that the wall is as high as it is long. Other study materials are perilously brief and shallow, giving the unsuspecting candidate a false sense of confidence while he or she merely attempts to step over the Great Wall, careful not to stub a toe. To help you avoid either misstep, *CISSP For Dummies* answers the question, "What level of knowledge must a CISSP candidate possess to succeed on the CISSP exam?"

Our goal in this book is simple: To help you prepare for and pass the CISSP examination so that you can join the ranks of respected certified security professionals who dutifully serve and protect organizations and industries around the world. Although we've stuffed it chock-full of good information, we don't expect that this book will be a weighty desktop reference on the shelf of every security professional — although we certainly wouldn't object.

And we don't intend for this book to be an all-purpose, be-all-and-end-all, one-stop shop that has all the answers to life's great mysteries. Given the broad base of knowledge required for the CISSP certification, we strongly recommend that you use multiple resources to prepare for the exam and study as much relevant information as your time and resources allow. *CISSP For Dummies*, 6th Edition, provides the framework and the blueprint for your study effort and sufficient information to help you pass the exam, but by itself, it won't make you an information security expert. That takes knowledge, skills, and experience!

Finally, as a security professional, earning your CISSP certification is only the beginning. Business and technology, which have associated risks and vulnerabilities, require that each of us — as security professionals — constantly press forward, consuming vast volumes of knowledge and information in a constant tug-of-war against the bad guys.

Foolish Assumptions

It's been said that most assumptions have outlived their uselessness, but we assume a few things nonetheless! Mainly, we assume the following:

>> You have at least five years of professional experience in two or more of the eight domains covered on the CISSP exam (corresponding to Chapters 3 through 10 of this book). Actually, this is more than an assumption, it's a requirement for CISSP certification. However, even if you don't yet have the minimum experience, some experience waivers are available for certain certifications and college education (we cover the specifics in Chapter 1), and you can still take the CISSP exam and then apply for certification after you meet the experience requirement.

>> You have general IT experience, perhaps even many years of experience. Passing the CISSP exam requires not only considerable knowledge of information security, but also underlying IT technologies and fundamentals such as networks, operating systems, and programming.

>> You have access to the Internet. Throughout this book, we provide lots of URLs for websites about technologies, standards, laws, tools, security associations, and other certifications that you'll find helpful as you prepare for the CISSP exam.

>> You are a "white hat" security professional. By this, we mean that you act lawfully and will have no problem abiding by the (ISC)² Code of Ethics (which is a requirement for CISSP certification).

If these assumptions describe you, then this book is for you! If none of these assumptions describes you, keep reading anyway. It's a great book and when you finish reading it, you'll know quite a bit about information security and the CISSP certification!

Icons Used in This Book

Throughout this book, you occasionally see icons in the left margin that call attention to important information that's particularly worth noting. No smiley faces winking at you or any other cute little emoticons, but you'll definitely want to take note! Here's what to look for and what to expect:

REMEMBER

This icon identifies general information and core concepts that are well worth committing to your non-volatile memory, your gray matter, or your noggin — along with anniversaries, birthdays, and other important stuff! You should certainly understand and review this information before taking your CISSP exam.

TIP

Tips are never expected but always appreciated, and we sure hope you'll appreciate these tips! This icon includes helpful suggestions and tidbits of useful information that may save you some time and headaches.

WARNING

This is the stuff your mother warned you about . . . well, okay — probably not, but you should take heed nonetheless. These helpful alerts point out easily confused or difficult-to-understand terms and concepts.

TECHNICAL STUFF

You won't find a map of the human genome or the secret to cold fusion in this book (or maybe you will, hmm), but if you're an insufferable insomniac, take note. This icon explains the jargon beneath the jargon and is the stuff legends — well, at least nerds — are made of. So, if you're seeking to attain the seventh level of NERD-vana, keep an eye out for these icons!

Beyond the Book

In addition to what you're reading right now, this book also comes with a free access-anywhere Cheat Sheet that includes tips to help you prepare for the CISSP exam and your date with destiny — well, your exam day. To get this Cheat Sheet, simply go to www.dummies.com and type *CISSP For Dummies Cheat Sheet* in the Search box.

You also get access to hundreds of practice CISSP exam questions, as well as dozens of flash cards. Use the exam questions to help you identify specific topics and domains in which you may need to spend a little more time studying, and to get familiar with the types of questions you'll encounter on the CISSP exam (including multiple choice, drag and drop, and hotspot). To gain access to the online practice, all you have to do is register. Just follow these simple steps:

1. **Find your PIN access code.**

   - **Print book users:** If you purchased a hard copy of this book, turn to the inside front cover to find your PIN.

   - **E-book users:** If you purchased this book as an e-book, you can get your PIN by registering your e-book at www.dummies.com/go/getaccess. Go to this website, find your book and click it, and answer the validation questions to verify your purchase. Then you'll receive an email with your PIN.

2. **Go to** www.dummies.com **and click Activate Now.**

3. **Find your product (*CISSP For Dummies*, 6th Edition), and then follow the onscreen prompts to activate your PIN.**

Now you're ready to go! You can come back to the program as often as you want — simply log on with the username and password you created during your initial login. No need to enter the access code a second time.

TIP

For technical support, please visit http://wiley.custhelp.com or call Wiley at 800-762-2974 (U.S.) or +1-317-572-3994 (international).

Your registration is good for one year from the day you activate your PIN. After that time frame has passed, you can renew your registration for a fee. The website gives you all the details about how to do so.

Where to Go from Here

If you don't know where you're going, any chapter will get you there — but Chapter 1 may be a good place to start! However, if you see a particular topic that piques your interest, feel free to jump ahead to that chapter. Each chapter is individually wrapped (but not packaged for individual sale) and written to stand on its own, so feel free to start reading anywhere and skip around! Read this book in any order that suits you (though we don't recommend upside down or backwards).

1

Getting Started with CISSP Certification

IN THIS PART . . .

Get acquainted with (ISC)² and the CISSP certification.

Advance your security career as a CISSP.

IN THIS CHAPTER

» **Learning about (ISC)² and the CISSP certification**

» **Understanding CISSP certification requirements**

» **Developing a study plan**

» **Registering for the exam**

» **Taking the CISSP exam**

» **Getting your exam results**

Chapter **1**

(ISC)² and the CISSP Certification

I n this chapter, you get to know the (ISC)² and learn about the CISSP certification including professional requirements, how to study for the exam, how to get registered, what to expect during the exam, and of course, what to expect after you pass the CISSP exam!

About (ISC)² and the CISSP Certification

The International Information System Security Certification Consortium (ISC)² (www.isc2.org) was established in 1989 as a not-for-profit, tax-exempt corporation chartered for the explicit purpose of developing a standardized security curriculum and administering an information security certification process for security professionals worldwide. In 1994, the Certified Information Systems Security Professional (CISSP) credential was launched.

The CISSP was the first information security credential to be accredited by the American National Standards Institute (ANSI) to the ISO/IEC 17024 standard. This international standard helps to ensure that personnel certification processes define specific competencies and identify required knowledge, skills, and personal attributes. It also requires examinations to be independently administered and designed to properly test a candidate's competence for the certification. This process helps a certification gain industry acceptance and credibility as more than just a marketing tool for certain vendor-specific certifications (a widespread criticism that has diminished the popularity of many vendor certifications over the years).

TECHNICAL STUFF

The ISO (International Organization for Standardization) and IEC (International Electrotechnical Commission) are two organizations that work together to prepare and publish international standards for businesses, governments, and societies worldwide.

The CISSP certification is based on a Common Body of Knowledge (CBK) identified by the (ISC)² and defined through eight distinct domains:

>> Security and Risk Management

>> Asset Security

>> Security Architecture and Engineering

>> Communication and Network Security

>> Identity and Access Management (IAM)

>> Security Assessment and Testing

>> Security Operations

>> Software Development Security

You Must Be This Tall to Ride This Ride (and Other Requirements)

The CISSP candidate must have a minimum of five cumulative years of professional (paid), *full-time*, direct work experience in two or more of the domains listed in the preceding section. The work experience requirement is a hands-on one — you can't satisfy the requirement by just having "information security" listed as one of your job responsibilities. You need to have *specific* knowledge of information security — and perform work that requires you to apply that knowledge regularly. Some examples of full-time information security roles that might satisfy the work experience requirement include (but aren't limited to)

>> Security Analyst

>> Security Architect

>> Security Auditor

>> Security Consultant

>> Security Engineer

>> Security Manager

Examples of information technology roles for which you can gain partial credit for security work experience include (but aren't limited to)

>> Systems Administrator

>> Network Administrator

>> Database Administrator

>> Software Developer

For any of these preceding job titles, your particular work experience might result in you spending some of your time (say, 25 percent) doing security-related tasks. This is perfectly legitimate for security work experience. For example, five years as a systems administrator, spending a quarter of your time doing security-related tasks, earns you 1.25 years of security experience.

Furthermore, you can get a waiver for a maximum of one year of the five-year professional experience requirement if you have one of the following:

>> A four-year college degree (or regional equivalent)

>> An advanced degree in information security from a U.S. National Centers of Academic Excellence in Cyber Defense (CAE-CD)

>> A credential that appears on the (ISC)²-approved list, which includes more than 45 technical and professional certifications, such as various SANS GIAC certifications, Cisco and Microsoft certifications, and CompTIA Security+ (For the complete list, go to www.isc2.org/Certifications/CISSP/Prerequisite-Pathway).

See Chapter 2 to learn more about relevant certifications on the (ISC)²-approved list for an experience waiver.

TIP

In the U.S., CAE-CD programs are jointly sponsored by the National Security Agency and the Department of Homeland Security. For more information, go to www.nsa.gov/resources/educators/centers-academic-excellence/cyber-defense.

Preparing for the Exam

Many resources are available to help the CISSP candidate prepare for the exam. Self-study is a major part of any study plan. Work experience is also critical to success, and you can incorporate it into your study plan. For those who learn best in a classroom or online training environment, (ISC)² offers CISSP training seminars.

We recommend that you commit to an intense 60-day study plan leading up to the CISSP exam. How intense? That depends on your own personal experience and learning ability, but plan on a minimum of two hours a day for 60 days. If you're a slow learner or reader, or perhaps find yourself weak in many areas, plan on four to six hours a day — and more on the weekends. But stick to the 60-day plan. If you feel you need 360 hours of study, you may be tempted to spread this study out over a six-month period for two hours a day. Consider, however, that committing to six months of intense study is much harder (on you, as well as your family and friends) than two months. In the end, you'll likely find yourself studying only as much as you would have in a 60-day period anyway.

Studying on your own

Self-study might include books and study references, a study group, and practice exams.

Begin by downloading the free official *CISSP Certification Exam Outline* from the (ISC)² website at www.isc2.org/exam-outline. This booklet provides a good basic outline of the exam and the subjects on which you'll be tested.

Next, read this (ISC)²-approved book and review the online practice at www.dummies.com (see the Introduction for more information). *CISSP For Dummies* is written to provide a thorough and essential review of all the topics covered on the CISSP exam. Then, read any additional study resources you can to further your knowledge and reinforce your understanding of the exam topics. You can find several excellent study resources in the official *CISSP Certification Exam Outline* and online at `www.cccure.org` and `http://resources.infosecinstitute.com`. Finally, rinse and repeat: Do another quick read of *CISSP For Dummies* as a final review before you take the actual CISSP exam.

WARNING

Don't rely on *CISSP For Dummies* (as awesome and comprehensive as it is!), or any other book — no matter how thick it is — as your single resource to prepare for the CISSP exam.

Joining a study group can help you stay focused and also provide a wealth of information from the broad perspectives and experiences of other security professionals. It's also an excellent networking opportunity (the talking-to-real-people type of network, not the TCP/IP type of network)! Study groups or forums can be hosted online or at a local venue. Find a group that you're comfortable with and that is flexible enough to accommodate your schedule and study needs. Or create your own study group!

Finally, answer *lots* of practice exam questions. There are many resources available for CISSP practice exam questions. Some practice questions are too hard, others are too easy, and some are just plain irrelevant. Don't despair! The repetition of practice questions helps reinforce important information that you need to know in order to successfully answer questions on the CISSP exam. For this reason, we recommend taking as many practice exams as possible. Start with the online practice at `www.dummies.com` (see the Introduction for more information), and try the practice questions at Clément Dupuis and Nathalie Lambert's CCCure website (`www.cccure.org`).

WARNING

No practice exams exactly duplicate the CISSP exam (and forget about brain dumps — using or contributing to brain dumps is unethical and is a violation of the (ISC)² non-disclosure agreement which could result in losing your CISSP certification permanently).

Getting hands-on experience

Getting hands-on experience may be easier said than done, but keep your eyes and ears open for learning opportunities while you prepare for the CISSP exam.

For example, if you're weak in networking or applications development, talk to the networking group or developers in your company. They may be able to show you a few things that can help make sense of the volumes of information that you're trying to digest.

TIP

Your company or organization should have a security policy that's readily available to its employees. Get a copy and review its contents. Are critical elements missing? Do any supporting guidelines, standards, and procedures exist? If your company doesn't have a security policy, perhaps now is a good time for you to educate management about issues of due care and due diligence as they relate to information security. For example, review your company's plans for business continuity and disaster recovery. They don't exist? Perhaps you can lead this initiative to help both you and your company.

Getting official (ISC)² CISSP training

Classroom-based CISSP training is available as a five-day, eight-hours-a-day seminar led by (ISC)²-Authorized Instructors at (ISC)² facilities and (ISC)² Official Training Providers worldwide. Private on-site training is also available, led by (ISC)²-Authorized Instructors, and taught in your office space or a local venue. This is a convenient and cost-effective option if your company is sponsoring your CISSP certification and has ten or more employees taking the CISSP exam. If you generally learn better in a classroom environment or find that you have knowledge or actual experience in only two or three of the domains, you might seriously consider classroom-based training or private on-site training.

If it's not convenient or practical for you to travel to a seminar, online training seminars provide the benefits of learning from an (ISC)²-Authorized Instructor at your computer. Online training seminars include real-time, instructor-led seminars offered on a variety of schedules with weekday, weekend, and evening options to meet your needs, and access to recorded course sessions for 60 days. Self-paced training is another convenient online option that provides virtual lessons taught by authorized instructors with modular training and interactive study materials. Self-paced online training can be accessed from any web-enabled device for 120 days and is available any time and as often as you need.

You can find information, schedules, and registration forms for official (ISC)² training at www.isc2.org/Certifications/CISSP.

TIP

The American Council on Education's College Credit Recommendation Service (ACE CREDIT) has evaluated and recommended three college credit hours for completing an Official (ISC)² CISSP Training Seminar. Check with your college or university to find out if these credits can be applied to your degree requirements.

Attending other training courses or study groups

Other reputable organizations offer high-quality training in both classroom and self-study formats. Before signing up and spending your money, we suggest that you talk to someone who has completed the course and can tell you about its quality. Usually, the quality of a classroom course depends on the instructor; for this reason, try to find out from others whether the proposed instructor is as helpful as he or she is reported to be.

Many cities have self-study groups, usually run by CISSP volunteers. You may find a study group where you live; or, if you know some CISSPs in your area, you might ask them to help you organize a self-study group.

TIP

Always confirm the quality of a study course or training seminar before committing your money and time.

Take the practice exam

Practice exams are a great way to get familiar with the types of questions and topics you'll need to be familiar with for the CISSP exam. Be sure to take advantage of the online practice exam questions that are included with this book (see the Introduction for more information). Although the practice exams don't simulate the adaptive testing experience, you can simulate a worst-case scenario by configuring the test engine to administer 150 questions (the maximum number of questions you might see on the CISSP exam) with a time limit of three hours (the maximum amount of time you'll have to complete the CISSP exam). Learn more about computer-adaptive testing for the CISSP exam in the "About the CISSP Examination" section later in this chapter and on the (ISC)² website at www.isc2. org/Certification/CISSP/CISSP-Cat.

REMEMBER

To successfully study for the CISSP exam, you need to know your most effective learning styles. "Boot camps" are best for some people, while others learn better over longer periods of time. Furthermore, some people get more value from group discussions, while reading alone works for others. *Know thyself*, and use what works best for you.

Are you ready for the exam?

Are you ready for the big day? We can't answer this question for you. You must decide, on the basis of your individual learning factors, study habits, and professional experience, when you're ready for the exam. Unfortunately, there is no magic formula for determining your chances of success or failure on the CISSP examination.

In general, we recommend a minimum of two months of focused study. Read this book and continue taking the practice exam on the Dummies website until you can consistently score 80 percent or better in all areas. *CISSP For Dummies* covers *all* the information you need to know if you want to pass the CISSP examination. Read this book (and reread it) until you're comfortable with the information presented and can successfully recall and apply it in each of the eight domains. Continue by reviewing other study materials (particularly in your weak areas) and actively participating in an online or local study group and take as many practice exams from as many different sources as possible.

Then, when you feel like you're ready for the big day, find a romantic spot, take a knee, and — wait, wrong big day! Find a secure Wi-Fi hot spot (or other Internet connection), take a seat, and register for the exam!

Registering for the Exam

The CISSP exam is administered via computer-adaptive testing (CAT) at local Pearson VUE testing centers worldwide. To register for the exam, go to the (ISC)² website (www.isc2.org/Register-For-Exam) and click the "Register" link, or go directly to the Pearson VUE website (www.pearsonvue.com/isc2).

On the Pearson VUE website, you first need to create an account for yourself; then you can register for the CISSP exam, schedule your test, and pay your testing fee. You can also locate a nearby test center, take a Pearson VUE testing tutorial, practice taking the exam (which you should definitely do if you've never taken a CBT), and then download and read the (ISC)² non-disclosure agreement (NDA).

TIP

Download and read the (ISC)² NDA when you register for the exam. Sure, it's boring legalese, but it isn't unusual for CISSPs to be called upon to read contracts, license agreements, and other "boring legalese" as part of their information security responsibilities — so get used to it (and also get used to not signing legal documents without actually reading them)! You're given five minutes to read and accept the agreement at the start of your exam, but why not read the NDA in advance so you can avoid the pressure and distraction on exam day, and simply accept the agreement. If you don't accept the NDA in the allotted five minutes, your exam will end and you forfeit your exam fees!

When you register, you're required to quantify your relevant work experience, answer a few questions regarding any criminal history and other potentially disqualifying background information, and agree to abide by the (ISC)² Code of Ethics.

The current exam fee in the U.S. is $699. You can cancel or re-schedule your exam by contacting Pearson VUE by telephone at least 24 hours in advance of your scheduled exam or online at least 48 hours in advance. The fee to re-schedule is $50. The fee to cancel your exam appointment is $100.

WARNING

If you fail to show up for your exam or you're more than 15 minutes late for your exam appointment, you'll forfeit your entire exam fee!

TIP

Great news! If you're a U.S. military veteran and are eligible for Montgomery GI Bill or Post-9/11 GI Bill benefits, the Veteran's Administration (VA) will reimburse you for the full cost of the exam, regardless of whether you pass or fail. In some cases, (ISC)² Official Training Providers also accept the GI Bill for in-person certification training.

About the CISSP Examination

The CISSP examination itself is a grueling three-hour, 100- to 150-question marathon. To put that into perspective, in three hours, you could run an actual (mini) marathon, watch *Gone with the Wind, The Godfather Part II, Titanic*, or one of the *Lord of the Rings* movies, or play "Slow Ride" 45 times on *Guitar Hero*. Each of these feats, respectively, closely approximates the physical, mental (not intellectual), and emotional toll of the CISSP examination.

The CISSP exam is now an adaptive exam, which means the test changes based on how you're doing on the exam. The exam starts out relatively easy, and then gets progressively harder as you answer questions correctly. That's right; The better you do on the exam, the harder it gets — but that's not a bad thing! Think of it like skipping a grade in school because you're smarter than the average bear. The CISSP exam assumes that if you can answer harder questions about a given topic, then logically, you can answer easier questions about that same topic, so why waste your time?

You'll have to answer a minimum of 100 questions. After you've answered the minimum number of questions, the testing engine will either conclude the exam if it determines with 95 percent confidence that you're statistically likely to either pass or fail the exam, or it will continue asking up to a maximum of 150 total questions until it reaches a 95 percent confidence level in either result. If you answer all 150 questions, the testing engine will determine whether you passed or failed based on your answers. If you run out of time (exceed the three-hour time limit) but you've answered the minimum number of questions (100), the testing engine will determine whether you passed or failed based on your answers to the questions you completed.

Only 75 percent of the questions on the exam are actually calculated toward your final result. The other 25 percent are trial questions for future versions of the CISSP examination (kind of like being a test "test dummy" — for dummies).

However, the exam doesn't identify which questions are real and which are trial questions, so you'll have to answer all questions truthfully and honestly and to the best of your ability!

There are three types of questions on the CISSP exam:

>> **Multiple-choice.** Select the *best* answer from four possible choices. For example:

Which of the following is the FTP control channel?

A TCP port 21

B UDP port 21

C TCP port 25

D IP port 21

The FTP control channel is port 21, but is it TCP, UDP, or IP?

>> **Drag and drop.** Drag and drop the correct answer (or answers) from a list of possible answers on the left side of the screen to a box for correct answers on the right side of the screen. For example:

Which of the following are message authentication algorithms? Drag and drop the correct answers from left to right.

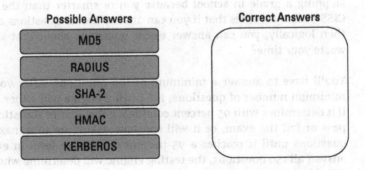

Possible Answers   Correct Answers

MD5

RADIUS

SHA-2

HMAC

KERBEROS

MD5, SHA-2, and HMAC are all correct. You must drag and drop all three answers to the box on the right for the answer to be correct.

>> **Hotspot.** Select the object in a diagram that best answers the question. For example:

Which of the following diagrams depicts a relational database model?

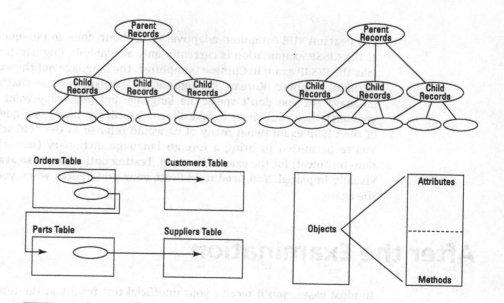

Click one of the four panels above to select your answer choice.

As described by (ISC)², you need a scaled score of 700 (out of 1000) or better to pass the examination. All three question *types* are weighted equally, but not all questions are weighted equally. Harder questions are weighted more heavily than easier questions, so there's no way to know how many correct answers are required for a passing score. But wait, it gets even better! On the adaptive exam, you no longer get a score when you complete the CISSP exam — you'll either get a pass or fail result. Think of it like watching a basketball game with no scoreboard — or a boxing match with no indication of the winner until the referee raises the victor's arm.

TIP

All questions on the CISSP exam require you to select the *best* answer (or answers) from the possible choices presented. The correct answer isn't always a straight-forward, clear choice. (ISC)² goes to great pains to ensure that you really, *really* know the material.

TIP

A common and effective test-taking strategy for multiple-choice questions is to carefully read each question and then eliminate any obviously wrong choices. The CISSP examination is no exception.

WARNING

Wrong choices aren't necessarily obvious on the CISSP examination. You may find a few *obviously* wrong choices, but they only stand out to someone who has studied thoroughly for the exam.

The Pearson VUE computer-adaptive, three-hour, 100- to 150-question version of the CISSP examination is currently only available in English. If you prefer to take the CISSP exam in Chinese (simplified, the language not the exam), French, German, Japanese, Korean, Portuguese, or Spanish, because that's your native language (or you don't speak the language but you *really* want to challenge yourself), then you'll have to take a form-based, six-hour, 250-question version of the CISSP exam (what many of us would refer to as the "old school" exam). You're permitted to bring a foreign language dictionary (non-electronic *and* non-technical) for the exam, if needed. Testing options are also available for the visually impaired. You need to indicate your preferences when you register for the exam.

After the Examination

In most cases, you'll receive your unofficial test results at the testing center as soon as you complete your exam, followed by an official email from (ISC)².

WARNING

In some rare instances, your unofficial results may not be immediately available. (ISC)² analyzes score data during each testing cycle; if they don't have enough test results early in the testing cycle, your results could be delayed up to eight weeks.

If, for some reason, you don't pass the CISSP examination — say, for example, you only read this chapter of *CISSP For Dummies* — you'll have to wait 30 days to try again. If that happens, we strongly recommend that you read the rest of this book during those 30 days! If you fail a second time, you'll have to wait 90 days to try again. If that happens, we most strongly recommend and highly urge you to read the rest of this book — perhaps a few times — during those 90 days! Finally, if you fail on your third attempt, you'll have to wait 180 days — no more excuses, you definitely need to read, re-read, memorize, comprehend, recite, ingest, and regurgitate this book several times if that happens!

After you earn your CISSP certification, you must remain an (ISC)² member in good standing and renew your certification every three years. You can renew the CISSP certification by accumulating 120 Continuing Professional Education (CPE) credits or by retaking the CISSP examination. You must earn a minimum of 40 CPE credits during each year of your three-year recertification cycle. You earn CPE credits for various activities, including taking educational courses or attending seminars and security conferences, belonging to association chapters and attending meetings, viewing vendor presentations, completing university or college courses, providing security training, publishing security articles or books, serving on relevant industry boards, taking part in self-study, and doing related volunteer work. You must document your annual CPE activities on the secure (ISC)² website to receive proper credit. You are also required to pay a U.S. $85 annual maintenance fee, payable to (ISC)². Maintenance fees are billed in arrears for the preceding year, and you can pay them online, also in the secure members area of the (ISC)² website.

WARNING

Be sure to be absolutely truthful on your CPE reporting and retain evidence of your training. (ISC)² audits some CPE submissions.

TIP

As soon as you receive your certification, register on the (ISC)² website and provide your contact information. (ISC)² reminds you of your annual maintenance fee, Board of Directors elections, annual meetings, and events, but *only* if you maintain your contact info — particularly your email address.

Chapter **2**

Putting Your Certification to Good Use

Although this book is devoted to helping you earn your CISSP certification, we thought it would be a good idea to include a few things you might consider doing after you've earned your CISSP.

So what do you do after you earn your CISSP? There are plenty of things you can do to enhance your professional career and the global community. Here are just a few ideas!

Networking with Other Security Professionals

Unless you work for a large organization, there probably aren't many other information security (infosec) professionals in your organization. In fact, you may be the only one! Yes, it can feel lonely at times, so we suggest you find ways to make connect with infosec professionals in your area and beyond. Many of the activities described in this chapter provide networking opportunities. If you haven't been much of a social butterfly before and your professional network is somewhat limited, get ready to take your career to a whole new level as you meet other likeminded security professionals and potentially build lifelong friendships. *Remember:* It's not what you know, but who you know — well, what you know matters, too!

THE POWER OF ONLINE BUSINESS NETWORKING

We promise that we have no affiliations with LinkedIn when we say this, but hear this: LinkedIn is one of the best business networking tools to come along since the telephone and the business card. LinkedIn can help you expand your networking horizons and help you make contacts with other business professionals in your company, your profession, your region, and far beyond.

Chances are, you aren't new to LinkedIn, so we'll skip the basics here. However, people in the infosec business are a bit particular, and that's what we want to discuss. Infosec professionals tend to be skeptical — after all, we're paid to be paranoid, as we sometimes say, because the bad guys (and gals) *are* out to get us. This relates to LinkedIn in this way: Most of us are wary of making connections with people we don't know. So, as you begin to network with other infosec professionals on LinkedIn, tread lightly and proceed slowly. It's best to start making connections with people you actually know and people you've actually met. If you make connection requests with infosec people you haven't met, there's a pretty good chance they'll ignore you or just decline the request. They're not being rude — they're just aware of the fact that there are a lot of scammers out there who will build fake connections in hopes of earning trust and pulling some kind of a ruse later on.

Similarly, if you've been one of those "open networkers" in the past, don't be surprised if others are a bit reluctant to connect with you, even those you've met. As you transition into an infosec career, you'll find that the rules are a bit different.

Bottom line: LinkedIn can be really fantastic for networking and learning, but do know that infosec professionals march to the beat of a different drummer.

If you're just getting started in your infosec career (regardless of your age or other career experience), you'll likely meet other infosec professionals that have at some point in their own careers been in your shoes, who will be happy to help you find answers and solutions to some of those elusive questions and challenges that may be perplexing you. You may find that you're initially doing more taking than giving, but make sure you're at least showing your appreciation and gratitude for their help — and remember to give back later in your career when someone new to infosec asks to pick *your* brain for some helpful insight.

So, as you venture out in search of other infosec professionals, put your smile on and bring plenty of business cards (print your own if your employer doesn't provide any). You're sure to make new friends and experience growth in the security business that may delight you.

Being an Active (ISC)² Member

Being an active (ISC)² member is easy! Besides volunteering (see the following section), you can participate in several other activities including:

>> **Attend the (ISC)² Congress.** For years, (ISC)² rode the coattails of ASIS (formerly the American Society for Industrial Security — we blame Kentucky Fried Chicken for becoming "KFC" and starting the trend of businesses and organizations dropping the original meaning behind their acronyms!) and occupied a corner of the ASIS annual conference. But in 2016, (ISC)² decided it was time to strike out on its own and run its own conference. In 2017, one of your authors (first name starts with a *P*) attended and spoke at the first (ISC)² Congress and found it to be a first-class affair that's every bit as good as those other great national and global conferences. Find out about the next (ISC)² Congress at http://congress.isc2.org.

>> **Vote in (ISC)² elections.** Every year, one-third of the (ISC)² Board of Directors is elected to serve three-year terms. As a CISSP in good standing, you've earned the right to vote in the (ISC)² elections. Exercise your right! The best part of this is becoming familiar with other CISSPs who run for board positions. You can read their biographies and understand their agendas if elected. With your vote, you're doing your part to make sure that the future of (ISC)² rests in good hands with directors that can provide capable leadership and vision.

>> **Attend (ISC)² events.** (ISC)² conducts several events each year, from networking receptions to conferences and educational events. (ISC)² often holds gatherings at larger industry conferences such as RSA and BlackHat. Check back regularly on the (ISC)² website to find out more about events in your area.

>> **Join an (ISC)² chapter.** (ISC)² has chapters around the world. You can find out more at www.isc2.org/chapters. There are many great opportunities to get involved in local chapters, including chapter leadership, participation in chapter activities, and participation in community outreach projects. Chapter events are also great opportunities to meet other infosec professionals.

It's important that (ISC)² has your correct contact information. As soon as you become a CISSP (or before, even), make sure your profile is correct and complete, so that you can receive announcements for these and other activities.

Considering (ISC)² Volunteer Opportunities

(ISC)² is much more than a certifying organization: It's a *cause*, and you might even say it's a *movement*. It's security professionals' *raison d'être*, the reason we exist — professionally, anyway. As one of us, consider throwing your weight into the cause.

Volunteers have made (ISC)² what it is today, and they make important contributions toward your certification. You can't stand on the sidelines and watch others do the work. Use your talents to help those who'll come after you. You can help in many ways. For information about volunteering, see the (ISC)² website (www.isc2.org).

Most sanctioned (ISC)² volunteer activities are eligible for CPE credits. Check with (ISC)² for details.

Writing certification exam questions

The state of technology, laws, and practices within the CISSP Common Body of Knowledge (CBK) is continually changing and advancing. In order to be effective and relevant, CISSP exams need to have fresh, new exam questions that reflect how security is done today. Therefore, people working in the industry — such as you — need to write new questions. If you're interested in being a question writer, visit the (ISC)² website and apply.

Speaking at events

(ISC)² now holds more security-related events around the world than it has at any other time in its history. More often than not, (ISC)² speakers are local volunteers — experts in their professions who want to share with others what they know and have learned. If you have an area of expertise or a unique perspective on CISSP-related issues, consider educating others with a speaking engagement. For more information, visit the (ISC)² website.

TIP

If you speak at an (ISC)² Congress, your conference fees are waived. You only need to pay for transportation, lodging, and meals.

Helping at (ISC)² conferences

(ISC)² puts on a fantastic annual conference that is called the (ISC)² Congress. This conference is an excellent opportunity to learn new topics and meet other infosec professionals. But this conference doesn't run itself — it's powered by volunteers! Go to the (ISC)² Congress website at `http://congress.isc2.org` to find information about volunteering.

Read and contribute to (ISC)² publications

(ISC)² publishes a quarterly online magazine called *INSIGHTS* that is associated with *InfoSecurity Professional*. You can find out more at `www.isc2.org/News-and-Events/Infosecurity-Professional-Insights`.

The *(ISC)² Blog* is a free online publication for all (ISC)² members. Find the blog, as well as information about writing articles, at `http://blog.isc2.org`.

The *Information Security Journal* is a fee-based publication that's published bimonthly. Find information about subscribing and writing articles on the journal's information page (`www.isc2.org/Member-Resources/Journal`). The annual subscription is currently U.S. $45.

Support the (ISC)² Center for Cyber Safety and Education

The Center for Cyber Safety and Education, formerly the (ISC)² Foundation, is a non-profit charity formed by (ISC)² in 2011. The Center is a conduit through which security professionals can reach society and empower students, teachers, and the general public to secure their online life with cybersecurity education and awareness programs in the community. The Center for Cyber Safety and Education was formed to meet those needs, and to expand altruistic programs, such as Safe and Secure Online, the Information Security Scholarship Program, and industry research — the Center's three core programs. Learn more at `www.iamcybersafe.org`.

Participating in (ISC)² focus groups

(ISC)² has developed focus groups and quality assurance (QA) testing opportunities. (ISC)² is developing new services, and it needs to receive early feedback during the requirements and design phases of its projects. By participating in these groups and tests, you can influence future (ISC)² services that will aid current and future certification holders.

Join the (ISC)² community

(ISC)² has developed a new interactive community that's full of discussion groups. With more than 16,000 members in the first year, the community is well designed and easy to use. You can sign up and join discussions at http://community. isc2.org.

Get involved with a CISSP study group

Many communities have CISSP study groups that consist of volunteer mentors and instructors who help those who want to earn the certification.

If your community doesn't have a CISSP study group, consider starting one. Many communities have them already, and the organizers there can give you advice on how to start your own. You can find out more at nearby (ISC)² chapters and other local security groups.

Help others learn more about data security

In no way are we being vain or arrogant when we say that we (the writers of this book, and you the readers) know more about data security and safe Internet usage than perhaps 99 percent of the general population. There are two main reasons for this:

» Security is our profession

» Security is not always easy to do

A legion of volunteer opportunities is available out there to help others keep their computers (and mobile computing devices) secure and to use the Internet safely. Here is a very short list of places where you can help:

» Service clubs

» Senior centers

>> Schools (be sure to read about Safe and Secure Online earlier in this chapter)

>> Alumni associations and groups

>> Your place of employment

Using a little imagination, you can certainly come up with additional opportunities. The world is hungry for the information you possess!

Becoming an Active Member of Your Local Security Chapter

In addition to (ISC)², many security organizations around the world have local chapters, perhaps in or near your community. Here's a short list of some organizations that you may be interested in:

>> **International Systems Security Association (ISSA):** www.issa.org

>> **ISACA (formerly Information Systems Audit and Control Association):** www.isaca.org

- » **Society for Information Management (SIM):** www.simnet.org

- » **InfraGard:** www.infragard.net

- » **Open Web Application Security Project (OWASP):** www.owasp.org

- » **ASIS International:** www.asisonline.org

- » **High Technology Crime Investigation Association (HTCIA):** www.htcia.org

- » **Risk and Insurance Management Society (RIMS):** www.rims.org

- » **Society of Information Risk Analysts (SIRA):** www.societyinforisk.org

- » **The Institute of Internal Auditors (IIA):** www.theiia.org

- » **International Association of Privacy Professionals (IAPP):** www.iapp.org

- » **Disaster Recovery Institute International (DRII):** www.drii.org

- » **Computer Technology Investigators Network (CTIN):** www.ctin.org

Local security groups provide excellent opportunities to find peers in other organizations and to discover more about your profession. Many people find that the contacts they make as part of their involvement with local security organizations can be especially valuable when looking for new career opportunities.

You certainly can find many, many more security organizations that have local chapters, beyond the ones we include in the preceding list. Ask your colleagues and others about security organizations and clubs in your community.

Spreading the Good Word about CISSP Certification

As popular as the CISSP certification is, there are people who still don't know about it. And many who may have heard of it don't understand what it's all about. Tell people about your CISSP certification and explain the certification process to your peers. Here are some facts that you can share with anyone and everyone you meet:

- » CISSP is *the* top-tier information security professional certification.

- » More than 112,000 security professionals around the world have the CISSP certification.

- » The CISSP certification started in 1994.

>> CISSP was the first credential to be accredited by the ANSI (American National Standards Institute) to ISO (International Organization for Standardization) Standard 17024.

>> The organization that manages the CISSP certification has other certifications for professionals who specialize in various fields of information security. The organization also promotes information security awareness through education programs and events.

Promote the fact that you're certified. How can you promote it? After you earn your CISSP, you can simply put the letters CISSP after your name on your business cards, stationery, email signature, resume, blog, and website. While you're at it, put the CISSP logo on there, too (just be sure to abide by any established terms of use).

TIP

There are many other certifications available from (ISC)² that are described in the next section.

Wear the colors proudly

The (ISC)² online store has a lot of neat stuff, from jackets to shirts to mugs to caps. There's something there for everyone. The organization introduces new items now and again, and it runs closeout specials. http://isc2education.org/shop.

Consider adding a few nice polo shirts that sport the (ISC)² and CISSP logos to your wardrobe. Or really splurge and consider buying a CISSP leather jacket (be cool like the Fonz — except when you say "Aaa!" you're of course referring to authentication, authorization, and accounting — which we discuss in Chapter 7) or backpack!

Lead by example

Like it or not, security professionals, particularly those with the CISSP, are role models for those around them. From a security perspective, whatever we do — and how we do it — is seen as the standard for correct behavior.

REMEMBER

Being mindful of this, we need to conduct ourselves as though someone were looking — even if no one is — in everything we do.

Using Your CISSP Certification to Be an Agent of Change

As a certified security professional, you're an *agent of change* in your organization: The state of threats and regulations is ever-changing, and you must respond by ensuring that your employer's environment and policies continue to defend your employer's assets against harm. Here are some of the important principles regarding successful agents of change:

» Identify and promote only essential changes.

» Promote only those changes that have a chance to succeed.

» Anticipate sources of resistance.

» Distinguish resistance from well-founded criticism.

» Involve all affected parties the right way.

» Don't promise what you can't deliver.

» Use sponsors, partners, and collaborators as co-agents of change.

» Change metrics and rewards to support the changing world.

» Provide training.

» Celebrate all successes.

REMEMBER

Your job as a security professional doesn't involve preaching; instead, you need to recognize opportunities for improvement and reduced risks to the business. Work within your organization's structure to bring about change in the right way. That's the best way to reduce security risks.

Earning Other Certifications

In business and technology, no one's career stays in one place. You're continuously growing and changing, and ever-changing technology also influences organizations and your role within them.

You shouldn't consider your quest for certifications finished when you earn your CISSP — even if it *is* the highest-level information security certification out there! Security is a journey, and your CISSP certification isn't the end goal, but a (major) milestone along the way. CISSP should be a part of your security *lifestyle.*

Other (ISC)² certifications

(ISC)² has several other certifications, including some that you may aspire to earn after (or instead of) receiving your CISSP. These certifications are

- » **Associate of (ISC)²:** If you can pass the CISSP or SSCP certification exams but don't yet possess the required professional experience, you can become an Associate of (ISC)². Read about this option on the (ISC)² website.

- » **CCSP (Certified Cloud Security Professional):** This certification on cloud controls and security practices was co-developed by (ISC)² and the Cloud Security Alliance.

- » **SSCP (Systems Security Certified Practitioner):** This certification is for hands-on security techs and analysts. SSCP has had the reputation for being a "junior" CISSP certification, but don't be fooled — it's anything but that. SSCP is highly technical, more so than CISSP. For some, SSCP may be a stepping stone to CISSP, but for others, it's a great destination all its own.

- » **CSSLP (Certified Secure Software Lifecycle Professional):** Designed for software development professionals, the CSSLP recognizes software development in which security is a part of the software requirements, design, and testing — so that the finished product has security designed in and built in, rather than added on afterward.

- » **HCISPP (HealthCare Information Security and Privacy Practitioner):** Designed for information security in the healthcare industry, the HCISPP recognizes knowledge and experience related to healthcare data protection regulations and the protection of patient data.

- » **JGISP (Japanese Government Information Security Professional):** A country-specific certification that validates a professional's knowledge, skills, and experience related to Japanese government regulations and standards.

- » **CAP (Certification and Accreditation Professional):** Jointly developed by the U.S. Department of State's Office of Information Assurance and (ISC)², the CAP credential reflects the skills required to assess risk and establish security requirements for complex systems and environments.

CISSP concentrations

(ISC)² has developed follow-on certifications (think *accessories*) that accompany your CISSP. (ISC)² calls these certifications *concentrations* because they represent the three areas you may choose to specialize in:

- » **ISSAP (Information Systems Security Architecture Professional):** Suited for technical systems security architects.

- » **ISSEP (Information Systems Security Engineering Professional):** Demonstrates competence for security engineers.

- » **ISSMP (Information Systems Security Management Professional):** About security management (of course!).

All the concentrations require that you first be a CISSP in good standing, and each has its own exam. Read about these concentrations and their exams on the (ISC)² website at www.isc2.org/Certifications/CISSP-Concentrations.

Non-(ISC)² certifications

Organizations other than (ISC)² have security-related certifications, one or more of which may be right for you. None of these certifications directly compete with CISSP, but some of them do overlap with CISSP somewhat.

Non-technical/non-vendor certifications

There are many other certifications available that are not tied to specific hardware or software vendors. Some of the better ones include

- » **CISA (Certified Information Systems Auditor):** Consider this certification if you work as an internal auditor or your organization is subject to one or more security regulations, such as Sarbanes-Oxley, HIPAA, GLBA, PCI, and so on. The Information Systems Audit and Control Association and Foundation (ISACA) manages this certification. Find out more about CISA at www.isaca.org/cisa.

- » **CISM (Certified Information Security Manager):** Similar to (ISC)²'s Information Systems Security Management Professional (ISSMP) certification (which we talk about in the section "CISSP concentrations," earlier in this chapter), you may want the CISM certification if you're in security management. Like CISA, ISACA manages this certification. Read more about it at www.isaca.org/cism.

- » **CRISC (Certified in Risk and Information Systems Control):** This is a relatively new certification that concentrates on organization risk management. Learn more at www.isaca.org/crisc.

- » **CGEIT (Certified in the Governance of Enterprise IT):** Look into this certification if you want to demonstrate your skills and knowledge in the areas of IT management and governance. Effective security in an IT organization definitely depends on *governance*, which involves the management and control of resources to meet long-term objectives. You can find out more about CGEIT at www.isaca.org/cgeit.

» **CPP (Certified Protection Professional):** Primarily a security management certification, CPP is managed by ASIS International, at www.asisonline.org/certification. The CPP certification designates individuals who have demonstrated competency in all areas constituting security management.

» **PSP (Physical Security Professional):** ASIS International also offers this certification, which caters to those professionals whose primary responsibility focuses on threat surveys and the design of integrated security systems. Read more at www.asisonline.org/certification.

» **CIPP (Certified Information Privacy Professional):** The International Association of Privacy Professionals (IAPP) has this and other country-specific privacy certifications for security professionals with knowledge and experience in personal data protection. Find out more at http://iapp.org/certify/cipp.

» **CIPP/E (Certified Information Privacy Professional/Europe):** Privacy in Europe is so important in our industry that the IAPP has developed a version of the CIPP especially for European privacy matters. Learn more at http://iapp.org/certify/cippe.

» **C|CISO (Certified Chief Information Security Officer):** This certification demonstrates the skills and knowledge required for the typical CISO position. Learn more at http://ciso.eccouncil.org.

» **CBCP (Certified Business Continuity Planner):** A business continuity planning certification offered by the Disaster Recovery Institute. You can find out more at http://drii.org/certification/cbcp.

» **DRCE (Disaster Recovery Certified Expert):** This certification is a recognition of knowledge and experience in disaster recovery planning. For more information, visit www.bcm-institute.org/certification.

» **PMP (Project Management Professional):** A good project manager — someone you can trust with organizing resources and schedules — is a wonderful thing, especially on large projects. The Project Management Institute, at www.pmi.org, offers this certification.

» **PCI-QSA (Payment Card Industry Qualified Security Assessor):** The Payment Card Industry Security Standards Council developed the QSA certification for professionals who audit organizations that store, transmit, or process credit card data. This certification is for PCI auditors. Find out more at www.pcisecuritystandards.org.

» **PCI-ISA (Payment Card Industry Internal Security Assessor):** This certification, also from The Payment Card Industry Security Standards Council, is for security professionals within organizations that store, transmit, or process cardholder data. Find out more at www.pcisecuritystandards.org.

>> **GIAC (Global Information Assurance Certification):** The GIAC family of certifications includes categories in Audit, Management, Operations, and Security Administration. One of the GIAC non-vendor-specific certifications that complement CISSP is the GIAC Certified Forensics Analyst (GCFA) and GIAC Certified Incident Handler (GCIH). Find more information at www.giac.org/certifications. There are also several vendor-related GIAC certifications mentioned in the next section.

Technical/vendor certifications

We won't even pretend to list all the technical and vendor certifications here. But these are some of the well-known vendor-related security certifications:

>> **CCIE (Cisco Certified Internetworking Expert) Security:** Cisco also offers several product-related certifications for specific products, including ASA firewalls and intrusion prevention systems. Find out more at www.cisco.com/certifications.

>> **Check Point Security Administration certifications:** You can earn certifications related to Check Point's firewall and other security products. Visit www.checkpoint.com/certification.

>> **C|EH (Certified Ethical Hacker):** We know, we know. A contradiction in terms to some, real business value for others. Read carefully before signing. Offered by the International Council of E-Commerce Consultants (EC-Council). You can find out more at http://cert.eccouncil.org.

>> **E|NSA (Network Security Administrator):** Also from EC Council, this is the certification that recognizes the defensive view — as opposed to the offensive view of C|EH. You can learn more at http://cert.eccouncil.org.

>> **L|PT (Licensed Penetration Tester):** Another certification from the EC Council, this takes penetration testing to a higher level than C|EH. Learn more at http://cert.eccouncil.org.

>> **C|HFI (Certified Hacking Forensics Investigator):** Also from EC Council, this certification recognizes the skills and knowledge of a forensic expert who can detect computer crime and gather forensic evidence. Find out more here: http://cert.eccouncil.org.

>> **CSFA (CyberSecurity Forensic Analyst):** This certification demonstrates the knowledge and skills for conducting computer forensic examinations. Part of the certification exam is an actual forensics assignment in the lab. Check out www.cybersecurityforensicanalyst.com for more.

>> **CompTIA Security+:** A security competency certification for PC techs and the like. We consider this an entry-level certification that may not be for you, but

you may well advise your aspiring colleagues who want to get into information security that this certification is a good place to start. You can find out more at http://certification.comptia.org.

>> **Security|5:** Like Security+, this is an entry-level security competency certification for anyone interested in learning computer networking and security basics. Find out more at http://cert.eccouncil.org.

You can find many other security certifications out there. Use your favorite search engine and search for phrases such as "security certification" to find information.

Choosing the right certifications

Regularly, technology and security professionals ask us which certifications they should earn next. Our answer is almost always the same: Your decision depends on where you are now and where you want your career to go. There is no single "right" certification for everyone — determining which certification you should seek is a very individual thing.

When considering other certifications, ask yourself the following questions:

>> **Where am I in my career right now?** Are you more focused on technology, policy, operations, development, or management?

>> **Where do I want my career to go in the future?** If (for example) you're stuck in operations but you want to be focusing on policy, let that goal be your guide.

>> **What qualifications for certifications do I possess right now?** Some people tackle certifications based on the skills they already possess, and they use those newly earned certifications to climb the career ladder.

>> **What do I need to do in my career to earn more qualifications?** You need to consider not only what certifications you may be qualified to earn right now, but also what experience you must develop in order to earn future certifications.

If you're honest with yourself, answering these questions should help you discern what certifications are right for you. We recommend that you take time every few years to do some long-term career planning; most people will find that the answers to the questions we've listed here will change.

You might even find that one or more of the certifications you have no longer reflect your career direction. If so, give yourself permission to let those certifications lapse. No sense hanging on to old certifications that no longer

Find a mentor, be a mentor

If you're somewhat new to infosec (and even if you're not!) and you find yourself asking a lot of questions about your career, perhaps you would benefit from a mentor. A mentor is someone who has lived your professional lifestyle and been on the security journey for many years.

We suggest you shop around for a mentor and that you decide on one after talking with a few prospects. Mentors often have different approaches, from casual discussions to more structured learning.

If you're not sure where to find a mentor, start with one or more of the local security organizations or activities in your area. If you live outside a major city, you may have to find a long-distance mentor. However, the experience can still be rewarding!

As you transition in your career from a security beginner to a security expert, consider being a mentor yourself. You'll find that, although you'll be helping another aspiring security professional get his or her career started, you'll also learn quite a bit about security and yourself along the way.

REMEMBER

Most non-technical certifications require you to prove that you *already* possess the required job experience in order to earn them. People make this common mistake: They want to earn a certification in order to land a particular kind of job. But that's not the purpose of a certification. Instead, a certification is evidence that you *already* possess both knowledge *and experience*.

Pursue Security Excellence

We think that the best way to succeed in a security career is to pursue excellence every day, regardless of whether you're already in your dream security job or just starting out.

The pursuit of excellence may sound like a lofty or vague term, but you can make a difference every day by doing the following:

>> **Do your best job daily.** No matter what you do for a living, be the very best at it.

>> **Maintain a positive outlook.** Happiness and job satisfaction are due in large part to your attitude. Having a good attitude helps make each day better and helps you to do a better job. Because optimism is contagious, your positive outlook will encourage your co-workers, and pretty soon everyone will be whistling, humming, or whatever they do when they like their jobs.

>> **Continually improve yourself.** Take the time to read about security practices, advances, developments, and changes in the industry. Try to figure out how innovation in the industry can help you and your organization reduce risk even more, with less effort.

>> **Understand your value.** Take the time to understand how your work adds value to the organization and try to come up with more ways to add value and reduce risk.

>> **Understand the security big picture in your organization.** Whether or not you're responsible for some aspect of security, take the time to understand the principles that your organization uses to increase security and reduce risk. Use the security and risk management principles in Chapter 3, and see how those principles can help improve security even more. Think about the role you can play in advancing the cause of asset and information protection in your organization.

If you make the pursuit of excellence a habit, you can slowly change for the better over time. You end up with an improved security career, and your organization gets better security and reduced risk.

2

Certification Domains

Understand security and risk management concepts and principles.

Make your knowledge of asset security one of your assets.

Design and implement secure software, systems, and facilities.

Learn communication and network security fundamentals.

Recognize identity and access management techniques.

Conduct security assessments, scans, testing, and audits.

Apply security operations concepts and controls.

Ensure secure software development throughout the development lifecycle.

Chapter **3**

Security and Risk Management

The Security and Risk Management domain addresses many fundamental security concepts and principles, as well as compliance, ethics, governance, security policies and procedures, business continuity planning, risk management, and security education, training, and awareness. This domain represents 15 percent of the CISSP certification exam.

Apply Security Governance Principles

For the CISSP exam, you must fully understand and be able to apply security governance principles including:

>> Alignment of security function to business strategy, goals, mission, and objectives

>> Organizational processes

>> Security roles and responsibilities

>> Control frameworks

>> Due care

>> Due diligence

Alignment of security function to business strategy, goals, mission, and objectives

In order for an information security program to be effective, it must be aligned with the organization's mission, strategy, goals, and objectives; thus you must understand the differences and relationships between an organization's mission statement, strategy, goals, and objectives. You also need to know how these elements can affect the organization's information security policies and program. Proper alignment with the organization's mission, strategy, goals, and objectives also helps to build business cases, secure budgets, and allocate resources for security program initiatives. With proper alignment, security projects and other activities are appropriately prioritized, and they fit better into organization policies, practices, and processes.

Mission (not-so-impossible) and strategy

Corny heading, yes, but there's a good chance you're humming the *Mission Impossible* theme song now — mission accomplished!

An organization's *mission statement* expresses its reason for existence. A good mission statement is an easily understood, general-purpose statement that says what the organization is, what it does, and why it exists, doing what it does in the way that it has chosen.

An organization's *strategy*, describes *how* it accomplishes its mission and is frequently adapted to address new challenges and business realities.

Goals and objectives

A *goal* is something (or many somethings) that an organization hopes to accomplish. A goal should be consistent with the organization's mission statement or philosophy, and it should help define a vision for the organization. It should also whip people into a wild frenzy, running around their offices, waving their arms in the air, and yelling "GOOOAAALLL!" (Well, maybe only if they're World Cup fans.)

An *objective* is a milestone or a specific result that is expected and, as such, helps an organization attain its goals and achieve its mission.

Security personnel should be acutely aware of their organizations' goals and objectives. Only then can security professionals ensure that security capabilities will work with and protect all the organization's current, changing, and new products, services, and endeavors.

WARNING

Organizations often use the terms *goals* and *objectives* interchangeably without distinction. Worse yet, some organizations refer to goals as long-term objectives, and objectives as short-term goals! For the CISSP exam, an *objective* (short-term) supports a *goal* (intermediate-term), which supports a *mission* (long-term), which is accomplished with a well-defined *strategy*. All of these fall under the umbrella of the organization's *mission statement*.

Organizational processes (security executive oversight)

In this section, we discuss key processes in the realm of security governance.

Governance committees and executive oversight

Security management starts (or should start!) at the top with executive management and board-level oversight. This generally takes the form of *security governance*, which simply means that the organization's governing body has set the direction and the organization has policies and processes in place to ensure that executive management is following that direction, is fully informed, and is in control of information security strategy, policy, and operations.

A governance committee is a group of executives and/or managers who regularly meet to review security incidents, projects, operational metrics, and other aspects of concern to them. The governance committee will occasionally issue mandates to security management about new business activities and shifts in priorities and strategic direction.

In practice, this is not much different from governance in IT or other departments. Governance is how executive management stays involved in the goings-on in IT, security, and other parts of the business.

Acquisitions and divestitures

Organizations, particularly in private industry, continually are reinventing themselves. More than ever before, it is important to be agile and competitive. This results in organizations acquiring other organizations, organizations splitting themselves into two (or more) separate companies, as well as internal reorganizations to change the alignment of teams, departments, divisions, and business units.

There are several security-related considerations that should be taken into account when an organization acquires another organization, or when two (or more) organizations merge:

>> **Security governance and management.** How is security managed in each organization, and what important differences are there?

>> **Security policy.** How do policies between the two organizations differ, and what issues will be encountered when merging the policies into one?

>> **Security posture.** Which security controls are present in each organization, and how different are they from one another?

>> **Security operations.** What security operations are in place today and how do they operate? This includes vulnerability management, event monitoring, identity and access management, third-party risk management, and incident management.

If the security of one organization is vastly different from another, the organization should not be too hasty to connect the two organizations' networks together.

Interestingly, when an organization divides itself into two (or more) separate organizations or sells off a division, it can be trickier. Each new company probably will need to duplicate the security governance, management, controls, operations, and tools that the single organization had before the split. This doesn't always mean that the two separate security functions need to be the same as the old; it is important to fully understand the business mission in each new organization, and what security regulations and standards apply to each new organization. Only then can information security align to each new organization.

Security roles and responsibilities

The truism that information security is "everyone's responsibility" is too often put into practice as *everyone is responsible, but no one is accountable*. To avoid this pitfall, specific roles and responsibilities for information security should be defined in an organization's security policy, individual job or position descriptions, and third-party contracts. These roles and responsibilities should apply to employees, consultants, contractors, interns, and vendors. And they should apply to every level of staff, from C-level executives to line employees.

Management

Senior-level management is often responsible for information security at several levels, including the role as an information owner, which we discuss in the following section. However, in this context, management has a responsibility to demonstrate a strong commitment to an organization's information security program through the following actions:

>> **Creating, mandating, and approving a corporate information security policy:** This policy should include a statement of support from management and should also be signed by the CEO, COO, CIO, or the Chairman of the Board.

>> **Leading by example:** A CEO who carries a mandatory identification badge and utilizes system access controls sets a good example.

>> **Rewarding compliance:** Management should expect proper security behavior and acknowledge, recognize, and/or reward employees accordingly.

REMEMBER

Management is always ultimately responsible for an organization's overall information security and for any information security decisions that are made (or not made). Our role as information security professionals is to report security issues and to make appropriate information security recommendations to management.

Users

An *end-user* (or *user*) includes just about everyone within an organization. Users aren't specifically designated. They can be broadly defined as anyone who has authorized access to an organization's internal information or information systems. Users include employees, contractors and other temporary help, consultants, vendors, customer, and anyone else with access. Some organizations call them employees, partners, associates, or what-have-you. Typical user responsibilities include

>> Complying with all applicable security requirements defined in organizational policies, standards, and procedures; applicable legislative or regulatory requirements; and contractual requirements (such as non-disclosure agreements and Service Level Agreements).

>> Exercising due care in safeguarding organizational information and information assets.

>> Participating in information security training and awareness efforts as required.

>> Reporting any suspicious activity, security violations, security problems, or security concerns to appropriate personnel.

Control frameworks

Organizations often adopt a control framework to aid in their legal and regulatory compliance efforts. Some examples of relevant security frameworks include

>> **COBIT 5.** Developed by ISACA (formerly known as the Information Systems Audit and Control Association) and the IT Governance Institute (ITGI), COBIT consists of several components, including:

- **Framework.** Organizes IT governance objectives and best practices.

- **Process descriptions.** Provides a reference model and common language.

- **Maturity models.** Assess organizational maturity/capability and address gaps.

The COBIT framework is popular in organizations that are subject to the Sarbanes-Oxley Act (SOX; discussed later in this chapter) or ICOFR.

>> **NIST (National Institute for Standards and Technology) Special Publication 800-53: Security and Privacy Controls for Federal Information Systems and Organizations.** Known among information security professionals as NIST 800-53, this is a very popular and comprehensive controls framework required by U.S. government agencies. It also is widely used in private industry, both in the U.S. and throughout the world.

>> **COSO (Committee of Sponsoring Organizations of the Treadway Commission).** Developed by the Institute of Management Accountants (IMA), the American Accounting Association (AAA), the American Institute of Certified Public Accountants (AICPA), The Institute of Internal Auditors (IIA), and Financial Executives International (FEI), the COSO framework consists of five components:

- **Control environment.** Provides the foundation for all other internal control components.

- **Risk assessment.** Establishes objectives through identification and analysis of relevant risks and determines whether anything will prevent the organization from meeting its objectives.

- **Control activities.** Policies and procedures that are created to ensure compliance with management directives. Various control activities are discussed in the other chapters of this book.

- **Information and communication.** Ensures appropriate information systems and effective communications processes are in place throughout the organization.

- **Monitoring activities.** Activities that assess performance over time and identify deficiencies and corrective actions.

» **ISO/IEC 27002 (International Organization for Standardization/ International Electrotechnical Commission).** Formally titled "Information technology — Security techniques — Code of practice for information security management," ISO/IEC 27002 documents security best practices in 14 domains, as follows:

- Information security policies

- Organization of information security

- Human resource security

- Asset management

- Access control

- Cryptography

- Physical and environmental security

- Operations security

- Communications security

- Systems acquisition, development, and maintenance

- Supplier relationships

- Information security incident management

- Information security aspects of business continuity management

- Compliance

» **ITIL (Information Technology Infrastructure Library).** A set of best practices for IT service management consisting of five volumes, as follows:

- **Service Strategy.** Addresses IT services strategy management, service portfolio management, IT services financial management, demand management, and business relationship management.

- **Service Design.** Addresses design coordination, service catalog management, service level management, availability management, capacity management, IT service continuity management, information security management system, and supplier management.

- **Service Transition.** Addresses transition planning and support, change management, service asset and configuration management, release and deployment management, service validation and testing, change evaluation, and knowledge management.

- **Service Operation.** Addresses event management, incident management, service request fulfillment, problem management, and access management.

- **Continual Service Improvement.** Defines a seven-step process for improvement initiatives, including identifying the strategy, defining what will be measured, gathering the data, processing the data, analyzing the information and data, presenting and using the information, and implementing the improvement.

Due care

Due care is the conduct that a reasonable person exercises in a given situation, which provides a standard for determining negligence. In the practice of information security, due care relates to the steps that individuals or organizations take to perform their duties and implement security best practices.

Another important aspect of due care is the principle of *culpable negligence*. If an organization fails to follow a standard of due care in the protection of its assets (or its personnel), the organization may be held culpably negligent. In such cases, jury awards may be adjusted accordingly, and the organization's insurance company may be required to pay only a portion of any loss — the organization may get stuck paying the rest of the bill!

Due diligence

Due diligence is the prudent management and execution of due care. It's most often used in legal and financial circles to describe the actions that an organization takes to research the viability and merits of an investment or merger/acquisition opportunity. In the context of information security, due diligence commonly refers to risk identification and risk management practices, not only in the day-to-day operations of an organization, but also in the case of technology procurement, as well as mergers and acquisitions.

WARNING

The concepts of *due care* and *due diligence* are related but distinctly different. For example, in practice, due care is turning on logging; due diligence is regularly reviewing the logs.

Understand and Apply Concepts of Confidentiality, Integrity, and Availability

The *CIA* triad (also referred to as *ICA*) forms the basis of information security (see Figure 3-1). The triad is composed of three fundamental information security concepts:

>> Confidentiality

>> Integrity

>> Availability

FIGURE 3-1:
The C-I-A triad.

As with any triangular shape, all three sides depend on each other (think of a three-sided pyramid or a three-legged stool) to form a stable structure. If one piece falls apart, the whole thing falls apart.

Confidentiality

Confidentiality limits access to information to subjects (users and machines) that require it. *Privacy* is a closely related concept that's most often associated with personal data. Various U.S. and international laws exist to protect the privacy (confidentiality) of personal data.

Personal data most commonly refers to *personally identifiable information* (PII) or *personal health information* (PHI). PII includes names, addresses, Social Security numbers, contact information (in some cases), and financial or medical data. PHI consists of many of the same data elements as PII, but also includes an individual patient's medical records and healthcare payment history. Personal data, in more comprehensive legal definitions (particularly in Europe), may also include race, marital status, sexual orientation or lifestyle, religious preference, political affiliations, and any number of other unique personal characteristics that may be collected or stored about an individual.

TIP

The U.S. Health Insurance Portability and Accountability Act (HIPAA), discussed later in this chapter, defines PHI as *protected health information*. In its more general context, PHI refers to *personal health information*.

The objective of privacy is the confidentiality and proper handling of personal data.

Integrity

Integrity safeguards the accuracy and completeness of information and processing methods. It ensures that

>> Unauthorized users or processes don't make modifications to data.

>> Authorized users or processes don't make unauthorized modifications to data.

>> Data is internally and externally consistent, meaning a given input produces an expected output.

Availability

Availability ensures that authorized users have reliable and timely access to information, and associated systems and assets, when and where needed. Availability is easily one of the most overlooked aspects of information security. In addition to Denial of Service attacks, other threats to availability include single points of failure, inadequate capacity (such as storage, bandwidth, and processing) planning, equipment malfunctions, and business interruptions or disasters.

THE INTERNET OF THINGS AND C-I-A

As the Internet of Things (IoT) evolves, an increasingly important aspect of security will be human safety.

As such, the CIA triad is likely to evolve as well, giving way to a four-part concept: *confidentiality, integrity, availability,* and *safety.*

Information security is rapidly including personal security and safety. Computer-controlled medical devices, self-driving cars, home automation and security, robotic surgery, and other innovations are taking information security far beyond information security to include the security of *us.*

Compliance

Compliance is composed of the set of activities undertaken by an organization in its attempts to abide by applicable laws, regulations, standards, and other legal obligations such as contract terms and conditions and service-level agreements (SLAs).

Because of the nature of compliance, and because there are many security- and privacy-related laws and standards, many organizations have adopted the fatally mistaken notion that to be compliant with security regulations is the same thing as being secure. However, it is appropriate to say that being compliant with security regulations and standards is a step in the right direction on the journey to becoming secure. The nature of threats today makes it plain that even organizations that are fully compliant with applicable security laws, regulations, and standards may be woefully unsecure.

Legislative and regulatory compliance

A basic understanding of the major types and classifications of U.S. and international law, including key concepts and terms, is required for the CISSP exam.

Common law

Common law (also known as *case law*) originated in medieval England, and is derived from the decisions (or *precedents*) of judges. Common law is based on the doctrine of *stare decisis* ("let the decision stand") and is often codified by statutes. Under the common law system of the United States, three major categories of laws are defined at the federal and state levels: *criminal*, *civil* (or *tort*), and *administrative* (or *regulatory*) laws.

Criminal law

Criminal law defines those crimes committed against society, even when the actual victim is a business or individual(s). Criminal laws are enacted to protect the general public. As such, in the eyes of the court, the victim is incidental to the greater cause.

CRIMINAL PENALTIES

Penalties under criminal law have two main purposes:

>> **Punishment:** Penalties may include jail/prison sentences, probation, fines, and/or financial restitution to the victim.

>> **Deterrence:** Penalties must be severe enough to dissuade any further criminal activity by the offender or anyone else considering a similar crime.

BURDEN OF PROOF UNDER CRIMINAL LAW

To be convicted under criminal law, a judge or jury must believe *beyond a reasonable doubt* that the defendant is guilty. Therefore, the burden of proof in a criminal case rests firmly with the prosecution.

CLASSIFICATIONS OF CRIMINAL LAW

Criminal law has two main classifications, depending on severity, such as type of crime/attack or total loss in dollars:

>> **Felony:** More serious crimes, normally resulting in jail/prison terms of more than one year.

>> **Misdemeanor:** Less serious crimes, normally resulting in fines or jail/prison terms of less than one year.

Civil law

Civil (tort) law addresses wrongful acts committed against an individual or business, either willfully or negligently, resulting in damage, loss, injury, or death.

CIVIL PENALTIES

Unlike criminal penalties, civil penalties don't include jail or prison terms. Instead, civil penalties provide financial restitution to the victim:

>> **Compensatory damages:** Actual damages to the victim, including attorney/legal fees, lost profits, investigative costs, and so on.

>> **Punitive damages:** Determined by a jury and intended to punish the offender.

>> **Statutory damages:** Mandatory damages determined by law and assessed for violating the law.

BURDEN OF PROOF UNDER CIVIL LAW

Convictions under civil law are typically easier to obtain than under criminal law because the burden of proof is much less. To be convicted under civil law, a jury must believe *based upon the preponderance of the evidence* that the defendant is guilty. This simply means that the available evidence leads the judge or jury to a conclusion of guilt.

LIABILITY AND DUE CARE

The concepts of liability and due care are germane to civil law cases, but they're also applicable under administrative law, which we discuss in the next section.

The standard criteria for assessing the legal requirements for implementing recommended safeguards is to evaluate the cost of the safeguard and the estimated loss from the corresponding threat, if realized. If the cost is less than the estimated loss and the organization doesn't implement a safeguard, then a legal liability may exist. This is based on the principle of *proximate causation*, in which an action taken or not taken was part of a sequence of events that resulted in negative consequences.

Under the Federal Sentencing Guidelines, senior corporate officers may be *personally* liable if their organization fails to comply with applicable laws. Such individuals must follow the prudent man (or person) rule, which requires them to perform their duties:

>> In good faith.

>> In the best interests of the enterprise.

>> With the care and diligence that ordinary, prudent people in a similar position would exercise under similar circumstances.

Administrative law

Administrative (regulatory) laws define standards of performance and conduct for major industries (including banking, energy, and healthcare), organizations, and government agencies. These laws are typically enforced by various government agencies, and violations may result in financial penalties and/or imprisonment.

International law

Given the global nature of the Internet, it's often necessary for countries to cooperate in order to bring a computer criminal to justice. But because practically every country in the world has its own unique legal system, such cooperation is always difficult and often impossible. As a starting point, countries sometimes disagree on exactly what justice is. Other problems include

>> **Lack of universal cooperation:** We can't answer the question, "Why can't we all just get along?" but we can tell you that it's highly unlikely that a 14-year-old hacker in some remote corner of the world will commit some dastardly crime that unites us all in our efforts to take him down, bringing about a lasting world peace.

LAWYER-SPEAK

Although the information in this sidebar is not tested on the CISSP examination, it may come in handy when you're attempting to learn the various laws and regulations in this domain. You'll find it helpful to know the correct parlance (fancy-speak for *jargon*) used in the U.S. For example:

18 U.S.C. § 1030 (1986) (the Computer Fraud and Abuse Act of 1986) refers to Section 1030 in Title 18 of the 1986 edition of the United States Code, not "18 University of Southern California squiggly-thingy 1030 (1986)."

Federal statutes and administrative laws are usually cited in the following format:

- **The title number:** Titles are grouped by subject matter.
- **The abbreviation for the code:** For example, *U.S.C.* is United States Code; *C.F.R.* is Code of Federal Regulations.
- **The section number:** *§* means "The Word Formerly Known as Section."
- **The year of publication:** Listed in parentheses.

Other important abbreviations to understand include

- **Fed. Reg.:** Federal Register.
- **Fed. R. Evid.:** Federal Rules of Evidence.
- **PL:** Public Law.
- **§§:** Sections; for example, 18 U.S.C. §§ 2701–11 refers to sections 2701 through 2711.
- **v.:** versus; for example, United States v. Moore. *Note:* The rest of the civilized world understands *vs.* to mean *versus* and *v.* to mean *version* or *volume*, but you need to remember two important points: Lawyers aren't part of the civilized world, and they apparently charge by the letter (as well as by the minute).

» **Differing interpretations of laws:** What's illegal in one country (or even in one state in the U.S.) isn't necessarily illegal in another.

» **Differing rules of evidence:** This problem can encompass different rules for obtaining and collecting evidence, as well as different rules for admissibility of evidence.

» **Low priority:** Different nations have different views regarding the seriousness of computer crimes; and in the realm of international relations, computer crimes are usually of minimal concern.

>> **Outdated laws and technology:** Related to the low-priority problem. Technology varies greatly throughout the world, and many countries (not only the Third World countries) lag far behind others. For this reason and many others, computer crime laws are often a low priority and aren't kept current. This problem is further exacerbated by the different technical capabilities of the various law enforcement agencies that may be involved in an international case.

>> **Extradition:** Many countries don't have extradition treaties and won't extradite suspects to a country that has different or controversial practices, such as capital punishment. Although capital punishment for a computer crime may sound extreme, recent events and the threat of cyberterrorism make this a very real possibility.

Besides common law systems (which we talk about in the section "Common law," earlier in this chapter), other countries throughout the world use legal systems including:

>> **Civil law systems:** Not to be confused with U.S. civil law, which is based on common law. *Civil law* systems use constitutions and statutes exclusively and aren't based on precedent. The role of a judge in a civil law system is to interpret the law. Civil law is the most widespread type of law system used throughout the world.

>> **Napoleonic code:** Originating in France after the French Revolution, the Napoleonic code has spread to many other countries in Europe and elsewhere. In this system, laws are developed by legislative bodies and interpreted by the courts. However, there is often no formal concept of legal precedent.

>> **Religious (or customary) law systems:** Derived from religious beliefs and values. Common religious law systems include *Sharia* in Islam, *Halakha* in Judaism, and *Canon law* in Christianity.

>> **Pluralistic (or mixed) law systems:** Combinations of various systems, such as civil and common law, civil and religious law, and common and religious law.

Privacy requirements compliance

Privacy and data protection laws are enacted to protect information collected and maintained on individuals from unauthorized disclosure or misuse. Privacy laws are one area in which the United States lags behind many others, particularly the European Union (EU) and its General Data Protection Regulation (GDPR), which has defined increasingly restrictive privacy regulations that regulate the transfer of personal information to countries (including the United States) that don't equally protect such information. The EU GDPR privacy rules include the following requirements about personal data and records:

>> Must be collected fairly and lawfully, and only after the subject has provided explicit consent.

>> Must only be used for the purposes for which it was collected and only for a reasonable period of time.

>> Must be accurate and kept up to date.

>> Must be accessible to individuals who request a report on personal information held about themselves.

>> Individuals must have the right to have any errors in their personal data corrected.

>> Individuals must have the right for their information to be expunged from an organization's information systems.

>> Personal data can't be disclosed to other organizations or individuals unless authorized by law or consent of the individual.

>> Transmission of personal data to locations where equivalent privacy protection cannot be assured is prohibited.

Specific privacy and data protection laws are discussed later in this chapter.

Understand Legal and Regulatory Issues that Pertain to Information Security in a Global Context

CISSP candidates are expected to be familiar with the laws and regulations that are relevant to information security throughout the world and in various industries. This could include national laws, local laws, and any laws that pertain to the types of activities performed by organizations.

Computer crimes

Computer crime consists of any criminal activity in which computer systems or networks are used as tools. Computer crime also includes crimes in which computer systems are targeted, or in which computers are the scene of the crime committed. That's a pretty wide spectrum.

The real world, however, has difficulty dealing with computer crimes. Several reasons why computer crimes are hard to cope with include

>> **Lack of understanding:** In general, legislators, judges, attorneys, law enforcement officials, and jurors don't understand the many different technologies and issues involved in a computer crime.

>> **Inadequate laws:** Laws are slow to change, and fail to keep pace with rapidly evolving new technology.

>> **Encryption:** Increasingly, there are cases where law enforcement organizations are hindered in their criminal investigations because of advanced encryption techniques in mobile devices.

>> **Multiple roles of computers in crime:** These roles include crimes committed *against* a computer (such as hacking into a system and stealing information) and crimes committed *by using* a computer (such as using a system to launch a Distributed Denial of Service attack). Computers may also *support* criminal enterprises, where criminals use computers for crime-related recordkeeping or communications.

Computer crimes are often difficult to prosecute for the reasons we just listed, and also because of the following issues:

>> **Lack of tangible assets:** Traditional rules of property often don't clearly apply in a computer crime case. However, property rules have been extended in many countries to include electronic information. Computing resources, bandwidth, and data (in the form of magnetic particles) are often the only assets at issue. These can be very difficult to quantify and assign a value to. The asset valuation process, which we discuss later in this chapter, can provide vital information for valuing electronic information.

>> **Rules of evidence:** Often, original documents aren't available in a computer crime case. Most evidence in such a case is considered hearsay evidence (which we discuss later in the upcoming section "Hearsay rule") and must meet certain requirements to be admissible in court. Often, evidence is a computer itself, or data on its hard drive.

>> **Lack of evidence:** Many crimes are difficult to prosecute because law enforcement agencies lack the skills or resources to even *identify* the perpetrator, much less gather sufficient evidence to bring charges and successfully prosecute. Frequently, skilled computer criminals use a long trail of compromised computers through different countries in order to make it as difficult as possible for even diligent law enforcement agencies to identify them. Further, encryption techniques sometimes prevent law enforcement from being able to search computers and mobile devices for evidence.

>> **Definition of loss:** A loss of confidentiality or integrity of data goes far beyond the normal definition of loss in a criminal or civil case.

>> **Location of perpetrators:** Often, the people who commit computer crimes against specific organizations do so from locations outside of the victim's country. Computer criminals do this, knowing that even if they make a mistake and create discoverable evidence that identifies them, the victim's country law enforcement agencies will have difficulty apprehending the criminal.

>> **Criminal profiles:** Computer criminals aren't necessarily hardened criminals and may include the following:

- **Juveniles:** Juvenile laws in many countries aren't taken seriously and are inadequate to deter crime. A busy prosecutor is unlikely to pursue a low-profile crime committed by a juvenile that results in a three-year probation sentence for the offender.

- **Trusted individuals:** Many computer criminals are individuals who hold a position of trust within a company and have no prior criminal record. Such an individual likely can afford a dream team for legal defense, and a judge may be inclined to levy a more lenient sentence for the first-time offender. However, recent corporate scandals in the U.S. have set a strong precedent for punishment at the highest levels.

Computer crimes are often classified under one of the following six major categories:

>> **Industrial espionage:** Businesses are increasingly the targets of industrial espionage. These attacks include competitive intelligence gathering, as well as theft of product specifications, plans, and schematics, and business information such as marketing and customer information. Businesses can be inviting targets for an attacker due to

- **Lack of expertise:** Despite heightened security awareness, a shortage of qualified security professionals exists and is getting worse. This results in organizations not having adequate preventive, detective, and response capabilities.

- **Lack of resources:** Businesses often lack the resources to prevent, or even detect, attacks against their systems.

- **Lack of concern:** Executive management and boards of directors in many organizations still turn a blind eye to requests for security resources.

- **Lack of reporting or prosecution:** Because of public relations concerns and the inability to prosecute computer criminals because of either a lack of evidence or a lack of properly handled evidence, the majority of business attacks still go unreported. Further, few jurisdictions require organizations to disclose break-ins involving intellectual property.

The cost to businesses can be significant, including loss of trade secrets or proprietary information, loss of revenue, and loss of reputation when intrusions are made public.

» **Financial attacks:** Banks, large corporations, and e-commerce sites are the targets of financial attacks, many of which are motivated by greed. Financial attacks may seek to steal or embezzle funds, gain access to online financial information, extort individuals or businesses, or obtain the personal credit card numbers of customers. Ransomware attacks are immensely successful forms of financial attacks that encrypt information and demand a cryptocurrency ransom for the key to decrypt the information. Destructware attacks are similar to ransomware in that they often demand ransoms but do not provide keys to recover the encrypted information.

» **"Fun" attacks:** "Fun" attacks are perpetrated by thrill-seekers and script kiddies who are motivated by curiosity or excitement. Although these attackers may not intend to do any harm or use any of the information that they access, they're still dangerous and their activities are still illegal.

These attacks can also be relatively easy to detect and prosecute. Because the perpetrators are often *script kiddies* (hackers who use scripts or programs written by other hackers because they don't have programming skills themselves) or otherwise-inexperienced hackers, they may not know how to cover their tracks effectively.

Also, because no real harm is normally done nor intended against the system, it may be tempting (although ill-advised) for a business to prosecute the individual and put a positive public relations spin on the incident. You've seen the film at 11:00: "We quickly detected the attack, prevented any harm to our network, and prosecuted the responsible individual; our security is *unbreakable!*" Such action, however, will likely motivate others to launch a more serious and concerted grudge attack against the business.

Many computer criminals in this category only seek notoriety. Although it's one thing to brag to a small circle of friends about defacing a public website, the wily hacker who appears on CNN reaches the next level of hacker celebrity-dom. These twisted individuals want to be caught to revel in their 15 minutes of fame.

» **Grudge attacks:** Grudge attacks are targeted at individuals or businesses, and the attacker is motivated by a desire to take revenge against a person or organization. A disgruntled employee, for example, may steal trade secrets, delete valuable data, or plant a *logic bomb* in a critical system or application.

Fortunately, these attacks (at least in the case of a disgruntled employee) can be easier to prevent or prosecute than many other types of attacks because:

- The attacker is often known to the victim.

- The attack has a visible impact that produces a viable evidence trail.

- Most businesses (already sensitive to the possibility of wrongful-termination suits) have well-established termination procedures.

- Specific laws (such as the U.S. Economic Espionage Act of 1996, which we discuss in the section "U.S. Economic Espionage Act of 1996," later in this chapter) provide very severe penalties for such crimes.

» **Ideological attacks and hacktivism:** Ideological attacks — commonly known as "hacktivism" — have become increasingly common in recent years. Hacktivists typically target businesses or organizations to protest a controversial position that does not agree with their own ideology. These attacks typically take the form of Distributed Denial-of-Service (DDoS) attacks, but can also include data theft. For example, the U.S. Senate and many businesses — including the Sony PlayStation Network — were targeted in 2011 and early 2012 because of their support for the Stop Online Piracy Act (SOPA).

» **Military and political intelligence attacks:** Military and political intelligence attacks are perpetrated by criminals, traitors, or foreign military and intelligence agents seeking classified government, law enforcement, or military information. Such attacks are often carried out by governments during times of war and conflict.

» **Terrorist attacks:** Terrorism exists at many levels on the Internet. Following the terrorist attacks against the U.S. on September 11, 2001, the general public became painfully aware of the extent of terrorism on the Internet. Terrorist organizations and cells use online capabilities to coordinate attacks, transfer funds, harm international commerce, disrupt critical systems, disseminate propaganda, recruit new members, and gain useful information about developing techniques and instruments of terror, including nuclear, biological, and chemical weapons.

Important international computer crime and information security laws and standards that the CISSP candidate should be familiar with include

» U.S. Computer Fraud and Abuse Act of 1986

» U.S. Electronic Communications Privacy Act (ECPA) of 1986

» U.S. Computer Security Act of 1987

» U.S. Federal Sentencing Guidelines of 1991 (not necessarily specific to computer crime, but certainly relevant)

» U.S. Economic Espionage Act of 1996

» U.S. Child Pornography Prevention Act of 1996

» USA PATRIOT Act of 2001

- >> U.S. Sarbanes-Oxley Act of 2002
- >> U.S. Homeland Security Act of 2002
- >> U.S. The Federal Information Security Management Act of 2002 (FISMA)
- >> U.S. Controlling the Assault of Non-Solicited Pornography and Marketing (CAN-SPAM) Act of 2003
- >> U.S. Identity Theft and Assumption Deterrence Act of 2003
- >> U.S. Intelligence Reform and Terrorism Prevention Act of 2004
- >> The Council of Europe's Convention on Cybercrime of 2001
- >> The Computer Misuse Act of 1990 (U.K.)
- >> Privacy and Electronic Communications Regulations of 2003 (U.K.)
- >> Information Technology Act 2000 (India)
- >> Cybercrime Act of 2001 (Australia)
- >> General Data Protection Regulation (GDPR) (EU)
- >> Payment Card Industry Data Security Standard (PCI DSS)

It is important to understand that cybersecurity and privacy laws change from time to time. The list of such laws in this book should not be considered complete or up to date. Instead, consider these a sampling of laws from the U.S. and elsewhere.

U.S. Computer Fraud and Abuse Act of 1986, 18 U.S.C. § 1030 (as amended)

In 1986, the first U.S. federal computer crime law, the U.S. Computer Fraud and Abuse Act, was passed. This intermediate act was narrowly defined and somewhat ambiguous. The law covered:

- >> Classified national defense or foreign relations information
- >> Records of financial institutions or credit reporting agencies
- >> Government computers

The U.S. Computer Fraud and Abuse Act of 1986 enhanced and strengthened the 1984 law, clarifying definitions of criminal fraud and abuse for federal computer crimes and removing obstacles to prosecution.

The Act established two new felony offenses for the unauthorized access of *federal interest* computers and a misdemeanor for unauthorized trafficking in computer passwords:

>> **Felony 1:** Unauthorized access, or access that exceeds authorization, of a federal interest computer to further an intended fraud, shall be punishable as a felony [Subsection (a)(4)].

>> **Felony 2:** Altering, damaging, or destroying information in a federal interest computer or preventing authorized use of the computer or information, that causes an aggregate loss of $1,000 or more during a one-year period or potentially impairs medical treatment, shall be punishable as a felony [Subsection (a)(5)].

This provision was stricken in its entirety and replaced with a more general provision, which we discuss later in this section.

>> **Misdemeanor:** Trafficking in computer passwords or similar information if it affects interstate or foreign commerce or permits unauthorized access to computers used by or for the U.S. government [Subsection (a)(6)].

TIP

The Act defines a *federal interest computer* (actually, the term was changed to *protected computer* in the 1996 amendments to the Act) as either a computer

>> "[E]xclusively for the use of a financial institution or the United States government, or, in the case of a computer not exclusively for such use, used by or for a financial institution or the United States government and the conduct constituting the offense affect that use by or for the financial institution or the government"

>> "[W]hich is used in interstate or foreign commerce or communication"

Several minor amendments to the U.S. Computer Fraud and Abuse Act were made in 1988, 1989, and 1990, and more significant amendments were made in 1994, 1996 (by the Economic Espionage Act of 1996), and 2001 (by the USA PATRIOT Act of 2001). The Act, in its present form, establishes eight specific computer crimes. In addition to the three that we discuss in the preceding list, these crimes include the following five provisions (we discuss subsection [a][5] in its current form in the following list):

>> Unauthorized access, or access that exceeds authorization, to a computer that results in *disclosure of U.S. national defense or foreign relations information* [Subsection (a)(1)].

>> Unauthorized access, or access that exceeds authorization, to a protected computer to *obtain any information on that computer* [Subsection (a)(2)].

>> Unauthorized access to a protected computer, or access that exceeds authorization, to a protected computer that *affects the use* of that computer by or for the U.S. government [Subsection (a)(3)].

>> Unauthorized access to a protected computer causing damage or reckless damage, or *intentionally transmitting malicious code* which causes damage to a protected computer [Subsection (a)(5), as amended].

>> Transmission of interstate or foreign commerce communication *threatening to cause damage* to a protected computer for the purpose of extortion [Subsection (a)(7)].

In the section "USA PATRIOT Act of 2001," later in this chapter, we discuss major amendments to the U.S. Computer Fraud and Abuse Act of 1986 (as amended) that Congress introduced in 2001.

The U.S. Computer Fraud and Abuse Act of 1986 is *the* major computer crime law currently in effect. The CISSP exam likely tests your knowledge of the Act in its original 1986 form, but you should also be prepared for revisions to the exam that may cover the more recent amendments to the Act.

U.S. Electronic Communications Privacy Act (ECPA) of 1986

The ECPA complements the U.S. Computer Fraud and Abuse Act of 1986 and prohibits eavesdropping, interception, or unauthorized monitoring of wire, oral, and electronic communications. However, the ECPA does provide specific statutory exceptions, allowing network providers to monitor their networks for legitimate business purposes if they notify the network users of the monitoring process.

The ECPA was amended extensively by the USA PATRIOT Act of 2001. These changes are discussed in the upcoming "USA PATRIOT Act of 2001" section.

The U.S. Electronic Communications Privacy Act (ECPA) provides the legal basis for network monitoring.

U.S. Computer Security Act of 1987

The U.S. Computer Security Act of 1987 requires federal agencies to take extra security measures to prevent unauthorized access to computers that hold sensitive information. In addition to identifying and developing security plans for sensitive systems, the Act requires those agencies to provide security-related awareness training for their employees. The Act also assigns formal government responsibility for computer security to the National Institute of Standards and Technology (NIST) for information security standards, in general, and to the National Security Agency (NSA) for cryptography in classified government/military systems and applications.

U.S. Federal Sentencing Guidelines of 1991

In November 1991, the United States Sentencing Commission published Chapter 8, "Federal Sentencing Guidelines for Organizations," of the U.S. Federal Sentencing Guidelines. These guidelines establish written standards of conduct for organizations, provide relief in sentencing for organizations that have demonstrated due diligence, and place responsibility for due care on senior management officials with penalties for negligence, including fines of up to $290 million.

U.S. Economic Espionage Act of 1996

The U.S. Economic Espionage Act (EEA) of 1996 was enacted to curtail industrial espionage, particularly when such activity benefits a foreign entity. The EEA makes it a criminal offense to take, download, receive, or possess trade secret information that's been obtained without the owner's authorization. Penalties include fines of up to $10 million, up to 15 years in prison, and forfeiture of any property used to commit the crime. The EEA also enacted the 1996 amendments to the U.S. Computer Fraud and Abuse Act, which we talk about in the section "U.S. Computer Fraud and Abuse Act of 1986, 18 U.S.C. § 1030 (as amended)," earlier in this chapter.

U.S. Child Pornography Prevention Act of 1996

The U.S. Child Pornography Prevention Act (CPPA) of 1996 was enacted to combat the use of computer technology to produce and distribute pornography involving children, including adults portraying children.

USA PATRIOT Act of 2001

Following the terrorist attacks against the United States on September 11, 2001, the USA PATRIOT Act of 2001 (Uniting and Strengthening America by Providing Appropriate Tools Required to Intercept and Obstruct Terrorism Act) was enacted in October 2001 and renewed in March 2006. (Many provisions originally set to expire have since been made permanent under the renewed Act.) This Act takes great strides to strengthen and amend existing computer crime laws, including the U.S. Computer Fraud and Abuse Act and the U.S. Electronic Communications Privacy Act (ECPA), as well as to empower U.S. law enforcement agencies, if only temporarily. U.S. federal courts have subsequently declared some of the Act's provisions unconstitutional. The sections of the Act that are relevant to the CISSP exam include

>> **Section 202 — Authority to Intercept Wire, Oral, and Electronic Communications Relating to Computer Fraud and Abuse Offenses:** Under previous law, investigators couldn't obtain a wiretap order for violations of the Computer Fraud and Abuse Act. This amendment authorizes such action for felony violations of that Act.

- » **Section 209 — Seizure of Voice-Mail Messages Pursuant to Warrants:** Under previous law, investigators could obtain access to e-mail under the ECPA but not voice-mail, which was covered by the more restrictive wiretap statute. This amendment authorizes access to voice-mail with a search warrant rather than a wiretap order.

- » **Section 210 — Scope of Subpoenas for Records of Electronic Communications:** Under previous law, subpoenas of electronic records were restricted to very limited information. This amendment expands the list of records that can be obtained and updates technology-specific terminology.

- » **Section 211 — Clarification of Scope:** This amendment governs privacy protection and disclosure to law enforcement of cable, telephone, and Internet service provider records.

- » **Section 212 — Emergency Disclosure of Electronic Communications to Protect Life and Limb:** Prior to this amendment, no special provisions existed that allowed a communications provider to disclose customer information to law enforcement officials in emergency situations, such as an imminent crime or terrorist attack, without exposing the provider to civil liability suits from the customer.

- » **Section 214 — Pen Register and Trap and Trace Authority under FISA (Foreign Intelligence Surveillance Act):** Clarifies law enforcement authority to trace communications on the Internet and other computer networks, and it authorizes the use of a pen/trap device nationwide, instead of limiting it to the jurisdiction of the court.

TECHNICAL STUFF

A *pen/trap device* refers to a *pen register* that shows outgoing numbers called from a phone and a *trap and trace device* that shows incoming numbers that called a phone. Pen registers and trap and trace devices are collectively referred to as pen/trap devices because most technologies allow the same device to perform both types of traces (incoming and outgoing numbers).

- » **Section 217 — Interception of Computer Trespasser Communications:** Under previous law, it was permissible for organizations to monitor activity on their own networks but not necessarily for law enforcement to assist these organizations in monitoring, even when such help was specifically requested. This amendment allows organizations to authorize persons "acting under color (pretense or appearance) of law" to monitor trespassers on their computer systems.

- » **Section 220 — Nationwide Service of Search Warrants for Electronic Evidence:** Removes jurisdictional issues in obtaining search warrants for e-mail. For an excellent example of this problem, read *The Cuckoo's Egg: Tracking a Spy Through the Maze of Computer Espionage,* by Clifford Stoll (Doubleday).

>> **Section 814 — Deterrence and Prevention of Cyberterrorism:** Greatly strengthens the U.S. Computer Fraud and Abuse Act, including raising the maximum prison sentence from 10 years to 20 years.

>> **Section 815 — Additional Defense to Civil Actions Relating to Preserving Records in Response to Government Requests:** Clarifies the "statutory authorization" (government authority) defense for violations of the ECPA.

>> **Section 816 — Development and Support of Cybersecurity Forensic Capabilities:** Requires the Attorney General to establish regional computer forensic laboratories, maintain existing laboratories, and provide forensic and training capabilities to Federal, State, and local law enforcement personnel and prosecutors.

WARNING

The USA PATRIOT Act of 2001 changes many of the provisions in the computer crime laws, particularly the U.S. Computer Fraud and Abuse Act, which we discuss in the section "U.S. Computer Fraud and Abuse Act of 1986, 18 U.S.C. § 1030 (as amended)," earlier in this chapter; and the Electronic Communications Privacy Act of 1986, which we detail in the section "U.S. Electronic Communications Privacy Act (ECPA) of 1986," earlier in this chapter. As a security professional, you must keep abreast of current laws and affairs to perform your job effectively.

U.S. Sarbanes-Oxley Act of 2002 (SOX)

In the wake of several major corporate and accounting scandals, SOX was passed in 2002 to restore public trust in publicly held corporations and public accounting firms by establishing new standards and strengthening existing standards for these entities including auditing, governance, and financial disclosures.

SOX established the Public Company Accounting Oversight Board (PCAOB), which is a private-sector, nonprofit corporation responsible for overseeing auditors in the implementation of SOX. PCAOB's "Accounting Standard 2" recognizes the role of information technology as it relates to a company's internal controls and financial reporting. The Standard identifies the responsibility of Chief Information Officers (CIOs) for the security of information systems that process and store financial data, and it has many implications for information technology security and governance.

U.S. Homeland Security Act of 2002

This law consolidated 22 U.S. government agencies to form the Department of Homeland Security (DHS). The law also provided for the creation of a privacy official to enforce the Privacy Act of 1974.

U.S. Federal Information Systems Management Act (FISMA) of 2002

FISMA extended the Computer Security Act of 1987 by requiring regular audits of both U.S. government information systems, and organizations providing information services to the U.S. federal government.

U.S. CAN-SPAM Act of 2003

The U.S. CAN-SPAM Act (Controlling the Assault of Non-Solicited Pornography and Marketing Act) establishes standards for sending commercial e-mail messages, charges the U.S. Federal Trade Commission (FTC) with enforcement of the provision, and provides penalties that include fines and imprisonment for violations of the Act.

U.S. Identity Theft and Assumption Deterrence Act of 2003

This law updated earlier U.S. laws on identity theft.

Directive 95/46/EC on the protection of personal data (1995, EU)

In 1995, the European Parliament ratified this essential legislation that protects personal information for all European citizens. The directive states that personal data should not be processed at all, except when certain conditions are met.

A legitimate concern about the disposition of European citizens' personal data when it leaves computer systems in Europe and enters computer systems in the U.S. led to the creation of the Safe Harbor program (discussed in the following section).

Safe Harbor (1998)

In an agreement between the European Union and the U.S. Department of Commerce in 1998, the U.S. Department of Commerce developed a certification program called *Safe Harbor*. This permits U.S.-based organizations to certify themselves as properly handling private data belonging to European citizens.

U.S. Intelligence Reform and Terrorism Prevention Act of 2004

This law facilitates the sharing of intelligence information between various U.S. government agencies, as well as protections of privacy and civil liberties.

The Council of Europe's Convention on Cybercrime (2001)

The Convention on Cybercrime is an international treaty, currently signed by more than 40 countries (the U.S. ratified the treaty in 2006), requiring criminal laws to be established in signatory nations for computer hacking activities, child pornography, and intellectual property violations. The treaty also attempts to improve international cooperation with respect to monitoring, investigations, and prosecution.

The Computer Misuse Act 1990 (U.K.)

The Computer Misuse Act 1990 (U.K.) defines three criminal offenses related to computer crime: unauthorized access (whether successful or unsuccessful), unauthorized modification, and hindering authorized access (Denial of Service).

Privacy and Electronic Communications Regulations of 2003 (U.K.)

Similar to U.S. "do not call" laws, this law makes it illegal to use equipment to make automated telephone calls that play recorded messages.

Information Technology Act 2000 (India)

This law modernized computer crimes and defined activities such as data theft, creation and spreading of malware, identity theft, pornography, child pornography, and cyber terrorism. This law also validated electronic contracts and electronic signatures.

Cybercrime Act 2001 (Australia)

The Cybercrime Act 2001 (Australia) establishes criminal penalties, including fines and imprisonment, for people who commit computer crimes (including unauthorized access, unauthorized modification, or Denial of Service) with intent to commit a serious offense.

Payment Card Industry Data Security Standard (PCI DSS)

Although not (yet) a legal mandate, the Payment Card Industry Data Security Standard (PCI DSS) is one example of an industry initiative for mandating and enforcing security standards. PCI DSS applies to any business worldwide that transmits, processes, or stores payment card (meaning credit card) transactions to conduct business with customers — whether that business handles thousands of credit card transactions a day or a single transaction a year. Compliance is mandated and enforced by the payment card brands (American Express, Master-Card, Visa, and so on) and each payment card brand manages its own compliance program.

TIP

Although PCI DSS is an industry standard rather than a legal mandate, many states are beginning to introduce legislation that would make PCI compliance (or at least compliance with certain provisions) mandatory for organizations that do business in that state.

PCI DSS requires organizations to submit an annual assessment and network scan, or to complete onsite PCI data security assessments and quarterly network scans. The actual requirements depend on the number of payment card transactions handled by an organization and other factors, such as previous data loss incidents.

PCI DSS version 3.2 consists of six core principles, supported by 12 accompanying requirements, and more than 200 specific procedures for compliance. These include

>> **Principle 1:** Build and maintain a secure network:

- **Requirement 1:** Install and maintain a firewall configuration to protect cardholder data.

- **Requirement 2:** Don't use vendor-supplied defaults for system passwords and other security parameters.

>> **Principle 2:** Protect cardholder data:

- **Requirement 3:** Protect stored cardholder data.

- **Requirement 4:** Encrypt transmission of cardholder data across open, public networks.

>> **Principle 3:** Maintain a vulnerability management program:

- **Requirement 5:** Use and regularly update antivirus software.

- **Requirement 6:** Develop and maintain secure systems and applications.

>> **Principle 4:** Implement strong access control measures:

- **Requirement 7:** Restrict access to cardholder data by business need-to-know.

- **Requirement 8:** Assign a unique ID to each person who has computer access.

- **Requirement 9:** Restrict physical access to cardholder data.

- **Principle 5:** Regularly monitor and test networks:

  - **Requirement 10:** Track and monitor all access to network resources and cardholder data.

  - **Requirement 11:** Regularly test security systems and processes.

- **Principle 6:** Maintain an information security policy:

  - **Requirement 12:** Maintain a policy that addresses information security.

Penalties for non-compliance are levied by the payment card brands and include not being allowed to process credit card transactions, fines up to $25,000 per month for minor violations, and fines up to $500,000 for violations that result in actual lost or stolen financial data.

Licensing and intellectual property

Given the difficulties in defining and prosecuting computer crimes, many prose-cutors seek to convict computer criminals on more traditional criminal statutes, such as theft, fraud, extortion, and embezzlement. Intellectual property rights and privacy laws, in addition to specific computer crime laws, also exist to protect the general public and assist prosecutors.

REMEMBER

The CISSP candidate should understand that because of the difficulty in prosecuting computer crimes, prosecutors often use more traditional criminal statutes, intellectual property rights, and privacy laws to convict criminals. In addition, you should also realize that specific computer crime laws do exist.

Intellectual property is protected by U.S. law under one of four classifications:

- Patents
- Trademarks
- Copyrights
- Trade secrets

Intellectual property rights worldwide are agreed upon, defined, and enforced by various organizations and treaties, including the World Intellectual Property Organization (WIPO), World Customs Organization (WCO), World Trade Organization (WTO), United Nations Commission on International Trade Law (UNCITRAL), European Union (EU), and Trade-Related Aspects of Intellectual Property Rights (TRIPs).

Licensing violations are among the most prevalent examples of intellectual property rights infringement. Other examples include plagiarism, software piracy, and corporate espionage.

Digital rights management (DRM) attempts to protect intellectual property rights by using access control technologies to prevent unauthorized copying or distribution of protected digital media.

Patents

A *patent*, as defined by the U.S. Patent and Trademark Office (PTO) is "the grant of a property right to the inventor." A patent grant confers upon the owner (either an individual or a company) "the right to exclude others from making, using, offering for sale, selling, or importing the invention." In order to qualify for a patent, an invention must be novel, useful, and not obvious. An invention must also be tangible — an idea cannot be patented. Examples of computer-related objects that may be protected by patents are computer hardware and physical devices in firmware.

A patent is granted by the U.S. PTO for an invention that has been sufficiently documented by the applicant and that has been verified as original by the PTO. A U.S. patent is generally valid for 20 years from the date of application and is effective only within the U.S., including territories and possessions. Patent applications must be filed with the appropriate patent office in various countries throughout the world to receive patent protection in that country. The owner of the patent may grant a license to others for use of the invention or its design, often for a fee.

U.S. patent (and trademark) laws and rules are covered in 35 U.S.C. and 37 C.F.R., respectively. The Patent Cooperation Treaty (PCT) provides some international protection for patents. More than 130 countries worldwide have adopted the PCT. Patent infringements are not prosecuted by the U.S. PTO. Instead, the holder of a patent must enforce their patent rights through the appropriate legal system.

REMEMBER

Patent grants were previously valid for only 17 years, but have recently been changed, for newly granted patents, to 20 years.

Trademarks

A *trademark*, as defined by the U.S. PTO, is "any word, name, symbol, or device, or any combination, used, or intended to be used, in commerce to identify and distinguish the goods of one manufacturer or seller from goods manufactured or sold by others." Computer-related objects that may be protected by trademarks include corporate brands and operating system logos. U.S. Public Law 105–330, the Trademark Law Treaty Implementation Act, provides some international protection for U.S. registered trademarks.

Copyrights

A *copyright* is a form of protection granted to the authors of "original works of authorship," both published and unpublished. A copyright protects a tangible form of expression rather than the idea or subject matter itself. Under the original Copyright Act of 1909, publication was generally the key to obtaining a federal copyright. However, the Copyright Act of 1976 changed this requirement, and copyright protection now applies to any original work of authorship immediately, from the time that it's created in a tangible form. Object code or documentation are examples of computer-related objects that may be protected by copyrights.

Copyrights can be registered through the Copyright Office of the Library of Congress, but a work doesn't need to be registered to be protected by copyright. Copyright protection generally lasts for the lifetime of the author plus 70 years.

Trade secrets

A *trade secret* is proprietary or business-related information that a company or individual uses and has exclusive rights to. To be considered a trade secret, the information must meet the following requirements:

>> **Must be genuine and not obvious:** Any unique method of accomplishing a task would constitute a trade secret, especially if it is backed up by copyrighted, patented, or proprietary software or methods that give that organization a competitive advantage.

>> **Must provide the owner a competitive or economic advantage and, therefore, have value to the owner:** For example, Google's search algorithms — the "secret sauce" that makes it popular with users (and therefore advertisers) — aren't universally known. Some secrets are protected.

>> **Must be reasonably protected from disclosure:** This doesn't mean that it must be kept absolutely and exclusively secret, but the owner must exercise due care in its protection.

Software source code or firmware code are examples of computer-related objects that an organization may protect as trade secrets.

Import/export controls

International import and export controls exist between countries to protect both intellectual property rights and certain sensitive technologies (such as encryption).

Information security professionals need to be aware of relevant import/export controls for any countries in which their organization operates or to which their employees travel. For example, it is not uncommon for laptops to be searched, and possibly confiscated, at airports to enforce various import/export controls.

Trans-border data flow

Related to import/export controls is the issue of trans-border data flow. As discussed earlier in this chapter, data privacy and breach disclosure laws vary greatly across different regions, countries, and U.S. states. Australia and European Union countries are two examples where data privacy regulations, in general, are far more stringent than in the U.S. Many countries restrict or completely forbid personal data of their citizens from leaving the country.

Issues of trans-border data flow, and data residency (where data is physically stored) are particularly germane for organizations operating in the public cloud. For these organizations, it is important to know — and have control over — where their data is stored. Issues of data residency and trans-border data flow should be addressed in any agreements or contracts with cloud service providers.

Privacy

Privacy in the context of electronic information about citizens is not well understood by everyone. Simply put, privacy has two main components:

>> **Data protection.** Here, we just mean the usual data security measures discussed in most of this book.

>> **Appropriate handling and use.** This refers to the ways in which information owners choose to process and distribute personal data.

Several important pieces of privacy and data protection legislation include the Federal Privacy Act, the Health Insurance Portability and Accountability Act (HIPAA), the Health Information Technology for Economic and Clinical Health Act (HITECH), and the Gramm-Leach-Bliley Act (GLBA) in the United States, and the Data Protection Act (DPA) in the United Kingdom. Finally, the Payment Card Industry Data Security Standard (PCI DSS) is an example of an industry policing itself — without the need for government laws or regulations.

Several privacy related laws that CISSP candidates should be familiar with include

>> U.S. Federal Privacy Act of 1974

>> U.S. Health Insurance Portability and Accountability Act (HIPAA) of 1996

>> U.S. Children's Online Privacy Protection Act (COPPA) of 1998

- » U.S. Gramm-Leach-Bliley Financial Services Modernization Act of 1999
- » U.S. Health Information Technology for Economic and Clinical Health Act (HITECH) of 2009
- » U.K. Data Protection Act of 1999
- » European General Data Protection Regulation (GDPR)

U.S. Federal Privacy Act of 1974, 5 U.S.C. § 552A

The Federal Privacy Act of 1974 protects records and information maintained by U.S. government agencies about U.S. citizens and lawful permanent residents. Except under certain specific conditions, no agency may disclose any record about an individual "except pursuant to a written request by, or with the prior written consent of, the individual to whom the record pertains." The Privacy Act also has provisions for access and amendment of an individual's records by that individual, except in cases of "information compiled in reasonable anticipation of a civil action or proceeding." The Privacy Act provides individual penalties for violations, including a misdemeanor charge and fines up to $5,000.

WARNING

Although the Federal Privacy Act of 1974 pre-dates the Internet as we know it today, don't dismiss its relevance. The provisions of the Privacy Act are as important as ever and remain in full force and effect today.

U.S. Health Insurance Portability and Accountability Act (HIPAA) of 1996, PL 104–191

HIPAA was signed into law effective August 1996. The HIPAA legislation provided Congress three years from that date to pass comprehensive health privacy legislation. When Congress failed to pass legislation by the deadline, the Department of Health and Human Services (HHS) received the authority to develop the privacy and security regulations for HIPAA. In October 1999, HHS released proposed HIPAA privacy regulations entitled "Privacy Standards for Individually Identifiable Health Information," which took effect in April 2003. HIPAA security standards were subsequently published in February 2003 and took effect in April 2003. Organizations that must comply with HIPAA regulations are referred to as *covered entities* and include

- » **Payers (or health plan):** An individual or group health plan that provides — or pays the cost of — medical care; for example, insurers.

- » **Healthcare clearinghouses:** A public or private entity that processes or facilitates the processing of nonstandard data elements of health information into standard data elements, such as data warehouses.

- » **Healthcare providers:** A provider of medical or other health services, such as hospitals, HMOs, doctors, specialists, dentists, and counselors.

Civil penalties for HIPAA violations include fines of $100 per incident, up to $25,000 per provision, per calendar year. Criminal penalties include fines up to $250,000 and potential imprisonment of corporate officers for up to ten years. Additional state penalties may also apply.

In 2009, Congress passed additional HIPAA provisions as part of the American Recovery and Reinvestment Act of 2009, requiring covered entities to publicly disclose security breaches involving personal information. (See the section "Disclosure laws" later in this chapter for a discussion of disclosure laws.)

Children's Online Privacy Protection Act (COPPA) of 1998

This law provides for protection of online information about children under the age of 13. The law defines rules for the collection of information from children and means for obtaining consent from parents. Organizations are also restricted from marketing to children under the age of 13.

U.S. Gramm-Leach-Bliley Financial Services Modernization Act (GLBA) of 1999, PL 106-102

Gramm–Leach–Bliley (known as GLBA) opened up competition among banks, insurance companies, and securities companies. GLBA also requires financial institutions to better protect their customers' personally identifiable information (PII) with three rules:

>> **Financial Privacy Rule:** Requires each financial institution to provide information to each customer regarding the protection of customers' private information.

>> **Safeguards Rule:** Requires each financial institution to develop a formal written security plan that describes how the institution will protect its customers' PII.

>> **Pretexting Protection:** Requires each financial institution to take precautions to prevent attempts by social engineers to acquire private information about institutions' customers.

Civil penalties for GLBA violations are up to $100,000 for each violation. Furthermore, officers and directors of financial institutions are personally liable for civil penalties of not more than $10,000 for each violation.

U.S. Health Information Technology for Economic and Clinical Health Act (HITECH) of 2009

The HITECH Act, passed as part of the American Recovery and Reinvestment Act of 2009, broadens the scope of HIPAA compliance to include the business associates of HIPAA covered entities. These include third-party administrators, pharmacy benefit managers for health plans, claims processing/billing/transcription companies, and persons performing legal, accounting and administrative work.

Another highly important provision of the HITECH Act promotes and, in many cases, funds the adoption of electronic health records (EHRs), in order to increase the effectiveness of individual medical treatment, improve efficiency in the U.S. healthcare system, and reduce the overall cost of healthcare. Anticipating that the widespread adoption of EHRs will increase privacy and security risks, the HITECH Act introduces new security and privacy-related requirements.

In the event of a breach of "unsecured protected health information," the HITECH Act requires covered entities to notify the affected individuals and the Secretary of the U.S. Department of Health and Human Services (HHS). The regulation defines *unsecured protected health information (PHI)* as PHI that is not secured through the use of a technology or methodology to render it unusable, unreadable, or indecipherable to unauthorized individuals.

The notification requirements vary according to the amount of data breached

» A data breach affecting more than 500 people must be reported immediately to the HHS, major media outlets and individuals affected by the breach, and must be posted on the official HHS website.

» A data breach affecting fewer than 500 people must be reported to the individuals affected by the breach, and to the HHS secretary.

Finally, the HITECH Act also requires the issuance of technical guidance on the technologies and methodologies "that render protected health information unusable, unreadable, or indecipherable to unauthorized individuals". The guidance specifies data destruction and encryption as actions that render PHI unusable if it is lost or stolen. PHI that is encrypted and whose encryption keys are properly secured provides a "safe harbor" to covered entities and does not require them to issue data-breach notifications.

U.K. Data Protection Act

Passed by Parliament in 1998, the U.K. Data Protection Act (DPA) applies to any organization that handles sensitive personal data about living persons. Such data includes

- » Names
- » Birth and anniversary dates
- » Addresses, phone numbers, and e-mail addresses
- » Racial or ethnic origins
- » Political opinions and religious (or similar) beliefs
- » Trade or labor union membership
- » Physical or mental condition
- » Sexual orientation or lifestyle
- » Criminal or civil records or allegations

The DPA applies to electronically stored information, but certain paper records used for commercial purposes may also be covered. The DPA consists of eight privacy and disclosure principles as follows:

- » "Personal data shall be processed fairly and lawfully and [shall not be processed unless certain other conditions (set forth in the Act) are met]."

- » "Personal data shall be obtained only for one or more specified and lawful purposes, and shall not be further processed in any manner incompatible with that purpose or those purposes."

- » "Personal data shall be adequate, relevant, and not excessive in relation to the purpose or purposes for which they are processed."

- » "Personal data shall be accurate and, where necessary, kept up-to-date."

- » "Personal data processed for any purpose or purposes shall not be kept for longer than is necessary for that purpose or those purposes."

- » "Personal data shall be processed in accordance with the rights of data subjects under this Act."

- » "Appropriate technical and organizational measures shall be taken against unauthorized or unlawful processing of personal data and against accidental loss or destruction of, or damage to, personal data."

- » "Personal data shall not be transferred to a country or territory outside the European Economic Area unless that country or territory ensures an adequate level of protection for the rights and freedoms of data subjects in relation to the processing of personal data."

DPA compliance is enforced by the Information Commissioner's Office (ICO), an independent official body. Penalties generally include fines which may also be imposed against the officers of a company.

European Union General Data Protection Regulation (GDPR)

The European Union General Data Protection Regulation, known as GDPR, represents a significant revision of the 1995 privacy directive. Highlights of GDPR include the following:

» Requires the enactment of a formal, documented data privacy program, which must direct all relevant business activities be designed with privacy by default and privacy by design.

» Requires that organizations that collect personally identifiable information from any European resident obtain explicit consent for the collection and use of such information. Organizations' collection of personally identifiable information must be *opt-in* as opposed to *opt-out*. In other words, users must choose to opt in to data collection and usage.

» Data subjects must have the ability to review information about themselves, be able to request that corrections be made, and be able to request that their data be expunged upon request.

» Definition of a *data controller*, an organization that stores and processes personally identifiable information.

» Definition of a *data processor*, an organization that stores and processes personally identifiable information as directed by a data controller.

» Requires the appointment of a *data protection officer* (DPO), an individual that oversees the creation and operation of an organization's data privacy program.

» Requires that all affected data subjects be notified within 72 hours of a data breach.

» Permits European authorities to levy fines on organizations that violate terms of GDPR, with those fines being as high as €20 million or 4 percent of the organization's annual turnover (revenue).

Data breaches

In an effort to combat identity theft, many U.S. states have passed disclosure laws that compel organizations to publicly disclose security breaches that may result in the compromise of personal data.

Although these laws typically include statutory penalties, the damage to an organization's reputation and the potential loss of business — caused by the public disclosure requirement of these laws — can be the most significant and damaging aspect to affected organizations. Thus, public disclosure laws shame organizations into implementing more effective information security policies and practices to lessen the risk of a data breach occurring in the first place.

By requiring organizations to notify individuals of a data breach, disclosure laws enable potential victims to take defensive or corrective action to help avoid or minimize the damage resulting from identity theft.

California Security Breach Information Act (SB-1386)

Passed in 2003, the California Security Breach Information Act (SB-1386) was the first U.S. state law to require organizations to notify all affected individuals "in the most expedient time possible and without unreasonable delay, consistent with the legitimate needs of law enforcement," if their confidential or personal data is lost, stolen, or compromised, unless that data is encrypted.

The law is applicable to any organization that does business in the state of California — even a single customer or employee in California. An organization is subject to the law even if it doesn't directly do business in California (for example, if it stores personal information about California residents for another company).

Other U.S. states have quickly followed suit, and 46 states, the District of Columbia, Puerto Rico, and the U.S. Virgin Islands now have public disclosure laws. However, these laws aren't necessarily consistent from one state to another, nor are they without flaws and critics.

For example, until early 2008, Indiana's Security Breach Disclosure and Identity Deception law (HEA 1101) did not require an organization to disclose a security breach "if access to the [lost or stolen] device is protected by a *password* [emphasis added] that has not been disclosed." Indiana's law has since been amended and is now one of the toughest state disclosure laws in effect, requiring public disclosure unless "all personal information . . . is protected by encryption."

Finally, a provision in California's and Indiana's disclosure laws, as well as in most other states' laws, allows an organization to avoid much of the cost of disclosure if the cost of providing such notice would exceed $250,000 or if more than 500,000 individuals would need to be notified. Instead, a substitute notice, consisting of e-mail notifications, conspicuous posting on the organization's website, and notification of major statewide media, is permitted.

Understand Professional Ethics

Ethics (or moral values) help to describe what you should do in a given situation based on a set of principles or values. Ethical behavior is important to maintaining credibility as an information security professional and is a requirement for maintaining your CISSP certification. An organization often defines its core values (along with its mission statement) to help ensure that its employees understand what is acceptable and expected as they work to achieve the organization's mission, goals, and objectives.

Ethics are not easily discerned, and a fine line often hovers between ethical and unethical activity. Unethical activity doesn't necessarily equate to illegal activity. And what may be acceptable in some organizations, cultures, or societies may be unacceptable or even illegal in others.

Ethical standards can be based on a common or national interest, individual rights, laws, tradition, culture, or religion. One helpful distinction between laws and ethics is that laws define what we *must* do and ethics define what we *should* do.

Many common fallacies abound about the proper use of computers, the Internet, and information, which contribute to this gray area:

>> **The Computer Game Fallacy:** Any system or network that's not properly protected is fair game.

>> **The Law-Abiding Citizen Fallacy:** If no physical theft is involved, an activity really isn't stealing.

>> **The Shatterproof Fallacy:** Any damage done will have a limited effect.

>> **The Candy-from-a-Baby Fallacy:** It's so easy, it can't be wrong.

>> **The Hacker's Fallacy:** Computers provide a valuable means of learning that will, in turn, benefit society.

The problem here lies in the distinction between *hackers* and *crackers*. Although both may have a genuine desire to learn, crackers do it at the expense of others.

>> **The Free Information Fallacy:** Any and all information should be free and thus can be obtained through any means.

REMEMBER

Almost every recognized group of professionals defines a code of conduct or standards of ethical behavior by which its members must abide. For the CISSP, it is the (ISC)² Code of Ethics. The CISSP candidate must be familiar with the (ISC)² Code of Ethics and Request for Comments (RFC) 1087 "Ethics and the Internet" for professional guidance on ethics (and information that you need to know for the exam).

Exercise the (ISC)² Code of Professional Ethics

As a requirement for (ISC)² certification, all CISSP candidates must subscribe to and fully support all portions of the (ISC)² Code of Ethics. Intentionally or knowingly violating any provision of the (ISC)² Code of Ethics may subject you to a peer review panel and revocation of your hard-earned CISSP certification.

The (ISC)² Code of Ethics consists of a preamble and four canons. The canons are listed in order of precedence, thus any conflicts should be resolved in the order presented below:

Preamble:

>> The safety and welfare of society and the common good, duty to our principals, and to each other, requires that we adhere, and be seen to adhere, to the highest ethical standards of behavior.

>> Therefore, strict adherence to this Code is a condition of certification.

Canons:

>> Protect society, the common good, necessary public trust and confidence, and the infrastructure.

>> Act honorably, honestly, justly, responsibly, and legally.

>> Provide diligent and competent service to principals.

>> Advance and protect the profession.

TIP

The best approach to complying with the (ISC)² Code of Professional Ethics is to never partake in any activity that provides even the *appearance* of an ethics violation. Making questionable moves puts your certification at risk, and it may also convey to others that such activity is acceptable. Remember to lead by example!

Support your organization's code of ethics

Just about every organization has a code of ethics, or a statement of values, which it requires its employees or members to follow in their daily conduct. As a CISSP-certified information security professional, you are expected to be a leader in your organization, which means you exemplify your organization's ethics (or values) and set a positive example for others to follow.

In addition to your organization's code of ethics, two other computer security ethics standards you should be familiar with for the CISSP exam and adhere to are the Internet Activities Board's (IAB) "Ethics and the Internet" (RFC 1087) and the Computer Ethics Institute's (CEI) "Ten Commandments of Computer Ethics".

Internet Architecture Board (IAB) — Ethics and the Internet (RFC 1087)

Published by the Internet Architecture Board (IAB) (www.iab.org) in January 1989, RFC 1087 characterizes as unethical and unacceptable any activity that purposely

> "Seeks to gain unauthorized access to the resources of the Internet."

> "Disrupts the intended use of the Internet."

> "Wastes resources (people, capacity, computer) through such actions."

> "Destroys the integrity of computer-based information."

> "Compromises the privacy of users."

Other important tenets of RFC 1087 include

> "Access to and use of the Internet is a privilege and should be treated as such by all users of [the] system."

> "Many of the Internet resources are provided by the U.S. Government. Abuse of the system thus becomes a Federal matter above and beyond simple professional ethics."

> "Negligence in the conduct of Internet-wide experiments is both irresponsible and unacceptable."

> "In the final analysis, the health and well-being of the Internet is the responsibility of its users who must, uniformly, guard against abuses which disrupt the system and threaten its long-term viability."

Computer Ethics Institute (CEI)

The Computer Ethics Institute (CEI; http://computerethicsinstitute.org) is a nonprofit research, education, and public policy organization originally founded in 1985 by the Brookings Institution, IBM, the Washington Consulting Group, and the Washington Theological Consortium. CEI members include computer science and information technology professionals, corporate representatives, professional industry associations, public policy groups, and academia.

CEI's mission is "to provide a moral compass for cyberspace." It accomplishes this mission through computer-ethics educational activities that include publications, national conferences, membership and certificate programs, a case study repository, the Ask an Ethicist online forum, consultation, and (most famously) its "Ten Commandments of Computer Ethics," which has been published in 23 languages (presented here in English):

1. Thou shalt not use a computer to harm other people.
2. Thou shalt not interfere with other people's computer work.
3. Thou shalt not snoop around in other people's computer files.
4. Thou shalt not use a computer to steal.
5. Thou shalt not use a computer to bear false witness.
6. Thou shalt not copy or use proprietary software for which you have not paid.
7. Thou shalt not use other people's computer resources without authorization or proper compensation.
8. Thou shalt not appropriate other people's intellectual output.
9. Thou shalt think about the social consequences of the program you are writing or the system you are designing.
10. Thou shalt always use a computer in ways that ensure consideration and respect for your fellow humans.

Develop and Implement Documented Security Policies, Standards, Procedures, and Guidelines

Policies, standards, procedures, and guidelines are all different from each other, but they also interact with each other in a variety of ways. It's important to understand these differences and relationships, and also to recognize the different types of policies and their applications. To successfully develop and implement information security policies, standards, guidelines, and procedures, you must ensure that your efforts are consistent with the organization's mission, goals, and objectives (discussed earlier in this chapter).

Policies, standards, procedures, and guidelines all work together as the blueprints for a successful information security program. They

>> Establish governance.

>> Provide valuable guidance and decision support.

>> Help establish legal authority.

>> Ensure that risks are kept to acceptable levels.

Too often, technical security solutions are implemented without these important blueprints. The results are often expensive and ineffective controls that aren't uniformly applied and don't support an overall security strategy.

Governance is a term that collectively represents the system of policies, standards, guidelines, and procedures — together with management oversight — that help steer an organization's day-to-day operations and decisions.

Policies

A *security policy* forms the basis of an organization's information security program. RFC 2196, *The Site Security Handbook*, defines a security policy as "a formal statement of rules by which people who are given access to an organization's technology and information assets must abide."

The four main types of policies are:

>> **Senior Management:** A high-level management statement of an organization's security objectives, organizational and individual responsibilities, ethics and beliefs, and general requirements and controls.

>> **Regulatory:** Highly detailed and concise policies usually mandated by federal, state, industry, or other legal requirements.

>> **Advisory:** Not mandatory, but highly recommended, often with specific penalties or consequences for failure to comply. Most policies fall into this category.

>> **Informative:** Only informs, with no explicit requirements for compliance.

REMEMBER

Standards, procedures, and guidelines are supporting elements of a policy and provide specific implementation details of the policy.

TIP

ISO/IEC 27002, *Information Technology — Security Techniques — Code of Practice for Information Security Management*, is an international standard for information security policy. ISO/IEC is the International Organization for Standardization and International Electrotechnical Commission. ISO/IEC 27002 consists of 12 sections that largely (but not completely) overlap the eight (ISC)[2] security domains.

Standards (and baselines)

Standards are specific, mandatory requirements that further define and support higher-level policies. For example, a standard may require the use of a specific technology, such as a minimum requirement for encryption of sensitive data using AES. A standard may go so far as to specify the exact brand, product, or protocol to be implemented. A device or system *hardening standard* would define specific security configuration settings for applicable systems.

Baselines are similar to and related to standards. A baseline can be useful for identifying a consistent basis for an organization's security architecture, taking into account system-specific parameters, such as different operating systems. After consistent baselines are established, appropriate standards can be defined across the organization.

TIP Some organizations call their configuration documents *standards* (and still others call them *standard operating environments*) instead of *baselines*. This is a common and acceptable practice.

Procedures

Procedures provide detailed instructions on how to implement specific policies and meet the criteria defined in standards. Procedures may include Standard Operating Procedures (SOPs), run books, and user guides. For example, a procedure may be a step-by-step guide for encrypting sensitive files by using a specific software encryption product.

Guidelines

Guidelines are similar to standards but they function as recommendations rather than as compulsory requirements. For example, a guideline may provide tips or recommendations for determining the sensitivity of a file and whether encryption is required.

Understand Business Continuity Requirements

Business continuity and disaster recovery (discussed in detail in Chapter 9) work hand in hand to provide an organization with the means to continue and recover business operations when a disaster strikes. Business continuity and disaster recovery are two sides of the same coin. Each springs into action when a disaster strikes. But they do have different goals:

>> **Business continuity** deals with keeping business operations running — perhaps in another location or by using different tools and processes — after a disaster has struck. This is sometimes called continuity of operations (COOP).

>> **Disaster recovery** deals with restoring normal business operations after the disaster takes place.

While the business continuity team is busy keeping business operations running via one of possibly several contingency plans, the disaster recovery team members are busy restoring the original facilities and equipment so that they can resume normal operations.

Here's an analogy. Two boys kick a big anthill — a disaster for the ant colony. Some of the ants scramble to save the eggs and the food supply; that's Ant City business continuity. Other ants work on rebuilding the anthill; that's Ant City disaster recovery. Both teams work to ensure the anthill's survival, but each team has its own role to play.

Business continuity and disaster recovery planning have these common elements:

>> **Identification of critical business functions:** The Business Impact Analysis (BIA) and Risk Assessment (discussed in the section "Conduct Business Impact Analysis," later in this chapter) identify these functions.

>> **Identification of possible scenarios:** The planning team identifies all the likely man-made and natural disaster activation scenarios, ranked by event probability and impact to the organization.

>> **Experts:** People who understand the organization's critical business processes.

The similarities end with this list. Business continuity planning concentrates on *continuing* business operations, whereas disaster recovery planning focuses on *recovering* the original business functions. Although both plans deal with the long-term survival of the business, they involve different activities. When a significant disaster occurs, both activities kick into gear at the same time, keeping vital business functions running (business continuity) and getting things back to normal as soon as possible (disaster recovery).

Business continuity (and disaster recovery) planning exist because bad things happen. Organizations that want to survive a disastrous event need to make formal and extensive plans — contingency plans to keep the business running and recovery plans to return operations to normal.

BUSINESS CONTINUITY AND DISASTER RECOVERY: A SIMPLE ILLUSTRATION

Here's a scenario: A business is a delivery service that has one delivery truck, which delivers goods around the city.

Business continuity deals with keeping the delivery service running in case something happens to the truck, presumably with a backup truck, substitute drivers, maps to get around traffic jams, and other contingencies to keep the delivery function running.

Disaster recovery, on the other hand, deals with fixing (or replacing) the original delivery truck, which might involve making repairs or even buying/leasing a new truck.

COOPERATION IS THE KEY

Like many disciplines based in technology, business continuity and disaster recovery planning are also changing rapidly. One new approach is COOP, or Continuity of Operations, which is a blending of business continuity and disaster recovery into a single mission: keeping the organization running after a disaster.

If you are interested in learning more, an excellent reference for added information on COOP is the FEMA (U.S. Federal Emergency Management Agency) guide IS-547, Introduction to COOP, which is available at https://training.fema.gov/is/courseoverview.aspx?code=IS-547.a.

Keeping a business operating during a disaster can be like juggling with one arm tied behind your back (we first thought of plate-spinning and one-armed paper hangers, but most of our readers are probably too young to understand these). You'd better plan in advance how you're going to do it, and practice! It could happen at night, you know (one-handed juggling in the dark is a lot harder).

Before business continuity planning can begin, everyone on the project team has to make and understand some basic definitions and assumptions. These critical items include

>> **Senior management support:** The development of a Business Continuity Plan (BCP) is time consuming, with no immediate or tangible *return on investment* (ROI). To ensure a successful business continuity planning project, you need the support of the organization's senior management, including

adequate budget, manpower, and visible statements backing the project. Senior management needs to make explicit statements identifying the responsible parties, as well as the importance of the business continuity planning project, budget, priorities, urgency, and timing.

>> **Senior management involvement:** Senior management can't just bless the business continuity planning project. Because senior managers and directors may have implicit and explicit responsibility for the organization's ability to recover from a disaster, senior management needs to have a degree of direct involvement in the business continuity planning effort. The careers that these people save may be their own.

>> **Project team membership:** Which people do you want to put on the business continuity planning project team? The team must represent all relevant functions and business units. Many of the team members probably have their usual jobs, too, so the team needs to develop a realistic timeline for how quickly the business continuity planning project can make progress.

>> **Who brings the donuts:** Because it's critical that business continuity planning meetings are well attended, quality donuts are an essential success component.

A business continuity planning project typically has four components: scope determination, the Business Impact Analysis (BIA), the Business Continuity Plan (BCP), and implementation. We discuss each of these components in the following sections.

Develop and document project scope and plan

The success and effectiveness of a business continuity planning project depends greatly on whether senior management and the project team properly define its scope. Business processes and technology can muddy the waters and make this task difficult. For instance, distributed systems dependence on at least some desktop systems for vital business functions expands the scope beyond core functions. Geographically dispersed companies — often the result of mergers — complicate matters as well.

Also, large companies are understandably more complex. The boundaries between where a function begins and ends are oftentimes fuzzy and sometimes poorly documented and not well understood.

Political pressures can influence the scope of the business continuity planning project as well. A department that *thinks* it's vital, but which falls outside the business continuity planning project scope, may lobby to be included in the project. Everybody wants to be important (and some just want to *appear* to be important).

You need senior management support of scope (what the project team *really* needs to include and what it doesn't) to put a stop to the political games.

Scope creep (what happens when a project's scope grows beyond the original intent) can become *scope leap* if you have a weak or inexperienced business continuity planning project team. For the success of the project, strong leaders must make rational decisions about the scope of the project. Remember, you can change the scope of the business continuity planning project in later iterations of the project.

The project team needs to find a balance between too narrow a scope, which makes the plan ineffective, and too wide a scope, which makes the plan too cumbersome.

A complete BCP consists of several components that handle not only the continuation of critical business functions, but also all the functions and resources that support those critical functions. The various elements of a BCP are described in the following sections.

Emergency response

Emergency response teams must be identified for every possible type of disaster. These response teams need *playbooks* (detailed written procedures and checklists) to keep critical business functions operating.

Written procedures are vital for two reasons. First, the people who perform critical functions after a disaster may not be familiar with them: They may not usually perform those functions. (During a disaster, the people who ordinarily perform the function may be unavailable.) Second, the team probably needs to use different procedures and processes for performing the critical functions during a disaster than they would under normal conditions. Also, the circumstances surrounding a disaster might have people feeling out-of-sorts; having a written procedure guides them into action (kind of like the "break glass" instructions on some fire alarms, in case you forget what to do).

Damage assessment

When a disaster strikes, experts need to be called in to inspect the premises and determine the extent of the damage. Typically, you need experts who can assess building damage, as well as damage to any special equipment and machinery.

Depending on the nature of the disaster, you may have to perform damage assessment in stages. A first assessment may involve a quick walkthrough to look for obvious damage, followed by a more time-consuming and detailed assessment to look for problems that you don't see right away.

Damage assessments determine whether an organization can still use buildings and equipment, whether they can use those items after some repairs, or whether they must abandon those items altogether.

Personnel safety

In any kind of disaster, the safety of personnel is the highest priority, ahead of buildings, equipment, computers, backup tapes, and so on. Personnel safety is critical not only because of the intrinsic value of human life, but also because people — not physical assets — make the business run.

Personnel notification

The BCP must have some provisions for notifying all affected personnel that a disaster has occurred. An organization needs to establish multiple methods for notifying key business-continuity personnel in case public communications infrastructures are interrupted.

Not all disasters are obvious: A fire or broken water main is a local event, not a regional one. And in an event such as a tornado or flood, employees who live even a few miles away may not know the condition of the business. Consequently, the organization needs a plan for communicating with employees, no matter what the situation.

Throughout a disaster and its recovery, management must be given regular status reports as well as updates on crucial tactical issues so that management can align resources to support critical business operations that function on a contingency basis. For instance, a manager of a corporate facilities department can loan equipment that critical departments need so that they can keep functioning.

Backups and media storage

Things go wrong with hardware and software, resulting in wrecked or unreachable data. When it's gone, it's gone! Thus IT departments everywhere make copies of their critical data on tapes, removable discs, or external storage systems, or in the cloud.

These backups must be performed regularly, usually once per day. For organizations with on-premises systems, backup media must also be stored off-site in the event that the facility housing the original systems is damaged. Having backup tapes *in* the data center may be convenient for doing a quick data restore but of little value if backup tapes are destroyed along with their respective systems. For organizations with cloud-based systems, the problem here is the same, but the technology differs a bit: It is imperative that data be backed up (or replicated) to a different geographic location, so that data can be recovered, no matter what happens.

For systems with large amounts of data, that data must be well *understood* in order to determine what kinds of backups need to be performed (real-time replication, full, differential, and incremental) and how frequently. Consider these factors:

>> The time that it takes to perform backups.

>> The effort required to restore data.

>> The procedures for restoring data from backups, compared with other methods for recovering the data.

For example, consider whether you can restore application software from backup tapes more quickly than by installing them from their release media (the original CD-ROMs or downloaded install files). Just make sure you can recover your configuration settings if you re-install software from release media. Also, if a large part of the database is static, do you really need to back it all up every day?

THE END OF MAGNETIC TAPE?

Magnetic tape has been the backup medium of choice since the 1960s. Gradually improving in reliability, capacity, and throughput, magnetic tape has hung in there as the mainstay of backup. But, the era of magnetic tape may be nearing its end.

The *linear access* property of magnetic tape means you have to read all the way through a tape to know its contents and to restore data that may be near the end. In addition, magnetic tape is somewhat fragile, and it is less tolerant of defects at higher storage densities.

Commercially viable alternatives to magnetic tape are emerging. Among them:

- **Virtual Tape Library (VTL):** This is really just disk-based storage; a VTL has the appearance of magnetic tape to backup programs. In a hot-pluggable RAID array, you could take these disks and send them offsite.

- **Replication:** An organization with two or more processing centers can consider replicating data from one location to another.

- **Cloud backup (also sometimes referred to as e-vaulting):** If data sets aren't too large and if Internet bandwidth is sufficient, data can be backed up to a cloud-based storage provider.

In comparison to these methods, proven but linear and relatively magnetic tape may soon be a part of the great data-processing museum in the sky.

You must choose off-site storage of backup media and other materials (documentation, and so on) carefully. Factors to consider include survivability of the off-site storage facility, as well as the distance from the off-site facility to the data center, media transportation, and alternate processing sites. The facility needs to be close enough so that media retrieval doesn't take too long (*how* long depends on the organization's recovery needs), but not so close that the facility becomes involved in the same natural disaster as the business.

Cloud-based data replication and backup services are a viable alternative to off-site backup media storage. Today's Internet speeds make it possible to back up critical data to a cloud-based storage provider — often faster than magnetic tapes can be returned from an off-site facility and data recovered from them.

TIP

Some organizations have one or more databases so large that the organizations literally can't (or, at any rate, don't) back them up to tape. Instead, they keep one or more replicated copies of their databases on other computers in other cities. Business continuity planners need to consider this possibility when developing continuity plans.

The purpose of off-site media storage is to ensure that up-to-date data is available in the event that systems in the primary data center are damaged.

Software escrow agreements

Your organization should consider *software escrow agreements* (wherein the software vendor sends a copy of its software code to a third-party escrow organization for safekeeping) with the software vendors whose applications support critical business functions. In the event that an insurmountable disaster (which could include bankruptcy) strikes the software vendor, your organization must consider all options for the continued maintenance of those critical applications, including in-house support.

External communications

The Corporate Communications, External Affairs, and (if applicable) Investor Relations departments should all have plans in place for communicating the facts about a disaster to the press, customers, and public. You need contingency plans for these functions if you want the organization to continue communicating to the outside world. Open communication during a disaster is vital so that customers, suppliers, and investors don't panic (which they might do if they don't know the true extent of the disaster).

The emergency communications plan needs to take into account the possibility that some corporate facilities or personnel may be unavailable. Thus you need to keep even the data and procedures related to the communications plan safe so that they're available in any situation.

Utilities

Data-processing facilities that support time-critical business functions must keep running in the event of a power failure. Although every situation is different, the principle remains the same: The business continuity planning team must determine for what period of time the data-processing facility must be able to continue operating without utility power. A power engineer can find out the length of typical (we don't want to say *routine*) power outages in your area and crunch the numbers to arrive at the mean time of outages. By using that information, as well as an inventory of the data center's equipment and environmental equipment, you can determine whether the organization needs an uninterruptible power supply (UPS) alone, or a UPS *and* an electric generator.

A business can use uninterruptible power supplies (UPSs) and emergency electric generators to provide electric power during prolonged power outages. A UPS is also good for a controlled shutdown, if the organization is better off having their systems powered off during a disaster. A business can also use a stand-alone power system (SPS), another term for an off-the-grid system that generates power with solar, wind, hydro, or employees madly pedaling stationary bicycles (we're kidding about that last one).

In a really long power outage (more than a day or two), it is also essential to have a plan for the replenishment of generator fuel.

Logistics and supplies

The business continuity planning team needs to study *every aspect* of critical functions that must be made to continue in a disaster. Every resource that's needed to sustain the critical operation must be identified and then considered against every possible disaster scenario to determine what special plans must be made. For instance, if a business operation relies upon a just-in-time shipment of materials for its operation and an earthquake has closed the region's only highway (or airport or sea/lake port), then alternative means for acquiring those materials must be determined in advance. Or, perhaps an emergency ration of those materials needs to be stockpiled so that the business function can continue uninterrupted.

Fire and water protection

Many natural disasters disrupt public utilities, including water supplies or delivery. In the event that a disaster has interrupted water delivery, new problems arise. Your facility may not be allowed to operate without the means for fighting a fire, should one occur.

In many places, businesses could be ordered to close if they can't prove that they can effectively fight a fire using other means, such as FM-200 inert gas. Then again, if water supplies have been interrupted, you have other issues to contend with, such as drinking water and water for restrooms. Without water, you're hosed!

We discuss fire protection in more detail in Chapter 5.

Documentation

Any critical business function must be able to continue operating after a disaster strikes. And to make sure you can sustain operations, you need to make available all relevant documentation for every critical piece of equipment, as well as every critical process and procedure that the organization performs in a given location.

Don't be lulled into taking for granted the emerging trend of hardware and software products that don't come with any documentation. Many vendors deliver their documentation *only* over the Internet, or they charge extra for a hard copy. But many types of disasters may disrupt Internet communications, thereby leaving an operation high and dry with no instructions for how to use and manage tools or applications.

At least one set of hard copy (or CD-ROM soft copy) documentation — including your BCP and Disaster Recovery Plan (DRP) — should be stored at the same off-site storage facility that stores the organization's backup tapes. It would also be smart to issue electronic copies of BCP and DRP documentation to all relevant personnel on USB storage devices (with encryption).

If the preceding sounds like the ancient past to you, then your organization may be fully in the cloud today. In such a case, you may be more inclined to maintain multiple soft copies of all required documentation so that personnel can use it when needed.

Continuity and recovery documentation must exist in hard copy in the event that it's unavailable via electronic means.

Data processing continuity planning

Data processing facilities are so vital to businesses today that a lot of emphasis is placed on them. Generally, this comes down to these variables: where and how the business will continue to sustain its data processing functions.

Because data centers are so expensive and time-consuming to build, better business sense dictates having an alternate processing site available. The types of sites are

>> **Cold site:** A *cold site* is basically an empty computer room with environmental facilities (UPS; heating, ventilation, and air conditioning [HVAC]; and so on) but no computing equipment. This is the least-costly option, but more time is required to assume a workload because computers need to be brought in from somewhere and set up, and data and applications need to be loaded. Connectivity to other locations also needs to be installed.

>> **Warm site:** A *warm site* is basically a cold site, but with computers and communications links already in place. In order to take over production operations, you must load the computers with application software and business data.

>> **Hot site:** Indisputably the most expensive option, you equip a *hot site* with the same computers as the production system, with application changes, operating system changes, and even patches kept in sync with their live production-system counterparts. You even keep business data up-to-date at the hot site by using some sort of mirroring or transaction replication. Because the organization trains its staff in how to operate the organization's business applications (and staff members have documentation), the operations staff knows what to do to take over data processing operations at a moment's notice. Hot sites may be cloud-based or in a co-location center.

>> **Reciprocal site:** Your organization and another organization sign a *reciprocal agreement* in which you both pledge the availability of your organization's data center in the event of a disaster. Back in the day, when data centers were rare, many organizations made this sort of arrangement, but it's fallen out of favor in recent years.

>> **Multiple data centers:** Larger organizations can consider the option of running daily operations out of two or more regional data centers that are hundreds (or more) of miles apart. The advantage of this arrangement is that the organization doesn't have to make arrangements with outside vendors for hot/warm/cold sites, and the organization's staff is already onsite and familiar with business and computer operations.

>> **Cloud site:** Organizations with primary information processing in the cloud are likely to employ cloud assets in multiple regions, and possibly with more than one cloud provider. Many organizations with primary processing on-premises employ hybrid cloud infrastructure for disaster recovery purposes — this is a common way for companies to ease their way into the cloud. Depending on the degree of readiness required, a cloud site can be as ready as a hot site, a warm site, or a cold site, as determined by the resources devoted to keeping the cloud site ready for production operations.

A hot site provides the most rapid recovery capability, but it also costs the most because of the effort required to maintain its readiness.

Table 3-1 compares these options side by side.

TABLE 3-1   Data Processing Continuity Planning Site Comparison

Feature	Hot Site	Warm Site	Cold Site	Multiple Data Centers	Cloud Site
Cost	Highest	Medium	Low	No additional	Variable
Computer-equipped	Yes	Yes	No	Yes	Yes
Connectivity-equipped	Yes	Yes	No	Yes	Yes
Data-equipped	Yes	No	No	Yes	Variable
Staffed	Yes	No	No	Yes	No
Typical lead time to readiness	Minutes to hours	Hours to days	Days to weeks	Minutes to hours or longer	Minutes to hours

Conduct Business Impact Analysis

The *Business Impact Analysis* (BIA) describes the impact that a disaster is expected to have on business operations. This important early step in business continuity planning helps an organization figure out which business processes are more resilient and which are more fragile.

A disaster's impact includes quantitative and qualitative effects. The *quantitative impact* is generally financial, such as loss of revenue or output of production. The *qualitative impact* has more to do with the quality of goods and/or services.

Any BIA worth its salt needs to perform the following tasks well:

>> Perform a Vulnerability Assessment — not so much an application/infrastructure vulnerability assessment, but a big-picture, business process vulnerability assessment.

>> Carry out a Criticality Assessment — determining how critically important a particular business function is to the ongoing viability of the organization.

>> Determine the Maximum Tolerable Downtime.

>> Establish recovery targets.

>> Determine resource requirements.

You can get the scoop on these activities in the following sections.

Vulnerability Assessment

Often, a BIA includes a *Vulnerability Assessment* that helps get a handle on obvious and not-so-obvious weaknesses in business critical systems. A Vulnerability Assessment has quantitative (financial) and qualitative (operational) sections, similar to a Risk Assessment, which is covered later in this chapter.

The purpose of a Vulnerability Assessment is to determine the impact — both quantitative and qualitative — of the loss of a critical business function.

Quantitative losses include

>> Loss of revenue

>> Loss of operating capital

>> Market share

>> Loss because of personal liabilities

>> Increase in expenses

>> Penalties because of violations of business contracts

>> Violations of laws and regulations (which can result in legal costs such as fines and civil penalties)

Qualitative losses include loss of

>> Service quality

>> Competitive advantages

>> Customer satisfaction

>> Prestige and reputation

The Vulnerability Assessment identifies *critical support areas*, which are business functions that, if lost, would cause significant harm to the business by jeopardizing critical business processes or the lives and safety of personnel. The Vulnerability Assessment should carefully study critical support areas to identify the resources that those areas require to continue functioning.

Quantitative losses include an increase in operating expenses because of any higher costs associated with executing the contingency plan. In other words, planners need to remember to consider operating costs that may be higher during a disaster situation.

Criticality Assessment

The business continuity planning team should inventory all high-level business functions (for example, customer support, order processing, returns, cash management, accounts receivable, payroll, and so on) and rank them in order of criticality. The team should also describe the impact of a disruption to each function on overall business operations.

REMEMBERING PAYROLL

Organizations that inventory and categorize their business processes usually look outward to the goods and services that they provide to their customers. During a disaster-related crisis, organizations that survive have effective contingency plans for these processes.

But some organizations overlook internal services that support ongoing operations. An important example is payroll. Some disasters can last weeks or even months while organizations rebuild their goods and services delivery. If you don't have payroll high on the list of processes to recover, employees could find themselves going without a paycheck for quite a while. An organization in this position may find itself losing the people it needs to get normal operations running again, which could precipitate a secondary disaster that has long-term consequences.

A retail organization that we're familiar with has an interesting contingency plan for paying its branch-office employees. Branch managers are authorized to pay their employees a fixed amount of cash each week if the organization's payroll system stops functioning. When automated payroll systems are restored, the cash payments are entered into the system, so that payroll records for each employee will be accurate.

The team members need to estimate the duration of a disaster event to effectively prepare the Criticality Assessment. Project team members need to consider the impact of a disruption based on the length of time that a disaster impairs specific critical business functions. You can see the vast difference in business impact of a disruption that lasts one minute, compared to one hour, one day, one week, or longer. Generally, the criticality of a business function depends on the degree of impact that its impairment has on the business.

REMEMBER

Planners need to consider disasters that occur at different times in the business cycle, whatever that might be for an organization. Response to a disaster at the busiest time of the month (or year) may vary quite a bit from response at other times.

Identifying key players

Although you can consider a variety of angles when evaluating vulnerability and criticality, commonly you start with a high-level organization chart. (Hip people call this chart the *org chart*). In most companies, the major functions pretty much follow the structure of the organization.

Following an org chart helps the business continuity planning project team consider all the steps in a critical process. Walk through the org chart, stopping at each manager's or director's position and asking, "What does he do?", "What does she do?", and "Who files the TPS reports?" This mental stroll can help jog your memory, and help you better see all the parts of the organization's big picture.

TIP

When you're cruising an org chart to make sure that it covers all areas of the organization, you may easily overlook outsourced functions that might not show up in the org chart. For instance, if your organization outsources accounts payable (A/P) functions, you might miss this detail if you don't see it on an org chart. Okay, you'd probably notice the absence of *all* A/P. But if your organization outsources only part of A/P — say, a group that detects and investigates A/P fraud (looking for payment patterns that suggest the presence of phony payment requests) — your org chart probably doesn't include that vital function.

Establishing Maximum Tolerable Downtime (MTD)

An extension of the Criticality Assessment (which we talk about in the section "Criticality Assessment," earlier in this chapter) is a statement of Maximum Tolerable Downtime (MTD — also known as Maximum Tolerable Period of Disruption or MTPD) for each critical business function. *Maximum Tolerable Downtime* is the maximum period of time that a critical business function can be inoperative before the company incurs significant and long-lasting damage.

For example, imagine that your favorite online merchant — a bookseller, an auction house, or an online trading company — goes down for an hour, a day, or a week. At some point, you have to figure that a prolonged disruption sinks the ship, meaning the business can't survive. Determining MTD involves figuring out at what point the organization suffers permanent, measurable loss as a result of a disaster. Online retailers know that even short outages may mean that some customers will switch brands and take their business elsewhere.

Make the MTD assessment a major factor in determining the criticality — and priority — of business functions. A function that can withstand only two hours of downtime obviously has a higher priority than another function that can withstand several days of downtime.

MTD is a measure of the longest period of time that a critical business function can be disrupted without suffering unacceptable consequences, perhaps threatening the actual survivability of the organization.

Determining Maximum Tolerable Outage (MTO)

During the Criticality Assessment, you establish a statement of Maximum Tolerable Outage (MTO) for each critical business function. *Maximum Tolerable Outage* is the maximum period of time that a critical business function can be operating in emergency or alternate processing mode. This matters because, in many cases, emergency or alternate processing mode performs at a lower level of throughput or quality, or at a higher cost. Although an organization's survival can be assured through an interim period in alternate processing mode, the long-term business model may not be able to sustain the differences in throughput, quality, cost, or whatever aspects of alternate processing mode are different from normal processing.

Establish recovery targets

When you establish the Criticality Assessment, MTD, and MTO for each business process (which we talk about in the preceding sections), the planning team can establish recovery targets. These targets represent the period of time from the onset of a disaster until critical processes have resumed functioning.

Two primary recovery targets are usually established for each business process: a Recovery Time Objective (RTO) and Recovery Point Objective (RPO). We discuss these targets in the following sections.

HOW BAD DOES IT HAVE TO BE?

Establishing reasonable MTD and MTO values can be difficult. The issue here is similar to pain threshold and the actual effects of a disaster. Years ago, we used to say that an MTD value was valid when its magnitude was sufficient to cause the complete failure of a business. Now we believe that's too high a threshold; after all, some organizations won't actually fail even in a huge disaster: for example, local governments and religious institutions won't go out of business and disappear from the landscape.

So what's a reasonable measure of MTD? It depends on your particular organization and situation, but here are some ideas:

- Threshold of public outcry
- Loss of a certain number of market-share points
- Loss of a certain percentage of constituents
- Loss of life

You need to identify a reasonable threshold of MTD — short of your organization ceasing to exist, but something more reasonable, such as a significant loss of business or loss of confidence in your organization.

Similarly, determining a reasonable MTO is far from simple. A disaster may result in an organization relying on emergency operations for an extended period of time, which may put financial strain on the organization. Higher costs or lower quality will take a toll, and organizations and their investors have to decide how much is enough before investors and executives throw in the towel.

RECOVERY TIME OBJECTIVE (RTO)

A *Recovery Time Objective* (RTO) is the maximum period of time in which a business process must be restored after a disaster.

An organization without a BCP that suffers a serious disaster, such as an earthquake or hurricane, could experience a recovery time of one to two weeks or more. An organization could possibly need this length of time to select a new location for processing data, purchase new systems, load application software and data, and resume processing. An organization that can't tolerate such a long outage needs to establish a shorter RTO and determine the level of investments required to meet that target.

RECOVERY POINT OBJECTIVE (RPO)

A *Recovery Point Objective* (RPO) is the maximum period of time in which data might be lost if a disaster strikes.

A typical schedule for backing up data is once per day. If a disaster occurs before backups are done, the organization can lose an entire day's worth of information. This is because system and data recovery are often performed using the last good set of backups. An organization that requires a shorter RPO needs to figure out a way to make copies of transaction data more frequently than once per day.

Here are some examples of how organizations might establish their RPOs:

>> **Keyed Invoices:** An accounts payable department opens the mail and manually keys in the invoices that it receives from its suppliers. Data entry clerks spend their entire day inputting invoices. If a disaster occurs before backups are run at the end of the business day (and if that disaster requires the organization to rebuild systems from backup tapes), those clerks have to redo that whole day's worth of data entry.

>> **Online orders:** A small business develops an online web application that customers can use to place orders. At the end of each day, the Orders department runs a program that prints out all the day's orders, and the Shipping department fills those orders on the following day. If a disaster occurs at any time during the day, the business loses all online orders placed since the previous day's backup.

If you establish the MTD for processes such as the ones in the preceding list as less than one business day, the organization needs to take some steps to save online data more than once per day.

Many organizations consider off-site backup media storage, where backup tapes are transported off-site as frequently as every day, or where electronic vaulting to an offsite location is performed several times each day. An event such as a fire can destroy computers as well as backup media if it is nearby.

HOW RTO AND RPO WORK TOGETHER

RPO and RTO targets are different measures of recovery for a system, but they work together. When the team establishes proposed targets, the team members need to understand how each target works.

At first glance, you might think that RPO should be a shorter time than RTO (or maybe the other way around). In fact, different businesses and applications present different business requirements that might make RPO less than RTO, equal to RTO, or greater than RTO. Here are some examples:

» **RPO greater than RTO:** A business can recover an application in 4 hours (RTO), and it has a maximum data loss (RPO) of 24 hours. So, if a disaster occurs, the business can get the application running again in 4 hours, but data recovered in the system consists of data entered prior to 24 hours before the incident took place.

» **RPO equal to RTO:** A business can recover an application in 12 hours (RTO), with a maximum data loss of 12 hours (RPO). You can probably imagine this scenario: An application mirrors (or replicates) data to a backup system in real-time. If a disaster occurs, the disaster recovery team requires 12 hours to start the backup system. After the team gets the system running, the business has data from until 12 hours in the past — the time when the primary system failed.

» **RPO less than RTO:** The disaster recovery team can recover an application in 4 hours (RTO), with a maximum data loss of 1 hour (RPO). How can this situation happen? Maybe a back-office transaction-posting application, which receives and processes data from order-processing applications, fails. If the back-office application is down for 4 hours, data coming from the order-processing applications may be buffered someplace else, and when the back-office application resumes processing, it can then receive and process the waiting input data.

THE HIGH COST OF RAPID RECOVERY

Business continuity planning teams often establish ambitious Recovery Point and Recovery Time Objectives (RPOs and RTOs, respectively) for systems. Teams working on recovery objectives need to understand that *the speed of recovery is directly proportional to its cost.*

For instance, an RPO for an application is established at two hours. To meet that goal, the organization has to purchase new storage systems, plus an expensive data connection from the main processing center to the backup processing center. But the cost of so short an RPO may not be warranted. The project team needs to understand the cost of downtime (in dollars per hour or per day) versus the cost of recovery. For instance, if the cost of downtime for an application is $40,000 per hour and a two-hour RPO requires a $500,000 investment in equipment and a $20,000-per-month expense, then the investment may be warranted. If, however, the cost of downtime for the application is $500 per hour, then the organization doesn't need this level of investment and should establish a longer RPO.

Defining Resource Requirements

The *Resource Requirements* portion of the BIA is a listing of the resources that an organization needs in order to continue operating each critical business function. In an organization that has finite resources (which is pretty much every organization), the most critical functions get first pick, and the lower-priority functions get the leftovers.

Understanding what resources are required to support a business process helps the project team to figure out what the contingency plan for that process needs to contain, and how the process can be operated in Emergency mode and then recovered.

Examples of required resources include

>> **Systems and applications:** In order for a business process to continue operating, it may require one or more IT systems or applications — not only the primary supporting application, but also other systems and applications that the primary application requires in order to continue functioning. Depending on the nature of the organization's primary and alternate processing resources, these systems may be physical, virtual, or cloud-based.

>> **Suppliers and partners:** Many business processes require a supply of materials or services from outside organizations, without which the business process can't continue operating.

>> **Key personnel:** Most business processes require a number of specifically trained or equipped staff members — or contingent workers such as contractors or personnel from another company — to run business processes and operate systems.

>> **Business equipment:** Anything from PBXs to copiers, postage machines, POS (point-of-sale) machines, red staplers, and any other machinery required to support critical business processes.

TIP

When you identify required resources for complex business processes, you may want to identify additional information about each resource, including resource owners, criticality, and dependencies.

Developing the Business Continuity Plan

After you define the scope of the business continuity planning project and develop the BIA, Criticality Assessment, MTDs, and MTOs, you know

>> What portion of the organization is included in the plan.

>> Of this portion of the organization, which business functions are so critical that the business would fail if these functions were interrupted for long (or even short) periods of time.

>> The general degree of impact on the business when one of the critical functions fails. This idea comes from quantitative and qualitative data.

The hard part of the business continuity planning project begins now: You need to develop the strategy for continuing each critical business function when disasters occur, which is known as the *Continuity Strategy*.

When you develop a Continuity Strategy, you must set politics aside and look at the excruciating details of critical business functions. You need lots of strong coffee, several pizzas, buckets of Rolaids, and cool heads.

Making your business continuity planning project a success

For the important and time-consuming Continuity Strategy phase of the project, you need to follow these guidelines:

>> **Call things like you see them.** No biases. No angles. No politics. No favorites. No favors. You're trying to ensure survival of the business before the disaster strikes.

>> **Build smaller teams of experts.** Each critical business function should have teams dedicated to just that function. That team's job is to analyze just one critical business function and figure out how you can keep it functioning despite a disaster of some sort. Pick the right people for each team — people who *really* understand the details of the business process that they're examining.

>> **Brainstorm.** Proper brainstorming considers all ideas, even silly ones (up to a point). Even a silly-sounding idea can lead to a *good* idea.

>> **Have teams share results with each other.** Teams working on individual continuity strategies can get ideas from each other. Each team can share highlights of its work over the past week or two. Some of the things that they say may spark ideas in other teams. You can improve the entire effort by holding these sharing sessions.

>> **Don't encourage competition or politics in or between teams.** Don't pit teams against each other. Identifying success factors isn't a zero-sum game: Everyone needs to do an excellent job.

>> **Retain a business continuity planning mentor/expert.** If your organization doesn't have experienced business continuity planners on staff, you need to bring in a consultant — someone who has helped develop plans for other organizations. Even more important than that, make sure the consultant you hire has been on the scene when disaster struck a business he or she was consulting for and has seen a BCP in action.

Simplifying large or complex critical functions

Some critical business functions may be too large and complex to examine in one big chunk. You can break down those complex functions into smaller components, perhaps like this:

>> **People:** Has the team identified the critical people — or more appropriately, the critical sub-functions — required to keep the function running?

>> **Facilities:** In the event that the function's primary facilities are unavailable, where can the business perform the function?

>> **Technology:** What hardware, software, and other computing/network components support the critical function? If parts or all of these components are unavailable, what other equipment can support the critical business functions? Do you need to perform the functions any differently?

>> **Miscellaneous:** What supplies, other equipment, and services do you need to support the critical business function?

Analyzing processes is like disassembling toy building block houses — you have to break them down to the level of their individual components. You really *do* need to understand each step in even the largest processes in order to be able to develop good continuity plans for them.

If a team that analyzes a large complex business function breaks it into groups, such as the groups in the preceding list, the team members need to get together frequently to ensure that their respective strategies for each group eventually become a cohesive whole. Eventually these groups need to come back together and integrate their separate materials into one complete, cohesive plan.

Documenting the strategy

Now for the part that everyone loves: documentation. The details of the continuity plans for each critical function must be described in minute detail, step by step by step.

Why? The people who develop the strategy may very well *not* be the people who execute it. The people who develop the strategy may change roles in the company or change jobs altogether. Or the scope of an actual disaster may be wide enough that the critical personnel just aren't available. Any skeptics should consider September 11 and the impact that this disaster had on a number of companies that lost practically every*one* and every*thing*.

REMEMBER

WHY HIRE AN EXPERT?

Most people don't do business continuity planning for a living. Although you may be the expert in your particular business processes, you don't necessarily know all the angles of contingency planning.

Turn this question around for a minute: What would you think if an IT shop developed a security strategy without having a security expert's help? Do you think they'd have a sound, viable strategy?

The same argument fits equally well with business continuity planning.

For the remaining skeptics, do yourself a favor: Hire a business continuity planning expert for just a short time to help validate your framework and plan. If your expert says that your plan is great, then you can consider it money well spent to confirm your suspicions. If the consultant says that your plan needs help, ask for details on where and how. Then, you can decide whether to rework and improve your plan.

When disaster strikes, it's too late to wish that you had a good BCP.

Best practices for documenting BCPs exist. For this reason, you may want to have an expert around. For $300 an hour, a consultant can spend a couple of weeks developing templates. But watch out — your consultant might just download templates from a business continuity planning website, tweak them a little bit, and spend the rest of his or her time playing Candy Crush. To be sure you get a solid consultant, do the old-fashioned things: check his references, ask for work samples, see if he has a decent LinkedIn page. (We're kidding about that last one!)

Implementing the BCP

It is an accomplishment indeed when the BCP documentation has been written, reviewed, edited, placed into three-ring binders, and distributed via thumb drives or online file storage accounts. However, the job isn't yet done. The BCP needs senior management buy-in, the plan must be announced and socialized throughout the organization, and one or more persons must be dedicated to keeping the plan up-to-date. Oh yeah, and the plan needs to be tested!

Securing senior management approval

After the entire plan has been documented and reviewed by all stakeholders, it's time for senior management to examine it and approve it. Not only must senior management approve the plan, but senior management must also *publicly* approve it. By "public" we don't mean the general public; instead, we mean that senior management should make it well known inside the business that they support the business continuity planning process.

Senior management's approval is needed so that all affected and involved employees in the organization understand the importance of emergency planning.

Promoting organizational awareness

Everyone in the organization needs to know about the plan and his or her role in it. You may need to establish training for potentially large numbers of people who need to *be there* when a disaster strikes.

All employees in the organization must know about the BCP.

Testing the plan

Regularly testing the BCP ensures that all essential personnel required to implement the plan understand their roles and responsibilities, and helps to ensure that the plan is kept up to date as the organization changes. BCP testing methods are similar to DRP testing methods (discussed in Chapter 9), and include

>> Read-through

>> Walkthrough

>> Simulation

>> Parallel

>> Full interruption

See Chapter 9 for a full explanation of these testing methods.

Maintaining the plan

No, the plan isn't finished. It has just begun! Now the business continuity planning *person* (the project team members by this time have collected their commemorative denim shirts, mugs, and mouse pads, and have moved on to other projects) needs to periodically *chase* The Powers That Be to make sure that they know about all significant changes to the environment.

In fact, if the business continuity planning person has any leadership left at this point in the process, he or she needs to start attending the Change Control Board and IT Steering Committee (or whatever that company calls them) meetings and to jot down notes that may mean that some detail in a BCP document may need some changes.

TIP

The BCP is easier to modify than it is to create out of thin air. Once or twice each year, someone knowledgeable needs to examine the detailed strategy and procedure documents in the BCP to make sure that they'll still work — and update them if necessary.

TIP

You can read more about business continuity and disaster recovery planning in *IT Disaster Recovery Planning For Dummies,* by Peter H. Gregory.

Contribute to Personnel Security Policies

An organization needs clearly documented personnel security policies and procedures in order to facilitate the use and protection of information. There are numerous essential practices for protecting the business and its important information assets. These essential practices all have to do with how people — not technology — work together to support the business.

This is collectively known as *administrative management and control.*

Note: We tend to use the term *essential practices* versus *best practices*. The reason is simple: *Best practices* refers to the very best practices and technologies that can be brought to bear against a business problem, whereas *essential practices* means those activities and technologies that are considered essential to implement in an organization. Best practices are nearly impossible to achieve, and few organizations attempt it. However, essential practices are, well, essential, and definitely achievable in many organizations.

Employment candidate screening

Even before posting a "Help Wanted" sign (Do people still do that?!) or an ad on a job search website, an employer should ensure that the position to be filled is clearly documented and contains a complete description of the job requirements, the qualifications, and the scope of responsibilities and authority.

The job (or position) description should be created as a collaborative effort between the hiring manager — who fully understands the functional requirements of the specific position to be filled — and the human resources manager — who fully understands the applicable employment laws and organizational requirements to be addressed.

Having a clearly documented job (or position) description can benefit an organization for many reasons:

>> The hiring manager knows (and can clearly articulate) exactly what skills a certain job requires.

>> The human resources manager can pre-screen job applicants quickly and accurately.

>> Potential candidates can ensure they apply only for positions for which they're qualified, and they can properly prepare themselves for interviews (for example, by matching their skills and experiences to the specific requirements of the position).

>> After the organization fills the position, the position description (in some cases, the employment contract) helps to reduce confusion about what the organization expects from the new employee and provides objective criteria for evaluating performance.

Concise job descriptions that clearly identify an individual's responsibility and authority, particularly on information security issues, can help:

>> Reduce confusion and ambiguity.

>> Provide legal basis for an individual's authority or actions.

>> Demonstrate any negligence or dereliction in carrying out assigned duties.

An organization should conduct background checks and verify application information for all potential employees and contractors. This process can help to expose any undesirable or unqualified candidates. For example:

>> A previous criminal conviction may immediately disqualify a candidate from certain positions within an organization.

>> Even when the existence of a criminal record itself doesn't automatically disqualify a candidate, if the candidate fails to disclose this information in the job application or interview, it should be a clear warning sign for a potential employer.

>> Some positions that require a U.S. government security clearance are available only to U.S. citizens.

>> A candidate's credit history should be examined if the position has significant financial responsibilities or handles high-value assets, or if a high opportunity for fraud exists.

>> It has been estimated that as many as 40 percent of job applicants "exaggerate the truth" on their résumés and applications. Common sources of omitted, exaggerated, or outright misleading information include employment dates, salary history, education, certifications, and achievements. Although the information itself may not be disqualifying, a dishonest applicant should not be given the opportunity to become a dishonest employee.

Most background checks require the written consent of the applicant and disclosure of certain private information (such as the applicant's Social Security or other retirement system number). Private information obtained for the purposes of a background check, as well as the results of the background check, must be properly handled and safeguarded in accordance with applicable laws and the organization's records retention and destruction policies.

Basic background checks and verification might include the following information:

>> Criminal record

>> Citizenship

>> Employment history

>> Education

>> Certifications and licenses

>> Financial history including judgments

>> Reference checks (personal and professional)

>> Union and association membership

Pre- and post-employment background checks can provide an employer with valuable information about an individual whom an organization is considering for a job or position within an organization. Such checks can give an immediate indication of an individual's integrity (for example, by providing verification of information in the employment application) and can help screen out unqualified and undesirable applicants.

Personnel who fill sensitive positions should undergo a more extensive pre-employment screening and background check, possibly including:

>> Credit records (minimally, including bankruptcies, foreclosures, judgments, and public records; possibly a full credit report, depending on the position).

>> Drug testing (even in countries or U.S. states where certain narcotics and other substances such as cannabis are legal, if the organization's policies prohibit their use, then drug testing should be used to enforce the policy).

>> Special background investigation (FBI and INTERPOL records, field interviews with former associates, or a personal interview with a private investigator).

Periodic post-employment screenings (such as credit records and drug testing) may also be necessary, particularly for personnel with access to financial data, cash, or high-value assets, or for personnel being considered for promotions to more sensitive or responsible positions.

Many organizations that did not perform drug screenings in the past do so today. Instead of drug testing all employees, some take a measured approach by screening employees when promoted to higher levels of responsibility, such as director or vice president.

Employment agreements and policies

Various employment agreements and policies should be signed when an individual joins an organization or is promoted to a more sensitive position within an organization. Employment agreements often include non-compete agreements, non-disclosure agreements, codes of conduct, and acceptable use policies. Typical employment policies might include Internet acceptable use, social media policy, remote access, mobile and personal device use (for example, "Bring Your Own Device," or BYOD), and sexual harassment/fraternization.

Employment termination processes

Formal employment termination procedures should be implemented to help protect the organization from potential lawsuits, property theft and destruction, unauthorized access, or workplace violence. Procedures should be developed for various scenarios including resignations, termination, layoffs, accident or death, immediate departures versus prior notification, and hostile situations. Termination procedures may include

>> Having the former employee surrender keys, security badges, and parking permits.

>> Conducting an exit interview.

>> Requiring that security escort the former employee to collect his or her personal belongings and/or to leave the premises.

>> Recovering company assets and materials including laptop computers, mobile phones, tablets, and so on.

>> Changing door locks and system passwords as needed.

>> Formally turning over duties and responsibilities.

>> Removing network and system access and disabling user accounts.

>> Enforcing policies regarding retention of e-mail, personal files, and employment records.

>> Notifying customers, partners, vendors, service providers, and contractors, as appropriate.

Vendor, consultant, and contractor controls

Organizations commonly outsource many IT functions, particularly data center hosting, call-center or contact-center support, and application development. Information security policies and procedures must address outsourcing security and the use of service providers, vendors and consultants, when appropriate. Access control, document exchange and review, maintenance hooks, on-site assessment, process and policy review, and service level agreements (SLAs) are good examples of outsourcing security considerations.

Compliance

Individual responsibilities for compliance with applicable policies and regulations within the organization should be understood by all personnel within an organization. Signed statements that attest to an individual's understanding, acknowledgement, and/or agreement to comply may be appropriate for certain regulations and policies.

Privacy

Applicable policy regulations and policy requirements should be documented and understood by all personnel within the organization. Signed statements that attest to an individual's understanding, acknowledgement, and/or agreement to comply may also be appropriate.

Understand and Apply Risk Management Concepts

Beyond basic security fundamentals, the concepts of risk management are perhaps the most important and complex part of the security and risk management domain. Indeed, risk management is the process from which decisions are made to establish what security controls are necessary, implement security controls, acquire and use security tools, and hire security personnel.

Risk can never be completely eliminated. Given sufficient time, resources, motivation, and money, any system or environment, no matter how secure, can eventually be compromised. Some threats or events, such as natural disasters, are entirely beyond our control and often unpredictable. Therefore, the main goal of risk management is *risk treatment*: making intentional decisions about specific risks that organizations identify. Risk management consists of three main elements (each treated in the upcoming sections):

>> Threat identification

>> Risk analysis

>> Risk treatment

Identify threats and vulnerabilities

The business of information security is all about risk management. A *risk* consists of a threat and a vulnerability of an asset:

>> **Threat:** Any natural or man-made circumstance or event that could have an adverse or undesirable impact, minor or major, on an organizational asset or process.

>> **Vulnerability:** The absence or weakness of a safeguard or control in an asset or process (or an intrinsic weakness) that makes a threat potentially more harmful or costly, more likely to occur, or likely to occur more frequently.

>> **Asset:** A resource, process, product, or system that has some value to an organization and must therefore be protected. Assets may be tangible (computers, data, software, records, and so on) or intangible (privacy, access, public image, ethics, and so on), and those assets may likewise have a tangible value (purchase price) or intangible value (competitive advantage).

Remember: Risk = Asset Value × Threat Impact × Threat Probability.

The *risk management triple* consists of an asset, a threat, and vulnerability.

Risk assessment/analysis (treatment)

Two key elements of risk management are the *risk assessment* and *risk treatment* (discussed in the following sections).

Risk assessment

A risk assessment begins with *risk identification* — detecting and defining specific elements of the three components of risk: assets, threats, and vulnerabilities.

The process of risk identification occurs during a *risk assessment*.

ASSET VALUATION

Identifying an organization's assets and determining their value is a critical step in determining the appropriate level of security. The value of an asset to an organization can be both *quantitative* (related to its cost) and *qualitative* (its relative importance). An inaccurate or hastily conducted asset valuation process can have the following consequences:

>> Poorly chosen or improperly implemented controls

>> Controls that aren't cost-effective

>> Controls that protect the wrong asset

A properly conducted asset valuation process has several benefits to an organization:

>> Supports quantitative and qualitative risk assessments, Business Impact Analyses (BIAs), and security auditing.

>> Facilitates cost-benefit analysis and supports management decisions regarding selection of appropriate safeguards.

>> Can be used to determine insurance requirements, budgeting, and replacement costs.

>> Helps demonstrate due care, thus (potentially) limiting personal liability on the part of directors and officers.

Three basic elements used to determine the value of an asset are

>> **Initial and maintenance costs:** Most often, a tangible dollar value that may include purchasing, licensing, development (or acquisition), maintenance, and support costs.

>> **Organizational (or internal) value:** Often a difficult and intangible value. It may include the cost of creating, acquiring, and re-creating information, and the business impact or loss if the information is lost or compromised. It can also include liability costs associated with privacy issues, personal injury, and death.

>> **Public (or external) value:** Another difficult and often intangible cost, public value can include loss of proprietary information or processes, as well as loss of business reputation.

>> **Contribution to revenue:** For instance, an asset worth $10,000 may be instrumental to the realization of $5 million in annual revenue. Hence, risk decisions for such an asset should consider not only its cost, but also its role in generating or protecting revenue.

THREAT ANALYSIS

To perform threat analysis, you follow these four basic steps:

1. **Define the actual threat.**
2. **Identify possible consequences to the organization if the threat event occurs.**
3. **Determine the probable frequency and impact of a threat event.**
4. **Assess the probability that a threat will actually materialize.**

For example, a company that has a major distribution center located along the Gulf Coast of the United States may be concerned about hurricanes. Possible consequences include power and communications outages, wind damage, and flooding. Using climatology, the company can determine that an annual average of three hurricanes pass within 50 miles of its location between June and September, and that a specific probability exists of a hurricane actually affecting the company's operations during this period. During the remainder of the year, the threat of hurricanes has a low probability.

The number and types of threats that an organization must consider can be overwhelming, but you can generally categorize them as

>> **Natural:** Earthquakes, floods, hurricanes, lightning, fire, and so on.

>> **Man-made:** Unauthorized access, data-entry errors, strikes/labor disputes, theft, terrorism, sabotage, arson, social engineering, malicious code and viruses, and so on.

WARNING

Not all threats can be easily or rigidly classified. For example, fires and utility losses can be both natural and man-made. See Chapter 9 for more on disaster recovery.

VULNERABILITY ASSESSMENT

A *vulnerability assessment* provides a valuable baseline for identifying vulnerabilities in an asset as well as identifying one or more potential methods for mitigating those vulnerabilities. For example, an organization may consider a Denial of Service (DoS) threat, coupled with a vulnerability found in Microsoft's implementation of Domain Name System (DNS). However, if an organization's DNS servers have been properly patched or the organization uses a UNIX-based DNSSEC server, the specific vulnerability may already have been adequately addressed, and no additional safeguards may be necessary for that threat.

Risk analysis

The next element in risk management is *risk analysis* — a methodical examination that brings together all the elements of risk management (identification, analysis, and control) and is critical to an organization for developing an effective risk management strategy.

Risk analysis involves the following four steps:

1. **Identify the assets to be protected, including their relative value, sensitivity, or importance to the organization.**

This component of risk identification is asset valuation.

2. **Define specific threats, including threat frequency and impact data.**

This component of risk identification is threat analysis.

3. **Calculate Annualized Loss Expectancy (ALE).**

The ALE calculation is a fundamental concept in risk analysis; we discuss this calculation later in this section.

4. **Select appropriate safeguards.**

This process is a component of both risk identification (vulnerability assessment) and risk control (which we discuss in the section "Risk control," later in this chapter).

The *Annualized Loss Expectancy (ALE)* provides a standard, quantifiable measure of the impact that a realized threat has on an organization's assets. Because it's the estimated annual loss for a threat or event, expressed in dollars, ALE is particularly useful for determining the cost-benefit ratio of a safeguard or control. You determine ALE by using this formula:

SLE × ARO = ALE

Here's an explanation of the elements in this formula:

>> **Single Loss Expectancy (SLE):** A measure of the loss incurred from a single realized threat or event, expressed in dollars. You calculate the SLE by using the formula Asset value × Exposure Factor (EF).

Exposure Factor (EF) is a measure of the negative effect or impact that a realized threat or event would have on a specific asset, expressed as a percentage.

>> **Annualized Rate of Occurrence (ARO):** The estimated annual frequency of occurrence for a threat or event.

The two major types of risk analysis are qualitative and quantitative, which we discuss in the following sections.

QUALITATIVE RISK ANALYSIS

Qualitative risk analysis is more subjective than a quantitative risk analysis; unlike quantitative risk analysis, this approach to analyzing risk can be purely qualitative and avoids specific numbers altogether. The challenge of such an approach is developing real scenarios that describe actual threats and potential losses to organizational assets.

Qualitative risk analysis has some advantages when compared with quantitative risk analysis; these include

>> No complex calculations are required.

>> Time and work effort involved is relatively low.

>> Volume of input data required is relatively low.

Disadvantages of qualitative risk analysis, compared with quantitative risk analysis, include

>> No financial costs are defined; therefore cost-benefit analysis isn't possible.

>> The qualitative approach relies more on assumptions and guesswork.

>> Generally, qualitative risk analysis can't be automated.

>> Qualitative analysis is less easily communicated. (Executives seem to understand *"This will cost us $3 million over 12 months"* better than *"This will cause an unspecified loss at an undetermined future date."*)

A distinct advantage of qualitative risk analysis is that a large set of identified risks can be charted and sorted by asset value, risk, or other means. This can help an organization identify and distinguish higher risks from lower risks, even though precise dollar amounts may not be known.

A qualitative risk analysis doesn't attempt to assign numeric values to the components (the assets and threats) of the risk analysis.

QUANTITATIVE RISK ANALYSIS

A fully quantitative risk analysis requires all elements of the process, including asset value, impact, threat frequency, safeguard effectiveness, safeguard costs, uncertainty, and probability, to be measured and assigned numeric values.

A *quantitative risk analysis* attempts to assign more objective numeric values (costs) to the components (assets and threats) of the risk analysis.

Advantages of a quantitative risk analysis, compared with qualitative risk analysis, include the following:

>> Financial costs are defined; therefore, cost-benefit analysis can be determined.

>> More concise, specific data supports analysis; thus fewer assumptions and less guesswork are required.

>> Analysis and calculations can often be automated.

>> Specific quantifiable results are easier to communicate to executives and senior-level management.

Disadvantages of a quantitative risk analysis, compared with qualitative risk analysis, include the following:

>> Human biases will skew results.

>> Many complex calculations are usually required.

>> Time and work effort involved is relatively high.

>> Volume of input data required is relatively high.

>> The probability of threat events is difficult to determine.

>> Some assumptions are required.

Purely quantitative risk analysis is generally not possible or practical. Primarily, this is because it is difficult to determine a precise probability of occurrence for any given threat scenario. For this reason, many risk analyses are a blend of qualitative and quantitative risk analysis, known as a hybrid risk analysis.

HYBRID RISK ANALYSIS

A hybrid risk analysis combines elements of both a quantitative and qualitative risk analysis. The challenges of determining accurate probabilities of occurrence, as well as the true impact of an event, compel many risk managers to take a middle ground. In such cases, easily determined quantitative values (such as asset value) are used in conjunction with qualitative measures for probability of occurrence and risk level. Indeed, many so-called quantitative risk analyses are more accurately described as hybrid.

Risk treatment

A properly conducted risk analysis provides the basis for the next step in the risk management process: deciding what to do about risks that have been identified. The decision-making process is known as *risk treatment*. The four general methods of risk treatment are

>> **Risk mitigation:** This involves the implementation of one or more policies, controls, or other measures to protect an asset. Mitigation generally reduces the probability of threat realization or the impact of threat realization to an acceptable level.

This is the most common risk control remedy.

>> **Risk assignment (or transference):** Transferring the potential loss associated with a risk to a third party, such as an insurance company or a service provider that explicitly agrees to accept risk.

>> **Risk avoidance:** Eliminating the risk altogether through a cessation of the activity or condition that introduced the risk in the first place.

>> **Risk acceptance:** Accepting the risk associated with a potential threat. This is sometimes done for convenience (not prudent) but more appropriately when the cost of other countermeasures is prohibitive, the probability or impact is low, or the benefits outweigh the costs.

Countermeasure selection

As stated in the preceding section, mitigation is the most common method of risk treatment. Mitigation involves the implementation of one or more countermeasures. Several criteria for selecting countermeasures include cost-effectiveness, legal liability, operational impact, and technical factors.

COST-EFFECTIVENESS

The most common criterion for countermeasure selection is cost-effectiveness, which is determined through cost-benefit analysis. Cost-benefit analysis for a given countermeasure (or collection of countermeasures) can be computed as follows:

ALE before countermeasure – ALE after countermeasure – Cost of countermeasure = Value of countermeasure to the organization

For example, if the ALE associated with a specific threat (data loss) is $1,000,000; the ALE after a countermeasure (enterprise tape backup) has been implemented is $10,000 (recovery time); and the cost of the countermeasure (purchase, installation, training, and maintenance) is $140,000; then the value of the countermeasure to the organization is $850,000.

When calculating the cost of the countermeasure, you should consider the *total cost of ownership* (TCO), including:

>> Purchase, development, and licensing

>> Architecture and design

>> Testing and installation

- » Normal operating costs
- » Resource allocation
- » Maintenance and repair
- » Production or service disruptions

The total cost of a countermeasure is normally stated as an annualized amount.

LEGAL LIABILITY

An organization that fails to implement a countermeasure against a threat is exposed to legal liability if the cost to implement a countermeasure is less than the loss resulting from a realized threat (see *due care* and *due diligence*, discussed earlier in this chapter). The legal liability we're talking about here could encompass statutory liability (as a result of failing to obey the law) or civil liability (as a result of failing to comply with a legal contract). A cost-benefit analysis is a useful tool for determining legal liability.

OPERATIONAL IMPACT

The operational impact of a countermeasure must also be considered. If a countermeasure is too difficult to implement and operate, or interferes excessively with normal operations or production, it may be circumvented or ignored and thus not be effective. The end result may be a risk that is higher than the original risk prior to the so-called mitigation.

TECHNICAL FACTORS

The countermeasure itself shouldn't, in principle (but often does, in practice), introduce new vulnerabilities. For example, improper placement, configuration, or operation of a countermeasure can cause new vulnerabilities; lack of fail-safe capabilities, insufficient auditing and accounting features, or improper reset functions can cause asset damage or destruction; finally, covert channel access or other unsafe conditions are technical issues that can create new vulnerabilities. Every new component in an environment, including security solutions, adds to the potential attack surface.

Implementation

After appropriate countermeasures have been selected, they need to be implemented in the organization and integrated with other systems and countermeasures, when appropriate. Organizations that implement countermeasures are making planned changes to their environment in specific ways. Examples of countermeasure implementation include

>> **Change to policy, standard, or procedure.** An update to an official policy, technology standard, or procedure will require planning to ensure that the change will not have unintended effects in the organization. There will be some level of review(s), analysis, and discussion before the changes are accepted, published, and communicated. Changes to policy, standard, or procedure may also require changes to technology, and vice versa.

>> **Change to technology.** An update to something as big as network architecture, or as focused as the configuration setting of an individual system, is used to mitigate risk. Changes to technology usually involve business processes such as change management and configuration management, and may also impact procedures or standards. Significant changes may also involve discussions or processes at the IT Steering Committee or Security Committee levels. Disaster recovery planning and the CMDB may also be impacted.

>> **Change to staff.** A change in staffing could include training, reallocation of responsibilities, the addition of temporary staff (contractors or consultants), or hiring of additional staff.

Types of controls

A *control* is defined as a safeguard that is used to ensure a desired outcome. A control can be implemented in technology (for example, a program that enforces password complexity policy by requiring users to employ complex passwords), in a procedure (for example, a security incident response process that requires an incident responder to inform upper management), or a policy (for example, a policy that requires users to report security incidents to management). Organizations typically will have dozens to hundreds or even thousands of controls. There are so many controls that, sometimes, it makes sense to categorize controls in various ways. This can help security professionals better understand the types and categories of controls used in their organization. A few of these category groupings are discussed here.

The major types of controls are

>> **Preventive controls:** Used to prevent errors, unwanted events, and unauthorized actions.

>> **Detective controls:** Used to detect errors, unwanted events, and unauthorized activities. An example of a detective control is a video surveillance system.

>> **Deterrent controls:** Used to discourage people from carrying out an activity. For example, a video surveillance system employs visibly placed monitors to inform and remind people that a video surveillance system is in place.

Other types of controls include

>> **Corrective controls:** Used to reverse or minimize the impact of errors and unauthorized events. These are also known as *recovery controls*. An example of a recovery control is the verification of successful data recovery after a hardware failure.

>> **Administrative controls:** These are policies, standards, or procedures (typically, just statements written down in some way).

>> **Compensating controls:** These are controls that are enacted when primary controls cannot be implemented for any reason, such as excessive cost.

Another way to think of controls is how they are enforced. These types are

>> **Automatic controls:** Some form of automated mechanism ensures their enforcement and effectiveness. For example, such a system may automatically display a login page that requires a user to successfully authenticate prior to accessing the system.

>> **Manual controls:** Controls must be performed manually. For example, there may be a mandatory review of proposed changes in the change control process.

Most organizations don't attempt to create their control frameworks from scratch; instead, they adopt one of these well-known industry standard control frameworks:

>> ISO/IEC 27002 (Code of practice for information security management).

>> NIST 800-53 (Security and Privacy Controls for Federal Information Systems and Organizations).

>> NIST 800-171 (Protecting Controlled Unclassified Information in Nonfederal Systems and Organizations).

>> COBIT 5 for Information Security.

>> PCI DSS (Payment Card Industry Data Security Standard).

>> HIPAA Security Rule controls.

>> CIS (Center for Internet Security) Security Controls.

Organizations typically start with one of these, then make individual additions, changes, or deletions to controls, until they arrive at the precise set of controls they deem sufficient.

Control assessment

An organization that implemented controls, but failed to periodically assess those controls, would be considered negligent. The periodic assessment of controls is a necessary part of a sound risk management system.

Control assessment approach

There are various approaches to security control assessments (SCA), including:

> » **Control self assessment.** Here, an organization examines its own controls to determine whether they are being followed and whether they are effective.

> » **External assessment.** An organization employs an external agency (which could be a different part of the organization, or an external entity such as an audit firm or a consulting firm) to assess its controls.

> » **Variations in assessment frequency.** Various circumstances will compel an organization to set schedules for control assessment. For example, highly critical controls may be assessed monthly or quarterly, other controls assessed annually, and low-risk controls assessed every other year.

Organizations often take a blended approach to control assessment: some controls may be assessed internally, others externally. There may be a mix of the two; some controls are assessed both internally *and* externally.

TIP

Laws, regulations, and standards often have requirements dictating the frequency of control assessment, as well as whether controls must be assessed internally or externally.

Control assessment methodology

It would take an entire book (a long chapter, anyway) to detail the methods used to assess controls. Most of this subject matter lies outside the realm of most CISSPs, so we'll just summarize here. If you are "fortunate" enough to work in a highly regulated environment, you may get exposure to these concepts, and more.

CONTROL ASSESSMENT TECHNIQUES

There are five basic techniques used to assess the effectiveness of a control:

> » **Observation.** Here, an auditor watches a control as it is being performed.

> » **Inquiry.** An auditor asks questions of control owners about the control, how it is performed, and how records (if any) are produced.

- » **Corroborative inquiry.** Here, an auditor asks other persons about a control, in order to see if their descriptions agree or conflict with those given by control owners.
- » **Inspection.** An auditor examines records, and other artifacts, to see whether the control is operating properly.
- » **Reperformance.** An auditor will perform actions associated with the control to see whether the results indicate proper control function.

Auditors often use more than one of the techniques above when testing control effectiveness. The method(s) used are sometimes determined by the auditor, but sometimes the law, regulation, or standard specifies the type of control testing required.

SAMPLING TECHNIQUES

Some controls are manifested in many physical locations, or are present in many separate information systems. Sometimes, an auditor will elect to examine a subset of systems or locations instead of all of them. In large organizations, or in organizations where controls are implemented identically in all locations, it makes sense to examine a subset of the total number of instances (auditors call the entire collection of instances the *population*).

The available techniques include the following:

- » **Statistical.** Random selection that represents the entire population.
- » **Judgmental.** Auditor selects samples based on specific criteria.
- » **Discovery.** In high-risk controls where even a single exception may represent a high risk, an auditor may continue to examine a large population in search of a single exception.

Some laws, regulations, and standards have their own rules about sampling and the techniques that are permitted.

REPORTING

Auditors will typically create formal reports that include several components, including:

- » Audit objectives
- » Personnel interviewed
- » Documents and records examined

- >> Dates of interviews and examinations
- >> Controls examined
- >> Findings for each control (whether effective or ineffective)

Some laws, regulations, and standards specify elements required in audit reports, and sometimes even the format of a report.

Monitoring and measurement

Any safeguards or controls that are implemented need to be managed and, as you know, you can't manage what you don't measure! Monitoring and measurement not only helps you manage safeguards and controls, it also helps you verify and prove effectiveness (for auditing and other purposes).

Monitoring and measurement refer to active, intentional steps in controls and processes, so that management can understand how controls and processes are operating. Depending on the control or process, one or more of the following will be recorded for management reporting:

- >> Number of events that occur
- >> Outcome of each event (for example, success or failure)
- >> Assets involved
- >> Persons, departments, business units, or customers involved
- >> Costs involved
- >> Length of time
- >> Location

For some controls, management may direct personnel (or systems, for automatic controls) to create alerts or exceptions in specific circumstances. This will inform management of specific events where they may wish to take action of some kind. For example, a bank's customer representative might be required to inform a branch manager if a customer asks for change for a ten-thousand dollar bill.

Asset valuation

Asset valuation is an important part of risk management, because managers and executives need to be aware of the tangible and intangible value of all assets involved in specific incidents of risk management.

Once in a while, an asset's valuation can come from the accounting department's balance sheet (for better organizations that have a good handle on asset inventory, value, and depreciation), but often that's only a part of the story. For example, if an older server is involved in an incident and must be replaced, that replacement cost will be far higher than the asset's depreciated value. Further, the time required to deploy and ready a replacement server, and the cost of downtime, also need to be considered.

There are sometimes other ways to assign values to assets. For example, an asset's contribution to revenue may change one's perspectives on an asset's value. If an asset with a $10,000 replacement cost is key in helping the organization realize $5 million in revenue, is it still worth just $10,000?

Reporting

Regular reporting is critical to ensure that risk management is always "top of mind" for management. Reports should be accurate and concise. Never attempt to hide or downplay an issue, incident, or other bad news. Any changes to the organization's risk posture — whether due to a new acquisition, changing technology, new threats, or the failure of a safeguard, among others — should be promptly reported and explained.

Potentially, there is a lot of reporting going on in a risk management process, including:

>> Additions and changes to the risk ledger

>> Risk treatment decisions

>> Internal audits

>> External audits

>> Changes to controls

>> Controls monitoring and key metrics

>> Changes in personnel related to the risk management program

You guessed it: Some laws, regulations, and standards may require these and other types of reports (and, in some cases, in specific formats).

Continuous improvement

Continuous (or continual) improvement is more than a state of mind or a philosophy. It is a way of thinking about security and risk management. Better organizations bake continual improvement into their business processes, as a way of intentionally seeking opportunities to do things better.

ISO/IEC 27001 (Information Security Management Systems [ISMS] requirements) specifically requires continual improvement in several ways:

>> It requires management to promote continual improvement.

>> It requires a statement of commitment to continual improvement in an organization's security policy.

>> It requires security planning to achieve continual improvement.

>> It requires that the organization provide resources in order to achieve continual improvement.

>> It requires that management reviews seek opportunities for continual improvement.

>> It requires a formal corrective action process that helps to bring about continual improvement.

Risk frameworks

If you ask an experienced security and risk professional about risk frameworks, chances are they will think you are talking about either risk assessment frameworks or risk management frameworks. These frameworks are distinct, but deal with the same general subject matter: identification of risk that can be treated in some way.

Risk assessment frameworks

Risk assessment frameworks are methodologies used to identify and assess risk in an organization. These methodologies are, for the most part, mature and well established.

Some common risk assessment methods include

>> **Factor Analysis of Information Risk (FAIR).** A proprietary framework for understanding, analyzing, and measuring information risk.

>> **OpenFAIR.** An open-source version of FAIR.

>> **Operationally Critical Threat, Asset and Vulnerability Evaluation (OCTAVE).** Developed by the CERT Coordination Center.

>> **Threat Agent Risk Assessment (TARA).** Developed by Intel, this is a newer kid on the block.

Risk management frameworks

A *risk framework* is a set of linked processes and records that work together to identify and manage risk in an organization. The activities in a typical risk management framework are

>> **Create** strategies and policies.

>> **Establish** risk tolerance.

>> **Categorize** systems and information.

>> **Select** a baseline set of security controls.

>> **Implement** security controls.

>> **Assess** security controls for effectiveness.

>> **Authorize** system operation.

>> **Monitor** security controls.

There is no need to build a risk management framework from scratch. Instead, there are several excellent frameworks available that can be adapted for any size and type of organization. These frameworks include

>> **NIST SP800-37,** Guide for Applying the Risk Management Framework to Federal Information Systems.

>> **ISO/IEC 27005** (Information Security Risk Management).

>> **Risk Management Framework (RMF)** from the National Institute of Standards and Technology (NIST).

>> **COBIT 5** from ISACA.

>> **Enterprise Risk Management — Integrated Framework** from COSO (Committee of Sponsoring Organizations of the Treadway Commission).

Understand and Apply Threat Modeling

Threat modeling is a type of risk analysis used to identify security defects in the design phase of an information system or business process. Threat modeling is most often applied to software applications, but it can be used for operating systems, devices, and business processes with equal effectiveness.

Threat modeling is typically attack-centric; threat modeling most often is used to identify vulnerabilities that can be exploited by an attacker in software applications.

Threat modeling is most effective when performed at the design phase of an information system, application, or process. When threats and their mitigation are identified at the design phase, much effort is saved through the avoidance of design changes and fixes in an existing system.

While there are different approaches to threat modeling, the typical steps are

- » Identifying threats
- » Determining and diagramming potential attacks
- » Performing reduction analysis
- » Remediation of threats

Identifying threats

Threat identification is the first step that is performed in threat modeling. Threats are those actions that an attacker may be able to successfully perform if there are corresponding vulnerabilities present in the application or system.

For software applications, there are two mnemonics used as a memory aid during threat modeling. They are

- » STRIDE, a list of basic threats (developed by Microsoft):
  - Spoofing of user identity
  - Tampering
  - Repudiation
  - Information disclosure
  - Denial of service
  - Elevation of privilege
- » DREAD, an older technique used for assessing threats:
  - Damage
  - Reproducibility

- Exploitability
- Affected users
- Discoverability

While these mnemonics themselves don't contain threats, they do assist the individual performing threat modeling, by reminding the individual of basic threat categories (STRIDE) and their analysis (DREAD).

TIP

Appendices D and E in NIST SP800-30, *Guide for Conducting Risk Assessments*, are an excellent general-purpose source for threats.

Determining and diagramming potential attacks

After threats have been identified, threat modeling continues through the creation of diagrams that illustrate attacks on an application or system. An *attack tree* can be developed. It outlines the steps required to attack a system. Figure 3-2 illustrates an attack tree of a mobile banking application.

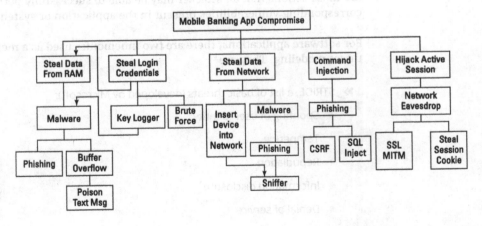

FIGURE 3-2: Attack tree for a mobile banking application.

REMEMBER

An attack tree illustrates the steps used to attack a target system.

Performing reduction analysis

When performing a threat analysis on a complex application or a system, it is likely that there will be many similar elements that represent duplications of technology. *Reduction analysis* is an optional step in threat modeling to avoid duplication of effort. It doesn't make sense to spend a lot of time analyzing different components in an environment if they are all using the same technology and configuration.

Here are typical examples:

>> An application contains several form fields (which are derived from the same source code) that request bank account number. Because all of the field input modules use the same code, detailed analysis only needs to be done once.

>> An application sends several different types of messages over the same TLS connection. Because the same certificate and connection are being used, detailed analysis of the TLS connection only needs to be done once.

Technologies and processes to remediate threats

Just as in routine risk analysis, the next step in threat analysis is the enumeration of potential measures to mitigate the identified threat. Because the nature of threats varies widely, remediation may consist of one or more of the following for each risk:

>> Change source code (for example, add functions to closely examine input fields and filter out injection attacks).

>> Change configuration (for example, switch to a more secure encryption algorithm, or expire passwords more frequently).

>> Change business process (for example, add or change steps in a process or procedure to record or examine key data).

>> Change personnel (for example, provide training, move responsibility for a task to another person).

Recall that the four options for risk treatment are mitigation, transfer, avoidance, and acceptance. In the case of threat modeling, some threats may be accepted as-is.

Integrate Security Risk Considerations into Supply Chain Management, Mergers, and Acquisitions

Integrating security risk considerations into supply chain management and merger and acquisition strategy helps to minimize the introduction of new or unknown risks into the organization.

It is often said that security in an organization is only as strong as its weakest link. In the context of service providers, mergers, and acquisitions, the security of all organizations in a given ecosystem will be dragged down by shoddy practices in any one of them. Connecting organizations together before sufficient analysis can result in significant impairment of the security capabilities overall.

REMEMBER

The task of reconciling policies, requirements, business processes, and procedures during a merger or acquisition is rarely straightforward. Further, there should be no assumption of one organization's policies, requirements, processes and procedures being the "right" or "best" way for all parties in the merger or acquisition – even if that organization is the acquiring entity.

Instead, each organization's individual policies, requirements, processes and procedures should be assessed to identify the best solution for the new formed organization going forward.

Hardware, software, and services

Any new hardware, software, or services being considered by an organization should be appropriately evaluated to determine both how it will impact the organization's overall security and risk posture, and how it will affect other hardware, software, services, and processes already in place within the organization. For example, integration issues can have a negative impact on a system's integrity and availability.

Third-party assessment and monitoring

It's important to consider the third parties that organizations use. Not only do organizations need to carefully examine their third-party risk programs, but also a fresh look of third parties themselves is needed, to ensure that the risk level related to each third party has not changed to the detriment of the organization.

Any new third-party assessments or monitoring should be carefully considered. Contracts (including privacy, non-disclosure requirements, and security requirements) and service-level agreements (SLAs, discussed later in this section) should be reviewed to ensure that all important security issues and regulatory requirements still are addressed adequately.

Minimum security requirements

Minimum security requirements, standards and baselines should be documented to ensure they are fully understood and considered in acquisition strategy and practice. Blending security requirements from two previously separate organizations is almost never as easy as simply combining them together into one document. Instead, there may be many instances of overlap, underlap, gaps, and contradiction that must all be reconciled. A transition period may be required, so that there is ample time to adjust the security configurations, architectures, processes, and practices to meet the new set of requirements after the merger or acquisition.

Service-level requirements

Service-level agreements (SLAs) establish minimum performance standards for a system, application, network, service, or process. An organization establishes internal SLAs and operating level agreements (OLAs) to provide its end-users with a realistic expectation of the performance of its information systems, services, and processes. For example, a help desk SLA might prioritize incidents as 1, 2, 3, and 4, and establish SLA response times of ten minutes, 1 hour, 4 hours, and 24 hours, respectively. In third-party relationships, SLAs provide contractual performance requirements that an outsourcing partner or vendor must meet. For example, an SLA with an Internet service provider might establish a maximum acceptable downtime which, if exceeded within a given period, results in invoice credits or (if desired) cancellation of the service contract.

Establish and Manage Information Security Education, Training, and Awareness

The CISSP candidate should be familiar with the tools and objectives of security awareness, training, and education programs. Adversaries are well aware that, as organizations' technical defenses improve, the most effective way to attack an organization is through its staff. Hence, all personnel in an organization need to be aware of attack techniques so that they can be on the lookout for these attacks and not be fooled by them.

Appropriate levels of awareness, training and education required within organization

REMEMBER

Security awareness is an often-overlooked factor in an information security program. Although security is the focus of security practitioners in their day-to-day functions, it's often taken for granted that common users possess this same level of security awareness. As a result, users can unwittingly become the weakest link in an information security program's defenses. Several key factors are critical to the success of a security awareness program:

>> **Senior-level management support:** Under ideal circumstances, senior management is seen attending and actively participating in training efforts.

>> **Clear demonstration of how security supports the organization's business objectives:** Employees need to understand why security is important to the organization and how it benefits the organization as a whole.

>> **Clear demonstration of how security affects all individuals and their job functions:** The awareness program needs to be relevant for everyone, so that everyone understands that "security is everyone's responsibility."

>> **Taking into account the audience's current level of training and understanding of security principles:** Training that's too basic will be ignored; training that's too technical will not be understood.

>> **Ensuring training is relevant and engaging:** Training needs to be relevant and engaging for all audiences, reflecting applicable regulations, technologies in use, and the organization's culture.

>> **Action and follow-up:** A glitzy presentation that's forgotten as soon as the audience leaves the room is useless. Find ways to incorporate the security information you present with day-to-day activities and follow-up plans.

The three main components of an effective security awareness program are a general awareness program, formal training, and education.

Awareness

A *general security awareness program* provides basic security information and ensures that everyone understands the importance of security. Awareness programs may include the following elements:

>> **Indoctrination and orientation:** New employees and contractors should receive basic indoctrination and orientation. During the indoctrination, they may receive a copy of the corporate information security policy, be required to acknowledge and sign acceptable-use statements and non-disclosure agreements, and meet immediate supervisors and pertinent members of the security and IT staff.

>> **Presentations:** Lectures, video presentations, and interactive computer-based training (CBTs) are excellent tools for disseminating security training and useful information. Employee bonuses and performance reviews are sometimes tied to participation in these types of security awareness programs.

>> **Printed materials:** Security posters, corporate newsletters, and periodic bulletins are useful for disseminating basic information such as security tips and promoting awareness of security.

Training

Formal training programs provide more in-depth information than an awareness program and may focus on specific security-related skills or tasks. Such training programs may include

>> **Classroom training:** Instructor-led or other formally facilitated training, possibly at corporate headquarters or a company training facility.

- **Self-paced training:** Usually web-based training where students can proceed at their own pace.
- **On-the-job training:** May include one-on-one mentoring with a peer or immediate supervisor.
- **Technical or vendor training:** Training on a specific product or technology provided by a third party.
- **Apprenticeship or qualification programs:** Formal probationary status or qualification standards that must be satisfactorily completed within a specified time period.

Education

An *education program* provides the deepest level of security training, focusing on underlying principles, methodologies, and concepts. In all but the largest organizations, this training is delivered by external agencies, as well as colleges, universities, and vocational schools.

An education program may include

- **Continuing education requirements:** Continuing Education Units (CEUs) are becoming popular for maintaining high-level technical or professional certifications such as the CISSP or Certified Information Systems Auditor (CISA).
- **Certificate programs:** Many colleges and universities offer adult education programs that have classes about current and relevant subjects for working professionals.
- **Formal education or degree requirements:** Many companies offer tuition assistance or scholarships for employees enrolled in classes that are relevant to their profession.

Measuring the effectiveness of security training

As we say often in this book, you can't manage what you don't measure. Security awareness training is definitely included here. It is vital that security awareness training include a number of different measurements so that security managers and company leadership know whether the effort is worth it. Some examples include

>> **Quizzes:** Whether delivered in the classroom or via on-demand web-based training, quizzes send a clear message that workers are expected to learn and retain security awareness knowledge. When minimum passing scores are enacted, this is made even more effective.

>> **Training metrics:** It's helpful to track completion rates to ensure that as many workers as possible complete required and optional training.

>> **Other security program metrics:** It may be interesting to track security awareness training metrics with other metrics such as security incidents, reports to ethics hot lines, and employees' reporting of security issues. It should be noted that some of these metrics may trend upward, which would represent workers' being more aware of security-related issues and a greater likelihood of their being reported.

Periodic reviews for content relevancy

Congratulations! You've chosen a profession that is constantly and rapidly changing! As such, security education, training, and awareness programs constantly must be reviewed and updated to ensure they remain relevant, and to ensure your own knowledge of current security concepts, trends, and technologies remains current. We suggest that the content of security education and training programs be examined at least once per year, to ensure that there is no mention of obsolete or retired technologies or systems, and that current topics are included.

IN THIS CHAPTER

» **Understanding commercial and government data classification**

» **Establishing ownership of data**

» **Addressing privacy issues**

» **Managing records retention**

» **Identifying appropriate data security controls**

» **Ensuring proper handling of sensitive information assets**

Chapter 4

Asset Security

The Asset Security domain addresses the collection, classification, handling, and protection of information assets throughout the information lifecycle. Important concepts within this domain include data ownership, privacy, data security controls, and cryptography. This domain represents 10 percent of the CISSP certification exam.

Classify Information and Supporting Assets

Information and data, in all their various forms, are valuable business assets. As with other, more tangible assets, the information's value determines the level of protection required by the organization.

A data classification scheme helps an organization assign a value to its information assets based on its *sensitivity* to loss or disclosure and its *criticality* to the organization's mission or purpose, and helps the organization determine the appropriate level of protection. Additionally, data classification schemes may be required for regulatory or other legal compliance.

Applying a single protection standard uniformly across all of an organization's assets is neither practical nor desirable. In such a case, either noncritical assets are over-protected or critical assets are under-protected.

An organization's employees also need to understand the classification schema being used, how to classify information assets, handling and safeguarding requirements, and proper destruction or disposal procedures.

Commercial data classification

Commercial data classification schemes are typically implemented to protect information that has a monetary value, to comply with applicable laws and protect privacy, and to limit liability. Criteria by which commercial data is classified include

>> **Value:** The most common classification criterion in commercial organizations. It's based on monetary value or some other value.

>> **Age/useful life:** Information that loses value over time, becomes obsolete or irrelevant, or becomes common/public knowledge is classified this way.

>> **Regulatory requirements:** Private information, such as medical records subject to HIPAA (Health Insurance Portability and Accountability Act of 1996) and HITECH (Health Information Technology for Economic and Clinical Health Act) regulations and educational records subject to the Privacy Act (see Chapter 3), may have legal requirements for protection. Classification of such information may be based not only on compliance but also on liability limits.

DATA CLASSIFICATION BEGETS SYSTEM CLASSIFICATION

Data classification is related to the identification of the sensitivity or criticality of data and proper procedures for handling that data. Asset classification, however, also applies to the information systems that store, process, and transmit this information. Better organizations go beyond data classification and implement system classification, and the two are distinctly related: Systems that store or process data at higher classification levels should be protected better than systems that do not store or process data at higher classification levels.

This practice has been around for quite a long time. In PCI, for example, systems that are in scope for PCI are required to have additional safeguards that an organization may not implement on its other systems. And, often, organizations place these systems in separate networks that have stricter network-level access controls.

Descriptive labels are often applied to company information, such as *Confidential and Proprietary* and *Internal Use Only*. However, the organizational requirements for protecting information labeled as such are often not formally defined. Organizations should formally identify standard classification levels as well as specific requirements for labeling, handling, storage, and destruction/disposal.

Government data classification

Government data classification schemes are generally implemented to

- » Protect national interests or security.
- » Comply with applicable laws.
- » Protect privacy.

REMEMBER

One of the more common systems, used within the U.S. Department of Defense (DoD), consists of five broad categories for information classification: Unclassified, Sensitive but Unclassified (SBU), Confidential, Secret, and Top Secret. We discuss all these categories in the following sections.

Within each classification level, certain safeguards are required in the use, handling, reproduction, transport, and destruction of Defense Department information. In addition to having an appropriate clearance level at or above the level of information being processed, individuals must have a need to know before they can access the information. Those who need to know are those who require the information so as to perform an assigned job function.

Unclassified

The lowest government data classification level is *Unclassified*. Unclassified information isn't sensitive, and unauthorized disclosure won't cause any harm to national security. Unclassified information may include information that was once classified at a higher level but has since been declassified by an appropriate authority. Unclassified information isn't automatically releasable to the public and may include additional modifiers such as *For Official Use Only* or *For Internal Use Only*.

Sensitive but Unclassified (SBU)

Sensitive but Unclassified information is a common modifier of unclassified information. It generally includes information of a private or personal nature. Examples include test questions, disciplinary proceedings, and medical records.

Confidential

Confidential information is information that, if compromised, could cause damage to national security. Confidential information is the lowest level of classified government information.

Secret

Secret information is information that, if compromised, could cause *serious* damage to national security. Secret information must normally be accounted for throughout its lifecycle, all the way to its destruction.

Top Secret

Top Secret information is information that, if compromised, could cause grave damage to national security. Top Secret information may require additional safeguards, such as special designations and handling restrictions.

REMEMBER

An individual must have the appropriate *clearance* level and *need-to-know* for access to classified information.

Determine and Maintain Ownership

Within an organization, *owners* and *custodians* of systems, data, and the business or mission (more specifically, a line of business or mission aspect) are implicitly or explicitly assigned.

TIP

Organizations should explicitly define owners and custodians of sensitive assets to avoid any confusion or ambiguity regarding roles, responsibilities, and accountability.

An *owner* is normally assigned at an executive or senior-management level within an organization, such as director or vice president. An owner doesn't legally *own* the asset assigned to him or her; the owner is ultimately responsible for safeguarding assigned assets and may have fiduciary responsibility or be held personally liable for negligence in protecting these assets under the concept of due care. For more on due care, read Chapter 3.

Typical responsibilities of an owner may include

>> Determining classification levels for assigned assets.

>> Determining policy for access to the asset.

>> Maintaining inventories and accounting for assigned assets.

>> Periodically reviewing classification levels of assigned assets for possible downgrading, destruction, or disposal.

>> Delegating day-to-day responsibility (but not accountability) and functions to a custodian.

A *custodian* is the individual who has day-to-day responsibility for protecting and managing assigned assets. IT systems administrators or network administrators often fill this role. Typical responsibilities may include

>> Performing regular backups and restoring systems and/or data, when necessary.

>> Ensuring that appropriate permissions are properly implemented on systems, directories, and files, and provide sufficient protection for the asset.

>> Ensuring that IT systems are adequately protected with system hardening and other safeguards.

>> Assigning new users to appropriate permission groups and revoking user privileges, when required.

>> Maintaining classified documents or other materials in a vault or secure file room.

REMEMBER

The distinction between owners and custodians, particularly regarding their different responsibilities, is an important concept in information security management. The data owner has ultimate responsibility for the security of the data, whereas the data custodian is responsible for the day-to-day security administration.

Protect Privacy

As discussed in Chapter 3, the concept of *privacy* is closely related to *confidentiality*, but is more specifically focused on preventing the unauthorized use or disclosure of personal data.

Personal data, commonly referred to as *personally identifiable information* (PII) may include

- » Name
- » Addresses
- » Contact information
- » Social Security Number
- » Financial account number
- » Birthdate and birthplace
- » Race
- » Marital status
- » Sexual orientation or lifestyle
- » Credit history and other financial information
- » Criminal records
- » Education
- » Employment records and history
- » Health records and medical data (known as *protected health information*, or PHI; known as *electronic protected health information*, or ePHI, when in electronic form)
- » Religious preference
- » Political affiliation
- » Other unique personal characteristics or traits

Every organization that collects any personal data about anyone (including employees, customers, and patients, among others) must have a well-defined, published, and distributed privacy policy that explains why the data is being collected, how it is being used, how it will be protected, and what the individual's rights are regarding the personal data that is being collected.

As with any other sensitive data, organizations must assign data owners and custodians (or processors) who are ultimately responsible for safeguarding personal data, and for the secure collection, processing, and use of the data. Anyone within an organization that has access to personal data in any capacity must be thoroughly familiar with established procedures for collecting, handling, and safeguarding such information throughout its entire lifecycle. This includes retention and destruction of private data, and technical issues such as *data remanence*.

REMEMBER

Data remanence refers to residual data that remains on storage media or in memory after a file or data has been deleted or erased. Data remanence occurs because standard delete routines only mark "deleted" data as storage or memory space that is available to be overwritten. To completely eliminate data remanence, the storage media and memory must be properly wiped, degaussed, encrypted, or physically (and completely) destroyed. *Object reuse* refers to an object (such as memory space in a program, or a storage block on media) that may present a risk of data remanence if it is not properly cleared.

Many privacy protection laws and regulations exist at continental (such as the European Union), country (or federal), state, and local levels throughout the world, as well as in various industries. Privacy protection laws are among some of the most rigorous laws enacted and legal requirements vary greatly. These laws also commonly limit the collection, use and retention of personal data, as well as trans-border information flows (or export) of personal data. Privacy laws are discussed in Chapter 3.

Finally, within an organization, certain employee privacy issues often arise regarding employee rights with respect to monitoring, search, drug testing, and other policies.

Monitoring commonly occurs in many forms within an organization including Internet, email, and general computer usage, as well as through surveillance cameras, access badges or keys, and time clocks, among others. Mandatory and random drug testing and searches of desks, lockers, work areas, and even personally-owned vehicles are other common policies that can evoke employee privacy concerns.

To reduce or eliminate employee privacy concerns, organizational policies should clearly define (and require written acknowledgement of) acceptable use policies (AUPs) for computer, Internet, and email usage. Additional policies should explain monitoring purposes, acceptable use or behavior, and potential disciplinary actions as a result of violations. Finally, organizational policies should clearly state that the employee has no *expectation of privacy* with regard to the organization's monitoring and search policies.

Ensure Appropriate Retention

Most organizations are bound by various laws, regulations and standards to collect and store certain information, as well as to keep it for specified periods of time. An organization must be aware of legal requirements and ensure that it's in compliance with all applicable regulations and standards.

Records retention policies should cover any electronic records that may be located on file servers, document management systems, databases, email systems, archives, and records management systems, as well as paper copies and backup media stored at off-site facilities.

Organizations that want to retain information longer than required by law should firmly establish *why* such information should be kept longer. Nowadays, just having information can be a liability, so keeping sensitive information longer should be the exception rather than the norm.

Data retention applies equally to the *minimum* as well as the *maximum* period of time that data may be retained in an organization. Retaining data longer than necessary (or permitted by law) increases an organization's liability, particularly where sensitive information is concerned. The Payment Card Industry Data Security Standard (PCI DSS) requires that credit card data be retained for as short a period of time as possible (and certain items like magnetic stripe data and PINs may not be retained at all!), whereas log data must be retained for at least one year (to aid in investigations).

At the opposite end of the records retention spectrum, many organizations now destroy records (including backup media) as soon as legally permissible in order to limit the scope (and cost) of any *future* discovery requests or litigation. Before implementing any such draconian retention policies that severely restrict your organization's retention periods, you should fully understand the negative implications such a policy has for your disaster recovery capabilities. Also, consult with your organization's legal counsel to ensure that you're in full compliance with all applicable laws and regulations.

WARNING

Although extremely short retention policies and practices may be prudent for limiting future discovery requests or litigation, they're *illegal* for limiting pending discovery requests or litigation (or even records that you have a reasonable expectation may become the subject of future litigation). In such cases, don't destroy pertinent records — otherwise, you go to jail. You go directly to jail! You don't pass Go, you don't collect $200, and (oh, yeah) you don't pass the CISSP exam, either — or even remain eligible for CISSP certification!

Determine Data Security Controls

Sensitive assets, including data, must be appropriately protected throughout their lifecycles. Information Lifecycle Management (ILM) covers data through the following five stages:

>> **Creation.** Data is created by an end user or application. Data needs to be classified at this time, based on the criticality and sensitivity of the data, and a data owner (usually, but not always, the creator) needs to be assigned. Data may exist in many forms such as in documents, spreadsheets, email and text messages, database records, forms, images, presentations (including video-conferences), and printed documents.

>> **Distribution ("data in motion").** Data may be distributed (or retrieved) internally within an organization or transmitted to external recipients. Distribution may be manual (such as via courier) or electronic (typically over a network). Data in transit is vulnerable to compromise, so appropriate safeguards must be implemented based on the classification of the data. For example, encryption may be required to send certain sensitive data over a public network. In such cases, appropriate encryption standards must be established. Data loss prevention (DLP) technologies may also be used to prevent accidental or intentional unauthorized distribution of sensitive data.

>> **Use ("data in use").** This stage refers to data that has been accessed by an end user or application and is being actively used (for example, read, analyzed, modified, updated, or duplicated) by that user or application. Data in use must be accessed only on systems that are authorized for the classification level of the data and only by users and applications that have appropriate permissions (clearance) and purpose (need-to-know).

>> **Maintenance ("data at rest").** Any time between the creation and disposition of data that it is not "in motion" or "in use", data is maintained "at rest". Maintenance includes the storage (on media such as a hard drive, removable USB thumb drive, backup magnetic tape, or paper) and filing (for example, in a directory and file structure) of data. Data may also be backed up, and the backup media transported to a secure off-site location (referred to as "data in transit"). Classification levels of data should also be routinely reviewed (typically by the data owner) to determine if a classification level needs to be upgraded (not common) or can be downgraded. Appropriate safeguards must be implemented and regularly audited to ensure:

- **Confidentiality (and privacy).** For example, using system, directory and file permissions, and encryption.

- **Integrity.** For example, using baselines, cryptographic hashes, cyclic redundancy checks (CRCs), and file locking (to prevent or control modification of data by multiple simultaneous users).

- **Availability.** For example, using database and file clustering (to eliminate single points of failure), backups and real-time replication (to prevent data loss).

>> **Disposition.** Finally, when data no longer has any value or is no longer useful to the organization, it needs to be properly destroyed in accordance with corporate retention and destruction policies, as well as any applicable laws and regulations. Certain sensitive data may require a final disposition determination by the data owner, and may require specific destruction procedures (such as witnesses, logging, and a magnetic wipe followed by physical destruction).

WARNING

Data that has merely been deleted HAS NOT been properly destroyed. It is merely "data at rest" waiting to be over-written — or inconveniently discovered by an unauthorized and potentially malicious third party!

REMEMBER

Data remanence refers to data that still exists on storage media or in memory after the data has been "deleted".

Baselines

Establishing a baseline is a standard business method used to compare an organization to a starting point or minimum standard, or for comparing progress within an organization over time. With security controls, these methods provide valuable insight:

>> **Comparing to other organizations.** Organizations can compare their control sets with other organizations, to see what differences exist in controls.

>> **Comparing internal controls over time.** An organization can baseline its set of controls, to see what changes occur in its control set over a period of years.

>> **Comparing control effectiveness over time.** An organization can compare its record of control effectiveness, to see where progress is being made, and where more effort is needed to make progress.

Scoping and tailoring

Because different parts of an organization and its underlying IT systems store and process different sets of data, it doesn't make sense for an organization to establish a single set of controls and impose them upon all systems. Like an oversimplified data classification program and its resulting overprotection and under-protection of data, organizations often divide themselves into logical zones, and then specify which controls and sets of controls are applied into these zones.

Another approach is to tailor controls and sets of controls to different IT systems and parts of the organization. For instance, controls on password strength can have categories that are applied to systems with varying security levels.

Both approaches for applying a complex control environment into a complex IT environment are valid – they're really just different ways of achieving the same objective: applying the right level of control to various systems and environments, based on the information they store and process or on other criteria.

Standards selection

Several excellent control frameworks are available for security professionals' use. In no circumstances is it necessary to start from scratch. Instead, the best approach is to start with one of several industry leading control frameworks, and then add or remove individual controls to suit the organization's needs.

Control framework standards include

- » **ISO/IEC 27002,** Code of practice for information security management.
- » **COBIT 5,** Control Objectives for Information and Related Technology.
- » **NIST SP800-53,** Recommended Security Controls for Federal Information Systems and Organizations.
- » **NIST SP800-171 Revision 1,** Protecting Controlled Unclassified Information in Nonfederal Systems and Organizations.
- » **NIST Cyber Security Framework (CSF),** Framework for Improving Critical Infrastructure Cybersecurity.

Cryptography

Crypto plays a critical role in data protection, whether we're talking about data in motion through a network, or at rest on a server or workstation. Cryptography is all about hiding data in plain sight, because there are situations where persons may be able to access sensitive data; crypto denies people that access unless they are in possession of an encryption key and the method for decrypting it.

Establish Handling Requirements

Sensitive information such as financial records, employee data, and information about customers must be clearly marked, properly handled and stored, and appropriately destroyed in accordance with established organizational policies, standards, and procedures:

» **Marking:** How an organization identifies sensitive information, whether electronic or hard copy. For example, a marking might read CONFIDENTIAL (discussed earlier in this chapter). The method for marking will vary, depending on the type of data we're talking about. For example, electronic documents can have a marking in the margin at the footer of every page. Where sensitive data is displayed by an application, it may be the application itself that informs the user of the classification of data being displayed.

» **Handling:** The organization should have established procedures for handling sensitive information. These procedures detail how employees can transport, transmit, and use such information, as well as any applicable restrictions.

» **Storage and Backup:** Similar to handling, the organization must have procedures and requirements specifying how sensitive information must be stored and backed up and how backup media must be protected.

» **Destruction:** Sooner or later, an organization must destroy a document that contains sensitive information. The organization must have procedures detailing how to destroy sensitive information that has been previously retained, regardless of whether the data is in hard copy or saved as an electronic file.

DETERMINING APPROPRIATE HANDLING REQUIREMENTS

You may be wondering, how do I determine what constitutes appropriate handling requirements for each classification level? There are two main ways to figure this out:

- **Applicable laws, regulations, and standards.** Oftentimes, regulations such as HIPAA and PCI contain specific requirements for handling sensitive information.

- **Risk assessment.** As described in Chapter 3, a risk assessment is used to identify relevant threats and vulnerabilities, as well as the establishment of controls to mitigate risks. Some of these controls may take the form of data handling requirements that would become a part of an organization's asset classification program.

Chapter **5**

Security Architecture and Engineering

Security must be part of the design of information systems, as well as the facilities housing information systems and workers, which is covered in the Security Architecture and Engineering domain. This domain represents 13 percent of the CISSP certification exam.

Implement and Manage Engineering Processes Using Secure Design Principles

It is a natural human tendency to build things without first considering their design or security implications. A network engineer who is building a new network may just start plugging cables into routers and switches without first thinking about the overall design — much less any security considerations. Similarly, a software engineer assigned to write a new program is apt to just begin coding without planning the program's design.

If we observe the outside world and the consumer products that are available, sometimes we see egregious usability and security flaws that make us wonder how the person or organization was ever allowed to participate in its design and development.

TIP

Security professionals need to help organizations understand that security-by-design principles are a vital component of the development of any system.

The engineering processes that require the inclusion of secure design principles include the following:

>> **Concept development.** From the idea stage, security considerations are vital to the success of any new IT engineering endeavor. Every project and product starts with something — a whiteboard session, sketches on cocktail napkins or pizza boxes, or a conference call. However the project starts, someone should ask how vital data, functions, and components will be protected in this new thing. We're not looking for detailed answers, but just enough confidence to know we aren't the latest lemmings rushing toward the nearest cliff.

>> **Requirements.** Before actual design begins, one or more persons will define the requirements for the new system or feature. Often, there are several categories of requirements. Security, privacy, and regulatory requirements need to be included.

>> **Design.** After all requirements have been established and agreed upon, formal design of the system or component can begin. Design must incorporate all requirements established in the preceding step.

>> **Development.** Depending on what is being built, development may take many forms, including creating

- System and device configurations

- Data center equipment racking diagrams

- Data flows for management and monitoring systems

>> **Testing.** Individual components and the entire system are tested to confirm that each and every requirement developed earlier has been achieved. Generally, someone other than the builder/developer should perform testing.

>> **Implementation.** When the system or component is placed into service, security considerations help ensure this does not place the new system/component or related things at risk. Implementation activities include

- Configuring and cabling network devices.

- Installing and configuring operating systems or subsystems, such as database management systems, web servers, or applications.

- Construction of physical facilities, work areas, or data centers.

>> **Maintenance and support.** After the system or facility is placed into service, all subsequent changes need to undergo similar engineering steps to ensure that new or changing security risks are quickly mitigated.

>> **Decommissioning.** When a system or facility reaches the end of its service life, it must be decommissioned without placing data, other systems, or personnel at risk.

TIP

The Building Security in Maturity Model (BSIMM) is a software security benchmarking tool that provides a framework for software security. It is composed of 256 measurements and 113 activities. The BSIMM activities consist of 12 practices organized into four domains including governance, intelligence, SSDL touchpoints, and deployment. Go to www.bsimm.com to learn more about BSIMM.

The application development lifecycle also includes security considerations that are nearly identical to security engineering principles here. Application development is covered in Chapter 10.

Understand the Fundamental Concepts of Security Models

Security models help us understand complex security mechanisms in information systems. Security models illustrate concepts that can be used when analyzing an existing system or designing a new one.

In this section, we describe the concepts of confidentiality, integrity, and availability (known together as *CIA*, or the *CIA Triad*), and access control models. Learn more about the CIA Triad in Chapter 3.

Confidentiality

Confidentiality refers to the concept that information and functions (objects) should be accessed only by authorized subjects. This is usually accomplished by several means, including:

>> **Access and authorization:** Ranging from physical access to facilities containing computers, to user account access, role-based access controls, and attribute-based access controls, the objective here is to make sure that only those persons with proper business authorization are permitted to access information. This topic is covered in Chapter 7.

>> **Vulnerability management:** This includes everything from system hardening to patch management and the elimination of vulnerabilities from applications. What we're trying to avoid here is any possibility that someone can attack the system and get to the data.

>> **Thorough system design:** The overall design of the system excludes unauthorized subjects from access to protected data.

>> **Sound data management practices:** The organization has established processes that define the use of the information it manages or controls.

These characteristics work together to ensure that secrets remain secrets.

Integrity

Integrity refers to the concept that information in a system will arrive or be created correctly and maintain that correctness throughout its lifetime. Systems storing the information will reject attempted changes by unauthorized parties or unauthorized means. The characteristics of data integrity that are ensured by systems are

>> Completeness

>> Timeliness

>> Accuracy

>> Validity

Some of the measures taken to ensure data integrity are

>> **Authorization:** This refers to whether data has proper authorization to enter a system. The integrity of a data record includes whether it should even be in the system.

>> **Input control:** This includes verifying that the new data entering the system is in the proper format and in the proper range.

>> **Access control:** This is used to control who (and what) is permitted to change the data and when the data can be changed.

>> **Output control:** This includes verifying that the data leaving the system is in the proper format and complete.

All of these steps help to ensure that the data in a system has the highest possible quality.

Availability

Availability refers to the concept that a system (and the data within it) will be accessible when and where users want to use it. The characteristics of a system that determine its availability include

>> **Resilient hardware design:** Features may include redundant power supplies, network adapters, processors and other components. These help to ensure that a system will keep running even if some of its internal components fail.

>> **Resilient software:** The operating system and other software components need to be designed and configured to be as reliable as possible incorporating techniques such as multithreading, multiprocessing, and multiprogramming.

>> **Resilient architecture:** We're talking big picture here. In addition to resilient hardware design, we would suggest that other components have redundancy including routers, firewalls, switches, telecommunications circuits, and whatever other items may otherwise be single points of failure.

>> **Sound configuration management, change management, and preventive maintenance processes:** Availability includes not only the components of the system itself, but is also reliant on good system management practices. After all, availability means avoiding unscheduled downtime, which is often a consequence of sloppy configuration management and change management practices, or neglected preventive maintenance.

>> **Established business continuity and disaster recovery plans:** Organizations need to ensure that natural and man-made disasters do not negatively affect the availability of critical systems and data. This topic is covered in detail later in this chapter.

REMEMBER

The CIA Triad comprises three principles of information protection: Confidentiality, Integrity, and Availability.

Access control models

Models are used to express access control requirements in a theoretical or mathematical framework that precisely describes or quantifies real access control systems. Common access control models include Bell-LaPadula, Access Matrix, Take-Grant, Biba, Clark-Wilson, Information Flow, and Non-interference.

REMEMBER

Bell-LaPadula, Access Matrix, and Take-Grant models address confidentiality of stored information. Biba and Clark-Wilson address integrity of stored information.

Bell-LaPadula

The Bell-LaPadula model was the first formal confidentiality model of a mandatory access control system. (We discuss mandatory and discretionary access controls in Chapter 7.) It was developed for the U.S. Department of Defense (DoD) to formalize the DoD multilevel security policy. As we discuss in Chapter 3, the DoD classifies information based on sensitivity at three basic levels: Confidential, Secret, and Top Secret. In order to access classified information (and systems), an individual must have access (a clearance level equal to or exceeding the classification of the information or system) and need-to-know (legitimately in need of access to perform a required job function). The Bell-LaPadula model implements the access component of this security policy.

Bell-LaPadula is a state machine model that addresses only the confidentiality of information. The basic premise of Bell-LaPadula is that information can't flow downward. This means that information at a higher level is not permitted to be copied or moved to a lower level. Bell-LaPadula defines the following two properties:

>> **Simple security property (ss property):** A subject can't read information from an object that has a higher sensitivity label than the subject (also known as *no read up,* or *NRU*).

>> ***-property (star property):** A subject can't write information to an object that has a lower sensitivity label than the subject (also known as *no write down,* or *NWD*).

Bell-LaPadula also defines two additional properties that give it the flexibility of a discretionary access control model:

>> **Discretionary security property:** This property determines access based on an *Access Matrix* — more on that model in the following section.

>> **Trusted subject:** A trusted subject is an entity that can violate the *-property but not its intent.

TIP

A *state machine* is an abstract model used to design computer programs; the state machine illustrates which "state" the program will be in at any time.

Access Matrix

An *Access Matrix model,* in general, provides object access rights (read/write/execute, or R/W/X) to subjects in a discretionary access control (DAC) system. An Access Matrix consists of access control lists (columns) and capability lists (rows). See Table 5-1 for an example.

TABLE 5-1   **An Access Matrix Example**

Subject/Object	Directory: H/R	File: Personnel	Process: LPD
Thomas	Read	Read/Write	Execute
Lisa	Read	Read	Execute
Harold	None	None	None

Take-Grant

Take–Grant systems specify the rights that a subject can transfer to or from another subject or object. These rights are defined through four basic operations: create, revoke, take, and grant.

Biba

The Biba integrity model (sometimes referred to as Bell–LaPadula upside down) was the first formal integrity model. Biba is a lattice-based model that addresses the first goal of integrity: ensuring that modifications to data aren't made by unauthorized users or processes. (See Chapter 3 for a complete discussion of the three goals of integrity.) Biba defines the following two properties:

>> **Simple integrity property:** A subject can't read information from an object that has a lower integrity level than the subject (also called *no read down*).

>> ***-integrity property (star integrity property):** A subject can't write information to an object that has a higher integrity level than the subject (also known as *no write up*).

Clark-Wilson

The *Clark-Wilson integrity model* establishes a security framework for use in commercial activities, such as the banking industry. Clark-Wilson addresses all three goals of integrity and identifies special requirements for inputting data based on the following items and procedures:

» **Unconstrained data item (UDI):** Data outside the control area, such as input data.

» **Constrained data item (CDI):** Data inside the control area. (Integrity must be preserved.)

» **Integrity verification procedures (IVP):** Checks validity of CDIs.

» **Transformation procedures (TP):** Maintains integrity of CDIs.

The Clark-Wilson integrity model is based on the concept of a *well-formed transaction*, in which a transaction is sufficiently ordered and controlled so that it maintains internal and external consistency.

Information Flow

An *Information Flow model* is a type of access control model based on the flow of information, rather than on imposing access controls. Objects are assigned a security class and value, and their direction of flow — from one application to another or from one system to another — is controlled by a security policy. This model type is useful for analyzing covert channels, through detailed analysis of the flow of information in a system, including the sources of information and the paths of flow.

Non-Interference

A *non-interference model* ensures that the actions of different objects and subjects aren't seen by (and don't interfere with) other objects and subjects on the same system.

Select Controls Based upon Systems Security Requirements

Designing and building secure software is critical to information security, but the systems that software runs on must themselves be securely designed and built. Selecting appropriate controls is essential to designing a secure computing architecture. Numerous systems security evaluation models exist to help you select the right controls and countermeasures for your environment.

Evaluation criteria

Evaluation criteria provide a standard for quantifying the security of a computer system or network. These criteria include the Trusted Computer System Evaluation Criteria (TCSEC), Trusted Network Interpretation (TNI), European Information Technology Security Evaluation Criteria (ITSEC), and the Common Criteria.

Trusted Computer System Evaluation Criteria (TCSEC)

The Trusted Computer System Evaluation Criteria (TCSEC), commonly known as the *Orange Book*, is part of the Rainbow Series developed for the U.S. DoD by the National Computer Security Center (NCSC). It's the formal implementation of the Bell–LaPadula model. The evaluation criteria were developed to achieve the following objectives:

>> **Measurement:** Provides a metric for assessing comparative levels of trust between different computer systems.

>> **Guidance:** Identifies standard security requirements that vendors must build into systems to achieve a given trust level.

>> **Acquisition:** Provides customers a standard for specifying acquisition requirements and identifying systems that meet those requirements.

The four basic control requirements identified in the Orange Book are

>> **Security policy:** The rules and procedures by which a trusted system operates. Specific TCSEC requirements include

- **Discretionary access control (DAC):** Owners of objects are able to assign permissions to other subjects.

- **Mandatory access control (MAC):** Permissions to objects are managed centrally by an administrator.

- **Object reuse:** Protects confidentiality of objects that are reassigned after initial use. For example, a deleted file still exists on storage media; only the file allocation table (FAT) and first character of the file have been modified. Thus residual data may be restored, which describes the problem of *data remanence*. Object-reuse requirements define procedures for actually erasing the data.

- **Labels:** Sensitivity labels are required in MAC-based systems. (Read more about information classification in Chapter 3.) Specific TCSEC labeling requirements include integrity, export, and subject/object labels.

>> **Assurance:** Guarantees that a security policy is correctly implemented. Specific TCSEC requirements (listed here) are classified as *operational assurance requirements:*

- **System architecture:** TCSEC requires features and principles of system design that implement specific security features.

- **System integrity:** Hardware and firmware operate properly and are tested to verify proper operation.

- **Covert channel analysis:** TCSEC requires covert channel analysis that detects unintended communication paths not protected by a system's normal security mechanisms. A *covert storage channel* conveys information by altering stored system data. A *covert timing channel* conveys information by altering a system resource's performance or timing.

REMEMBER

A systems or security architect must understand covert channels and how they work in order to prevent the use of covert channels in the system environment.

- **Trusted facility management:** The assignment of a specific individual to administer the security-related functions of a system. Closely related to the concepts of *least privilege, separation of duties,* and *need-to-know.*

- **Trusted recovery:** Ensures that security isn't compromised in the event of a system crash or failure. This process involves two primary activities: failure preparation and system recovery.

- **Security testing:** Specifies required testing by the developer and the National Computer Security Center (NCSC).

- **Design specification and verification:** Requires a mathematical and automated proof that the design description is consistent with the security policy.

- **Configuration management:** Identifying, controlling, accounting for, and auditing all changes made to the Trusted Computing Base (TCB) during the design, development, and maintenance phases of a system's lifecycle.

- **Trusted distribution:** Protects a system during transport from a vendor to a customer.

>> **Accountability:** The ability to associate users and processes with their actions. Specific TCSEC requirements include

- **Identification and authentication (I&A):** Systems need to track who performs what activities. We discuss this topic in Chapter 7.

- **Trusted Path:** A direct communications path between the user and the Trusted Computing Base (TCB) that doesn't require interaction with untrusted applications or operating-system layers.

- **Audit:** Recording, examining, analyzing, and reviewing security-related activities in a trusted system.

>> **Documentation:** Specific TCSEC requirements include

- **Security Features User's Guide (SFUG):** User's manual for the system.

- **Trusted Facility Manual (TFM):** System administrator's and/or security administrator's manual.

- **Test documentation:** According to the TCSEC manual, this documentation must be in a position to "show how the security mechanisms were tested, and results of the security mechanisms' functional testing."

- **Design documentation:** Defines system boundaries and internal components, such as the Trusted Computing Base (TCB).

REMEMBER

The Orange Book defines four major hierarchical classes of security protection and numbered subclasses (higher numbers indicate higher security):

>> **D:** Minimal protection

>> **C:** Discretionary protection (C1 and C2)

>> **B:** Mandatory protection (B1, B2, and B3)

>> **A:** Verified protection (A1)

These classes are further defined in Table 5-2.

TIP

You don't need to know specific requirements of each TCSEC level for the CISSP exam, but you should know at what levels DAC and MAC are implemented and the relative trust levels of the classes, including numbered subclasses.

Major limitations of the Orange Book include that

>> It addresses only confidentiality issues. It doesn't include integrity and availability.

>> It isn't applicable to most commercial systems.

>> It emphasizes protection from unauthorized access, despite statistical evidence that many security violations involve insiders.

>> It doesn't address networking issues.

TABLE 5-2   TCSEC Classes

Class	Name	Sample Requirements
D	Minimal protection	Reserved for systems that fail evaluation.
C1	Discretionary protection (DAC)	System doesn't need to distinguish between individual users and types of access.
C2	Controlled access protection (DAC)	System must distinguish between individual users and types of access; object reuse security features required.
B1	Labeled security protection (MAC)	Sensitivity labels required for all subjects and storage objects.
B2	Structured protection (MAC)	Sensitivity labels required for all subjects and objects; trusted path requirements.
B3	Security domains (MAC)	Access control lists (ACLs) are specifically required; system must protect against covert channels.
A1	Verified design (MAC)	Formal Top-Level Specification (FTLS) required; configuration management procedures must be enforced throughout entire system lifecycle.
Beyond A1		Self-protection and reference monitors are implemented in the Trusted Computing Base (TCB). TCB verified to source-code level.

Trusted Network Interpretation (TNI)

Part of the Rainbow Series, like TCSEC (discussed in the preceding section), Trusted Network Interpretation (TNI) addresses confidentiality and integrity in trusted computer/communications network systems. Within the Rainbow Series, it's known as the *Red Book*.

Part I of the TNI is a guideline for extending the system protection standards defined in the TCSEC (the *Orange Book*) to networks. Part II of the TNI describes additional security features such as communications integrity, protection from denial of service, and transmission security.

European Information Technology Security Evaluation Criteria (ITSEC)

Unlike TCSEC, the European Information Technology Security Evaluation Criteria (ITSEC) addresses confidentiality, integrity, and availability, as well as evaluating an entire system, defined as a *Target of Evaluation* (TOE), rather than a single computing platform.

ITSEC evaluates *functionality* (security objectives, or *why*; security-enforcing functions, or *what*; and security mechanisms, or *how*) and *assurance* (effectiveness and correctness) separately. The ten functionality (F) classes and seven evaluation (E) (assurance) levels are listed in Table 5-3.

TABLE 5-3

ITSEC Functionality (F) Classes and Evaluation (E) Levels mapped to TCSEC levels

(F) Class	(E) Level	Description
NA	E0	Equivalent to TCSEC level D
F-C1	E1	Equivalent to TCSEC level C1
F-C2	E2	Equivalent to TCSEC level C2
F-B1	E3	Equivalent to TCSEC level B1
F-B2	E4	Equivalent to TCSEC level B2
F-B3	E5	Equivalent to TCSEC level B3
F-B3	E6	Equivalent to TCSEC level A1
F-IN	NA	TOEs with high integrity requirements
F-AV	NA	TOEs with high availability requirements
F-DI	NA	TOEs with high integrity requirements during data communication
F-DC	NA	TOEs with high confidentiality requirements during data communication
F-DX	NA	Networks with high confidentiality and integrity requirements

You don't need to know specific requirements of each ITSEC level for the CISSP exam, but you should know how the basic functionality levels (F–C1 through F–B3) and evaluation levels (E0 through E6) correlate to TCSEC levels.

Common Criteria

The Common Criteria for Information Technology Security Evaluation (usually just called *Common Criteria*) is an international effort to standardize and improve existing European and North American evaluation criteria. The Common Criteria has been adopted as an international standard in ISO 15408. The Common Criteria defines eight *evaluation assurance levels* (EALs), which are listed in Table 5-4.

You don't need to know specific requirements of each Common Criteria level for the CISSP exam, but you should understand the basic evaluation hierarchy (EAL0 through EAL7, in order of increasing levels of trust).

System certification and accreditation

System *certification* is a formal methodology for comprehensive testing and documentation of information system security safeguards, both technical and nontechnical, in a given environment by using established evaluation criteria (the TCSEC).

TABLE 5-4   **The Common Criteria**

Level	TCSEC Equivalent	ITSEC Equivalent	Description
EAL0	N/A	N/A	Inadequate assurance
EAL1	N/A	N/A	Functionally tested
EAL2	C1	E1	Structurally tested
EAL3	C2	E2	Methodically tested and checked
EAL4	B1	E3	Methodically designed, tested, and reviewed
EAL5	B2	E4	Semi-formally designed and tested
EAL6	B3	E5	Semi-formally verified design and tested
EAL7	A1	E6	Formally verified design and tested

Accreditation is an official, written approval for the operation of a specific system in a specific environment, as documented in the certification report. Accreditation is normally granted by a senior executive or Designated Approving Authority (DAA). The term *DAA* is used in the U.S. military and government. A DAA is normally a senior official, such as a commanding officer.

System certification and accreditation must be updated when any changes are made to the system or environment, and they must also be periodically re-validated, which typically happens every three years.

The certification and accreditation process has been formally implemented in U.S. military and government organizations as the Defense Information Technology Security Certification and Accreditation Process (DITSCAP) and National Information Assurance Certification and Accreditation Process (NIACAP), respectively. U.S. government agencies utilizing cloud-based systems and services are required to undergo FedRAMP certification and accreditation processes (described in this chapter). These important processes are used to make sure that a new (or changed) system has the proper design and operational characteristics, and that it's suitable for a specific task.

DITSCAP

The Defense Information Technology Security Certification and Accreditation Process (DITSCAP) formalizes the certification and accreditation process for U.S. DoD information systems through four distinct phases:

>> **Definition:** Security requirements are determined by defining the organization and system's mission, environment, and architecture.

>> **Verification:** Ensures that a system undergoing development or modification remains compliant with the System Security Authorization Agreement (SSAA), which is a baseline security-configuration document.

>> **Validation:** Confirms compliance with the SSAA.

>> **Post-Accreditation:** Represents ongoing activities required to maintain compliance, and address new and evolving threats, throughout a system's lifecycle.

NIACAP

The National Information Assurance Certification and Accreditation Process (NIA-CAP) formalizes the certification and accreditation process for U.S. government national security information systems. NIACAP consists of four phases (Definition, Verification, Validation, and Post-Accreditation) that generally correspond to the DITSCAP phases. Additionally, NIACAP defines three types of accreditation:

>> **Site accreditation:** All applications and systems at a specific location are evaluated.

>> **Type accreditation:** A specific application or system for multiple locations is evaluated.

>> **System accreditation:** A specific application or system at a specific location is evaluated.

FedRAMP

The Federal Risk and Authorization Management Program (FedRAMP) is a standardized approach to assessments, authorization, and continuous monitoring of cloud-based service providers. This represents a change from controls-based security to risk-based security.

DCID 6/3

The Director of Central Intelligence Directive 6/3 is the process used to protect sensitive information that's stored on computers used by the U.S. Central Intelligence Agency (CIA).

Security controls and countermeasures

Various security controls and countermeasures that should be applied to security architecture, as appropriate, include defense in depth, system hardening, implementation of heterogeneous environments, and designing system resilience.

Defense in depth

Defense in depth is a strategy for resisting attacks. A system that employs defense in depth will have two or more layers of protective controls that are designed to protect the system or data stored there.

An example defense-in-depth architecture would consist of a database protected by several components, such as:

>> Screening router

>> Firewall

>> Intrusion prevention system

>> Hardened operating system

>> OS-based network access filtering

All the layers listed here help to protect the database. In fact, each one of them by itself offers nearly complete protection. But when considered together, all these controls offer a varied (in effect, deeper) defense, hence the term *defense in depth*.

REMEMBER

Defense in depth refers to the use of multiple layers of protection.

System hardening

Most types of information systems, including computer operating systems, have several general-purpose features that make it easy to set up the systems. But systems that are exposed to the Internet should be "hardened," or configured according to the following concepts:

>> Remove all unnecessary components.

>> Remove all unnecessary accounts.

>> Close all unnecessary network listening ports.

>> Change all default passwords to complex, difficult to guess passwords.

>> All necessary programs should run at the lowest possible privilege.

>> Security patches should be installed as soon as they are available.

System hardening guides can be obtained from a number of sources, such as:

>> The Center for Internet Security (www.cisecurity.org).

>> Information Assurance Support Environment, from the U.S. Defense Information Security Agency (https://iase.disa.mil/stigs).

TIP

Software and operating system vendors often provide their own hardening guides, which may also be useful.

Heterogeneous environment

Rather than containing systems or components of a single type, a *heterogeneous environment* contains a variety of different types of systems. Contrast an environment that consists only of Windows 2016 servers and the latest SQL Server and IIS Server, to a more complex environment that contains Windows, Linux, and Solaris servers with Microsoft SQL Server, MySQL, and Oracle databases.

The advantage of a heterogeneous environment is its variety of systems; for one thing, the various types of systems probably won't possess common vulnerabilities, which makes them harder to attack. However, the complexity of a heterogeneous environment also negatively impacts security, as there are more components that potentially can fail or be compromised.

The weakness of a *homogeneous environment* (one where all of the systems are the same) is its uniformity. If a weakness in one of the systems is discovered, all systems may have the weakness. If one of the systems is attacked and compromised, all may be attacked and compromised.

You can liken homogeneity to a herd of animals; if they are genetically identical, then they may all be susceptible to a disease that could wipe out the entire herd. If they are genetically diverse, then perhaps some will be able to survive the disease.

System resilience

The *resilience* of a system is a measure of its ability to keep running, even under less-than-ideal conditions. Resilience is important at all levels, including network, operating system, subsystem (such as database management system or web server), and application.

Resilience can mean a lot of different things. Here are some examples:

>> **Filter malicious input:** System can recognize and reject input that may be an attack. Examples of suspicious input include what you get typically in an injection attack, buffer-overflow attack, or Denial of Service attack.

>> **Data replication:** System copies critical data to a separate storage system in the event of component failure.

» **Redundant components:** System contains redundant components that permit the system to continue running even when hardware failures or malfunctions occur. Examples of redundant components include multiple power supplies, multiple network interfaces, redundant storage techniques such as RAID, and redundant server architecture techniques such as clustering.

» **Maintenance hooks:** Hidden, undocumented features in software programs that are intended to inappropriately expose data or functions for illicit use.

» **Security countermeasures:** Knowing that systems are subject to frequent or constant attack, systems architects need to include several security countermeasures in order to minimize system vulnerability. Such countermeasures include

- Revealing as little information about the system as possible. For example, don't permit the system to ever display the version of operating system, database, or application software that's running.

- Limiting access to only those persons who must use the system in order to fulfill needed organizational functions.

- Disabling unnecessary services in order to reduce the number of attack targets.

- Using strong authentication in order to make it as difficult as possible for outsiders to access the system.

TEMPEST IN A TEAPOT?

The U.S. military conducted a series of experiments to determine whether emanations from computer equipment would reveal activities taking place. These experiments were controlled through a project named TEMPEST. Standards have been developed in the U.S. and other NATO countries that provide three levels of protection, depending upon the distance between a potential attacker and a target system. The Level I standard is for systems with only 1 meter of safe distance; Level II is for systems with 20 meters; Level III is for systems with 100 meters of safe distance between systems and potential attackers. Systems can be certified to these standards in the U.S. and other NATO countries.

Understand Security Capabilities of Information Systems

Basic concepts related to security architecture include the Trusted Computing Base (TCB), Trusted Platform Module (TPM), secure modes of operation, open and closed systems, protection rings, security modes, and recovery procedures.

Computer architecture

Basic computer (system) *architecture* refers to the structure of a computer system and comprises its hardware, firmware, and software.

TIP

The CompTIA A+ certification exam covers computer architecture in depth and is an excellent way to prepare for this portion of the CISSP examination.

Hardware

Hardware consists of the physical components in computer architecture. The main components of the computer architecture include the CPU, memory, and bus.

CPU

The *CPU* (Central Processing Unit) or microprocessor is the electronic circuitry that performs a computer's arithmetic, logic, and computing functions. As shown in Figure 5-1, the main components of a CPU include

>> **Arithmetic Logic Unit (ALU):** Performs numerical calculations and comparative logic functions, such as ADD, SUBTRACT, DIVIDE, and MULTIPLY.

>> **Bus Interface Unit (BIU):** Supervises data transfers over the bus system between the CPU and I/O devices.

>> **Control Unit:** Coordinates activities of the other CPU components during program execution.

>> **Decode Unit:** Converts incoming instructions into individual CPU commands.

>> **Floating-Point Unit (FPU):** Handles higher math operations for the ALU and control unit.

>> **Memory Management Unit (MMU):** Handles addressing and cataloging data that's stored in memory and translates logical addressing into physical addressing.

>> **Pre-Fetch Unit:** Preloads instructions into CPU registers.

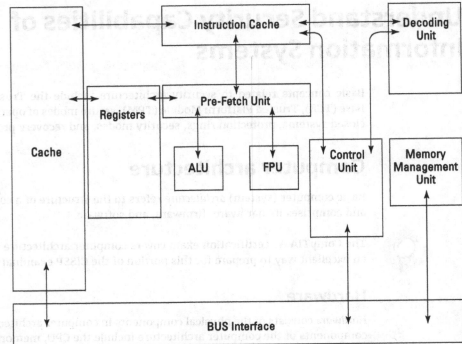

FIGURE 5-1:
The main
components of
a CPU.

>> **Protection Test Unit (PTU):** Monitors all CPU functions to ensure that they're properly executed.

>> **Registers:** Hold CPU data, addresses, and instructions temporarily, in special buffers.

The basic operation of a microprocessor consists of two distinct phases: *fetch* and *execute*. (It's not too different from what your dog does: You throw the stick, and he fetches the stick.) During the fetch phase, the CPU locates and retrieves a required instruction from memory. During the execute phase, the CPU decodes and executes the instruction. These two phases make up a basic *machine cycle* that's controlled by the CPU clock signals. Many complex instructions require more than a single machine cycle to execute.

The four operating states for a computer (CPU) are

>> **Operating (or run) state:** The CPU executes an instruction or instructions.

>> **Problem (or application) state:** The CPU calculates a solution to an application-based problem. During this state, only a limited subset of instructions (non-privileged instructions) is available.

>> **Supervisory state:** The CPU executes a *privileged* instruction, meaning that instruction is available only to a system administrator or other authorized user/process.

>> **Wait state:** The CPU hasn't yet completed execution of an instruction and must extend the cycle.

The two basic types of CPU designs used in modern computer systems are

>> **Complex-Instruction-Set Computing (CISC):** Can perform multiple operations per single instruction. Optimized for systems in which the fetch phase is the longest part of the instruction execution cycle. CPUs that use CISC include Intel x86, PDP-11, and Motorola 68000.

>> **Reduced-Instruction-Set Computing (RISC):** Uses fewer, simpler instructions than CISC architecture, requiring fewer clock cycles to execute. Optimized for systems in which the fetch and execute phases are approximately equal. CPUs that have RISC architecture include Alpha, PowerPC, and SPARC.

Microprocessors are also often described as scalar or superscalar. A *scalar* processor executes a single instruction at a time. A *superscalar* processor can execute multiple instructions concurrently.

Finally, many systems (microprocessors) are classified according to additional functionality (which must be supported by the installed operating system):

>> **Multitasking:** Alternates the execution of multiple subprograms or tasks on a single processor.

>> **Multiprogramming:** Alternates the execution of multiple programs on a single processor.

>> **Multiprocessing:** Executes multiple programs on multiple processors simultaneously.

Two related concepts are multistate and multiuser systems that, more correctly, refer to operating system capabilities:

>> **Multistate:** The operating system supports multiple operating states, such as single-user and multiuser modes in the UNIX/Linux world and Normal and Safe modes in the Windows world.

>> **Multiuser:** The operating system can differentiate between users. For example, it provides different shell environments, profiles, or privilege levels for each user, as well as process isolation between users.

An important security issue in multiuser systems involves privileged accounts, and programs or processes that run in a privileged state. Programs such as su (UNIX/Linux) and RunAs (Windows) allow a user to switch to a different account, such as root or administrator, and execute privileged commands in this context. Many programs rely on privileged service accounts to function properly. Utilities such as IBM's Superzap, for example, are used to install fixes to the operating system or other applications.

BUS

The *bus* is a group of electronic conductors that interconnect the various components of the computer, transmitting signals, addresses, and data between these components. Bus structures are organized as follows:

>> **Data bus:** Transmits data between the CPU, memory, and peripheral devices.

>> **Address bus:** Transmits addresses of data and instructions between the CPU and memory.

>> **Control bus:** Transmits control information (device status) between the CPU and other devices.

Main memory

Main memory (also known as *main storage*) is the part of the computer that stores programs, instructions, and data. The two basic types of *physical* (or real — as opposed to virtual — more on that later) memory are

>> **Random Access Memory (RAM):** *Volatile* memory (data is lost if power is removed) is memory that can be directly addressed and whose stored data can be altered. RAM is typically implemented in a computer's architecture as cache memory and primary memory. The two main types of RAM are

  • **Dynamic RAM (DRAM):** Must be *refreshed* (the contents rewritten) every two milliseconds because of capacitance decay. Refreshing is accomplished by using multiple clock signals known as multiphase clock signals.

  • **Static RAM (SRAM):** Faster than DRAM and uses circuit latches to represent data, so it doesn't need to be refreshed. Because SRAM doesn't need to be refreshed, a single-phase clock signal is used.

>> **Read-Only Memory (ROM):** *Nonvolatile* memory (data is retained, even if power is removed) is memory that can be directly addressed but whose stored data can't be easily altered. ROM is typically implemented in a computer's architecture as firmware (which we discuss in the following section). Variations of ROM include

- **Programmable Read-Only Memory (PROM):** This type of ROM can't be rewritten.

- **Erasable Programmable Read-Only Memory (EPROM):** This type of ROM is erased by shining ultraviolet light into the small window on the top of the chip. (No, we aren't kidding.)

- **Electrically Erasable Programmable Read-Only Memory (EEPROM):** This type of ROM was one of the first that could be changed without UV light. Also known as Electrically Alterable Read-Only Memory (EAROM).

- **Flash Memory:** This type of memory is used in USB thumb drives.

REMEMBER

Be sure you don't confuse the term "main storage" with the storage provided by hard drives.

SECONDARY MEMORY

Secondary memory (also known as *secondary storage*) is a variation of these two basic types of physical memory. It provides dynamic storage on nonvolatile magnetic media such as hard drives, solid-state drives, or tape drives (which are considered *sequential memory* because data can't be directly accessed — instead, you must search from the beginning of the tape). *Virtual memory* (such as a paging file, swap space, or swap partition) is a type of secondary memory that uses both installed physical memory and available hard-drive space to present a larger apparent memory space to the CPU than actually exists in main storage.

Two important security concepts associated with memory are the protection domain (also called protected memory) and memory addressing.

A *protection domain* prevents other programs or processes from accessing and modifying the contents of address space that's already been assigned to another active program or process. This protection can be performed by the operating system or implemented in hardware. The purpose of a protection domain is to protect the memory space assigned to a process so that no other process can read from the space or alter it. The memory space occupied by each process can be considered private.

Memory space describes the amount of physical memory available in a computer system (for example, 2 GB), whereas *address space* specifies where memory is located in a computer system (a memory address). *Memory addressing* describes the method used by the CPU to access the contents of memory. A *physical* memory address is a hard-coded address assigned to physically installed memory. It can only be accessed by the operating system that maps physical addresses to virtual addresses. A *virtual* (or *symbolic*) memory address is the address used by applications (and programmers) to specify a desired location in memory. Common virtual memory addressing modes include

>> **Base addressing:** An address used as the origin for calculating other addresses.

>> **Absolute addressing:** An address that identifies a location without reference to a base address — or it may be a base address itself.

>> **Indexed addressing:** Specifies an address relative to an index register. (If the index register changes, the resulting memory location changes.)

>> **Indirect addressing:** The specified address contains the address to the final desired location in memory.

>> **Direct addressing:** Specifies the address of the final desired memory location.

REMEMBER

Don't confuse the concepts of virtual memory and virtual addressing. *Virtual memory* combines physical memory and hard drive space to create more apparent memory (or *memory space*). *Virtual addressing* is the method used by applications and programmers to specify a desired location in physical memory.

Firmware

Firmware is a program or set of computer instructions stored in the physical circuitry of ROM memory. These types of programs are typically changed infrequently or not at all. In servers and user workstations, firmware usually stores the initial computer instructions that are executed when the server or workstation is powered on; the firmware starts the CPU and other onboard chips, and establishes communications by using the keyboard, monitor, network adaptor, and hard drive. The firmware retrieves blocks of data from the hard drive that are then used to load and start the operating system.

A computer's BIOS is a common example of firmware. *BIOS*, or Basic Input-Output System, contains instructions needed to start a computer when it's first powered on, initialize devices, and load the operating system from secondary storage (such as a hard drive).

Firmware is also found in devices such as smartphones, tablets, DSL/cable modems, and practically every other type of Internet-connected device, such as automobiles, thermostats, and even your refrigerator.

Firmware is typically stored on one or more ROM chips on a computer's *motherboard* (the main circuit board containing the CPU(s), memory, and other circuitry).

Software

Software includes the operating system and programs or applications that are installed on a computer system. We cover software security in Chapter 10.

OPERATING SYSTEMS

A computer *operating system* (OS) is the software that controls the workings of a computer, enabling the computer to be used. The operating system can be thought of as a logical platform, through which other programs can be run to perform work.

The main components of an operating system are

>> **Kernel:** The core component of the operating system that allows processes, control of hardware devices, and communications to external devices and systems to run.

>> **Device drivers:** Software modules used by the kernel to communicate with internal and external devices that may be connected to the computer.

>> **Tools:** Independent programs that perform specific maintenance functions, such as filesystem repair or network testing. Tools can be run automatically or manually.

The operating system controls a computer's resources. The main functions of the operating system are

>> **Process management:** Sets up an environment in which multiple independent processes (programs) can run.

>> **Resource management:** Controls access to all available resources, using schemes that may be based on priority or efficiency.

>> **I/O device management:** Controls communication to all devices that are connected to the computer, including hard drives, printers, monitors, keyboard, mouse, and so on.

>> **Memory management:** Controls the allocation and access to main memory (RAM), allocating it to processes, as well as general uses such as disk caching.

>> **File management:** Controls the file systems that are present on hard drives and other types of devices, and performs all file operations on behalf of individual processes.

>> **Communications management:** Controls communications on all available communications media on behalf of processes.

VIRTUALIZATION

A *virtual machine* is a software implementation of a computer, enabling many running copies of an operating system to execute on a single running computer without interfering with each other. Virtual machines are typically controlled by a *hypervisor*, a software program that allocates resources for each resident operating system (called a *guest*).

A hypervisor serves as an operating system for multiple operating systems. One of the strengths of virtualization is that the resident operating system has little or no awareness of the fact that it's running as a guest — instead, it may believe that it has direct control of the computer's hardware. Only your system administrator knows for sure.

CONTAINERIZATION

A *container* is a lightweight, standalone executable package of a piece of software that includes everything it needs to run. A container is essentially a bare-bones virtual machine that only has the minimum software installed necessary to deploy a given application. Popular container platforms include Docker and Kubernetes.

Trusted Computing Base (TCB)

A *Trusted Computing Base* (TCB) is the entire complement of protection mechanisms within a computer system (including hardware, firmware, and software) that's responsible for enforcing a security policy. A *security perimeter* is the boundary that separates the TCB from the rest of the system.

A Trusted Computing Base (TCB) is the total combination of protection mechanisms within a computer system (including hardware, firmware, and software) that's responsible for enforcing a security policy.

REMEMBER

Access control is the ability to permit or deny the use of an *object* (a passive entity, such as a system or file) by a *subject* (an active entity, such as an individual or a process).

Access control is the ability to permit or deny the use of an object (a system or file) by a subject (an individual or a process).

REMEMBER

A *reference monitor* is a system component that enforces access controls on an object. Stated another way, a reference monitor is an abstract machine that mediates all access to an object by a subject.

A reference monitor is a system component that enforces access controls on an object.

REMEMBER

A *security kernel* is the combination of hardware, firmware, and software elements in a Trusted Computing Base that implements the reference monitor concept. Three requirements of a security kernel are that it must:

>> Mediate all access

>> Be protected from modification

>> Be verified as correct

REMEMBER

A *security kernel* is the combination of hardware, firmware, and software elements in a Trusted Computing Base (TCB) that implements the reference monitor concept.

Trusted Platform Module (TPM)

A Trusted Platform Module (TPM) performs sensitive cryptographic functions on a physically separate, dedicated microprocessor. The TPM specification was written by the Trusted Computing Group (TCG) and is an international standard (ISO/IEC 11889 Series).

A TPM generates and stores cryptographic keys, and performs the following functions:

>> **Attestation.** Enables third-party verification of the system state using a cryptographic hash of the known good hardware and software configuration.

>> **Binding.** Binds a unique cryptographic key to specific hardware.

>> **Sealing.** Encrypts data with a unique cryptographic key and ensures that ciphertext can only be decrypted if the hardware is in a known good state.

Common TPM uses include ensuring platform integrity, full disk encryption, password and cryptographic key protection, and digital rights management.

Secure modes of operation

Security modes are used in mandatory access control (MAC) systems to enforce different levels of security. Techniques and concepts related to secure modes of operation include:

>> **Abstraction.** The process of viewing an application from its highest-level functions, which makes all lower-level functions into abstractions. Lower-level functions are treated as black boxes — known to work, even if we don't know how.

>> **Data hiding.** An object-oriented term that refers to the practice of encapsulating an object within another, in order to hide the first object's functioning details.

>> **System high mode.** A system that operates at the highest level of information classification. Any user who wants to access such a system must have clearance at, or above, the information classification level.

>> **Security kernel.** Composed of hardware, software, and firmware components that mediate access and functions between subjects and objects. The security kernel is a part of the protection rings model, in which the operating system kernel occupies the innermost ring, and rings farther from the innermost ring represent fewer access rights. The *security kernel* is the innermost ring, and has full access to all system hardware and data. User programs occupy outer rings, and have fewer access privileges.

>> **Reference monitor.** A component implemented by the security kernel that enforces access controls on data and devices on a system. In other words, when a user tries to access a file, the reference monitor ultimately performs the "Is this person allowed to access this file?" function.

The system's reference monitor enforces access controls on a system.

REMEMBER

Open and closed systems

An *open system* is a vendor-independent system that complies with a published and accepted standard. This compliance with open standards promotes interoperability between systems and components made by different vendors. Additionally, open systems can be independently reviewed and evaluated, which facilitates identification of bugs and vulnerabilities and the rapid development of solutions and updates. Examples of open systems include the Linux operating system, the Open Office desktop productivity system, and the Apache web server.

A *closed system* uses proprietary hardware and/or software that may not be compatible with other systems or components. Source code for software in a closed system isn't normally available to customers or researchers. Examples of closed systems include the Microsoft Windows operating system, Oracle database management system, and Apple iTunes.

The terms *open systems* and *closed systems* also refer to a system's access model. A closed system does not allow access by default, whereas an open system does.

TECHNICAL STUFF

Protection rings

The concept of protection rings implements multiple concentric domains with increasing levels of trust near the center. The most privileged ring is identified as Ring 0 and normally includes the operating system's security kernel. Additional system components are placed in the appropriate concentric ring according to the principle of least privilege and to provide isolation, so that a breach of a component in one protection ring does not automatically provide access to components in more privileged rings. The MIT MULTICS operating system implements the concept of protection rings in its architecture, as did Novell Netware.

Security modes

A system's *security mode of operation* describes how a system handles stored information at various classification levels. Several security modes of operation, based on the classification level of information being processed on a system and the clearance level of authorized users, have been defined. These designations are typically used for U.S. military and government systems, and include

>> **Dedicated:** All authorized users must have a clearance level equal to or higher than the highest level of information processed on the system and a valid need-to-know.

>> **System High:** All authorized users must have a clearance level equal to or higher than the highest level of information processed on the system, but a valid need-to-know isn't necessarily required.

>> **Multilevel:** Information at different classification levels is stored or processed on a *trusted computer system* (a system that employs all necessary hardware and software assurance measures and meets the specified requirements for reliability and security). Authorized users must have an appropriate clearance level, and access restrictions are enforced by the system accordingly.

>> **Limited access:** Authorized users aren't required to have a security clearance, but the highest level of information on the system is Sensitive but Unclassified (SBU).

A trusted computer system is a system with a Trusted Computing Base (TCB).

REMEMBER Security modes of operation generally come into play in environments that contain highly sensitive information, such as government and military environments. Most private and education systems run in *multilevel mode*, meaning they contain information at all sensitivity levels. See Chapter 3 for more on security clearance levels.

Recovery procedures

A hardware or software failure can potentially compromise a system's security mechanisms. Security designs that protect a system during a hardware or software failure include

>> **Fault-tolerant systems:** These systems continue to operate after the failure of a computer or network component. The system must be capable of detecting and correcting — or circumventing — a fault.

>> **Fail-safe systems:** When a hardware or software failure is detected, program execution is terminated, and the system is protected from compromise.

>> **Fail-soft (resilient) systems:** When a hardware or software failure is detected, certain noncritical processing is terminated, and the computer or network continues to function in a degraded mode.

>> **Failover systems:** When a hardware or software failure is detected, the system automatically transfers processing to a component, such as a clustered server.

Vulnerabilities in security architectures

Unless detected (and corrected) by an experienced security analyst, many weaknesses may be present in a system and permit exploitation, attack, or malfunction. We discuss the most important problems in the following list:

>> **Covert channels:** Unknown, hidden communications that take place within the medium of a legitimate communications channel.

>> **Rootkits:** By their very nature, rootkits are designed to subvert system architecture by inserting themselves into an environment in a way that makes it difficult or impossible to detect. For instance, some rootkits run as a hypervisor and change the computer's operating system into a guest, which changes the basic nature of the system in a powerful but subtle way. We wouldn't normally discuss malware in a chapter on computer and security architecture, but rootkits are a game-changer that warrants mention: They use various techniques to hide themselves from the target system.

>> **Race conditions:** Software code in multiprocessing and multiuser systems, unless very carefully designed and tested, can result in critical errors that are difficult to find. A *race condition* is a flaw in a system where the output or result of an activity in the system is unexpectedly tied to the timing of other events. The term *race condition* comes from the idea of two events or signals that are racing to influence an activity.

The most common race condition is the time-of-check-to-time-of-use bug caused by changes in a system between the checking of a condition and the use of the results of that check. For example, two programs that both try to open a file for exclusive use may both open the file, even though only one should be able to.

» **State attacks:** Web-based applications use session management to distinguish users from one another. The mechanisms used by the web application to establish sessions must be able to resist attack. Primarily, the algorithms used to create session identifiers must not permit an attacker from being able to steal session identifiers, or guess other users' session identifiers. A successful attack would result in an attacker taking over another user's session, which can lead to the compromise of confidential data, fraud, and monetary theft.

» **Emanations:** The unintentional emissions of electromagnetic or acoustic energy from a system can be intercepted by others and possibly used to illicitly obtain information from the system. A common form of undesired emanations is radiated energy from CRT (cathode-ray tube, yes. . . they're still out there, and not just in old movies!) computer monitors. A third party can discover what data is being displayed on a CRT by intercepting radiation emanating from the display adaptor or monitor from as far as several hundred meters. A third party can also eavesdrop on a network if it has one or more un-terminated coaxial cables in its cable plant.

Assess and Mitigate the Vulnerabilities of Security Architectures, Designs, and Solution Elements

In this section, we discuss the techniques used to identify and fix vulnerabilities in systems. We will lightly discuss techniques for security assessments and testing, which is fully explored in Chapter 8.

Client-based systems

The types of design vulnerabilities often found on endpoints involve defects in client-side code that is present in browsers and applications. The defects most often found include these:

» **Sensitive data left behind in the file system.** Generally, this consists of temporary files and cache files, which may be accessible by other users and processes on the system.

>> **Unprotected local data.** Local data stores may have loose permissions and lack encryption.

>> **Vulnerable applets.** Many browsers and other client applications often employ applets for viewing documents and video files. Often, the applets themselves may have exploitable weaknesses.

>> **Unprotected or weakly protected communications.** Data transmitted between the client and other systems may use weak encryption, or use no encryption at all.

>> **Weak or nonexistent authentication.** Authentication methods on the client, or between the client and server systems, may be unnecessarily weak. This permits an adversary to access the application, local data, or server data without first authenticating.

Other weaknesses may be present in client systems. For a more complete understanding of application weaknesses, consult www.owasp.org.

Identifying weaknesses like the preceding examples will require one or more of the following techniques:

>> Operating system examination

>> Network sniffing

>> Code review

>> Manual testing and observation

Server-based systems

Design vulnerabilities found on servers fall into the following categories:

>> **Sensitive data left behind in the file system.** Generally, this consists of temporary files and cache files, which may be accessible by other users and processes on the system.

>> **Unprotected local data.** Local data stores may have loose permissions and also lack encryption.

>> **Unprotected or weakly protected communications.** Data transmitted between the server and other systems (including clients) may use weak encryption, or use no encryption at all.

>> **Weak or nonexistent authentication.** Authentication methods on the server may be unnecessarily weak. This permits an adversary to access the application, local data, or server data without first authenticating.

These defects are similar to those in the preceding Client-based section. This is because the terms *client* and *server* have only to do with perspective: in both cases, software is running on a system.

Database systems

Database management systems are nearly as complex as the operating systems on which they reside. Vulnerabilities in database management systems include these:

>> **Loose access permissions.** Like applications and operating systems, database management systems have schemes of access controls that are often designed far too loosely, which permits more access to critical and sensitive information than is appropriate. Another aspect of loose access permissions is an excessive number of persons with privileged access. Finally, there can be failures to implement cryptography as an access control when appropriate.

>> **Excessive retention of sensitive data.** Keeping sensitive data longer than necessary increases the impact of a security breach.

>> **Aggregation of personally identifiable information.** The practice known as *aggregation* of data about citizens is a potentially risky undertaking that can result in an organization possessing sensitive personal information. Sometimes, this happens when an organization deposits historic data from various sources into a data warehouse, where this disparate sensitive data is brought together for the first time. The result is a gold mine or a time bomb, depending on how you look at it.

Database security defects can be identified through manual examination or automated tools. Mitigation may be as easy as changing access permissions or as complex as redesigning the database schema and related application software programs.

Large-scale parallel data systems

Large-scale parallel data systems are systems with large numbers of processors. The processors may either reside in one physical location or be geographically distributed. Vulnerabilities in these systems include

>> **Loose access permissions.** Management interfaces or the processing systems themselves may have either default, easily guessed, or shared logon credentials that would permit an intruder to easily attack the system.

>> **Unprotected or weakly protected communications.** Data transmitted between systems may be using either weak encryption or no encryption at all. This could enable an attacker to obtain sensitive data in transit or enough knowledge to compromise the system.

Security defects in parallel systems can be identified through manual examination and mitigated through either configuration changes or system design changes.

Distributed systems

Distributed systems are simply systems with components scattered throughout physical and logical space. Oftentimes, these components are owned and/or managed by different groups or organizations, sometimes in different countries. Some components may be privately used while others represent services available to the public (for example, Google Maps). Vulnerabilities in distributed systems include these:

>> **Loose access permissions.** Individual components in a distributed system may have individual, separate access control systems, or there may be one overarching access control system for all of the distributed system's components. Either way, there are too many opportunities for access permissions to be too loose, thereby enabling some subjects access to more data and functions than they need.

>> **Unprotected or weakly protected communications.** Data transmitted between the server and other systems (including clients) may be using either weak encryption or no encryption at all.

>> **Weak security inheritance.** What we mean here is that in a distributed system, one component having weak security may compromise the security of the entire system. For example, a publicly accessible component may have direct open access to other components, bypassing local controls in those other components.

>> **Lack of centralized security and control.** A distributed system that is controlled by more than one organization often lacks overall oversight for security management and security operations.

This is especially true of peer-to-peer systems that are often run by end users on lightly managed or unmanaged endpoints.

>> **Critical paths.** A critical path weakness is one where a system's continued operation depends on the availability of a single component.

All of these weaknesses can also be present in simpler environments. These weaknesses and other defects can be detected through either the use of security scanning tools or manual techniques, and corrective actions taken to mitigate those defects.

High quality standards for cloud computing — for cloud service providers as well as organizations using cloud services — can be found at the Cloud Security Alliance (www.cloudsecurityalliance.org) and the European Network and Information Security Agency (ENISA — www.enisa.europa.eu).

Cryptographic systems

Cryptographic systems are especially apt to contain vulnerabilities, for the simple reason that people focus on the cryptographic algorithm but fail to implement it properly. Like any powerful tool, if the operator doesn't know how to use it, it can be useless at best and dangerous at its worst.

The ways in which a cryptographic system may be vulnerable include these:

>> **Use of outdated algorithm.** Developers and engineers must be careful to select encryption algorithms that are robust. Furthermore, algorithms in use should be reviewed at least once per year to ensure they continue to be sufficient.

>> **Use of untested algorithm.** Engineers sometimes make the mistake of either home-brewing their own cryptographic system or using one that is clearly insufficient. It's best to use one of many publicly available cryptosystems that have stood the test of repeated scrutiny.

>> **Failure to encrypt encryption keys.** A proper cryptosystem sometimes requires that encryption keys themselves be encrypted.

>> **Weak cryptographic keys.** Choosing a great algorithm is all but undone if the initialization vector is too small, or too-short keys or too-simple keys are used.

>> **Insufficient protection of cryptographic keys.** A cryptographic system is only as strong as the protection of its encryption keys. If too many people have access to keys, or if the keys are not sufficiently protected, an intruder may be able to compromise the system simply by stealing and using the keys. Separate encryption keys should be used for the data encryption key (DEK) used to encrypt/decrypt data and the key encryption key (KEK) used to encrypt/decrypt the DEK.

These and other vulnerabilities in cryptographic systems can be detected and mitigated through peer reviews of cryptosystems, assessments by qualified external parties, and the application of corrective actions to fix defects.

Industrial control systems

Industrial control systems (ICS) represent a wide variety of means for monitoring and controlling machinery of various kinds, including power generation, distribution, and consumption; natural gas and petroleum pipelines; municipal water, irrigation, and waste systems; traffic signals; manufacturing; and package distribution.

Weaknesses in industrial control systems include the following:

>> **Loose access permissions.** Access to monitoring or controls of ICS's are often set too loosely, thereby enabling some users or systems access to more data and control than they need.

>> **Failure to change default access credentials.** All too often, organizations implement ICS components and fail to change the default administrative credentials on those components. This makes it far too easy for intruders to take over the ICS.

>> **Access from personally owned devices.** In the name of convenience, some organizations permit personnel to control machinery from personally owned smartphones and tablets. This vastly increases the ICS's attack surface and provides opportunities for intruders to access and control critical machinery.

>> **Lack of malware control.** Many ICS's lack security components that detect and block malware and other malicious activity, resulting in intruders having too easy a time getting into the ICS.

>> **Failure to air gap the ICS.** Many organizations fail to air gap (isolate) the ICS from the rest of its corporate network, thereby enabling excessive opportunities for malware and intruders to access the ICS via a corporate network where users invite malware through phishing and other means.

>> **Failure to update ICS components.** While the manufacturers of ICS components are notorious for failing to issue security patches, organizations are equally culpable in their failure to install these patches when they do arrive.

These vulnerabilities can be mitigated through a systematic process of establishing good controls, testing control effectiveness, and applying corrective action when controls are found to be ineffective.

Cloud-based systems

The U.S. National Institute of Standards and Technology (NIST) defines three cloud computing service models as follows:

>> **Software as a Service (SaaS):** Customers are provided access to an application running on a cloud infrastructure. The application is accessible from various client devices and interfaces, but the customer has no knowledge of, and does not manage or control, the underlying cloud infrastructure. The customer may have access to limited user-specific application settings.

>> **Platform as a Service (PaaS):** Customers can deploy supported applications onto the provider's cloud infrastructure, but the customer has no knowledge of, and does not manage or control, the underlying cloud infrastructure. The customer has control over the deployed applications and limited configuration settings for the application-hosting environment.

>> **Infrastructure as a Service (IaaS):** Customers can provision processing, storage, networks, and other computing resources and deploy and run operating systems and applications, but the customer has no knowledge of, and does not manage or control, the underlying cloud infrastructure. The customer has control over operating systems, storage, and deployed applications, as well as some networking components (for example, host firewalls).

NIST further defines four cloud computing deployment models as follows:

>> **Public:** A cloud infrastructure that is open to use by the general public. It's owned, managed, and operated by a third party (or parties) and exists on the cloud provider's premises.

>> **Community:** A cloud infrastructure that is used exclusively by a specific group of organizations.

>> **Private:** A cloud infrastructure that is used exclusively by a single organization. It may be owned, managed, and operated by the organization or a third party (or a combination of both), and may exist on or off premises.

>> **Hybrid:** A cloud infrastructure that is composed of two or more of the aforementioned deployment models, bound together by standardized or proprietary technology that enables data and application portability (for example, failover to a secondary data center for disaster recovery or content delivery networks across multiple clouds).

Major public cloud service providers such as Amazon Web Services, Microsoft Azure, Google Cloud Platform, and Oracle Cloud Platform provide customers not only with virtually unlimited compute and storage at scale, but also a depth and breadth of security capabilities that often exceeds the capabilities of the customers themselves. However, this does not mean that cloud-based systems are inherently secure. The shared responsibility model is used by public cloud service providers to clearly define which aspects of security the provider is responsible for, and which aspects the customer is responsible for. SaaS models place the most responsibility on the cloud service provider, typically including securing the following:

>> Applications and data

>> Runtime and middleware

>> Servers, virtualization, and operating systems

» Storage and networking

» Physical data center

However, the customer is always ultimately responsible for the security and privacy of its data. Additionally, identity and access management (IAM) is typically the customer's responsibility.

In a PaaS model, the customer is typically responsible for the security of its applications and data, as well as IAM, among others.

In an IaaS model, the customer is typically responsible for the security of its applications and data, runtime and middleware, and operating systems. The cloud service provider is typically responsible for the security of networking and the data center (although cloud service providers generally do not provide firewalls). Virtualization, server, and storage security may be managed by either the cloud service provider or customer.

TIP

The Cloud Security Alliance (CSA) publishes the Cloud Controls Matrix, which provides a framework for information security that is specifically designed for the cloud industry.

Internet of Things

The security of Internet of Things (IoT) devices and systems is a rapidly evolving area of information security. IoT sensors and devices collect large amounts of both potentially sensitive data and seemingly innocuous data. However, under certain circumstances practically any data that is collected can be used for nefarious purposes, security must be a critical design consideration for IoT devices and systems. This includes not only securing the data stored on the systems, but also how the data is collected, transmitted, processed, and used. There are many networking and communications protocols commonly used in IoT devices, including the following:

» IPv6 over Low power Wireless Personal Area Networks (6LoWPAN)

» 5G

» Wi-Fi

» Bluetooth Mesh and Bluetooth Low-Energy (BLE)

» Thread

» Zigbee, and many others

The security of these various protocols and their implementations must also be carefully considered in the design of secure IoT devices and systems.

Assess and Mitigate Vulnerabilities in Web-Based Systems

Web-based systems contain many components, including application code, database management systems, operating systems, middleware, and the web server software itself. These components may, individually and collectively, have security design or implementation defects. Some of the defects present include these:

» **Failure to block injection attacks.** Attacks such as JavaScript injection and SQL injection can permit an attacker to cause a web application to malfunction and expose sensitive internally stored data.

» **Defective authentication.** There are many, many ways in which a web site can implement authentication — they are too numerous to list here. Authentication is essential to get right; many sites fail to do so.

» **Defective session management.** Web servers create logical "sessions" to keep track of individual users. Many web sites' session management mechanisms are vulnerable to abuse, most notably that permit an attacker to take over another user's session.

» **Failure to block cross-site scripting attacks.** Web sites that fail to examine and sanitize input data. As a result, attackers can sometimes create attacks that send malicious content to the user.

» **Failure to block cross-site request forgery attacks.** Web sites that fail to employ proper session and session context management can be vulnerable to attacks in which users are tricked into sending commands to web sites that may cause them harm.

The example we like to use is where an attacker tricks a user into clicking a link that actually takes the user to a URL like this: `http://bank.com/transfer?tohackeraccount:amount=99999.99`.

» **Failure to protect direct objects references.** Web sites can sometimes be tricked into accessing and sending data to a user who is not authorized to view or modify it.

These vulnerabilities can be mitigated in three main ways:

» Developer training on the techniques of safer software development.

» Including security in the development lifecycle.

» Use of dynamic and static application scanning tools.

For a more in-depth review of vulnerabilities in web-based systems, read the "Top 10" list at www.owasp.org.

TIP

Assess and Mitigate Vulnerabilities in Mobile Systems

Mobile systems include the operating systems and applications on smartphones, tablets, phablets, smart watches, and wearables. The most popular operating system platforms for mobile systems are Apple iOS, Android, and Windows 10.

The vulnerabilities that are found on mobile systems include

>> **Lack of robust resource access controls.** History has shown us that some mobile OSs lack robust controls that govern which apps are permitted to access resources on the mobile device, including:

- Locally stored data
- Contact list
- Camera roll
- Email messages
- Location services
- Camera
- Microphone

>> **Insufficient security screening of applications.** Some mobile platform environments are quite good at screening out applications that contain security flaws or outright break the rules, but other platforms have more of an "anything goes" policy, apparently. The result is *buyer beware*: Your mobile app may be doing more than advertised.

>> **Security settings defaults too lax.** Many mobile platforms lack enforcement of basic security and, for example, don't require devices to automatically lock or have lock codes.

In a managed corporate environment, the use of a mobile device management (MDM) system can mitigate many or all of these risks. For individual users, mitigation is up to individual users to do the right thing and use strong security settings.

Assess and Mitigate Vulnerabilities in Embedded Devices

Embedded devices encompass the wide variety of systems and devices that are Internet connected. Mainly, we're talking about devices that are not human connected in the computing sense. Examples of such devices include

>> Automobiles and other vehicles.

>> Home appliances, such as clothes washers and dryers, ranges and ovens, refrigerators, thermostats, televisions, video games, video surveillance systems, and home automation systems.

>> Medical care devices, such as IV infusion pumps and patient monitoring.

>> Heating, ventilation, and air conditioning (HVAC) systems.

>> Commercial video surveillance and key card systems.

>> Automated payment kiosks, fuel pumps, and automated teller machines (ATMs).

>> Network devices such as routers, switches, modems, firewalls, and so on.

These devices often run embedded systems, which are specialized operating systems designed to run on devices lacking computer-like human interaction through a keyboard or display. They still have an operating system that is very similar to that found on endpoints like laptops and mobile devices.

Some of the design defects in this class of device include

>> **Lack of a security patching mechanism.** Most of these devices utterly lack any means for remediating security defects that are found after manufacture.

>> **Lack of anti-malware mechanisms.** Most of these devices have no built-in defenses at all. They're completely defenseless against attack by an intruder.

>> **Lack of robust authentication.** Many of these devices have simple, easily-guessed default login credentials that cannot be changed (or, at best, are rarely changed by their owners).

>> **Lack of monitoring capabilities.** Many of these devices lack any means for sending security and event alerts.

Because the majority of these devices cannot be altered, mitigation of these defects typically involves isolation of these devices on separate, heavily guarded networks that have tools in place to detect and block attacks.

TIP

Many manufacturers of embedded, network-enabled devices do not permit customers to alter their configuration or apply security settings. This compels organizations to place these devices on separate, guarded networks.

Apply Cryptography

Cryptography (from the Greek *kryptos*, meaning *hidden*, and *graphia*, meaning *writing*) is the science of encrypting and decrypting communications to make them unintelligible for all but the intended recipient.

Cryptography can be used to achieve several goals of information security, including confidentiality, integrity, and authentication.

>> **Confidentiality:** First, cryptography protects the confidentiality (or secrecy) of information. Even when the transmission or storage medium has been compromised, the encrypted information is practically useless to unauthorized persons without the proper keys for decryption.

>> **Integrity:** Cryptography can also be used to ensure the integrity (or accuracy) of information through the use of hashing algorithms and message digests.

>> **Authentication:** Finally, cryptography can be used for authentication (and non-repudiation) services through digital signatures, digital certificates, or a Public Key Infrastructure (PKI).

HE SAID, SHE SAID: THE CONCEPT OF NON-REPUDIATION

To *repudiate* is to deny; *non-repudiation* means that an action (such as an online transaction, email communication, and so on) or occurrence can't be easily denied. Non-repudiation is a related function of identification and authentication (I&A) and accountability. For example, it's difficult for a user to deny sending an email message that was digitally signed with that user's private key. Likewise, it's difficult to deny responsibility for an enterprise-wide outage if the accounting logs positively identify you (from username and strong authentication) as the poor soul who inadvertently issued the write-erase command on the core routers two seconds before everything dropped!

REMEMBER

The CISSP exam tests the candidate's ability to apply general cryptographic concepts to real-world issues and problems. You don't have to memorize cryptographic algorithms or the step-by-step operation of various cryptographic systems. However, you should have a firm grasp of cryptographic concepts and technologies, as well as their specific strengths, weaknesses, uses, and applications.

WARNING

Don't confuse these three points with the C-I-A triad, which we discuss in Chapter 3: The C-I-A triad deals with confidentiality, integrity, and *availability*; cryptography does nothing to ensure availability.

TALES FROM THE CRYPT-O: A BRIEF HISTORY OF CRYPTOGRAPHY

Cryptography dates back over 4,000 years to the ancient Egyptians when hieroglyphs were used not to protect messages but to add mystique.

Around 400 B.C., the Spartans began using a military cryptography system known as the *scytale,* which consisted of a strip of parchment wrapped around a wooden rod of a specified secret length and diameter. The message to be encoded was written on the strip of parchment vertically down the rod and then unwrapped and sent by messenger to the intended recipient. The recipient had an identical rod to wrap the strip of parchment around and decode the message.

Around 50 B.C., Julius Caesar used a substitution cipher to transmit secret messages. This system involved substituting letters of the message with other letters from the same alphabet. For example, a simple encryption scheme may have required the sender to shift each letter three spaces to the right: so, A = D, B = E, C = F, and so on. The recipient would then shift the letters three spaces to the left to decrypt and read the message.

This system, which uses only a single alphabet to encrypt and decrypt an entire message, is known as a *monoalphabetic substitution.* This system was particularly effective for Caesar because most of the population was illiterate at the time.

In the 15th century, a cryptographic system utilizing concentric disks to provide substitution was used in Italy. In 1790, Thomas Jefferson invented an encryption device by using a stack of 26 individually rotating disks. The Japanese Purple Machine and German Enigma Machine are two examples of cryptographic devices used successfully during World War II — at least, until the Allies cracked the codes. More recently, Quaker Oats developed the Cap'n Crunch Magic Decoder Ring for encrypting and decrypting simple messages!

THE SCIENCE OF CRYPTO

Cryptography is the science of encrypting and decrypting information, such as a private message, to protect its confidentiality, integrity, and/or authenticity. Practitioners of cryptography are known as *cryptographers*.

Cryptanalysis is the science of deciphering (or breaking) ciphertext without the cryptographic key. Practitioners of cryptanalysis are known as *cryptanalysts*.

Cryptology is the science that encompasses both cryptography and cryptanalysis. Practitioners of cryptology are known as *cryptologists*.

Cryptography today has evolved into a complex science (some say an art) presenting many great promises and challenges in the field of information security. The basics of cryptography include various terms and concepts, the individual components of the cryptosystem, and the classes and types of ciphers.

Cryptographic lifecycle

The cryptographic lifecycle is the sequence of events that occurs throughout the use of cryptographic controls in a system. These steps include

>> Development of requirements for a cryptosystem.

>> Selection of cryptographic controls.

>> Implementation of cryptosystem.

>> Examination of cryptosystem for proper implementation, effective key management, and efficacy of cryptographic algorithms.

>> Rotation of cryptographic keys.

>> Mitigation of any defects identified.

These steps are not altogether different from the selection, implementation, examination, and correction of any other type of security control in a network and computing environment. Like virtually any other component in a network and computing environment, components in a cryptosystem must be periodically examined to ensure that they are still effective and being operated properly.

Plaintext and ciphertext

A *plaintext* message is a message in its original readable format or a ciphertext message that has been properly decrypted (unscrambled) to produce the original readable plaintext message.

A *ciphertext* message is a plaintext message that has been transformed (encrypted) into a scrambled message that's unintelligible. This term doesn't apply to messages from your boss that may also happen to be unintelligible!

Encryption and decryption

Encryption (or *enciphering*) is the process of converting plaintext communications into ciphertext. *Decryption* (or *deciphering*) reverses that process, converting ciphertext into plaintext. (See Figure 5-2.)

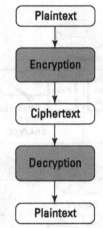

FIGURE 5-2:
Encryption and decryption.

Traffic on a network can be encrypted by using either *end-to-end* or *link encryption*.

End-to-end encryption

With *end-to-end encryption*, packets are encrypted once at the original encryption source and then decrypted only at the final decryption destination. The advantages of end-to-end encryption are its speed and overall security. However, in order for the packets to be properly routed, only the data is encrypted, not the routing information.

Link encryption

Link encryption requires that each node (for example, a router) has separate key pairs for its upstream and downstream neighbors. Packets are encrypted and decrypted, then re-encrypted at every node along the network path.

The following example, as shown in Figure 5-3, illustrates link encryption:

1. Computer 1 encrypts a message by using Secret Key A, and then transmits the message to Router 1.

2. Router 1 decrypts the message by using Secret Key A, re-encrypts the message by using Secret Key B, and then transmits the message to Router 2.

3. Router 2 decrypts the message by using Secret Key B, re-encrypts the message by using Secret Key C, and then transmits the message to Computer 2.

4. Computer 2 decrypts the message by using Secret Key C.

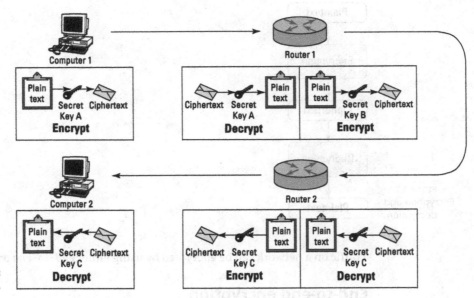

FIGURE 5-3:
Link encryption.

The advantage of using link encryption is that the entire packet (including routing information) is encrypted. However, link encryption has the following two disadvantages:

>> **Latency:** Packets must be encrypted/decrypted at every node, which creates latency (delay) in the transmission of those packets.

>> **Inherent vulnerability:** If a node is compromised or a packet's decrypted contents are cached in a node, the message can be compromised.

Putting it all together: The cryptosystem

A *cryptosystem* is the hardware or software implementation that transforms plaintext into ciphertext (encrypting it) and back into plaintext (decrypting it).

An effective cryptosystem must have the following properties:

TIP

>> The encryption and decryption process is efficient for all possible keys within the cryptosystem's keyspace.

A *keyspace* is the range of all possible values for a key in a cryptosystem.

>> The cryptosystem is easy to use. A cryptosystem that is difficult to use might be used improperly, leading to data loss or compromise.

>> The strength of the cryptosystem depends on the secrecy of the *cryptovariables* (or keys), rather than the secrecy of the algorithm.

TIP

A *restricted algorithm* refers to a cryptographic algorithm that must be kept secret in order to provide security. Restricted or proprietary algorithms are not very effective, because the effectiveness depends on keeping the algorithm itself secret rather than the complexity and high number of variable solutions of the algorithm, and therefore are not commonly used today. They are generally used only for applications that require minimal security.

Cryptosystems are typically composed of two basic elements:

>> **Cryptographic algorithm:** Also called a *cipher*, the *cryptographic algorithm* details the step-by-step mathematical function used to produce

- Ciphertext (encipher)

- Plaintext (decipher)

>> **Cryptovariable:** Also called a *key*, the *cryptovariable* is a secret value applied to the algorithm. The strength and effectiveness of the cryptosystem largely depend on the secrecy and strength of the cryptovariable.

Key clustering (or simply *clustering*) occurs when identical ciphertext messages are generated from a plaintext message by using the same encryption algorithm but different encryption keys. Key clustering indicates a weakness in a cryptographic algorithm because it statistically reduces the number of key combinations that must be attempted in a brute force attack.

REMEMBER

A *cryptosystem* consists of the cryptographic algorithm (cipher) and the cryptovariable (key), as well as all the possible plaintexts and ciphertexts produced by the cipher and key.

REMEMBER

An analogy of a cryptosystem is a deadbolt lock. A deadbolt lock can be easily identified, and its inner working mechanisms aren't closely guarded state secrets. What makes a deadbolt lock effective is the individual key that controls a specific lock on a specific door. However, if the key is weak (imagine only one or two notches on a flat key) or not well protected (left under your doormat), the lock won't protect your belongings. Similarly, if an attacker is able to determine what cryptographic algorithm (lock) was used to encrypt a message, it should still be protected because you're using a strong key that you've kept secret, rather than a six-character password that you wrote on a scrap of paper and left under your mouse pad.

Classes of ciphers

Ciphers are cryptographic transformations. The two main classes of ciphers used in symmetric key algorithms are *block* and *stream* (see the section "Not Quite the Metric System: Symmetric and Asymmetric Key Systems," later in this chapter), which describe how the ciphers operate on input data.

REMEMBER

The two main classes of ciphers are block ciphers and stream ciphers.

BLOCK CIPHERS

Block ciphers operate on a single fixed block (typically 128 bits) of plaintext to produce the corresponding ciphertext. Using a given key in a block cipher, the same plaintext block always produces the same ciphertext block. Advantages of block ciphers compared with stream ciphers are

>> **Reusable keys:** Key management is much easier.

>> **Interoperability:** Block ciphers are more widely supported.

Block ciphers are typically implemented in software. Examples of block ciphers include AES, DES, Blowfish, Twofish, and RC5.

A DISPOSABLE CIPHER: THE ONE-TIME PAD

A *one-time pad* (key) is a keystream (a stream of random or pseudo-random characters) that can be used only once. Considered unbreakable because it's completely random and is used only once and then destroyed, it consists of a pad of the same length as the message to which it's applied. Both the sender and receiver have an identical pad, which is used by the sender to encrypt the message and by the receiver to decrypt the message. This type of cipher is very effective for short messages but is impractical for larger (several megabytes) messages (due to the computing resources required to create unique keystreams for such messages). One-time pads are typically implemented as stream ciphers.

STREAM CIPHERS

Stream ciphers operate in real time on a continuous stream of data, typically bit by bit. Stream ciphers generally work faster than block ciphers and require less code to implement. However, the keys in a stream cipher are generally used only once (see the sidebar "A disposable cipher: The one-time pad") and then discarded. Key management becomes a serious problem. Using a stream cipher, the same plaintext bit or byte will produce a different ciphertext bit or byte every time it is encrypted. Stream ciphers are typically implemented in hardware.

Examples of stream ciphers include Salsa20 and RC4.

A one-time pad is an example of a stream cipher and is considered unbreakable.

REMEMBER

Types of ciphers

The two basic types of ciphers are *substitution* and *transposition*. Both are involved in the process of transforming plaintext into ciphertext.

Most modern cryptosystems use both substitution and permutation to achieve encryption.

REMEMBER

SUBSTITUTION CIPHERS

Substitution ciphers replace bits, characters, or character blocks in plaintext with alternate bits, characters, or character blocks to produce ciphertext. A classic example of a substitution cipher is one that Julius Caesar used: He substituted letters of the message with other letters from the same alphabet. (Read more about this in the sidebar "Tales from the crypt-o: A brief history of cryptography," earlier in this chapter.) In a simple substitution cipher using the standard English alphabet, a *cryptovariable* (key) is added *modulo 26* to the plaintext message. In modulo 26 addition, the remainder is the final result for any sum equal to or greater than 26.

For example, a basic substitution cipher in which the word *BOY* is encrypted by adding three characters using modulo 26 math produces the following result:

	B	O	Y	PLAINTEXT
	2	15	25	NUMERIC VALUE
+	<u>3</u>	<u>3</u>	<u>3</u>	SUBSTITUTION VALUE
	5	18	2	MODULO 26 RESULT
	E	R	B	CIPHERTEXT

A substitution cipher may be either monoalphabetic or polyalphabetic:

>> **Monoalphabetic:** A single alphabet is used to encrypt the entire plaintext message.

>> **Polyalphabetic:** A more complex substitution that uses a different alphabet to encrypt each bit, character, or character block of a plaintext message.

A more modern example of a substitution cipher is the S-boxes (Substitution boxes) employed in the Data Encryption Standard (DES) algorithm. The S-boxes in DES produce a nonlinear substitution (6 bits in, 4 bits out). *Note:* Do *not* attempt to sing this to the tune "Shave and a Haircut" to improve the strength of the encryption by hiding any statistical relationship between the plaintext and cipher-text characters.

TRANSPOSITION (OR PERMUTATION) CIPHERS

Transposition ciphers rearrange bits, characters, or character blocks in plaintext to produce ciphertext. In a simple columnar transposition cipher, a message might be read horizontally but written vertically to produce the ciphertext as in the following example:

```
THE QUICK BROWN FOX JUMPS OVER THE LAZY DOG
```

written in 9 columns as

```
THEQUICKB
ROWNFOXJU
MPSOVERTH
ELAZYDOG
```

then transposed (encrypted) vertically as

```
TRMEHOPLEWSAQNOZUFVYIOEDCXROKJTGBUH
```

The original letters of the plaintext message are the same; only the order has been changed to achieve encryption.

DES performs permutations through the use of P-boxes (Permutation boxes) to spread the influence of a plaintext character over many characters so that they're not easily traced back to the S-boxes used in the substitution cipher.

Other types of ciphers include

- **Codes:** Includes words and phrases to communicate a secret message.

- **Running (or book) ciphers:** For example, the key is page 137 of *The Catcher in the Rye*, and text on that page is added modulo 26 to perform encryption/decryption.

- **Vernam ciphers:** Also known as *one-time pads*, which are keystreams that can be used only once. We discuss these more in the earlier sidebar "A disposable cipher: The one-time pad."

- **Concealment ciphers:** These ciphers include *steganography*, which we discuss in the section "Steganography: A picture is worth a thousand (hidden) words," later in this chapter.

Cryptography alternatives

Technology does provide valid and interesting alternatives to cryptography when a message needs to be protected during transmission. Some useful options are listed in the following sections.

Steganography: A picture is worth a thousand (hidden) words

Steganography is the art of hiding the very existence of a message. It is related to but different from cryptography. Like cryptography, one purpose of steganography is to protect the contents of a message. However, unlike cryptography, the contents of the message aren't encrypted. Instead, the existence of the message is hidden in some other communications medium.

For example, a message may be hidden in a graphic or sound file, in slack space on storage media, in traffic noise over a network, or in a digital image. By using the example of a digital image, the least significant bit (the right-most bit) of each byte in the image file can be used to transmit a hidden message without noticeably altering the image. However, because the message itself isn't encrypted, if it is discovered, its contents can be easily compromised.

Digital watermarking: The (ouch) low watermark

Digital watermarking is a technique similar (and related) to steganography that can be used to verify the authenticity of an image or data, or to protect the intellectual property rights of the creator. Watermarking is the visible cousin of steganography — no attempt is made to hide its existence. Watermarks have long been used on paper currency and office letterhead or paper stock.

Within the last decade, the use of digital watermarking has become more widespread. For example, to display photo examples on the Internet without risking intellectual property theft, a copyright notice may be prominently imprinted across the image. As with steganography, nothing is encrypted using digital watermarking; the confidentiality of the material is not protected with a watermark.

Not quite the metric system: Symmetric and asymmetric key systems

Cryptographic algorithms are broadly classified as either symmetric or asymmetric key systems.

Symmetric key cryptography

Symmetric key cryptography, also known as *symmetric algorithm*, *secret key*, *single key*, and *private key* cryptography, uses a single key to both encrypt and decrypt information. Two parties (for our example, Thomas and Richard) can exchange an encrypted message by using the following procedure:

1. The sender (Thomas) encrypts the plaintext message with a secret key known only to the intended recipient (Richard).

2. The sender then transmits the encrypted message to the intended recipient.

3. The recipient decrypts the message with the same secret key to obtain the plaintext message.

In order for an attacker (Harold) to read the message, he must either guess the secret key (by using a brute-force attack, for example), obtain the secret key from Thomas or Richard using the rubber hose technique (another form of uh, brute-force attack — humans are typically the weakest link, and neither Thomas nor Richard have much tolerance for pain) or through social engineering (Thomas and Richard both like money and may be all too willing to help Harold's Nigerian uncle claim his vast fortune) or intercept the secret key during the initial exchange.

The following list includes the main disadvantages of symmetric systems:

>> **Distribution:** Secure distribution of secret keys is absolutely required either through out-of-band methods or by using asymmetric systems.

>> **Scalability:** A different key is required for each pair of communicating parties.

>> **Limited functionality:** Symmetric systems can't provide authentication or non-repudiation (see the earlier sidebar "He said, she said: The concept of non-repudiation").

Of course, symmetric systems do have many advantages:

>> **Speed:** Symmetric systems are much faster than asymmetric systems.

>> **Strength:** Strength is gained when used with a large key (128 bit, 192 bit, 256 bit, or larger).

>> **Availability:** There are many algorithms available for organizations to select and use.

Symmetric key algorithms include Data Encryption Standard (DES), Triple DES (3DES), Advanced Encryption Standard (AES), International Data Encryption Algorithm (IDEA), and Rivest Cipher 5 (RC5).

Symmetric key systems use a shared secret key.

REMEMBER

DATA ENCRYPTION STANDARD (DES)

In the early 1970s, the National Institute of Standards and Technology (NIST) solicited vendors to submit encryption algorithm proposals to be evaluated by the National Security Agency (NSA) in support of a national cryptographic standard. This new encryption standard was used for private-sector and Sensitive but Unclassified (SBU) government data. In 1974, IBM submitted a 128-bit algorithm originally known as *Lucifer*. After some modifications (the algorithm was shortened to 56 bits and the S-boxes were changed), the IBM proposal was endorsed by the NSA and formally adopted as the Data Encryption Standard. It was published in *Federal Information Processing Standard* (FIPS) PUB 46 in 1977 (updated and revised in 1988 as FIPS PUB 46-1) and *American National Standards Institute* (ANSI) X3.92 in 1981.

DES is a block cipher that uses a 56-bit key.

REMEMBER

The DES algorithm is a symmetric (or private) key cipher consisting of an algorithm and a key. The algorithm is a 64-bit block cipher based on a 56-bit symmetric key. (It consists of 56 key bits plus 8 parity bits . . . or think of it as 8 bytes, with each byte containing 7 key bits and 1 parity bit.) During encryption, the original message (plaintext) is divided into 64-bit blocks. Operating on a single block at a time, each 64-bit plaintext block is split into two 32-bit blocks. Under control of the 56-bit symmetric key, 16 rounds of transpositions and substitutions are performed on each individual character to produce the resulting ciphertext output.

TECHNICAL STUFF

A *parity bit* is used to detect errors in a bit pattern. For example, if the bit pattern has 55 key bits (ones and zeros) that add up to an even number, an *odd-parity bit* should be a one, making the total of the bits — including the parity bit — an odd number. For an *even-parity bit*, if the 55 key bits add up to an even number, the parity bit should be a zero, making the total of the bits — including the parity bit — an even number. If an algorithm uses even parity and the resulting bit pattern (including the parity bit) is an odd number, then the transmission has been corrupted.

TECHNICAL STUFF

A *round* is a transformation (permutations and substitutions) that an encryption algorithm performs on a block of plaintext to convert (encrypt) it into ciphertext.

The four distinct modes of operation (the mode of operation defines how the plaintext/ciphertext blocks are processed) in DES are Electronic Code Book, Cipher Block Chaining, Cipher Feedback, and Output Feedback.

REMEMBER

The four modes of DES are ECB, CBC, CFB, and OFB. ECB and CBC are the most commonly used.

The original goal of DES was to develop an encryption standard that could be used for 10 to 15 years. Although DES far exceeded this goal, in 1999, the Electronic Frontier Foundation achieved the inevitable, breaking a DES key in only 23 hours.

Electronic Code Book (ECB)

Electronic Code Book (ECB) mode is the native mode for DES operation and normally produces the highest throughput. It is best used for encrypting keys or small amounts of data. ECB mode operates on 64-bit blocks of plaintext independently and produces 64-bit blocks of ciphertext. One significant disadvantage of ECB is that the same plaintext, encrypted with the same key, always produces the same ciphertext. If used to encrypt large amounts of data, it's susceptible to Chosen Text Attacks (CTA) (discussed in the section "Chosen Text Attack (CTA)," later in this chapter) because certain patterns may be revealed.

Cipher Block Chaining (CBC)

Cipher Block Chaining (CBC) mode is the most common mode of DES operation. Like ECB mode, CBC mode operates on 64-bit blocks of plaintext to produce 64-bit blocks of ciphertext. However, in CBC mode, each block is XORed (see the following sidebar "The XORcist,") with the ciphertext of the preceding block to create a dependency, or *chain*, thereby producing a more random ciphertext result. The first block is encrypted with a random block known as the *initialization vector* (IV). One disadvantage of CBC mode is that errors propagate. However, this problem is limited to the block in which the error occurs and the block that immediately follows, after which, the decryption resynchronizes.

Cipher Feedback (CFB)

Cipher Feedback (CFB) mode is a stream cipher most often used to encrypt individual characters. In this mode, previously generated ciphertext is used as feedback for key generation in the next keystream. The resulting ciphertext is chained together, which causes errors to be multiplied throughout the encryption process.

Output Feedback (OFB)

Output Feedback (OFB) mode is also a stream cipher very similar to CFB. It is often used to encrypt satellite communications. In this mode, previous plaintext is used as feedback for key generation in the next keystream. Because the resulting ciphertext is not chained together, errors don't spread throughout the encryption process.

TRIPLE DES (3DES)

Triple Data Encryption Standard (3DES) effectively extended the life of the DES algorithm. In Triple DES implementations, a message is encrypted by using one key, encrypted by using a second key, and then again encrypted by using either the first key or a third key.

THE XORCIST

The *Exclusive Or (XOR) function* is a binary operation applied to two input bits: for example, a plaintext bit and a key bit. If the two bits are equal, the result is 0 (zero). If the two bits aren't equal, the result is 1.

Input A (Plaintext)	Input B (Key)	Output C (Ciphertext)
0	0	0
0	1	1
1	0	1
1	1	0

YOU SAY TO-*MAY*-TO, I SAY TO-*MAH*-TO: 3DES VARIATIONS

The several variations of Triple DES (3DES) are as follows:

- DES-EEE2 (Encrypt-Encrypt-Encrypt), using 1st key, 2nd key, 1st key

- DES-EDE2 (Encrypt-Decrypt-Encrypt), using 1st key, 2nd key, 1st key

- DES-EEE3 (Encrypt-Encrypt-Encrypt), using 1st key, 2nd key, 3rd key

- DES-EDE3 (Encrypt-Decrypt-Encrypt), using 1st key, 2nd key, 3rd key

The basic function of Triple DES is sometimes explained like this: The message is encrypted using one key, decrypted using a second key, and again encrypted using the first key. The differences in syntax (and operation) are subtle but important: The second key (in an EDE implementation) doesn't truly decrypt the original message because the output is still gibberish (ciphertext). This variation was developed for backwards compatibility with single DES cryptosystems. Also, you should understand that use of the first key twice (in EDE2 and EEE2) is one common implementation, but use of a third distinct key is also possible (in EDE3 and EEE3).

The use of three separate 56-bit encryption keys produces an effective key length of 168 bits. But Triple DES doesn't just triple the work factor required to crack the DES algorithm (see the sidebar "Work factor: Force × effort = work!" in this chapter). Because the attacker doesn't know whether he or she successfully cracked even the first 56-bit key (pick a number between 0 and 72 quadrillion!) until all three keys are cracked and the correct plaintext is produced, the work factor required is more like $2^{56} \times 2^{56} \times 2^{56}$, or 72 quadrillion x 72 quadrillion x 72 quadrillion. (Don't try this multiplication on a calculator; just trust us on this one.)

WARNING

Double DES wasn't a significant improvement to DES. In fact, by using a Meet-in-the-Middle Attack (see the section "Meet-in-the-Middle Attack," later in this chapter), the work factor required to crack Double DES is only slightly greater than for DES. For this reason, Double DES isn't commonly used.

Using Triple DES (officially known as the Triple Data Encryption Algorithm, or TDEA) would seem enough to protect even the most sensitive data for at least a few lifetimes, but a few problems exist with Triple DES. First, the performance cost is significant. Although Triple DES is faster than many other symmetric encryption algorithms, it's still unacceptably slow and therefore doesn't work with many applications that require high-speed throughput of large volumes of data.

Second, a weakness exists in the implementation that allows a cryptanalyst to reduce the effective key size to 108 bits in a brute force attack. Although a 108-bit key size still requires a significant amount of time to crack (theoretically, several million millennia), it's still a weakness.

ADVANCED ENCRYPTION STANDARD (AES)

In May 2002, NIST announced the Rijndael Block Cipher as the new standard to implement the *Advanced Encryption Standard (AES)*, which replaced DES as the U.S. government standard for encrypting Sensitive but Unclassified data. AES was subsequently approved for encrypting classified U.S. government data up to the Top Secret level (using 192- or 256-key lengths).

The *Rijndael Block Cipher*, developed by Dr. Joan Daemen and Dr. Vincent Rijmen, uses variable block and key lengths (128, 192, or 256 bits) and between 10 and 14 rounds. It was designed to be simple, resistant to known attacks, and fast. It can be implemented in either hardware or software and has relatively low memory requirements.

REMEMBER

AES is based on the Rijndael Block Cipher.

Until recently, the only known successful attacks against AES were *side-channel attacks*, which don't directly attack the encryption algorithm, but instead attack the system on which the encryption algorithm is implemented. Side-channel attacks using cache-timing techniques are most common against AES implementations. In 2009, a theoretical related-key attack against AES was published. The attack method is considered theoretical because, although it reduces the mathematical complexity required to break an AES key, it is still well beyond the computational capability available today.

BLOWFISH AND TWOFISH ALGORITHMS

The *Blowfish Algorithm* operates on 64-bit blocks, employs 16 rounds, and uses variable key lengths of up to 448 bits. The *Twofish Algorithm*, a finalist in the AES selection process, is a symmetric block cipher that operates on 128-bit blocks, employing 16 rounds with variable key lengths up to 256 bits. Both Blowfish and Twofish were designed by Bruce Schneier (and others) and are freely available in the public domain (neither algorithm has been patented). To date, there are no known successful cryptanalytic attacks against either algorithm.

RIVEST CIPHERS

Drs. Ron Rivest, Adi Shamir, and Len Adleman invented the RSA algorithm and founded the company RSA Data Security (RSA = *R*ivest, *S*hamir, *A*dleman).

The Rivest Ciphers are a series of symmetric algorithms that include RC2, RC4, RC5, and RC6 (RC1 was never published and RC3 was broken during development):

>> **RC2:** A block-mode cipher that encrypts 64-bit blocks of data by using a variable-length key.

>> **RC4:** A stream cipher (data is encrypted in real time) that uses a variable-length key (128 bits is standard).

>> **RC5:** Similar to RC2, but includes a variable-length key (0 to 2,048 bits), variable block size (32, 64, or 128 bits), and variable number of processing rounds (0 to 255).

>> **RC6:** Derived from RC5 and a finalist in the AES selection process. It uses a 128-bit block size and variable-length keys of 128, 192, or 256 bits.

IDEA CIPHER

The *International Data Encryption Algorithm (IDEA)* Cipher evolved from the Proposed Encryption Standard and the Improved Proposed Encryption Standard (IPES) originally developed in 1990. IDEA is a block cipher that operates on 64-bit plaintext blocks by using a 128-bit key. IDEA performs eight rounds on 16-bit sub-blocks and can operate in four distinct modes similar to DES. The IDEA Cipher provides stronger encryption than RC4 and Triple DES, but because it's patented, it's not widely used today. However, the patents were set to expire in various countries between 2010 and 2012. It is currently used in some software applications, including Pretty Good Privacy (PGP) email.

Asymmetric key cryptography

Asymmetric key cryptography (also known as *asymmetric algorithm cryptography* or *public key cryptography*) uses two separate keys: one key to encrypt and a different key to decrypt information. These keys are known as *public* and *private key pairs*. When two parties want to exchange an encrypted message by using asymmetric key cryptography, they follow these steps:

1. The sender (Thomas) encrypts the plaintext message with the intended recipient's (Richard) public key.

2. This produces a ciphertext message that can then be transmitted to the intended recipient (Richard).

3. The recipient (Richard) then decrypts the message with his private key, known only to him.

Only the private key can decrypt the message; thus, an attacker (Harold) possessing only the public key can't decrypt the message. This also means that not even the original sender can decrypt the message. This use of an asymmetric key system is known as a *secure message*. A secure message guarantees the confidentiality of the message.

Asymmetric key systems use a public key and a private key.

Secure message format uses the recipient's private key to protect confidentiality.

If the sender wants to guarantee the authenticity of a message (or, more correctly, the authenticity of the sender), he or she can sign the message with this procedure:

1. The sender (Thomas) encrypts the plaintext message with his own private key.

2. This produces a ciphertext message that can then be transmitted to the intended recipient (Richard).

3. To verify that the message is in fact from the purported sender, the recipient (Richard) applies the sender's (Thomas's) public key (which is known to every Tom, Dick, and Harry).

Of course, an attacker can also verify the authenticity of the message. This use of an asymmetric key system is known as an *open message format* because it guarantees only the authenticity, not the confidentiality.

Open message format uses the sender's private key to ensure authenticity.

If the sender wants to guarantee both the confidentiality and authenticity of a message, he or she can do so by using this procedure:

1. The sender (Thomas) encrypts the message first with the intended recipient's (Richard's) public key and then with his own private key.

2. This produces a ciphertext message that can then be transmitted to the intended recipient (Richard).

3. The recipient (Richard) uses the sender's (Thomas's) public key to verify the authenticity of the message, and then uses his own private key to decrypt the message's contents.

If an attacker intercepts the message, he or she can apply the sender's public key, but then has an encrypted message that he or she can't decrypt without the intended recipient's private key. Thus, both confidentiality and authenticity are assured. This use of an asymmetric key system is known as a *secure and signed message format.*

REMEMBER

A secure and signed message format uses the sender's private key and the recipient's public key to protect confidentiality and ensure authenticity.

A public key and a private key are mathematically related, but theoretically, no one can compute or derive the private key from the public key. This property of asymmetric systems is based on the concept of a one-way function. A *one-way function* is a problem that you can easily compute in one direction but not in the reverse direction. In asymmetric key systems, a *trapdoor* (private key) resolves the reverse operation of the one-way function.

Because of the complexity of asymmetric key systems, they are more commonly used for key management or digital signatures than for encryption of bulk information. Often, a *hybrid* system is employed, using an asymmetric system to securely distribute the secret keys of a symmetric key system that's used to encrypt the data.

The main disadvantage of asymmetric systems is their lower speed. Because of the types of algorithms that are used to achieve the one-way hash functions, very large keys are required. (A 128-bit symmetric key has the equivalent strength of a 2,304-bit asymmetric key.) Those large keys, in turn, require more computational power, causing a significant loss of speed (up to 10,000 times slower than a comparable symmetric key system).

However, the many significant advantages of asymmetric systems include

>> **Extended functionality:** Asymmetric key systems can provide both confidentiality and authentication; symmetric systems can provide only confidentiality.

>> **Scalability:** Because symmetric key systems require secret key exchanges between all of the communicating parties, their scalability is limited. Asymmetric key systems, which do not require secret key exchanges, resolve key management issues associated with symmetric key systems, and are therefore more scalable.

Asymmetric key algorithms include RSA, Diffie-Hellman, El Gamal, Merkle-Hellman (Trapdoor) Knapsack, and Elliptic Curve, which we talk about in the following sections.

RSA

Drs. Ron Rivest, Adi Shamir, and Len Adleman published the RSA algorithm, which is a *key transport* algorithm based on the difficulty of factoring a number that's the product of two large prime numbers (typically 512 bits). Two users (Thomas and Richard) can securely transport symmetric keys by using RSA, like this:

1. Thomas creates a symmetric key, encrypts it with Richard's public key, and then transmits it to Richard.

2. Richard decrypts the symmetric key by using his own private key.

REMEMBER

RSA is an asymmetric key algorithm based on factoring prime numbers.

DIFFIE-HELLMAN KEY EXCHANGE

Drs. Whitfield Diffie and Martin Hellman published a paper, entitled "New Directions in Cryptography," that detailed a new paradigm for secure key exchange based on discrete logarithms. *Diffie–Hellman* is described as a key agreement algorithm. Two users (Thomas and Richard) can exchange symmetric keys by using Diffie–Hellman, like this:

1. Thomas and Richard obtain each other's public keys.

2. Thomas and Richard then combine their own private keys with the public key of the other person, producing a symmetric key that only the two users involved in the exchange know.

Diffie–Hellman key exchange is vulnerable to Man-in-the-Middle Attacks, in which an attacker (Harold) intercepts the public keys during the initial exchange and substitutes his own private key to create a session key that can decrypt the session. (You can read more about these attacks in the section "Man-in-the-Middle Attack," later in this chapter.) A separate authentication mechanism is necessary to protect against this type of attack, ensuring that the two parties communicating in the session are, in fact, the legitimate parties.

REMEMBER

Diffie–Hellman is an asymmetric key algorithm based on discrete logarithms.

EL GAMAL

El Gamal is an unpatented, asymmetric key algorithm based on the discrete logarithm problem used in Diffie–Hellman (discussed in the preceding section). El Gamal extends the functionality of Diffie–Hellman to include encryption and digital signatures.

MERKLE-HELLMAN (TRAPDOOR) KNAPSACK

The *Merkle-Hellman (Trapdoor) Knapsack*, published in 1978, employs a unique approach to asymmetric cryptography. It's based on the problem of determining what items, in a set of items that have fixed weights, can be combined in order to obtain a given total weight. Knapsack was broken in 1982.

Knapsack is an asymmetric key algorithm based on fixed weights.

ELLIPTIC CURVE (EC)

Elliptic curves (EC) are far more difficult to compute than conventional discrete logarithm problems or factoring prime numbers. (A 160-bit EC key is equivalent to a 1,024-bit RSA key.) The use of smaller keys means that EC is significantly faster than other asymmetric algorithms (and many symmetric algorithms), and can be widely implemented in various hardware applications including wireless devices and smart cards.

Elliptic Curve is more efficient than other asymmetric key systems and many symmetric key systems because it can use a smaller key.

Message authentication

Message authentication guarantees the authenticity and integrity of a message by ensuring that

>> A message hasn't been altered (either maliciously or accidentally) during transmission.

>> A message isn't a replay of a previous message.

>> The message was sent from the origin stated (it's not a forgery).

>> The message is sent to the intended recipient.

Checksums, CRC-values, and parity checks are examples of basic message authentication and integrity controls. More advanced message authentication is performed by using digital signatures and message digests.

Digital signatures and message digests can be used to provide message authentication.

Digital signatures

The *Digital Signature Standard* (DSS), published by the National Institute of Standards and Technology (NIST) in Federal Information Processing Standard (FIPS) 186-4, specifies three acceptable algorithms in its standard: the RSA Digital Signature Algorithm, the Digital Signature Algorithm (DSA, which is based on a modified El Gamal algorithm), and the Elliptic Curve Digital Signature Algorithm (ECDSA).

A digital signature is a simple way to verify the authenticity (and integrity) of a message. Instead of encrypting a message with the intended receiver's public key, the sender encrypts it with his or her own private key. The sender's public key properly decrypts the message, authenticating the originator of the message. This process is known as an *open message format* in asymmetric key systems, which we discuss in the section "Asymmetric key cryptography," earlier in this chapter.

Message digests

It's often impractical to encrypt a message with the receiver's public key to protect confidentiality, and then encrypt the entire message again by using the sender's private key to protect authenticity and integrity. Instead, a representation of the encrypted message is encrypted with the sender's private key to produce a digital signature. The intended recipient decrypts this representation by using the sender's public key, and then independently calculates the expected results of the decrypted representation by using the same, known, one-way hashing algorithm. If the results are the same, the integrity of the original message is assured. This representation of the entire message is known as a *message digest*.

To *digest* means to reduce or condense something, and a message digest does precisely that. (Conversely, *indigestion* means to expand . . . like gases . . . how do you spell *relief?*) A message digest is a condensed representation of a message; think *Reader's Digest*. Ideally, a message digest has the following properties:

» The original message can't be re-created from the message digest.

» Finding a message that produces a particular digest shouldn't be computationally feasible.

» No two messages should produce the same message digest (known as a *collision*).

» The message digest should be calculated by using the entire contents of the original message — it shouldn't be a representation of a representation.

Message digests are produced by using a one-way hash function. There are several types of one-way hashing algorithms (digest algorithms), including MD5, SHA-2 variants, and HMAC.

WARNING

The SHA-1 digest algorithm is now considered obsolete. SHA-3 should be used instead.

WARNING

A *collision* results when two messages produce the same digest or when a message produces the same digest as a different message.

REMEMBER

A *one-way function* ensures that the same key can't encrypt and decrypt a message in an asymmetric key system. One key encrypts the message (produces ciphertext), and a second key (the trapdoor) decrypts the message (produces plaintext), effectively reversing the one-way function. A one-way function's purpose is to ensure confidentiality.

A *one-way hashing algorithm* produces a hashing value (or message digest) that can't be reversed; that is, it can't be decrypted. In other words, no trapdoor exists for a one-way hashing algorithm. The purpose of a one-way hashing algorithm is to ensure integrity and authentication.

REMEMBER

MD5, SHA-2, SHA-3, and HMAC are all examples of commonly used message authentication algorithms.

MD FAMILY

MD (Message Digest) is a family of one-way hashing algorithms developed by Dr. Ron Rivest that includes MD (obsolete), MD2, MD3 (not widely used), MD4, MD5, and MD6:

>> **MD2:** Developed in 1989 and still widely used today, MD2 takes a variable size input (message) and produces a fixed-size output (128-bit message digest). MD2 is very slow (it was originally developed for 8-bit computers) and is highly susceptible to collisions.

>> **MD4:** Developed in 1990, MD4 produces a 128-bit digest and is used to compute NT-password hashes for various Microsoft Windows operating systems, including NT, XP, and Vista. An MD4 hash is typically represented as a 32-digit hexadecimal number. Several known weaknesses are associated with MD4, and it's also susceptible to collision attacks.

>> **MD5:** Developed in 1991, MD5 is one of the most popular hashing algorithms in use today, commonly used to store passwords and to check the integrity of files. Like MD2 and MD4, MD5 produces a 128-bit digest. Messages are processed in 512-bit blocks, using four rounds of transformation. The resulting hash is typically represented as a 32-digit hexadecimal number. MD5 is also susceptible to collisions and is now considered "cryptographically broken" by the U.S. Department of Homeland Security.

>> **MD6:** Developed in 2008, MD6 uses very large input message blocks (up to 512 *bytes*) and produces variable-length digests (up to 512 bits). MD6 was originally

submitted for consideration as the new SHA-3 standard but was eliminated from further consideration after the first round in July 2009. Unfortunately, the first widespread use of MD6 (albeit, unauthorized and illicit) was in the Conficker.B worm in late 2008, shortly after the algorithm was published!

SHA FAMILY

Like MD, SHA (Secure Hash Algorithm) is another family of one-way hash functions. The SHA family of algorithms is designed by the U.S. National Security Agency (NSA) and published by NIST. The SHA family of algorithms includes SHA-1, SHA-2, and SHA-3:

>> **SHA-1:** Published in 1995, SHA-1 takes a variable size input (message) and produces a fixed-size output (160-bit message digest, versus MD5's 128-bit message digest). SHA-1 processes messages in 512-bit blocks and adds padding to a message length, if necessary, to produce a total message length that's a multiple of 512. Note that SHA-1 is no longer considered a viable hash algorithm.

>> **SHA-2:** Published in 2001, SHA-2 consists of four hash functions — SHA-224, SHA-256, SHA-384, and SHA-512 — that have digest lengths of 224, 256, 384, and 512 bits, respectively. SHA-2 processes messages in 512-bit blocks for the 224, 256, and 384 variants, and 1,024-bit blocks for SHA-512.

>> **SHA-3:** Published in 2015, SHA-3 includes SHA3-224, SHA3-256, SHA3-384, and SHA3-512, which produce digests of 224, 256, 384, and 512 bits, respectively. SHAKE128 and SHAKE256 are also variants of SHA3.

HMAC

The Hashed Message Authentication Code (or Checksum) (HMAC) further extends the security of the MD5 and SHA-1 algorithms through the concept of a *keyed digest*. HMAC incorporates a previously shared secret key and the original message into a single message digest. Thus, even if an attacker intercepts a message, modifies its contents, and calculates a new message digest, the result doesn't match the receiver's hash calculation because the modified message's hash doesn't include the secret key.

Public Key Infrastructure (PKI)

A *Public Key Infrastructure (PKI)* is an arrangement whereby a designated authority stores encryption keys or *certificates* (an electronic document that uses the public key of an organization or individual to establish identity, and a digital signature to establish authenticity) associated with users and systems, thereby enabling secure communications through the integration of digital signatures, digital certificates, and other services necessary to ensure confidentiality, integrity, authentication, non-repudiation, and access control.

REMEMBER

The four basic components of a PKI are the Certification Authority, Registration Authority, repository, and archive:

>> **Certificate Authority (CA):** The Certificate Authority (CA) comprises hardware, software, and the personnel administering the PKI. The CA issues certificates, maintains and publishes status information and Certificate Revocation Lists (CRLs), and maintains archives.

>> **Registration Authority (RA):** The Registration Authority (RA) also comprises hardware, software, and the personnel administering the PKI. It's responsible for verifying certificate contents for the CA.

>> **Repository:** A *repository* is a system that accepts certificates and CRLs from a CA and distributes them to authorized parties.

>> **Archive:** An *archive* offers long-term storage of archived information from the CA.

Key management functions

Like physical keys, encryption keys must be safeguarded. Most successful attacks against encryption exploit some vulnerability in *key management* functions rather than some inherent weakness in the encryption algorithm. The following are the major functions associated with managing encryption keys:

>> **Key generation:** Keys must be generated randomly on a secure system, and the generation sequence itself shouldn't provide potential clues regarding the contents of the keyspace. Generated keys shouldn't be displayed in the clear.

>> **Key distribution:** Keys must be securely distributed. This is a major vulnerability in symmetric key systems. Using an asymmetric system to securely distribute secret keys is one solution.

>> **Key installation:** Key installation is often a manual process. This process should ensure that the key isn't compromised during installation, incorrectly entered, or too difficult to be used readily.

>> **Key storage:** Keys must be stored on protected or encrypted storage media, or the application using the keys should include safeguards that prevent extraction of the keys.

>> **Key change:** Keys, like passwords, should be changed regularly, relative to the value of the information being protected and the frequency of use. Keys used frequently are more likely to be compromised through interception and statistical analysis.

>> **Key control:** Key control addresses the proper use of keys. Different keys have different functions and may only be approved for certain levels of classification.

>> **Key disposal:** Keys (and any distribution media) must be properly disposed of, erased, or destroyed so that the key's contents are not disclosed, possibly providing an attacker insight into the key management system.

The seven key management issues are generation, distribution, installation, storage, change, control, and disposal.

Key escrow and key recovery

Law enforcement has always been concerned about the potential use of encryption for criminal purposes. To counter this threat, NIST published the Escrowed Encryption Standard (EES) in Federal Information Processing Standards (FIPS) Publication 185 (1994). The premise of the EES is to divide a secret key into two parts and place those two parts into escrow with two separate, trusted organizations. With a court order, the two parts can be obtained by law enforcement officials, the secret key recovered, and the suspected communications decrypted. One implementation of the EES is the Clipper Chip proposed by the U.S. government. The Clipper Chip uses the Skipjack Secret Key algorithm for encryption and an 80-bit secret key.

Methods of attack

Attempts to crack a cryptosystem can be generally classified into four classes of attack methods:

>> **Analytic attacks:** An *analytic attack* uses algebraic manipulation in an attempt to reduce the complexity of the algorithm.

>> **Brute-force attacks:** In a *brute-force* (or *exhaustion*) *attack,* the cryptanalyst attempts every possible combination of key patterns, sometimes utilizing rainbow tables, and specialized or scalable computing architectures. This type of attack can be very time-intensive (up to several hundred million years) and resource-intensive, depending on the length of the key, the speed of the attacker's computer . . . and the lifespan of the attacker.

WORK FACTOR: FORCE × EFFORT = WORK!

Work factor (discussed earlier in this chapter) describes the expenditure required — in terms of time, effort, and resources — to break a cryptosystem. Given enough time, effort, and resources, any cryptosystem can be broken. The goal of all cryptosystems, then, is to achieve a work factor that sufficiently protects the encrypted information against a reasonable estimate of available time, effort, and resources. However, *reasonable* can be difficult to estimate as technology continues to improve rapidly.

Moore's Law is based on an observation by Gordon Moore, one of the founders of Intel, that processing power seems to double about every 18 months. To compensate for Moore's Law, some *really* hard encryption algorithms are used. Today, encrypted information is valuable for perhaps only three months with encryption algorithms that (theoretically) would take several hundred millennia to break; everybody's confident in the knowledge that by tomorrow such a feat will be mere child's play.

>> **Implementation attacks:** *Implementation attacks* attempt to exploit some weakness in the cryptosystem such as vulnerability in a protocol or algorithm.

>> **Statistical attacks:** A *statistical attack* attempts to exploit some statistical weakness in the cryptosystem, such as a lack of randomness in key generation.

TECHNICAL STUFF

A *rainbow table* is a precomputed table used to reverse cryptographic hash functions in a specific algorithm. Examples of password-cracking programs that use rainbow tables include Ophcrack and RainbowCrack.

The specific attack methods discussed in the following sections employ various elements of the four classes we describe in the preceding list.

The Birthday Attack

The *Birthday Attack* attempts to exploit the probability of two messages producing the same message digest by using the same hash function. It's based on the statistical probability (greater than 50 percent) that in a room containing 23 or more people, 2 people in that room have the same birthday. However, for 2 people in a room to share a specific birthday (such as August 3rd), 253 or more people must be in the room to have a statistical probability of greater than 50 percent (even if one of the birthdays is on February 29).

Ciphertext Only Attack (COA)

In a *Ciphertext Only Attack* (COA), the cryptanalyst obtains the ciphertext of several messages, all encrypted by using the same encryption algorithm, but he or she doesn't have the associated plaintext. The cryptanalyst then attempts to decrypt the data by searching for repeating patterns and using statistical analysis. For example, certain words in the English language, such as *the* and *or*, occur frequently. This type of attack is generally difficult and requires a large sample of ciphertext.

Chosen Text Attack (CTA)

In a *Chosen Text Attack* (CTA), the cryptanalyst selects a sample of plaintext and obtains the corresponding ciphertext. Several types of Chosen Text Attacks exist, including Chosen Plaintext, Adaptive Chosen Plaintext, Chosen Ciphertext, and Adaptive Chosen Ciphertext:

>> **Chosen Plaintext Attack (CPA):** The cryptanalyst chooses plaintext to be encrypted, and the corresponding ciphertext is obtained.

>> **Adaptive Chosen Plaintext Attack (ACPA):** The cryptanalyst chooses plaintext to be encrypted; then based on the resulting ciphertext, he chooses another sample to be encrypted.

>> **Chosen Ciphertext Attack (CCA):** The cryptanalyst chooses ciphertext to be decrypted, and the corresponding plaintext is obtained.

>> **Adaptive Chosen Ciphertext Attack (ACCA):** The cryptanalyst chooses ciphertext to be decrypted; then based on the resulting ciphertext, he chooses another sample to be decrypted.

Known Plaintext Attack (KPA)

In a *Known Plaintext Attack* (KPA), the cryptanalyst has obtained the ciphertext and corresponding plaintext of several past messages, which he or she uses to decipher new messages.

Man-in-the-Middle Attack

A *Man-in-the-Middle Attack* involves an attacker intercepting messages between two parties on a network and potentially modifying the original message.

Meet-in-the-Middle Attack

A *Meet-in-the-Middle Attack* involves an attacker encrypting known plaintext with each possible key on one end, decrypting the corresponding ciphertext with each possible key, and then comparing the results *in the middle*. Although commonly classified as a brute-force attack, this kind of attack may also be considered an analytic attack because it does involve some differential analysis.

THE RUBBER HOSE ATTACK

No discussion of cryptanalysis would be complete without mentioning the "rubber hose" attack. This is a tongue-in-cheek term that implies coercion of some sort that compels the owner of a cryptosystem to relinquish encryption keys to an adversary.

Replay Attack

A *Replay Attack* occurs when a session key is intercepted and used against a later encrypted session between the same two parties. Replay attacks can be countered by incorporating a time stamp in the session key.

Apply Security Principles to Site and Facility Design

Finally, securely designed and built software running on securely designed and built systems must be operated in securely designed and build facilities. Otherwise, an adversary with unrestricted access to a system and its installed software will inevitably succeed in compromising your security efforts. Astute organizations involve security professionals during the design, planning, and construction of new or renovated locations and facilities. Proper site- and facility-requirements planning during the early stages of construction helps ensure that a new building or data center is adequate, safe, and secure — all of which can help an organization avoid costly situations later.

The principles of Crime Prevention Through Environmental Design (CPTED) have been widely adopted by security practitioners in the design of public and private buildings, offices, communities, and campuses since CPTED was first published in 1971. CPTED focuses on designing facilities by using techniques such as unobstructed areas, creative lighting, and functional landscaping, which help to naturally deter crime through positive psychological effects. By making it difficult for a criminal to hide, gain access to a facility, escape a location, or otherwise perpetrate an illegal and/or violent act, such techniques may cause a would-be criminal to decide against attacking a target or victim, and help to create an environment that's perceived as (and that actually is) safer for legitimate people who regularly use the area. CPTED is comprised of three basic strategies:

>> **Natural access control:** Uses security zones (or *defensible space*) to limit or restrict movement and differentiate between public, semi-private, and private areas that require differing levels of protection. For example, this natural

access control can be accomplished by limiting points of entry into a building and using structures such as sidewalks and lighting to guide visitors to main entrances and reception areas. *Target hardening* complements natural access controls by using mechanical and/or operational controls, such as window and door locks, alarms, picture identification requirements, and visitor sign-in/out procedures.

>> **Natural surveillance:** Reduces criminal threats by making intruder activity more observable and easily detected. Natural surveillance can be accomplished by maximizing visibility and activity in strategic areas, for example, by placing windows to overlook streets and parking areas, landscaping to eliminate hidden areas and create clear lines of sight, installing open railings on stairways to improve visibility, and using numerous low-intensity lighting fixtures to eliminate shadows and reduce security-camera glare or blind spots (particularly at night).

>> **Territorial reinforcement:** Creates a sense of pride and ownership, which causes intruders to more readily stand out and encourages people to report suspicious activity, instead of ignoring it. Territorial reinforcement is accomplished through maintenance activities (picking up litter, cleaning up graffiti, repairing broken windows, and replacing light bulbs), assigning individuals responsibility for an area or space, placing amenities (such as benches and water fountains) in common areas, and displaying prominent signage (where appropriate). It can also include scheduled activities, such as corporate-sponsored beautification projects and company picnics.

FIXING BROKEN WINDOWS IN NYC

CPTED is the multi-disciplinary culmination of a number of works from criminologists, archaeologists, social psychologists, and many others that began in the 1960s. One of its tenets, the Broken Windows theory, was successfully put to the test by Mayor Rudy Giuliani in the early 1990s on a large scale — New York City! Mayor Giuliani's crime-fighting initiatives included cleaning vandalized subway rail cars, citing subway fare jumpers and other minor offenders, and clearing the streets of public nuisances — drunks and New York's infamous "squeegee men." These efforts demoralized and discouraged gang members and vandals who saw their subway "artwork" quickly eradicated, led to an increase in arrests because many fare jumpers and other minor offenders also had more serious criminal backgrounds, and created a safer environment for New York City's residents, commuters, and tourists. The significant reduction in crime that resulted from these and other unconventional crime-fighting methods has had a positive and enduring impact.

Choosing a secure location

Location, location, location! Although, to a certain degree, this bit of conventional business wisdom may be less important to profitability in the age of e-commerce, it's still a critical factor in physical security. Important factors when considering a location include

>> **Climatology and natural disasters:** Although an organization is unlikely to choose a geographic location solely based on the likelihood of hurricanes or earthquakes, these factors must be considered when designing a safe and secure facility. Other related factors may include flood plains, the location of evacuation routes, and the adequacy of civil and emergency preparedness.

>> **Local considerations:** Is the location in a high-crime area? Are hazards nearby, such as hazardous materials storage, railway freight lines, or flight paths for the local airport? Is the area heavily industrialized (will air and noise pollution, including vibration, affect your systems)?

>> **Visibility:** Will your employees and facilities be targeted for crime, terrorism, or vandalism? Is the site near another high-visibility organization that may attract undesired attention? Is your facility located near a government or military target? Keeping a low profile is generally best because you avoid unwanted and unneeded attention; avoid external building markings, if possible.

>> **Accessibility:** Consider local traffic patterns, convenience to airports, proximity to emergency services (police, fire, and medical facilities), and availability of adequate housing. For example, will on-call employees have to drive for an hour to respond when your organization needs them?

>> **Utilities:** Where is the facility located in the power grid? Is electrical power stable and clean? Is sufficient fiber optic cable already in place to support telecommunications requirements?

>> **Joint tenants:** Will you have full access to all necessary environmental controls? Can (and should) physical security costs and responsibilities be shared between joint tenants? Are other tenants potential high-visibility targets? Do other tenants take security as seriously as your organization?

Designing a secure facility

Many of the physical and technical controls that we discuss in the section "Implement Site and Facility Security Controls" later in this chapter, should be considered during the initial design of a secure facility. Doing so often helps reduce the costs and improves the overall effectiveness of these controls. Other building design considerations include

>> **Exterior walls:** Ideally, exterior walls should be able to withstand high winds (tornadoes and hurricanes/typhoons) and reduce electronic emanations that can be detected and used to re-create high-value data (for example government or military data). If possible, exterior windows should be avoided throughout the building, particularly on lower levels. Metal bars over windows or reinforced windows on lower levels may be necessary. Any windows should be *fixed* (meaning you can't open them), shatterproof, and sufficiently opaque to conceal inside activities.

>> **Interior walls:** Interior walls adjacent to secure or restricted areas must extend from the floor to the ceiling (through raised flooring and drop ceilings) and must comply with applicable building and fire codes. Walls adjacent to storage areas (such as closets containing janitorial supplies, paper, media, or other flammable materials) must meet minimum fire ratings, which are typically higher than for other interior walls. Ideally, Kevlar (bulletproof) walls should protect the most sensitive areas.

>> **Floors:** Flooring (both slab and raised) must be capable of bearing loads in accordance with local building codes (typically 150 pounds per square foot). Additionally, raised flooring must have a nonconductive surface and be properly grounded to reduce personnel safety risks.

>> **Ceilings:** Weight-bearing and fire ratings must be considered. Drop ceilings may temporarily conceal intruders and small water leaks; conversely, stained drop-ceiling tiles can reveal leaks while temporarily impeding water damage.

>> **Doors:** Doors and locks must be sufficiently strong and well-designed to resist forcible entry, and they need a fire rating equivalent to adjacent walls. Emergency exits must remain unlocked from the inside and should also be clearly marked, as well as monitored or alarmed. Electronic lock mechanisms and other access control devices should fail open (unlock) in the event of an emergency to permit people to exit the building. Many doors swing out to facilitate emergency exiting; thus door hinges are located on the outside of the room or building. These hinges must be properly secured to prevent an intruder from easily lifting hinge pins and removing the door.

>> **Lighting:** Exterior lighting for all physical spaces and buildings in the security perimeter (including entrances and parking areas) should be sufficient to provide safety for personnel, as well as to discourage prowlers and casual intruders.

>> **Wiring:** All wiring, conduits, and cable runs must comply with building and fire codes, and be properly protected. Plenum cabling must be used below raised floors and above drop ceilings because PVC-clad cabling releases toxic chemicals when it burns.

A *plenum* is the vacant area above a drop ceiling or below a raised floor. A fire in these areas can spread very rapidly and can carry smoke and noxious fumes to other areas of a burning building. For this reason, non-PVC-coated cabling, known as *plenum cabling*, must be used in these areas.

>> **Electricity and HVAC:** Electrical load and HVAC requirements must be carefully planned to ensure that sufficient power is available in the right locations and that proper climate ranges (temperature and humidity) are maintained.

>> **Pipes:** Locations of shutoff valves for water, steam, or gas pipes should be identified and appropriately marked. Drains should have *positive flow*, meaning they carry drainage away from the building.

>> **Lightning strikes:** Approximately 10,000 fires are started every year by lightning strikes in the United States alone, despite the fact that only 20 percent of all lightning ever reaches the ground. Lightning can heat the air in immediate contact with the stroke to 54,000° Fahrenheit (F), which translates to 30,000° Celsius (C), and lightning can discharge 100,000 amperes of electrical current. Now *that's* an inrush!

>> **Magnetic fields:** Monitors and storage media can be permanently damaged or erased by magnetic fields.

>> **Sabotage/terrorism/war/theft/vandalism:** Both internal and external threats must be considered. A heightened security posture is also prudent during certain other disruptive situations — including labor disputes, corporate downsizing, hostile terminations, bad publicity, demonstrations/protests, and civil unrest.

>> **Equipment failure:** Equipment failures are inevitable. Maintenance and support agreements, ready spare parts, and redundant systems can mitigate the effects.

>> **Loss of communications and utilities:** Including voice and data; electricity; and heating, ventilation, and air conditioning (HVAC). Loss of communications and utilities may happen because of any of the factors discussed in the preceding bullets, as well as human errors and mistakes.

>> **Vibration and movement:** Causes may include earthquakes, landslides, and explosions. Equipment may also be damaged by sudden or severe vibrations, falling objects, or equipment racks tipping over. More seriously, vibrations or movement may weaken structural integrity, causing a building to collapse or otherwise be unusable.

>> **Severe weather:** Includes hurricanes, tornadoes, high winds, severe thunderstorms and lightning, rain, snow, sleet, and ice. Such forces of nature may cause fires, water damage and flooding, structural damage, loss of communications and utilities, and hazards to personnel.

>> **Personnel loss:** Can happen because of illness, injury, death, transfer, labor disputes, resignations, and terminations. The negative effects of a personnel loss can be mitigated through good security practices, such as documented procedures, job rotations, cross-training, and redundant functions.

Implement Site and Facility Security Controls

The CISSP candidate must understand the various threats to physical security; the elements of site- and facility-requirements planning and design; the various physical security controls, including access controls, technical controls, environmental and life safety controls, and administrative controls; as well as how to support the implementation and operation of these controls, as covered in this section.

TIP

Although much of the information in this section may seem to be common sense, the CISSP exam asks very specific and detailed questions about physical security, and many candidates lack practical experience in fighting fires, so don't underestimate the importance of physical security — in real life and on the CISSP exam!

Wiring closets, server rooms, media storage facilities, and evidence storage

Wiring closets, server rooms, and media and evidence storage facilities contain high-value equipment and/or media that is critical to ongoing business operations or in support of investigations. Physical security controls often found in these locations include

>> **Strong access controls.** Typically, this includes the use of key cards, plus a PIN pad or biometric.

>> **Fire suppression.** Often, you'll find inert gas fire suppression instead of water sprinklers, because water can damage computing equipment in case of discharge.

>> **Video surveillance.** Cameras fixed at entrances to wiring closets and data center entrances, as well as the interior of those facilities, to observe the goings-on of both authorized personnel and intruders.

> » **Visitor log.** All visitors, who generally require a continuous escort, often are required to sign a visitor log.

> » **Asset check-in / check-out log.** All personnel are required to log the introduction and removal of any equipment and media.

Restricted and work area security

High–security work areas often employ physical security controls above and beyond what is seen in ordinary work areas. In addition to key card access control systems and video surveillance, additional physical security controls may include

> » **Multi-factor key card entry.** Together with key cards, employees may be required to use a PIN Pad or biometric to access restricted areas.

> » **Security guards.** There may be more guards present at ingress / egress points, as well as roaming within the facility, to be on the alert for unauthorized personnel or unauthorized activities.

> » **Guard dogs.** These provide additional deterrence against unauthorized entry, and also assist in the capture of unauthorized personnel in a facility.

> » **Security walls and fences.** Restricted facilities may employ one or more security walls and fences to keep unauthorized personnel away from facilities. General height requirements for fencing are listed in Table 5-5.

> » **Security lighting.** Restricted facilities may have additional lighting, to expose and deter any would-be intruders.

> » **Security gates, crash gates, and bollards.** These controls limit the movement of vehicles near a facility to reduce vehicle-borne threats.

TABLE 5-5 **General Fencing Height Requirements**

Height	General Effect
3–4 ft (1m)	Deters casual trespassers
6–7 ft (2m)	Too high to climb easily
8 ft (2.4m) + three-strand barbed wire	Deters more determined intruders

Utilities and HVAC considerations

Environmental and life safety controls, such as utilities and HVAC (heating, ventilation, and air conditioning) are necessary for maintaining a safe and acceptable operating environment for computers and personnel.

Electrical power

General considerations for electrical power include having one or more dedicated feeders from one or more utility substations or power grids, as well as ensuring that adequate physical access controls are implemented for electrical distribution panels and circuit breakers. An Emergency Power Off (EPO) switch should be installed near major systems and exit doors to shut down power in case of fire or electrical shock. Additionally, a backup power source should be established, such as a diesel or natural-gas power generator. Backup power should be provided for critical facilities and systems, including emergency lighting, fire detection and suppression, mainframes and servers (and certain workstations), HVAC, physical access control systems, and telecommunications equipment.

WARNING

Although natural gas can be a cleaner alternative than diesel for backup power, in terms of air and noise pollution, it's generally not acceptable for emergency life systems (such as emergency lighting and fire protection systems) because the fuel source (natural gas) can't be locally stored, so the system relies instead on an external fuel source that must be supplied by pipelines.

Protective controls for electrostatic discharge (ESD) include

>> Maintain proper humidity levels (40 to 60 percent).

>> Ensure proper grounding.

>> Use anti-static flooring, anti-static carpeting, and floor mats.

Protective controls for electrical noise include

>> Install power line conditioners.

>> Ensure proper grounding.

>> Use shielded cabling.

Using an Uninterruptible Power Supply (UPS) is perhaps the most important protection against electrical anomalies. A UPS provides clean power to sensitive systems and a temporary power source during electrical outages (blackouts, brownouts, and sags); this power supply must be sufficient to properly shut down the protected systems. *Note:* A UPS shouldn't be used as a backup power source. A UPS — even a building UPS — is designed to provide temporary power, typically for 5 to 30 minutes, in order to give a backup generator time to start up or to allow a controlled and proper shutdown of protected systems.

Electrical hazards

Sensitive equipment can be damaged or affected by various electrical hazards and anomalies, including:

» **Electrostatic discharge (ESD):** The ideal humidity range for computer equipment is 40 to 60 percent. Higher humidity causes condensation and corrosion. Lower humidity increases the potential for ESD (static electricity). A static charge of as little as 40V (volts) can damage sensitive circuits, and 2,000V can cause a system shutdown. The minimum discharge that can be felt by humans is 3,000V, and electrostatic discharges of over 25,000V are possible — so if you can feel it, it's a problem for your equipment!

REMEMBER

The ideal humidity range for computer equipment is 40 to 60 percent.

» **Electrical noise:** Includes Electromagnetic Interference (EMI) and Radio Frequency Interference (RFI). EMI is generated by the different charges between the three electrical wires (hot, neutral, and ground) and can be either *common-mode noise* (caused by hot and ground) or *traverse-mode noise* (caused by a difference in power between the hot and neutral wires). RFI is caused by electrical components, such as fluorescent lighting and electric cables. A *transient* is a momentary line-noise disturbance.

» **Electrical anomalies:** These anomalies include the ones listed in Table 5-6.

TABLE 5-6

Electrical Anomalies

Electrical Event	Definition
Blackout	Total loss of power
Fault	Momentary loss of power
Brownout	Prolonged drop in voltage
Sag	Short drop in voltage
Inrush	Initial power rush
Spike	Momentary rush of power
Surge	Prolonged rush of power

TIP

You may want to come up with some meaningless mnemonic for the list in Table 5-6, such as *Bob Frequently Buys Shoes In Shoe Stores.* You need to know these terms for the CISSP exam.

REMEMBER

It's not the volts that kill — it's the amps!

WARNING

Surge protectors and surge suppressors provide only minimal protection for sensitive computer systems, and they're more commonly (and dangerously) used to overload an electrical outlet or as a daisy-chained extension cord. The protective circuitry in most of these units costs less than one dollar (compare the cost of a low-end surge protector with that of a 6-foot extension cord), and you get what you pay for — these glorified extension cords provide only minimal spike protection. True, a surge protector does provide more protection than nothing at all, but don't be lured into complacency by these units — check them regularly for proper use and operation, and don't accept them as a viable alternative to a UPS.

HVAC

Heating, ventilation, and air conditioning (HVAC) systems maintain the proper environment for computers and personnel. HVAC-requirements planning involves complex calculations based on numerous factors, including the average BTUs (British Thermal Units) produced by the estimated computers and personnel occupying a given area, the size of the room, insulation characteristics, and ventilation systems.

The ideal temperature range for computer equipment is between 50°F and 80°F (10°C and 27°C). At temperatures as low as 100°F (38°C), magnetic storage media can be damaged.

REMEMBER

The ideal temperature range for computer equipment is between 50°F and 80°F (10°C and 27°C).

The ideal humidity range for computer equipment is between 40 and 60 percent. Higher humidity causes condensation and corrosion. Lower humidity increases the potential for ESD (static electricity).

Doors and side panels on computer equipment racks should be kept closed (and locked, as a form of physical access control) to ensure proper airflow for cooling and ventilation. When possible, empty spaces in equipment racks (such as a half-filled rack or gaps between installed equipment) should be covered with blanking panels to reduce hot and cold air mixing between the hot side (typically the power-supply side of the equipment) and the cold side (typically the front of the equipment); such mixing of hot and cold air can reduce the efficiency of cooling systems.

Heating and cooling systems should be properly maintained, and air filters should be cleaned regularly to reduce dust contamination and fire hazards.

Most gas-discharge fire suppression systems automatically shut down HVAC systems prior to discharging, but a separate Emergency Power Off (EPO) switch should be installed near exits to facilitate a manual shutdown in an emergency.

Ideally, HVAC equipment should be dedicated, controlled, and monitored. If the systems aren't dedicated or independently controlled, proper liaison with the building manager is necessary to ensure that everyone knows who to call when there are problems. Monitoring systems should alert the appropriate personnel when operating thresholds are exceeded.

Water issues

Water damage (and damage from liquids in general) can occur from many different sources, including pipe breakage, firefighting efforts, leaking roofs, spilled drinks, flooding, and tsunamis. Wet computers and other electrical equipment pose a potentially lethal hazard.

Both preventive as well as detective controls are used to ensure that water in unwanted places does not disrupt business operations or destroy expensive assets. Common features include

>> **Water diversion.** Barriers of various types help to prevent water from entering sensitive areas.

>> **Water detection alarms.** Sensors that detect the presence of water can alert personnel of the matter and provide valuable time before damage occurs.

Fire prevention, detection, and suppression

Threats from fire can be potentially devastating and lethal. Proper precautions, preparation, and training not only help limit the spread of fire and damage, but more important, can also save lives.

REMEMBER

Saving human lives is the first priority in any life-threatening situation.

Other hazards associated with fires include smoke, explosions, building collapse, release of toxic materials or vapors, and water damage.

For a fire to burn, it requires three elements: heat, oxygen, and fuel. These three elements are sometimes referred to as the *fire triangle*. (See Figure 5-4.) Fire suppression and extinguishing systems fight fires by removing one of these three elements or by temporarily breaking up the chemical reaction between these three elements (separating the fire triangle). Fires are classified according to the fuel type, as listed in Table 5-7.

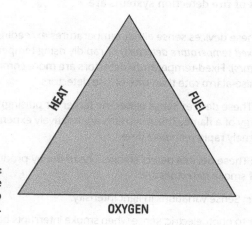

FIGURE 5-4:
A fire needs these three elements to burn.

TABLE 5-7   **Fire Classes and Suppression/Extinguishing Methods**

Class	Description (Fuel)	Extinguishing Method
A	Common combustibles, such as paper, wood, furniture, and clothing	Water or soda acid
B	Burnable fuels, such as gasoline or oil	CO_2 or soda acid
C	Electrical fires, such as computers or electronics	CO_2 (*Note:* The most important step to fight a fire in this class: Turn off electricity first!)
D	Special fires, such as combustible metals	May require total immersion or other special techniques
K (or F)	Cooking oils or fats	Water mist or fire blankets

Saving human lives is the first priority in any life-threatening situation.

REMEMBER

You must be able to describe Class A, B, and C fires and their primary extinguishing methods. The CISSP exam doesn't ask about Class D and K (or F) fires (they aren't too common as it relates to computer fires — unless your server room happens to be located directly above the deep fat fryers of a local bar and hot wings restaurant).

TIP

Fire detection and suppression

Fire detection and suppression systems are some of the most essential life safety controls for protecting facilities, equipment, and (most important) human lives.

The three main types of fire detection systems are

>> **Heat-sensing:** These devices sense either temperatures exceeding a predetermined level *(fixed-temperature detectors)* or rapidly rising temperatures *(rate-of-rise detectors)*. Fixed-temperature detectors are more common and exhibit a lower false-alarm rate than rate-of-rise detectors.

>> **Flame-sensing:** These devices sense either the flicker (or pulsing) of flames or the infrared energy of a flame. These systems are relatively expensive but provide an extremely rapid response time.

>> **Smoke-sensing:** These devices detect smoke, one of the by-products of fire. The four types of smoke detectors are

- **Photoelectric:** Sense variations in light intensity.

- **Beam:** Similar to photoelectric; sense when smoke interrupts beams of light.

- **Ionization:** Detect disturbances in the normal ionization current of radioactive materials.

- **Aspirating:** Draw air into a sampling chamber to detect minute amounts of smoke.

REMEMBER

The three main types of fire detection systems are heat–sensing, flame–sensing, and smoke–sensing.

The two primary types of fire suppression systems are

>> **Water sprinkler systems:** Water extinguishes fire by removing the heat element from the fire triangle, and it's most effective against Class A fires. Water is the primary fire-extinguishing agent for all business environments. Although water can potentially damage equipment, it's one of the most effective, inexpensive, readily available, and least harmful (to humans) extinguishing agents available. The four variations of water sprinkler systems are

- **Wet-pipe (or closed-head):** Most commonly used and considered the most reliable. Pipes are always charged with water and ready for activation. Typically, a fusible link in the nozzle melts or ruptures, opening a gate valve that releases the water flow. Disadvantages include flooding because of nozzle or pipe failure and because of frozen pipes in cold weather.

- **Dry-pipe:** No standing water in the pipes. At activation, a clapper valve opens, air is blown out of the pipe, and water flows. This type of system is less efficient than the wet pipe system but reduces the risk of accidental flooding; the time delay provides an opportunity to shut down computer systems (or remove power), if conditions permit.

- **Deluge:** Operates similarly to a dry-pipe system but is designed to deliver large volumes of water quickly. Deluge systems are typically not used for computer-equipment areas.

- **Preaction:** Combines wet- and dry-pipe systems. Pipes are initially dry. When a heat sensor is triggered, the pipes are charged with water, and an alarm is activated. Water isn't actually discharged until a fusible link melts (as in wet-pipe systems). This system is recommended for computer-equipment areas because it reduces the risk of accidental discharge by permitting manual intervention.

REMEMBER

The four main types of water sprinkler systems are wet-pipe, dry-pipe, deluge, and preaction.

» **Gas discharge systems:** Gas discharge systems may be portable (such as a CO_2 extinguisher) or fixed (beneath a raised floor). These systems are typically classified according to the extinguishing agent that's employed. These agents include

- **Carbon dioxide (CO_2):** CO_2 is a commonly used colorless, odorless gas that extinguishes fire by removing the oxygen element from the fire triangle. (Refer to Figure 5-4.) CO_2 is most effective against Class B and C fires. Because it removes oxygen, its use is potentially lethal and therefore best suited for unmanned areas or with a delay action (that includes manual override) in manned areas.

  CO_2 is also used in portable fire extinguishers, which should be located near all exits and within 50 feet (15 meters) of any electrical equipment. All portable fire extinguishers (CO_2, water, and soda acid) should be clearly marked (listing the extinguisher type and the fire classes it can be used for) and periodically inspected. Additionally, all personnel should receive training in the proper use of fire extinguishers.

- **Soda acid:** Includes a variety of chemical compounds that extinguish fires by removing the fuel element (suppressing the flammable components of the fuel) of the fire triangle. (Refer to Figure 5-4.) Soda acid is most effective against Class A and B fires. It is not used for Class C fires because of the highly corrosive nature of many of the chemicals used.

- **Gas-discharge:** Gas-discharge systems suppress fire by separating the elements of the fire triangle (a chemical reaction); they are most effective against Class B and C fires. (Refer to Figure 5-4.) Inert gases don't damage computer equipment, don't leave liquid or solid residue, mix thoroughly with the air, and spread extremely quickly. However, these gases in concentrations higher than 10 percent are harmful if inhaled, and some types degrade into toxic chemicals (hydrogen fluoride, hydrogen bromide, and bromine) when used on fires that burn at temperatures above 900°F (482°C).

Halon used to be the gas of choice in gas-discharge fire suppression systems. However, because of Halon's ozone-depleting characteristics, the Montreal Protocol of 1987 prohibited the further production and installation of Halon systems (beginning in 1994) and encouraging the replacement of existing systems. Acceptable replacements for Halon include FM-200 (most effective), CEA-410 or CEA-308, NAF-S-III, FE-13, Argon or Argonite, and Inergen.

REMEMBER

Halon is an ozone-depleting substance. Acceptable replacements include FM-200, CEA-410 or CEA-308, NAF-S-III, FE-13, Argon or Argonite, and Inergen.

Chapter **6**

Communication and Network Security

The Communication and Network Security domain requires a thorough understanding of network fundamentals, secure network design, concepts of network operation, networking technologies and network management techniques. This domain represents 14 percent of the CISSP certification exam.

TIP

A thorough understanding of networking protocols, services, practices, and architecture will definitely help you pass the exam. If your network experience is light, we recommend that you pick up a copy of *Networking All-In-One For Dummies*. Also, consider earning a networking certification, such as CompTIA Network+ or Cisco Certified Network Associate (CCNA), before taking the CISSP exam. These materials are extremely helpful in preparing for this portion of the CISSP exam if your background is light in networking.

Implement Secure Design Principles in Network Architectures

A solid understanding of networking concepts and fundamentals is essential for creating a secure network architecture. This requires knowledge of network topologies, IP addressing, various networking protocols (including multilayer and converged protocols), wireless networks, communication security, and new and evolving networking trends, such as software-defined networks, microsegmentation, and cloud computing.

Data networks are commonly classified as local area networks (LANs) and wide area networks (WANs). Although these are basic classifications, you should understand the fundamental distinctions between these two types of networks.

A *local area network* (LAN) is a data network that operates across a relatively small geographic area, such as a single building or floor. A LAN connects workstations, servers, printers, and other devices so that network resources, such as files and email, can be shared. Key characteristics of LANs include the following:

>> Can connect networked resources over a small geographic area, such as a floor, a building, or a group of buildings.

>> Are relatively inexpensive to set up and maintain, typically consisting of readily available equipment such as servers, desktop PCs, printers, switches, hubs, bridges, repeaters, wireless access points (WAPs or simply, APs), and various security devices such as firewalls and intrusion prevention systems (IPSs).

>> Can be wired, wireless, or a combination of both wired and wireless.

>> Perform at relatively high speeds — typically 10 megabits per second (Mbps), 100 Mbps, 1000 Mbps (also referred to as 1 gigabit per second [1 Gbps]), 10 Gbps, and 40 Gbps for wired networks, and 11 Mbps, 54 Mbps, or 600 Mbps for wireless networks. We cover LAN speeds in the section "Physical Layer (Layer 1)," later in this chapter.

WARNING

Be careful when referring to data capacity (and their abbreviations) and data storage. 100 Mbps is "100 megabits per second," and 100 MB is "100 megabytes." The distinction is subtle (a little b versus a big B, bits rather than bytes), but the difference is significant: A byte is equal to 8 bits. Data speeds are typically referred to in bits per second; data storage is typically referred to in bytes.

REMEMBER

A *local area network* (LAN) is a data network that operates across a relatively small geographic area, such as a building or group of buildings.

A *wide area network* (WAN) connects multiple LANs and other WANs by using telecommunications devices and facilities to form an internetwork. Key characteristics of WANs include the following:

>> Connect multiple LANs over large geographic areas, such as a small city (for example, a metropolitan area network [or MAN]), a region or country, a global corporate network, the entire planet (for example, the Internet), or beyond (for example, the International Space Station via satellite).

>> Can be relatively expensive to set up and maintain, typically consisting of equipment such as routers, Channel Service Unit/Data Service Unit (CSU/DSU) devices, firewalls, virtual private network (VPN) concentrators, and various other security devices.

>> Perform at relatively low speeds by using various technologies, such as dial-up (56 kilobits per second [Kbps]); digital subscriber line, or DSL (for example, 128 Kbps to 16 Mbps); T-1 (1.544 Mbps); DS-3 (approximately 45 Mbps); OC-12 (approximately 622 Mbps); and OC-255 (approximately 13 Gbps). We cover WAN speeds in the section "Data Link Layer (Layer 2)," later in this chapter.

Examples of WANs include

>> **Internet:** The mother of all WANs, the *Internet* is the global network of public networks originally developed by the U.S. Department of Defense (DoD) Advanced Research Projects Agency (DARPA). Users and systems connect to the Internet via *Internet service providers* (ISPs).

>> **Intranet:** An *intranet* can be thought of as a private Internet. An *intranet* typically uses web-based technologies to disseminate company information that's available only to authorized users on an internal company network.

>> **Extranet:** An *extranet* extends the basic concept of an intranet to include partners, vendors, or other related parties. For example, an automobile manufacturer may operate an extranet that connects networks belonging to parts manufacturers, distributors, and dealerships. Extranets are commonly operated across the Internet by using a virtual private network (VPN) — discussed later in this chapter — or other secure connection.

A *wide area network* (WAN) is a data network that operates across a relatively large geographic area, and includes portions supplied by telecommunications carriers.

OSI and TCP/IP models

The OSI and TCP/IP models define standard protocols for network communication and interoperability by using a layered approach. This approach divides complex networking issues into simpler functional components that help the understanding, design, and development of networking solutions and provides the following specific advantages:

>> Clarifies the general functions of a communications process, instead of focusing on specific issues.

>> Reduces complex networking processes into simpler sub-layers and components.

FILL-IN-THE-BLANK AREA NETWORKS (__AN)

Although networks are generally classified as LANs or WANs, you should familiarize yourself with a number of variations (and acronyms) — if for no other reason than to put together a winning combination in a friendly game of Scrabble:

- **Personal area network (PAN) and wireless personal area network (WPAN):** Connects an individual's electronic devices to each other or to a larger network, such as the Internet and the Internet of Things (IoT). Examples of devices that might be connected via a PAN include laptop computers, smartphones, tablets, wearable technology, virtual personal assistants (such as Amazon Alexa, Apple Siri, Google Assistant, and Microsoft Cortana) home appliances, smart thermostats, and home security cameras. These devices can be connected via wired technologies such as USB and FireWire, or wireless technologies such as Wi-Fi, Bluetooth, IrDA (Infrared Data Association), 6LoWPAN (IPv6 over Low power Wireless Personal Area Networks), Bluetooth Low-Energy (BLE, also known as Bluetooth Smart or Bluetooth 4.0+), Bluetooth Mesh, Thread, ZigBee, and Open Connectivity Foundation (OCF). A wireless PAN is also sometimes referred to as a WPAN (that's worth nine points in Scrabble!).

- **Storage area network (SAN):** Connects servers to a separate physical storage device (typically a disk array). The server operating system sees the storage as if it were directly attached to the server. SANs typically comprise several terabytes or more of disk storage and incorporate highly sophisticated design architectures for fault tolerance and redundancy. Communications protocols used in SANs typically include SCSI (Small Computer System Interface, pronounced "Scuzzy"), iSCSI (IP-based SCSI), Fibre Channel Protocol (FCP, SCSI over Fibre Channel), and FCoE (Fibre Channel over Ethernet). SANs are highly scalable, enable technologies such as virtualization and snapshots, provide flexibility in server deployment options, facilitate disaster recovery (for example, with real-time replication), and tend to reduce the overall cost of data storage.

- **Virtual local area network (VLAN):** Implemented on network switches in a LAN as a way of logically grouping users and resources in a broadcast domain. Often, such VLANs correlate to department functions (such as Accounting, Sales, and Research & Development) and/or IP subnets. VLANs provide scalability, segmentation, and (some) security at Layer 2 (see the section "The OSI Reference Model," in this chapter) and can also work to limit the size of your Ethernet broadcast domains. VLANs are implemented by using Institute of Electrical and Electronics Engineers (IEEE) 802.1q tagging to tag Ethernet frames with VLAN information. *Note:* The IEEE is an international organization that defines many standards, including numerous 802 networking standards.

- **Wireless local area network (WLAN):** Also known as a *Wi-Fi network*. A wireless LAN that uses wireless access points (WAPs, or simply APs) to connect wireless-enabled devices to a wired LAN. We cover WLANs in more detail later in this chapter.

- **Wireless wide area network (WWAN):** A wireless network that typically uses mobile cellular technologies such as 4G Long-Term Evolution (LTE), Global System for Mobile Communications (GSM), Universal Mobile Telecommunications System (UMTS), or Code Division Multiple Access (CDMA2000), to extend wireless network coverage regionally, nationally, and/or globally.

- **Campus area network (CAN) and wireless campus area network (WCAN):** Connects multiple buildings across a high-performance backbone.

- **Metropolitan area network (MAN) and wireless metropolitan area network (WMAN):** Extends across a large area, such as a small city.

- **Value-added network (VAN):** A type of extranet that allows businesses within an industry to share information or integrate shared processes. For example, Electronic Data Interchange (EDI) allows organizations to exchange structured documents — such as order forms, purchase orders, bills of lading, and invoices — over a secure network.

>> Promotes interoperability by defining standard interfaces.

>> Aids development by allowing vendors to change individual features at a single layer, instead of rebuilding the entire protocol stack.

>> Facilitates easier (and more logical) troubleshooting.

TIP

The OSI model isn't just a theoretical model to be pondered by intellectuals — it really is helpful for explaining complex networking topics. For this reason, much of the information you need to know for the Communication and Network Security domain is presented in this chapter in the context of the OSI model. You don't necessarily need to know which protocols and equipment belong to which layers of the OSI model for the CISSP exam or in your day-to-day work. We've just presented it this way to help logically organize the information you need to know for this domain.

The OSI Reference Model

In 1984, the International Organization for Standardization (ISO) adopted the Open Systems Interconnection (OSI) Reference Model (or simply, the *OSI model*) to facilitate interoperability between network devices independent of the manufacturer.

The OSI model consists of seven distinct layers that describe how data is communicated between systems and applications on a computer network, as shown in Figure 6-1. These layers include

» Application (Layer 7)

» Presentation (Layer 6)

» Session (Layer 5)

» Transport (Layer 4)

» Network (Layer 3)

» Data Link (Layer 2)

» Physical (Layer 1)

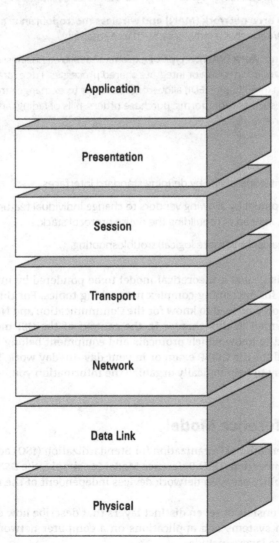

FIGURE 6-1:
The seven layers
of the OSI model.

Application

Presentation

Session

Transport

Network

Data Link

Physical

TIP

Try creating a mnemonic to recall the layers of the OSI model, such as *All People Seem To Need Delicious Pizza*, and in reverse, *Please Do Not Throw Sausage Pizza Away*.

In the OSI model, data is passed from the highest layer (Application; Layer 7) downward through each layer to the lowest layer (Physical; Layer 1), and is then transmitted across the network medium to the destination node, where it's passed upward from the lowest layer to the highest layer. Each layer communicates only with the layer immediately above and below it *(adjacent layers)*. This communication is achieved through a process known as data encapsulation. *Data encapsulation wraps protocol information from the layer immediately above in the data section of the layer immediately below.* Figure 6-2 illustrates this process.

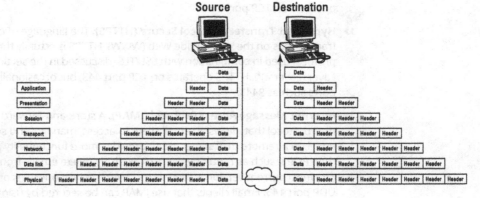

FIGURE 6-2:
Data encapsulation in the OSI model.

APPLICATION LAYER (LAYER 7)

The Application Layer (Layer 7) is the highest layer of the OSI model. It supports the components that deal with the communication aspects of an application that requires network access, and it provides an interface to the user. So, both the Application Layer and the end-user interact directly with the application.

The Application Layer is responsible for the following:

>> Identifying and establishing availability of communication partners

>> Determining resource availability

>> Synchronizing communication

REMEMBER

The Application Layer is responsible for identifying and establishing availability of communication partners, determining resource availability, and synchronizing communication.

Don't confuse the Application Layer with software applications such as Microsoft Word or Excel. Applications that function at the Application Layer include

>> **File transfer protocol (FTP):** A program used to copy files from one system to another over a network. FTP operates on TCP ports 20 (the data port) and 21 (the control port).

>> **HyperText Transfer Protocol (HTTP):** The language of the World Wide Web (WWW), used by web servers and browsers for non-sensitive content. HTTP operates on TCP port 80.

>> **HyperText Transfer Protocol Secure (HTTPS):** The language of commercial transactions on the World Wide Web (WWW). HTTPS is actually the HTTP protocol used in combination with SSL/TLS (discussed in the section "Transport Layer (Layer 4)"). HTTPS operates on TCP port 443, but occasionally on other ports such as 8443.

>> **Internet Message Access Protocol (IMAP):** A store-and-forward electronic mail protocol that allows an email client to access, manage, and synchronize email on a remote mail server. IMAP provides more functionality and security than POP3, such as requiring users to explicitly delete emails from the server. The most current version is IMAPv4 (or IMAP4), which operates on TCP and UDP port 143. Email clients that use IMAP can be secured by using TLS or SSL encryption over TCP/UDP port 993.

>> **Post Office Protocol Version 3 (POP3):** An email retrieval protocol that allows an email client to access email on a remote mail server by using TCP port 110. Inherently insecure, POP3 allows users to authenticate over the Internet by using plaintext passwords. Email clients that use POP3 can be secured by using TLS or SSL encryption over TCP/UDP port 995.

>> **Privacy Enhanced Mail (PEM):** *PEM* is an IETF (Internet Engineering Task Force) standard for providing email confidentiality and authentication. PEM is not widely used.

>> **Secure HyperText Transfer Protocol (S-HTTP):** *S-HTTP* is an Internet protocol that provides a method for secure communications with a web server. S-HTTP is a connectionless-oriented protocol that encapsulates data after security properties for the session have been successfully negotiated.

WARNING

Do not confuse HTTPS and S-HTTP. They are two distinctly different protocols with several differences. For example, HTTPS encrypts an entire communications session and is commonly used in VPNs, whereas S-HTTP encrypts individual messages between a client and server pair.

- » **Secure Multipurpose Internet Mail Extensions (S/MIME):** *S/MIME* is a secure method of sending email incorporated into several popular browsers and email applications.

- » **Simple Mail Transfer Protocol (SMTP):** Used to send and receive email across the Internet. This protocol has several well-known vulnerabilities that make it inherently insecure. SMTP operates on TCP/UDP port 25. SMTP over SSL/TLS (SMTPS) uses TCP/UDP port 465.

- » **Simple Network Management Protocol (SNMP):** Used to collect network information by polling stations and sending *traps* (or alerts) to a management station. SNMP has many well-known vulnerabilities, including default cleartext community strings (passwords). SNMP operates on TCP/UDP ports 161 (agent) and 162 (manager). Secure SNMP uses TCP/UDP ports 10161 (agent) and 10162 (manager).

- » **Telnet:** Provides terminal emulation for remote access to system resources. Telnet operates on TCP/UDP port 23. Because Telnet transmits passwords in cleartext, it is no longer considered safe; instead SSH (discussed in the section "Session Layer (Layer 5)" later in this chapter) is preferred.

- » **Trivial File Transfer Protocol (TFTP):** A lean, mean version of FTP without directory-browsing capabilities or user authentication. Generally considered less secure than FTP, TFTP operates on UDP port 69.

PRESENTATION LAYER (LAYER 6)

The Presentation Layer (Layer 6) provides coding and conversion functions that are applied to data being presented to the Application Layer (Layer 7). These functions ensure that data sent from the Application Layer of one system are compatible with the Application Layer of the receiving system.

REMEMBER

The Presentation Layer is responsible for coding and conversion functions.

Tasks associated with this layer include

- » **Data representation:** Use of common data representation formats (standard image, sound, and video formats) enable application data to be exchanged between different types of computer systems.

- » **Character conversion:** Information is exchanged between different systems by using common character conversion schemes.

- » **Data compression:** Common data compression schemes enable compressed data to be properly decompressed at the destination.

- » **Data encryption:** Common data encryption schemes enable encrypted data to be properly decrypted at the destination.

Some examples of Presentation Layer protocols include

>> **American Standard Code for Information Interchange (ASCII):** A character-encoding scheme based on the English alphabet, consisting of 128 characters.

>> **Extended Binary-Coded Decimal Interchange Code (EBCDIC):** An 8-bit character-encoding scheme largely used on mainframe and mid-range computers.

>> **Graphics Interchange Format (GIF):** A widely used bitmap image format that allows up to 256 colors and is suitable for images or logos (but not photographs).

>> **Joint Photographic Experts Group (JPEG):** A photographic compression method widely used to store and transmit photographs.

>> **Motion Picture Experts Group (MPEG):** An audio and video compression method widely used to store and transmit audio and video files.

SESSION LAYER (LAYER 5)

The Session Layer (Layer 5) establishes, coordinates, and terminates communication sessions (service requests and service responses) between networked systems.

REMEMBER

The Session Layer is responsible for establishing, coordinating, and terminating communication sessions between systems.

A communication session is divided into three distinct phases:

>> **Connection establishment:** Initial contact between communicating systems is made, and the end devices agree on communications parameters and protocols to be used, including the mode of operation:

  • **Simplex mode:** In simplex mode, a one-way communications path is established with a transmitter at one end of the connection and a receiver at the other end. An analogy is AM radio, where a radio station broadcasts music and the radio receiver can only receive the broadcast.

  • **Half-duplex mode:** In half-duplex mode, both communicating devices are capable of transmitting and receiving messages, but they can't do it at the same time. An analogy is a two-way radio in which a button must be pressed to transmit and then released to receive a signal.

  • **Full-duplex mode:** In full-duplex mode, both communicating devices are capable of transmitting and receiving simultaneously. An analogy is a telephone with which you can transmit and receive signals (but not necessarily communicate) at the same time.

>> **Data transfer:** Information is exchanged between end devices.

>> **Connection release:** After data transfer is completed, end devices systematically end the session.

Some examples of Session Layer protocols include

>> **NetBIOS:** Network Basic Input/Output System (NetBIOS) is a Microsoft protocol that allows applications to communicate over a LAN. When NetBIOS is combined with other protocols such as TCP/IP, known as NetBIOS over TCP/IP (or NBT), applications can communicate over large networks.

>> **Network File System (NFS):** Developed by Sun Microsystems to facilitate transparent user access to remote resources on a UNIX-based TCP/IP network.

>> **Remote Procedure Call (RPC):** A client-server network redirection tool. Procedures are created on clients and performed on servers.

>> **Secure Remote Procedure Call (S-RPC):** *S-RPC* is a secure client-server protocol that's defined at multiple upper layers of the OSI model. RPC is used to request services from another computer on the network. S-RPC provides public and private keys to clients and servers by using Diffie-Hellman. After S-RPC operations initially authenticate, they're transparent to the end-user.

>> **Secure Shell (SSH and SSH-2):** SSH provides a secure alternative to Telnet (discussed in the section "Application Layer (Layer 7)" later in this chapter) for remote access. SSH establishes an encrypted tunnel between the client and the server, and can also authenticate the client to the server. SSH can be used to protect the confidentiality and integrity of network communications. SSH-2 establishes an encrypted tunnel between the SSH client and SSH server and can also authenticate the client to the server. SSH version 1 is also widely used but has inherent vulnerabilities that are easily exploited.

REMEMBER

SSH-2 (or simply SSH) is an Internet security application that provides secure remote access.

>> **Session Initiation Protocol (SIP):** An open signaling protocol standard for establishing, managing and terminating real-time communications — such as voice, video, and text — over large IP-based networks.

TRANSPORT LAYER (LAYER 4)

The Transport Layer (Layer 4) provides transparent, reliable data transport and end-to-end transmission control. The Transport Layer hides the details of the lower layer functions from the upper layers.

Specific Transport Layer functions include

>> **Flow control:** Manages data transmission between devices, ensuring that the transmitting device doesn't send more data than the receiving device can process.

>> **Multiplexing:** Enables data from multiple applications to be transmitted over a single physical link.

>> **Virtual circuit management:** Establishes, maintains, and terminates virtual circuits.

>> **Error checking and recovery:** Implements various mechanisms for detecting transmission errors and taking action to resolve any errors that occur, such as requesting that data be retransmitted.

REMEMBER

The Transport Layer is responsible for providing transparent data transport and end-to-end transmission control.

Several important protocols defined at the Transport Layer include

>> **Transmission Control Protocol (TCP):** A *full-duplex* (capable of simultaneous transmission and reception), connection-oriented protocol that provides reliable delivery of packets across a network. A *connection-oriented* protocol requires a direct connection between two communicating devices before any data transfer occurs. In TCP, this connection is accomplished via a *three-way handshake*. The receiving device acknowledges packets, and packets are retransmitted if an error occurs. The following characteristics and features are associated with TCP:

   • **Connection-oriented:** Establishes and manages a direct virtual connection to the remote device.

   • **Reliable:** Guarantees delivery by acknowledging received packets and requesting retransmission of missing or corrupted packets.

   • **Slow:** Because of the additional overhead associated with initial handshaking, acknowledging packets, and error correction, TCP is generally slower than connectionless protocols, such as User Datagram Protocol (UDP).

REMEMBER

TECHNICAL STUFF

TCP is a connection-oriented protocol.

A *three-way handshake* is the method used to establish a TCP connection. A PC attempting to establish a connection with a server initiates the connection by sending a TCP SYN (Synchronize) packet. This is the first part of the handshake. In the second part of the handshake, the server replies to the PC with a SYN ACK packet (Synchronize Acknowledgement). Finally, the PC completes the handshake by sending an ACK or SYN-ACK-ACK packet, acknowledging the server's acknowledgement, and the data communications commence.

A *socket* is a logical endpoint on a system or device used to communicate over a network to another system or device (or even on the same device). A socket usually is expressed as an IP address and port number, such as *192.168.100.2:25*.

» **User Datagram Protocol (UDP):** A connectionless protocol that provides fast best-effort delivery of datagrams across a network. A connectionless protocol doesn't guarantee delivery of transmitted packets (datagrams) and is thus considered unreliable. It doesn't

- Attempt to establish a connection with the destination network prior to transmitting data.
- Acknowledge received datagrams.
- Perform re-sequencing.
- Perform error checking or recovery.
- A *datagram* is a self-contained unit of data that is capable of being routed between a source and a destination. Similar to a packet, which is used in the Internet Protocol (IP), datagrams are commonly used in UDP and other protocols.

TECHNICAL STUFF

TECHNICAL STUFF

The term Protocol Data Unit (PDU) is used to describe the unit of data used at a particular layer of a protocol. For instance, in OSI, the layer 1 PDU is a bit, layer 2's PDU is a frame, layer 3's is a packet, and layer 4's is a segment or datagram, and layer 7's PDU.

UDP is ideally suited for data that requires fast delivery, as long as that data isn't sensitive to packet loss and doesn't need to be fragmented. Examples of applications that use UDP include Domain Name System (DNS), Simple Network Management Protocol (SNMP), and streaming audio or video. The following characteristics and features are associated with UDP:

- **Connectionless:** Doesn't pre-establish a communication circuit with the destination network.
- **Best effort:** Doesn't guarantee delivery and is thus considered unreliable.
- **Fast:** Has no overhead associated with circuit establishment, acknowledgement, sequencing, or error-checking and recovery.

TECHNICAL STUFF

Jitter in streaming audio and video is caused by variations in the delay of received packets, which is a negative characteristic of UDP.

» **Sequenced Packet Exchange (SPX):** The protocol used to guarantee data delivery in older Novell NetWare IPX/SPX networks. SPX sequences transmitted packets, reassembles received packets, confirms all packets are received, and requests retransmission of packets that aren't received. SPX is to IPX as TCP is to IP, though it might be confusing because the order is stated as IPX/SPX, rather than SPX/IPX (as in TCP/IP): SPX and TCP are Layer 4 protocols, and IPX and IP are Layer 3 protocols. Just think of it as yang and yin, rather than yin and yang!

Several examples of connection-oriented and connectionless-oriented protocols are identified in Table 6-1.

» **Secure Sockets Layer/Transport Layer Security (SSL/TLS):** The SSL/TLS protocol provides session-based encryption and authentication for secure communication between clients and servers on the Internet. SSL/TLS provides server authentication with optional client authentication.

» **Stream Control Transmission Protocol (SCTP):** A message-oriented protocol (similar to UDP) that ensures reliable, in-sequence transport with congestion control (similar to TCP). Also provides multi-homing and redundant paths for resiliency and reliability.

TABLE 6-1   **Connection-Oriented and Connectionless-Oriented Protocols**

Protocol	Layer	Type
TCP (Transmission Control Protocol)	4 (Transport)	Connection-oriented
UDP (User Datagram Protocol)	4 (Transport)	Connectionless-oriented
IP (Internet Protocol)	3 (Network)	Connectionless-oriented
ICMP (Internet Control Message Protocol)	3 (Network)	Connectionless-oriented
IPX (Internetwork Packet Exchange)	3 (Network)	Connectionless-oriented
SPX (Sequenced Packet Exchange)	4 (Transport)	Connection-oriented

NETWORK LAYER (LAYER 3)

The Network Layer (Layer 3) provides routing and related functions that enable data to be transported between systems on the same network or on interconnected networks (or *internetworks*). *Routing* protocols, such as the Routing Information Protocol (RIP), Open Shortest Path First (OSPF), and Border Gateway Protocol (BGP), are defined at this layer. Logical addressing of devices on the network is accomplished at this layer by using *routed* protocols, including the Internet Protocol (IP) and Internetwork Packet Exchange (IPX).

The Network Layer is primarily responsible for routing.

Routing protocols move *routed* protocol messages across a network. Routing protocols include RIP, OSPF, IS-IS, IGRP, and BGP. Routed protocols include IP and IPX.

Routing protocols

Routing protocols are defined at the Network Layer and specify how routers communicate with one another on a WAN. Routing protocols are classified as static or dynamic.

A *static* routing protocol requires an administrator to create and update routes manually on the router. If the route is down, the network is down. The router can't reroute traffic dynamically to an alternate destination (unless a different route is specified manually). Also, if a given route is congested, but an alternate route is available and relatively fast, the router with static routes can't route data dynamically over the faster route. Static routing is practical only in very small networks or for very limited, special-case routing scenarios (for example, a destination that's reachable only via a single router). Despite the limitations of static routing, it has a few advantages, such as low bandwidth requirements (routing information isn't broadcast across the network) and some built-in security (users can only get to destinations that are specified in the routing table).

A *dynamic* routing protocol can discover routes and determine the best route to a given destination at any given time. The routing table is periodically updated with current routing information. Dynamic routing protocols are further classified as link-state and distance-vector (for intra-domain routing) and path-vector (for inter-domain routing) protocols.

A *distance-vector* protocol makes routing decisions based on two factors: the distance (hop count or other metric) and vector (the egress router interface). It periodically informs its peers and/or neighbors of topology changes. *Convergence,* the time it takes for all routers in a network to update their routing tables with the most current information (such as link status changes), can be a significant problem for distance-vector protocols. Without convergence, some routers in a network may be unaware of topology changes, causing the router to send traffic to an invalid destination. During convergence, routing information is exchanged between routers, and the network slows down considerably.

Routing Information Protocol (RIP) is a distance-vector routing protocol that uses hop count as its routing metric. In order to prevent *routing loops,* in which packets effectively get stuck bouncing between various router nodes, RIP implements a hop limit of 15, which significantly limits the size of networks that RIP can support. After a data packet crosses 15 router nodes (hops) between a source and a destination, the destination is considered unreachable. In addition to hop limits, RIP employs three other mechanisms to prevent routing loops:

>> **Split horizon:** Prevents a router from advertising a route back out through the same interface from which the route was learned.

>> **Route poisoning:** Sets the hop count on a bad route to 16, effectively advertising the route as unreachable if it takes more than 15 hops to reach.

>> **Holddown timers:** Cause a router to start a timer when the router first receives information that a destination is unreachable. Subsequent updates about that destination will not be accepted until the timer expires. This also helps avoid problems associated with *flapping*. Flapping occurs when a route (or interface) repeatedly changes state (up, down, up, down) over a short period of time.

RIP uses UDP port 520 as its transport protocol and port, and thus is a connectionless-oriented protocol. Other disadvantages of RIP include slow convergence and insufficient security (RIPv1 has no authentication, and RIPv2 transmits passwords in cleartext). RIP is a legacy protocol, but it's still in widespread use on networks today, despite its limitations, because of its simplicity.

TECHNICAL STUFF

Hop count generally refers to the number of router nodes that a packet must pass through to reach its destination.

A *link-state* protocol requires every router to calculate and maintain a complete map, or *routing table*, of the entire network. Routers that use a link-state protocol periodically transmit updates that contain information about adjacent connections (these are called *link states*) to all other routers in the network. Link-state protocols are computation-intensive but can calculate the most efficient route to a destination, taking into account numerous factors such as link speed, delay, load, reliability, and cost (an arbitrarily assigned weight or metric). Convergence occurs very rapidly (within seconds) with link-state protocols; distance-vector protocols usually take longer (several minutes, or even hours in very large networks). Two examples of link-state routing protocols are:

>> **Open Shortest Path First (OSPF).** OSPF is a link-state routing protocol widely used in large enterprise networks. It's considered an Interior Gateway Protocol (IGP) because it performs routing within a single autonomous system (AS). OSPF is encapsulated directly into IP datagrams, as opposed to using a Transport Layer protocol such as TCP or UDP. OSPF networks are divided into areas identified by 32-bit area identifiers. *Area identifiers* can (but don't have to) correspond to network IP addresses and can duplicate IP addresses without conflicts. Special OSPF areas include the *backbone area* (also known as *area 0*), *stub area*, and *not-so-stubby area* (NSSA).

>> **Intermediate System to Intermediate System (IS-IS).** IS-IS is a link-state routing protocol used to route datagrams through a packet-switched network. It is an interior gateway protocol used for routing within an autonomous system, used extensively in large service-provider backbone networks.

TECHNICAL STUFF

An *autonomous system (AS)* is a group of contiguous IP address ranges under the control of a single Internet entity. Individual autonomous systems are assigned a 16-bit or 32-bit AS Number (ASN) that uniquely identifies the network on the Internet. ASNs are assigned by the Internet Assigned Numbers Authority (IANA).

A *path-vector* protocol is similar in concept to a distance-vector protocol, but without the scalability issues associated with limited hop counts. *Border Gateway Protocol* (BGP) is an example of a path-vector protocol.

BGP is a path-vector routing protocol used between separate autonomous systems (ASs). It's considered an Exterior Gateway Protocol (EGP) because it performs routing between separate autonomous systems. It's the core protocol used by Internet service providers (ISPs), network service providers (NSPs), and on very large private IP networks. When BGP runs between autonomous systems (such as between ISPs), it's called external BGP (eBGP). When BGP runs within an AS (such as on a private IP network), it's called internal BGP (iBGP).

Routed protocols

Routed protocols are Network Layer protocols, such as *Internetwork Packet Exchange* (IPX) and *Internet Protocol* (IP) which address packets with routing information and allow those packets to be transported across networks using routing protocols (discussed in the preceding section).

Internetwork Packet Exchange (IPX) is a connectionless protocol used primarily in older Novell NetWare networks for routing packets across the network. It's part of the IPX/SPX (Internetwork Packet Exchange/Sequenced Packet Exchange) protocol suite, which is analogous to the TCP/IP suite.

Internet Protocol (IP) contains addressing information that enables packets to be routed. IP is part of the TCP/IP (Transmission Control Protocol/Internet Protocol) suite, which is the language of the Internet. IP has two primary responsibilities:

>> Connectionless, best-effort (no guarantee of) delivery of datagrams.

>> Fragmentation and reassembly of datagrams.

IP Version 4 (IPv4), which is currently the most commonly used version, uses a 32-bit logical IP address that's divided into four 8-bit sections (*octets*) and consists of two main parts: the network number and the host number. The first four bits in an octet are known as the high-order bits and the last four bits in an octet are known as the low-order bits. The first bit in the octet is referred to as the most significant bit, and the last bit in the octet is referred to as the least significant bit. Each bit position represents its value (see Table 6-2) if the bit is "on" (1); otherwise, its value is zero ("off" or 0).

TABLE 6-2 **Bit Position Values in an IPv4 Address**

High-Order Bits				Low-Order Bits			
Most significant bit							Least significant bit
128	64	32	16	8	4	2	1

Each octet contains an 8-bit number with a value of 0 to 255. Table 6-3 shows a partial list of octet values in binary notation.

TABLE 6-3 **Binary Notation of Octet Values**

Decimal	Binary	Decimal	Binary	Decimal	Binary
255	1111 1111	200	1100 1000	9	0000 1001
254	1111 1110	180	1011 0100	8	0000 1000
253	1111 1101	160	1010 0000	7	0000 0111
252	1111 1100	140	1000 1100	6	0000 0110
251	1111 1011	120	0111 1000	5	0000 0101
250	1111 1010	100	0110 0100	4	0000 0100
249	1111 1001	80	0101 0000	3	0000 0011
248	1111 1000	60	0011 1100	2	0000 0010
247	1111 0111	40	0010 1000	1	0000 0001
246	1111 0110	20	0001 0100	0	0000 0000

IPv4 addressing supports five different address classes, indicated by the high-order (leftmost) bits in the IP address, as listed in Table 6-4.

TABLE 6-4 **IP Address Classes**

Class	Purpose	High-Order Bits	Address Range	Maximum Number of Hosts
A	Large networks	0	1 to 126	16,777,214 (224-2)
B	Medium networks	10	128 to 191	65,534 (216-2)
C	Small networks	110	192 to 223	254 (28-2)
D	Multicast	1110	224 to 239	N/A
E	Experimental	1111	240 to 254	N/A

TECHNICAL STUFF

The address range 127.0.0.1 to 127.255.255.255 is a *loopback* network used for testing and troubleshooting. Packets sent to a 127 address are immediately routed back to the source device. The most commonly used loopback (or localhost) address for devices is 127.0.0.1 (sometimes called *home*), although any address in the 127 network range can be used for this purpose.

Several IPv4 address ranges are also reserved for use in *private networks*, including:

» 10.0.0.0–10.255.255.255 (Class A)

» 172.16.0.0–172.31.255.255 (Class B)

» 192.168.0.0–192.168.255.255 (Class C)

These addresses aren't routable on the Internet and are thus often implemented behind firewalls and gateways by using Network Address Translation (NAT) to conserve IP addresses, mask the network architecture, and enhance security. NAT translates private, non-routable addresses on internal network devices to registered IP addresses when communication across the Internet is required. The widespread use of NAT and private network addresses) somewhat delayed the inevitable depletion of IPv4 addresses, which is limited to approximately 4.3 billion due to it's 32-bit format (2^{32} = 4,294,967,296 possible addresses). But the thing about inevitability is that it's, well, inevitable. Factors such as the proliferation of mobile devices worldwide, always-on Internet connections, inefficient use of assigned IPv4 addresses, and the spectacular miscalculation of IBM's Thomas Watson — who, in 1943, predicted that there would be a worldwide market for "maybe five computers" (he was no Nostradamus) — have led to the depletion of IPv4 addresses.

The Asia-Pacific Network Information Centre (APNIC) was the first regional Internet Registry to run out of IPv4 addresses, on April 15, 2011. Réseaux IP Européens Network Coordination Centre (RIPE NCC), the regional Internet registry for Europe exhausted its pool of IPv4 addresses on September 14, 2012, followed by the Latin America and Caribbean Network Information Centre (LACNIC) on June 10, 2014, and the American Registry for Internet Numbers (ARIN) on

September 24, 2015. The African Network Information Centre (AFRINIC) was expected to deplete its IPv4 pools in 2018.

TECHNICAL STUFF

Technically, we're not completely out of IPv4 addresses. Each regional Internet registry has reserved a very small pool of IPv4 addresses to facilitate the transition to IPv6.

In 1998, the IETF formally defined the IP Version 6 (IPv6) specification as the replacement for IPv4. IPv6 uses a 128-bit hexadecimal IP address (versus 32 bits for IPv4) and incorporates additional functionality to provide security, multimedia support, plug-and-play compatibility, and backward compatibility with IPv4. The main reason for developing IPv6 was to provide infinitely more network addresses than are available with IPv4 addresses. Okay, it's not infinite, but it is ginormous — 2^{128} or approximately 3.4×10^{38} (that's 340 hundred undecillion) unique addresses!

IPv6 addresses consist of 32 hexadecimal numbers grouped into eight blocks (sometimes referred to as *hextels*) of four hexadecimal digits, separated by a colon. *Remember:* A hexadecimal digit is represented by 4 bits (see Table 6-5), so each hextel is 16 bits (four 4-bit hexadecimal digits) and eight 16-bit hextels equals 128 bits. An IPv6 address is further divided into two 64-bit segments: The first (also referred to as the "top" or "upper") 64 bits represent the network part of the address, and the last (also referred to as the "bottom" or "lower") 64 bits represent the node or interface part of the address. The network part is further subdivided into a 48-bit global network address and a 16-bit subnet. The node or interface part of the address is based on the IEEE Extended Unique Identifier (EUI-64) physical or media access control (MAC) address (discussed in the "Data Link Layer (Layer 2)" section later in this chapter) of the node or interface.

The basic format for an IPv6 address is:

xxxx:xxxx:xxxx:xxxx:xxxx:xxxx:xxxx:xxxx

where x represents a hexadecimal digit (0–f).

The following is an example of an IPv6 address:

2001:0db8:0000:0000:0008:0800:200c:417a

There are several rules the IETF has defined to shorten an IPv6 address:

>> **Leading zeroes in an individual hextel can be omitted, but there must be at least one hexadecimal digit in each hextel, except as noted in the next rule.** Applying this rule to the previous example would yield the following result: 2001:db8:0:0:8:800:200c:417a.

TABLE 6-5 **Decimal, Hexadecimal, and Binary Notation**

Decimal	Hexadecimal	Binary
0	0	0000
1	1	0001
2	2	0010
3	3	0011
4	4	0100
5	5	0101
6	6	0110
7	7	0111
8	8	1000
9	9	1001
10	A	1010
11	B	1011
12	C	1100
13	D	1101
14	E	1110
15	F	1111

>> **Two colons (::) can be used to represent one or more groups of 16 bits of zeros, as well as leading or trailing zeroes in an address; the :: can only appear once in an IPv6 address.** Applying this rule to the previous example would yield the following result: 2001:db8::8:800:200c:417a.

>> **In mixed IPv4 and IPv6 environments, the form x:x:x:x:x;x:d.d.d.d can be used, in which x represents the six high-order 16-bit hextels of the address and d represents the four low-order 8-bit octets (in standard IPv4 notation) of the address.** For example, 0db8:0:0:0:0:FFFF:129.144.52.38 is a valid IPv6 address. Applying the previous two rules to this example would yield the following result: db8::ffff:129.144.52.38.

Letters in hexadecimal notation are not case-sensitive (A is the same as a, B is the same as b, and so on), so either form can be used in IPv6 addresses, although IETF recommends using lowercase letters.

Security features in IPv6 include network-layer security via Internet Protocol Security (IPsec) and requirements defined in Request For Comments (RFC) 7112 to prevent fragmentation exploits in IPv6 headers.

TIP

Although you don't need to know all the intricate details of IPv6 addressing for the CISSP exam, as its use becomes more commonplace — particularly in IoT devices — you need to be familiar with the security enhancements in IPv6 and be able to recognize a valid IPv6 address.

Multilayer protocols

Multilayer protocols are groups of protocols that are purpose-built for some type of specialized communications need. Multilayer protocols have their own schemes for encapsulation, just like TCP/IP itself.

One good example of a multilayer protocol is DNP3 (Distributed Network Protocol), which is used in industrial control systems (ICS) and supervisory control and data acquisition (SCADA) networks. DNP3 has a layer 2 framing layer, a layer 4 transport layer, and a layer 7 application layer.

DNP3's original design lacks security features, such as authentication and encryption. Recent updates to the standard have introduced security protocols. Without security features, relatively simple attacks (such as eavesdropping, spoofing, and perhaps denial of service) can be easily carried out on specialized multiprotocol networks.

Converged protocols

Converged protocols refers to an implementation of two or more protocols for a specific communications purpose. Some examples of converged protocols include

>> MPLS (Multiprotocol Label Switching).

>> FCoE (Fibre Channel over Ethernet).

>> VoIP (Voice over Internet Protocol).

>> SIP (Session Initiation Protocol).

>> iSCSI (Internet Small Computer System Interface).

Software-defined networks

Software-defined networks, or SDN, represent the ability to create, configure, manage, secure, and monitor network elements rapidly and efficiently. SDN utilizes an open standards architecture that enables intelligent network functions, such as routing, switching, and load balancing (the overlay function), to be performed on virtual software that is installed on commodity network hardware (the physical underlay), similar to server virtualization. In SDN, network elements and network architectures are virtual; this enables organizations to quickly build and modify their networks and network elements.

Like other virtualization technologies, SDN requires policy, process, and discipline to manage it correctly, in order to avoid *network sprawl* (the phenomenon where undisciplined administrators bypass change control processes and unilaterally create virtual network elements).

Other network layer protocols

Other protocols defined at the Network Layer include the *Internet Control Message Protocol* (ICMP) and *Simple Key Management for Internet Protocols* (SKIP).

ICMP is a Network Layer protocol that is used for network control and diagnostics. Commonly used ICMP commands include ping and traceroute. Although ICMP is very helpful in troubleshooting routing and connectivity issues in a network, it is also commonly used by attackers for network reconnaissance, device discovery, and denial-of-service (DoS) attacks (such as an ICMP flood).

SKIP is a Network Layer key management protocol used to share encryption keys. An advantage of SKIP is that it doesn't require a prior communication session to be established before it sends encrypted keys or packets. However, SKIP is bandwidth-intensive because of the size of additional header information in encrypted packets.

Networking equipment at the network layer

The primary networking equipment defined at Layer 3 are *routers* and *gateways*.

Routers are intelligent devices that link dissimilar networks and use logical or physical addresses to forward data packets only to the destination network (or along the network path). Routers employ various routing algorithms (for example, RIP, OSPF, and BGP) to determine the best path to a destination, based on different variables that include bandwidth, cost, delay, and distance.

Gateways are created with software running on a computer (workstation or server) or router. Gateways link dissimilar programs and protocols by examining the entire layer 7 data packet so as to translate incompatibilities. For example, a gateway can be used to link an IP network to an IPX network or a Microsoft Exchange mail server to a Lotus Notes server (a mail gateway).

DATA LINK LAYER (LAYER 2)

The Data Link Layer ensures that messages are delivered to the proper device across a physical network link. This layer also defines the networking protocol (for example, Ethernet, USB, and token ring) used to send and receive data between individual devices. The Data Link Layer formats messages from layers above into frames for transmission, handles point-to-point synchronization and error control, and can perform link encryption.

The IEEE 802 standards and protocols further divide the Data Link Layer into two sub-layers: the Logical Link Control (LLC) and Media Access Control (MAC) sub-layers (see Figure 6-3).

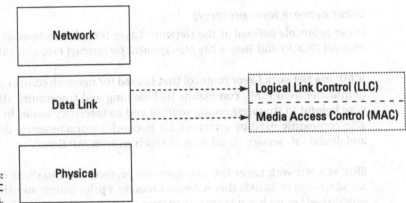

FIGURE 6-3:
The LLC and MAC sub-layers.

REMEMBER

The Data Link Layer is responsible for ensuring that messages are delivered to the proper device across a physical network link.

The LLC sub-layer operates between the Network Layer above and the MAC sub-layer below. The LLC sub-layer performs the following three functions:

>> Provides an interface for the MAC sub-layer by using Source Service Access Points (SSAPs) and Destination Service Access Points (DSAPs).

>> Manages the control, sequencing, and acknowledgement of frames being passed up to the Network Layer or down to the Physical Layer.

>> Bears responsibility for timing and flow control. *Flow control* monitors the flow of data between devices to ensure that a receiving device, which may not necessarily be operating at the same speed as the transmitting device, isn't overwhelmed and dropping packets.

REMEMBER

The Logical Link Control (LLC) and Media Access Control (MAC) are sub-layers of the Data Link Layer.

The MAC sub-layer operates between the LLC sub-layer above and the Physical Layer below. It's primarily responsible for framing and has the following three functions:

>> **Performs error control:** Error control uses a cyclic redundancy check (CRC). A *CRC* is a simple mathematical calculation or checksum used to create a message profile. The CRC is recalculated by the receiving device. If the calculated CRC doesn't match the received CRC, the packet is dropped and a request to re-send is transmitted back to the device that sent it.

>> **Identifies hardware device (or MAC) addresses:** A *MAC address* (also known as a *hardware address* or *physical address*) is a 48-bit address that's encoded on each device by its manufacturer. The first 24 bits identify the manufacturer or vendor. The second 24 bits uniquely identify the device.

>> **Controls media access:** The three basic types of media access are

- **Contention:** In contention-based networks such as Ethernet, individual devices must vie for control of the physical network medium. This type of network is ideally suited for networks characterized by small bursts of traffic. Ethernet networks use a contention-based method, known as *Carrier Sense Multiple Access with Collision Detection* (CSMA/CD), in which all stations listen for traffic on the physical network medium. If the line is clear, any station can transmit data. However, if another station attempts to transmit data at the same time, a collision occurs, the traffic is dropped, and both stations must wait a random period of time before attempting to re-transmit. Another method, used in Apple LocalTalk and Wi-Fi networks, is known as *Carrier Sense Multiple Access with Collision Avoidance* (CSMA/CA).

- **Token-passing:** In token passing networks such as token ring and Fiber Distributed Data Interface (FDDI), individual devices must wait for a special frame, known as a *token*, before they transmit data across the physical network medium. This type of network is considered *deterministic* (transmission delay can be reliably calculated, and collisions don't occur) and is ideally suited for networks that have large, bandwidth-consuming applications that are delay-sensitive. Token ring, FDDI, and ARCnet networks all use various token passing methods for media access control.

- **Polling:** In polling networks, individual devices (secondary hosts) are polled by a primary host to see whether they have data to be transmitted. Secondary hosts can't transmit until permission is granted by the primary host. Polling is typically used in mainframe environments and wireless networks.

LAN protocols and transmission methods

Common LAN protocols are defined at the Data Link (and Physical) Layer. They include the following:

» **Ethernet:** The Ethernet protocol transports data to the physical LAN medium by using CSMA/CD (discussed in the preceding section). It is designed for networks characterized by sporadic, sometimes heavy traffic requirements. Ethernet is by far the most common LAN protocol used today — most often implemented with twisted-pair cabling (discussed in the section "Cable and connector types"). Ethernet operates at speeds up to 10 Mbps, Fast Ethernet operates at speeds up to 100 Mbps (over Cat 5 twisted-pair or fiber-optic cabling), and Gigabit Ethernet operates at speeds up to 40 Gbps (over Cat 5e, Cat 6, or Cat 7 twisted-pair or fiber-optic cabling).

» **ARCnet:** The ARCnet protocol is one of the earliest LAN technologies developed. It transports data to the physical LAN medium by using the token passing media access method that we discuss in the preceding section. It's implemented in a star topology by using coaxial cable. ARCnet provides slow-but-predictable network performance.

» **Token Ring:** The Token Ring protocol transports data to the physical LAN medium by using the token passing media access method that we discuss in the preceding section. In a token ring network, all nodes are attached to a Multistation Access Unit (MAU) in a logical ring (but physical star) topology. One node on the token ring network is designated as the *active monitor* and ensures that no more than one token is on the network at any given time. (Variations permit more than one token on the network.) If the token is lost, the active monitor is responsible for ensuring that a replacement token is generated. Token ring networks operate at speeds of 4 and 16 Mbps — pretty slow by today's standards. Token ring networks are not often seen nowadays.

» **Fiber Distributed Data Interface (FDDI):** The FDDI protocol transports data to the physical LAN medium by using the token passing media access method that we discuss in the preceding section. It's implemented as a dual counter-rotating ring over fiber-optic cabling at speeds up to 100 Mbps. All stations on a FDDI network are connected to both rings. During normal operation, only one ring is active. In the event of a network break or fault, the ring wraps back through the nearest node onto the second ring.

» **Address Resolution Protocol (ARP):** ARP maps Network Layer IP addresses to MAC addresses. ARP discovers physical addresses of attached devices by broadcasting ARP query messages on the network segment. IP-address-to-MAC-address translations are then maintained in a dynamic table that's cached on the system.

>> **Reverse Address Resolution Protocol (RARP):** RARP maps MAC addresses to IP addresses. This process is necessary when a system, such as a diskless machine, needs to discover its IP address. The system broadcasts a RARP message that provides the system's MAC address and requests to be informed of its IP address. A RARP server replies with the requested information.

REMEMBER

Both ARP and RARP are Layer 2 protocols. ARP maps an IP address to a MAC address and is used to identify a device's hardware address when only the IP address is known. RARP maps a MAC address to an IP address and is used to identify a device's IP address when only the MAC address is known.

LAN data transmissions are classified as

>> **Unicast:** Packets are sent from the source to a single destination device by using a specific destination IP address.

>> **Multicast:** Packets are copied and sent from the source to multiple destination devices by using a special multicast IP address that the destination stations have been specifically configured to use.

>> **Broadcast:** Packets are copied and sent from the source to every device on a destination network by using a broadcast IP address.

REMEMBER

LAN data transmissions are classified as unicast, multicast, or broadcast.

WLAN technologies and protocols

WLAN (wireless LAN) technologies, commonly known as Wi-Fi, function at the lower layers of the OSI Reference Model. WLAN protocols define how frames are transmitted over the air. See Table 6-6 for a description of the most common IEEE 802.11 WLAN standards.

TABLE 6-6 ## Wireless LAN Standards

Type	Speed	Description
802.11a	54 Mbps	Operates at 5 GHz (less interference than at 2.4 GHz)
802.11b	11 Mbps	Operates at 2.4 GHz (first widely used protocol)
802.11g	54 Mbps	Operates at 2.4 GHz (backward-compatible with 802.11b)
802.11n	600 Mbps	Operates at 5 GHz or 2.4 GHz
802.11ac	1 Gbps	Operates at 5 GHz

WLAN networks were first encrypted with the WEP (Wired Equivalent Privacy) protocol, which was soon proven to be insufficient. New standards of encryption include WPA (Wi-Fi protected access) and WPA2. WPA using TKIP (Temporal Key Integrity Protocol) is also considered insufficient; AES (Advanced Encryption Standard) should be used instead. *Wireless Networks For Dummies,* by our friends Barry Lewis and Peter T. Davis, is a great book for more information on wireless networks.

WAN technologies and protocols

WAN technologies function at the lower three layers of the OSI Reference Model (the Physical, Data Link, and Network Layers), primarily at the Data Link Layer. WAN protocols define how frames are carried across a single data link between two devices. These protocols include

>> **Point-to-point links:** These links provide a single, pre-established WAN communications path from the customer's network, across a carrier network (such as a Public Switched Telephone Network [PSTN]), to a remote network. These point-to-point links include

- **Layer 2 Forwarding Protocol (L2F):** A tunneling (data encapsulation) protocol developed by Cisco and used to implement VPNs, specifically Point-to-Point Protocol (PPP, discussed later in this section) traffic. L2F provides encapsulation but doesn't provide encryption or confidentiality.

- **Layer 2 Tunneling Protocol (L2TP):** A tunneling protocol used to implement VPNs. L2TP is derived from L2F (described in the preceding item) and PPTP (described in this list) and uses UDP port 1701 (see the section "Network Layer (Layer 3)" earlier in this chapter) to create a tunneling session. L2TP is commonly implemented along with an encryption protocol, such as IPsec, because it doesn't encrypt traffic or provide confidentiality by itself. We discuss L2TP and IPsec in more detail in the section "Remote access" later in this chapter.

- **Point-to-Point Protocol (PPP):** The successor to SLIP (see the discussion later in this section), PPP provides router-to-router and host-to-network connections over synchronous and asynchronous circuits. It's a more robust protocol than SLIP and provides additional built-in security mechanisms. PPP is far more common than SLIP in modern networking environments.

- **Point-to-Point Tunneling Protocol (PPTP):** A tunneling protocol developed by Microsoft and commonly used to implement VPNs, specifically PPP traffic. PPTP doesn't provide encryption or confidentiality, instead relying on other protocols, such as PAP, CHAP, and EAP, for security. We discuss PPTP, PAP, CHAP, and EAP in more detail in the section "Remote access," later in this chapter.

- **Serial Line IP (SLIP):** The predecessor of Point-to-Point Protocol (PPP), SLIP was originally developed to support TCP/IP networking over low-speed asynchronous serial lines (such as dial-up modems) for Berkeley UNIX computers. SLIP is rarely seen today, except in computer museums.

» **Circuit-switched networks:** In a circuit-switched network, a dedicated physical circuit path is established, maintained, and terminated between the sender and receiver across a carrier network for each communications session (the *call*). This network type is used extensively in telephone company networks and functions similarly to a regular telephone call. Examples include

- **Digital Subscriber Line (xDSL):** xDSL uses existing analog phone lines to deliver high-bandwidth connectivity to remote customers. Table 6-7 describes several types of xDSL lines that are currently available.
- **Data Over Cable Service Interface Specification (DOCSIS):** DOCSIS is a communications protocol for transmitting high speed data over an existing cable TV system.

TABLE 6-7   **xDSL Examples**

Type	Characteristics	Description
ADSL and ADSL2	Downstream rate: 1.5 to 12 Mbps Upstream rate: 0.5 to 3.5 Mbps Operating range: Up to 14,400 ft	Asymmetric Digital Subscriber Line; designed to deliver higher bandwidth downstream (as from a central office to a customer site) than upstream
SDSL	Downstream rate: 1.544 Mbps Upstream rate: 1.544 Mbps Operating range: Up to 10,000 ft	Single-line Digital Subscriber Line; designed to deliver high bandwidth both upstream and downstream over a single copper twisted pair
HDSL	Downstream rate: 1.544 Mbps Upstream rate: 1.544 Mbps Operating range: Up to 12,000 ft	High-rate Digital Subscriber Line; designed to deliver high bandwidth both upstream and downstream over two copper twisted pairs; commonly used to provide local access to T1 services
VDSL	Downstream rate: 13 to 52 Mbps Upstream rate: 1.5 to 2.3 Mbps Operating range: 1,000 to 4,500 ft	Very high Data-rate Digital Subscriber Line; designed to deliver extremely high bandwidth over a single copper twisted pair; VDSL2 provides simultaneous upstream and downstream data rates in excess of 100 Mbps

- **Integrated Services Digital Network (ISDN):** ISDN is a communications protocol that operates over analog phone lines that have been converted to use digital signaling. ISDN lines are capable of transmitting both voice and data traffic. ISDN defines a B-channel for data, voice, and other services, and a D-channel for control and signaling information. Table 6-8 describes the two levels of ISDN service that are currently available.

  With the introduction and widespread adoption of DSL and DOCSIS, ISDN has largely fallen out of favor in the United States and is no longer available in many areas.

Circuit-switched networks are ideally suited for *always-on* connections that experience constant traffic.

>> **Packet-switched networks:** In a packet-switched network, devices share bandwidth (by using statistical multiplexing) on communications links to transport packets between a sender and receiver across a carrier network. This type of network is more resilient to error and congestion than circuit-switched networks. We compare packet-switched and circuit-switched networks in Table 6-9.

Examples of packet-switched networks include

- **Asynchronous Transfer Mode (ATM):** A very high-speed, low-delay technology that uses switching and multiplexing techniques to rapidly relay fixed-length (53-byte) cells that contain voice, video, or data. Cell processing occurs in hardware that reduces transit delays. ATM is ideally suited for fiber-optic networks that carry bursty (uneven) traffic.

TABLE 6-8   **ISDN Service Levels**

Level	Description
Basic Rate Interface (BRI)	One 16-Kbps D-channel and two 64-Kbps B-channels (maximum data rate of 128 Kbps)
Primary Rate Interface (PRI)	One 64-Kbps D-channel and either 23 64-Kbps B-channels (U.S.) or 30 64-Kbps B-channels (EU), with a maximum data rate of 1.544 Mbps (U.S.) or 2.048 Mbps (EU)

TABLE 6-9   **Circuit Switching versus Packet Switching**

Circuit Switching	Packet Switching
Ideal for always-on connections, constant traffic, and voice communications	Ideal for bursty traffic and data communications
Connection-oriented	Connectionless-oriented
Fixed delays	Variable delays

- **Frame Relay:** A packet-switched, standard protocol that handles multiple virtual circuits by using High-level Data Link Control (HDLC) encapsulation (which we discuss later in this section) between connected devices. Frame Relay utilizes a simplified framing approach that has no error correction and Data Link Connection Identifiers (DLCIs) to achieve high speeds across the WAN. Frame Relay can be used on *Switched Virtual Circuits* (SVCs) or *Permanent Virtual Circuits* (PVCs). An *SVC* is a temporary connection that's dynamically created (in the circuit establishment phase) to transmit data (which happens during the data transfer phase) and then disconnected (in the circuit termination phase). PVCs are permanently established connections. Because the connection is permanent, a PVC doesn't require the bandwidth overhead associated with circuit establishment and termination. However, PVCs are generally a more expensive option than SVCs.

- **Multi-Protocol Label Switching (MPLS):** A packet-switched, high-speed, highly scalable and highly versatile technology used to create fully meshed Virtual Private Networks (VPNs). It can carry IP packets, as well as ATM, SONET (Synchronous Optical Networking), or Ethernet frames. MPLS is specified at both Layer 2 and Layer 3. Label Edge Routers (LERs) in an MPLS network push or encapsulate a packet (or frame) with an MPLS label. The label information is used to switch the payload through the MPLS cloud at very high speeds. Label Switch Routers (LSRs) within the MPLS cloud make routing decisions based solely on the label information, without actually examining the payload. At the egress point, an LER *pops* (decapsulates) the packet, removing the MPLS label when the packet exits the MPLS network. One ntntage of an MPLS network is that a customer loses visibility into the Cloud. Or, if you're a glass-is-half-full type, one advantage of an MPLS network is that an attacker loses visibility into the Cloud.

- **Synchronous Optical Network (SONET) and Synchronous Digital Hierarchy (SDH):** A high-availability, high-speed, multiplexed, low-latency technology used on fiber-optic networks. SONET was originally designed for the public telephone network and is widely used throughout the U.S. and Canada, particularly within the energy industry. SDH was developed after SONET and is used throughout the rest of the world. Data rates for SONET and SDH are defined at OC (optical carrier) levels (see Table 6-10).

- **Switched Multimegabit Data Service (SMDS):** A high-speed, packet-switched, connectionless-oriented, datagram-based technology available over public switched networks. Typically, companies that exchange large amounts of data bursts with other remote networks use SMDS.

TABLE 6-10   Common Telecommunications Circuits

Type	Speed	Description
DS0	64 Kbps	Digital Signal Level 0. Framing specification used in transmitting digital signals over a single channel at 64 Kbps on a T1 facility.
DS1	1.544 Mbps or 2.048 Mbps	Digital Signal Level 1. Framing specification used in transmitting digital signals at 1.544 Mbps on a T1 facility (U.S.) or at 2.048 Mbps on an E1 facility (EU).
DS3	44.736 Mbps	Digital Signal Level 3. Framing specification used in transmitting digital signals at 44.736 Mbps on a T3 facility.
T1	1.544 Mbps	Digital WAN carrier facility. Transmits DS1-formatted data at 1.544 Mbps (24 DS0 user channels at 64 Kbps each).
T3	44.736 Mbps	Digital WAN carrier facility. Transmits DS3-formatted data at 44.736 Mbps (672 DS0 user channels at 64 Kbps each).
E1	2.048 Mbps	Wide-area digital transmission scheme used primarily in Europe that carries data at a rate of 2.048 Mbps.
E3	34.368 Mbps	Wide-area digital transmission scheme used primarily in Europe that carries data at a rate of 34.368 Mbps (16 E1 signals).
OC-1	51.84 Mbps	SONET (Synchronous Optical Networking) Optical Carrier WAN specification
OC-3	155.52 Mbps	SONET
OC-12	622.08 Mbps	SONET
OC-48	2.488 Gbps	SONET
OC-192	9.9 Gbps	SONET
OC-768	39 Gbps	SONET

- **X.25:** The first packet-switching network, X.25 is an International Telecommunication Union – Telecommunications (ITU-T) standard that defines how point-to-point connections between data terminal equipment (DTE) and data carrier equipment (DCE) are established and maintained. X.25 specifies the Link Access Procedure, Balanced (LAPB) protocol at the Data Link Layer and the Packet Level Protocol (PLP; also known as X.25 Level 3) at the Network Layer. X.25 is more common outside the United States but largely has been superseded by MPLS and Frame Relay.

REMEMBER

Packet-switched networks are ideally suited for on-demand connections that have bursty traffic.

» **Other WAN protocols:** Two other important WAN protocols defined at the Data Link Layer include

- **High-level Data Link Control (HDLC):** A bit-oriented, synchronous protocol that was created by the ISO to support point-to-point and multipoint configurations. Derived from SDLC, it specifies a data encapsulation method for synchronous serial links and is the default for serial links on Cisco routers. Unfortunately, various vendor implementations of the HDLC protocol are incompatible.

- **Synchronous Data Link Control (SDLC):** A bit-oriented, full-duplex serial protocol that was developed by IBM to facilitate communications between mainframes and remote offices. It defines and implements a polling method of media access, in which the *primary* (front end) polls the *secondaries* (remote stations) to determine whether communication is required.

WAN protocols and technologies are implemented over telecommunications circuits. Refer to Table 6-10 for a description of common telecommunications circuits and speeds.

Networking equipment at the Data Link Layer

Networking devices that operate at the Data Link Layer include bridges, switches, DTEs/DCEs, and wireless equipment:

>> A *bridge* is a semi-intelligent repeater used to connect two or more (similar or dissimilar) network segments. A bridge maintains an Address Resolution Protocol (ARP) cache that contains the MAC addresses of individual devices on connected network segments. When a bridge receives a data signal, it checks its ARP cache to determine whether the destination MAC address is on the local network segment. If the data signal turns out to be local, it isn't forwarded to a different network; if the MAC address isn't local, however, the bridge forwards (and amplifies) the data signal to all other connected network segments. A serious networking problem associated with bridges is a *broadcast storm,* in which broadcast traffic is automatically forwarded by a bridge, effectively flooding a network. Network bridges have been superseded by switches (discussed next).

ASYNCHRONOUS AND SYNCHRONOUS COMMUNICATIONS

Asynchronous communication transmits data in a serial stream that has control data (start and stop bits) embedded in the stream to indicate the beginning and end of characters. Asynchronous devices must communicate at the same speed, which is controlled by the slower of the two communicating devices. Because no internal clocking signal is used, parity bits are used to reduce transmission errors.

Synchronous communications utilize an internal clocking signal to transmit large blocks of data, known as *frames*. Synchronous communication is characterized by very high-speed transmission rates.

>> *Data Terminal Equipment* (DTE) is a general term used to classify devices at the user end of a user-to-network interface (such as computer workstations). A DTE connects to *Data Carrier Equipment* (DCE; also known as Data Circuit-Terminating Equipment), which consists of devices at the network end of a user-to-network interface. The DCE provides the physical connection to the network, forwards network traffic, and provides a clocking signal to synchronize transmissions between the DCE and the DTE. Examples of DCEs include NICs (Network Interface Cards), modems, and CSUs/DSUs (Channel Service Units/Data Service Units).

>> *Wireless Access Points* (APs) are transceivers that connect wireless clients to the wired network. Access points are base stations for the wireless network. They're essentially hubs (or routers) operating in half-duplex mode — they can only receive or transmit at a given time; they can't do both at the same time (unless they have multiple antennas). Wireless access points use antennas to transmit and receive data. The four basic types of wireless antennas include

- **Omni-directional:** The most common type of wireless antenna, *omni-directional antennas* are essentially short poles that transmit and receive wireless signals with equal strength in all directions around a horizontal axis. Omni-directional antennas are often a dipole design.

- **Parabolic:** Also known as dish antennas, *parabolic antennas* are directional dish antennas made of meshed wire grid or solid metal. Parabolic antennas are used to extend wireless ranges over great distances.

- **Sectorized:** Similar in shape to omni-directional antennas, *sectorized antennas* have reflectors that direct transmitted signals in a specific direction (usually a 60- to 120-degree pattern) to provide additional range and decrease interference in a specific direction.

- **Yagi:** Similar in appearance to a small aerial TV antenna, *yagi antennas* are used for long distances in point-to-point or point-to-multipoint wireless applications.

Client devices in a Wi-Fi network include desktop and laptop PCs, as well as mobile devices and other endpoints (such as smartphones, medical devices, barcode scanners, and many so-called "smart" devices such as thermostats and other home automation devices). Wireless network interface cards (WNICs), or wireless cards, come in a variety of form factors such as PCI adapters, PC cards, and USB adapters, or they are built into wireless-enabled devices, such as laptop PCs, tablets, and smartphones.

Access points and the wireless cards that connect to them must use the same WLAN 802.11 standard or be backward-compatible. See the section "WLAN technologies and protocols," earlier in this chapter, for a list of the 802.11 specifications.

Access points (APs) can operate in one of four modes:

- **Root mode:** The default configuration for most APs. The AP is directly connected to the wired network, and wireless clients access the wired network via the wireless access point. Also known as *infrastructure* mode.

- **Repeater mode:** The AP doesn't connect directly to the wired network, but instead provides an upstream link to another AP, effectively extending the range of the WLAN. Also known as *stand-alone* mode.

- **Bridge mode:** A rare configuration that isn't supported in most APs. Bridge mode is used to connect two separate wired network segments via a wireless access point.

- **Mesh mode:** Multiple APs work together to create the appearance of a single Wi-Fi network for larger homes and workspaces.

TIP

Ad hoc is a type of WLAN architecture that doesn't have any APs. The wireless devices communicate directly with each other in a peer-to-peer network, such as between two notebook computers.

PHYSICAL LAYER (LAYER 1)

The Physical Layer sends and receives bits across the network medium (cabling or wireless links) from one device to another.

It specifies the electrical, mechanical, and functional requirements of the network, including network topology, cabling and connectors, and interface types, as well as the process for converting bits to electrical (or light) signals that can be transmitted across the physical medium. Various network topologies, made from copper or fiber-optic wires and cables, hubs, and other physical materials, comprise the Physical Layer.

Network topologies

There are four basic network topologies defined at the Physical Layer. Although there are many variations of the basic types — such as Fiber Distributed Data Interface (FDDI), star-bus (or tree), and star-ring — we stick to the basics here:

>> **Star.** Each individual node on the network is directly connected to a switch, hub, or concentrator. All data communications must pass through the switch (or hub), which can become a bottleneck or single point of failure. A star topology is ideal for practically any size environment and is the most common basic topology in use today. A star topology is also easy to install and maintain, and network faults are easily isolated without affecting the rest of the network.

>> **Mesh.** All systems are interconnected to provide multiple paths to all other resources. In most networks, a partial mesh is implemented for only the most critical network components, such as routers, switches, and servers (by using multiple network interface cards [NICs] or server clustering) to eliminate single points of failure.

>> **Ring.** A closed loop that connects end devices in a continuous ring. Functionally, this is achieved by connecting individual devices to a Multistation Access Unit (MSAU or MAU). Physically, this setup gives the ring topology the appearance of a star topology. Ring topologies are common in token ring and FDDI networks. In a ring topology, all communication travels in a single direction around the ring.

>> **Bus.** In a *bus* (or *linear bus*) topology, all devices are connected to a single cable (the *backbone*) that's terminated on both ends. Bus networks were commonly used for very small networks because they're inexpensive and easy to install. However, in large environments, they're impractical because the media has physical limitations (namely, the length of the cabling), the backbone is a single point of failure (a break anywhere on the network affects the entire network), and tracing a fault in a large network can be extremely difficult. Bus networks are extremely rare today and are no longer the least-expensive or easiest-to-install network option.

Cable and connector types

Cables carry the electrical or light signals that represent data between devices on a network. Data signaling is described by several characteristics, including type (see the sidebar "Analog and digital signaling," in this chapter), control mechanism (see the sidebar "Asynchronous and synchronous communications," in this chapter), and classification (either baseband or broadband). *Baseband* signaling uses a single channel for transmission of digital signals and is common in LANs that use twisted-pair cabling. *Broadband* signaling uses many channels over a range of frequencies for transmission of analog signals, including voice, video, and data. The four basic cable types used in networks include

>> **Coaxial cable.** Coaxial (abbreviated as coax and pronounced *KOH-axe*) cable consists of a single, solid-copper-wire core, surrounded by a plastic or Teflon insulator, braided-metal shielding, and (sometimes) a metal foil wrap, all covered with a plastic sheath. This construction makes the cable very durable and resistant to Electromagnetic Interference (EMI) and Radio Frequency Interference (RFI) signals. Coax cable is commonly used to connect cable or satellite television receivers (the cable that goes from the black box to the wall). Note that coax cable used for television signals is not compatible with coax cable used for computer networking due to different capacitance. Coax cable comes in two flavors, thick and thin:

- **Thick:** Also known as *RG8* or *RG11* or *thicknet*. Thicknet cable uses a screw-type connector, known as an *Attachment Unit Interface (AUI)*.

- **Thin:** Also known as *RG58* or *thinnet*. Thinnet cable is typically connected to network devices by using a bayonet-type connector, known as a *BNC (Bayonet Neill-Concelman) connector*.

» **Twinaxial cable.** Twinaxial (also known as twinax) cable is very similar to coax cable, but it consists of *two* solid copper-wire cores, rather than a single core. Twinax is used to achieve high data transmission speeds (for example, 10 Gb Ethernet [abbreviated as GE, GbE or GigE]) over very short distances (for example, 10 meters) at a relatively low cost. Typical applications for twinax cabling include SANs and top-of-rack network switches that connect critical servers to a high-speed core. Other advantages of twinax cabling include lower transceiver latency (delay in transmitter/receiver devices) and power consumption (compared to 10 GbE twisted-pair cables), and low bit error ratios (BERs).

TECHNICAL
STUFF

Bit error ratio (BER) is the ratio of incorrectly received bits to total received bits over a specified period of time.

» **Twisted-pair cable.** Twisted-pair cable is the most popular LAN cable in use today. It's lightweight, flexible, inexpensive, and easy to install. One easily recognized example of twisted-pair cable is common telephone wire.

Twisted-pair cable consists of four copper-wire pairs that are twisted together to improve the transmission quality of the cable by reducing crosstalk and attenuation. The tighter the twisted pairs, the better the transmission speed and quality.

TECHNICAL
STUFF

Crosstalk occurs when a signal transmitted over one channel or circuit negatively affects the signal transmitted over another channel or circuit. An (ancient) example of crosstalk occurred over analog phone lines when you could hear parts of other conversations over the phone. *Attenuation* is the gradual loss of intensity of a wave (for example, electrical or light) while it travels over (or through) a medium.

Currently, ten categories of twisted-pair cabling exist, but only Cat 5/5e, Cat 6/6a, and Cat 7/7a cable are typically used for networking today (see Table 6-11).

Twisted-pair cable can be either unshielded (UTP) or shielded (STP). UTP cabling is more common because it's easier to work with and less expensive than STP. STP is used when noise is a problem or when security is a major concern, and is popular in IBM rings. Noise is produced by external sources and can distort or otherwise impair the quality of a signal. Examples of noise include RFI and EMI from sources such as electrical motors, radio signals, fluorescent lights, microwave ovens, and electronic equipment. Shielded cabling also reduces electromagnetic emissions that may be intercepted by an attacker.

TABLE 6-11 Commonly Used Twisted-Pair Cable Categories

Category	Use and Speed	Example
5 (not a TIA/EIA standard)	Data (up to 100 Mbps)	Fast Ethernet
5e	Data (up to 1000 Mbps at 100 MHz)	Gigabit Ethernet
6	Data (up to 1000 Mbps at 250 MHz)	Gigabit Ethernet
6a	Data (up to 10 Gbps at 500 MHz)	10 Gigabit Ethernet
7	Data (up to 10 Gbps at 600 MHz up to 100 meters)	10 Gigabit Ethernet
7a	Data (up to 100 Gbps at 1000 MHz up to 15 meters)	40 Gigabit Ethernet

REMEMBER

TEMPEST is a (previously classified) U.S. military term that refers to the study of electromagnetic emissions from computers and related equipment.

Twisted-pair cable is terminated with an RJ-type terminator. The three common types of RJ-type connectors are RJ-11, RJ-45, and RJ-49. Although these connectors are all similar in appearance (particularly RJ-45 and RJ-49), only RJ-45 connectors are used for LANs. RJ-11 connectors are used for analog phone lines, and RJ-49 connectors are commonly used for Integrated Services Digital Network (ISDN) lines and WAN interfaces.

>> **Fiber-optic cable.** Fiber-optic cable is typically used in backbone networks and high-availability networks (such as FDDI). Fiber-optic cable carries data as light signals, rather than as electrical signals. Fiber-optic cable consists of a glass or plastic core or bundle, a glass insulator (commonly known as *cladding*), Kevlar fiber strands (for strength), and a polyvinyl chloride (PVC) or Teflon outer sheath. Advantages of fiber-optic cable include high speeds, long distances, and resistance to interception and interference. Fiber-optic cable is terminated with an SC-type (square connector), ST-type (straight tip), or LC-type (Lucent, little, or local connector) connector (see Table 6-12 for a comparison of the various cable types and their characteristics).

TECHNICAL STUFF

Ethernet designations, such as 10Base-T or 100Base-TX, refer to the capacity of the cable and the signaling type (baseband). The last part of the designation is less strictly defined. It may refer to the approximate maximum length (as in 10Base-2 and 10Base-5), the type of connector (as in 10Base-T, 100Base-TX, and 100Base-F), or the type and speed of the connector (as in 1000Base-T/GbE).

TABLE 6-12   **Cable Types and Characteristics**

Cable Type	Ethernet Designation	Maximum Length	EMI/RFI Resistance
RG58 (thinnet)	10Base-2	185 m	Good
RG8/11 (thicknet)	10Base-5	500 m	Better
UTP	10Base-T 100Base-TX 1000Base-T 10GbE	100 m	Poor
STP	10Base-T 100Base-TX 1000Base-T 10GbE	100 m	Fair to good
Fiber-optic	100Base-F	2,000 m	Best (EFI and RFI have no effect on fiber-optic cable)

ANALOG AND DIGITAL SIGNALING

Analog signaling conveys information through a continuous signal by using variations of wave amplitude, frequency, and phase.

Digital signaling conveys information in pulses through the presence or absence (on-off) of electrical signals.

Interface types

The interface between the Data Terminal Equipment (DTE) and Data Communications Equipment (DCE), which we discuss in the following section, is specified at the Physical Layer.

REMEMBER

Network topologies, cable and connector types, and interfaces are defined at the Physical Layer of the OSI model.

Common interface standards include

» **EIA/TIA-232-F:** This standard supports circuits at signal speeds of up to 115,200 bits per second (formerly known as *RS-232*).

» **V.24. ITU-T:** This standard is essentially the same as the EIA/TIA-232 standard.

» **V.35. ITU-T:** This standard describes a synchronous communications protocol between network access devices and a packet network that supports speeds of up to 48 Kbps.

>> **X.21bis. ITU-T:** Formerly CCITT. This standard defines the communications protocol between DCE and DTE in an X.25 network. It's essentially the same as the EIA/TIA-232 standard.

>> **High-Speed Serial Interface (HSSI):** This network standard was developed to address the need for high-speed (up to 52 Mbps) serial connections over WAN links.

Networking equipment

Networking devices that operate at the Physical Layer include network interface cards (NICs), network media (cabling, connectors, and interfaces, all of which we discuss in the section "Cable and connector types," earlier in this chapter), repeaters, and hubs.

Network interface cards (NICs) are used to connect a computer to the network. NICs may be integrated on a computer motherboard or installed as an adapter card, such as an ISA, PCI, or PC card. Similar to a NIC, a WIC (WAN interface card) contains a built-in CSU/DSU and is used to connect a router to a digital circuit. Variations of WICs include HWICs (high-speed WAN interface cards) and VWICs (voice WAN interface cards).

A *repeater* is a non-intelligent device that simply amplifies a signal to compensate for *attenuation* (signal loss) so that one can extend the length of the cable segment.

A *hub* (or *concentrator*) is used to connect multiple LAN devices together, such as servers and workstations. The two basic types of hubs are

>> **Passive:** Data enters one port and exits all other ports without any signal amplification or regeneration.

>> **Active:** Combines the features of a passive hub and repeater. Also known as a *multi-port repeater*.

A *switch* is used to connect multiple LAN devices together. Unlike a hub, a switch doesn't send outgoing packets to all devices on the network, but instead sends packets only to actual destination devices.

The TCP/IP Model

The Transmission Control Protocol/Internet Protocol (TCP/IP) Model is similar to the OSI Reference Model. It was originally developed by the U.S. Department of Defense and actually preceded the OSI model. However, the TCP/IP model is not as widely used as a learning and troubleshooting tool as the OSI model today. The most notable difference between the TCP/IP model and the OSI model is that the TCP/IP model consists of only four layers, rather than seven (see Figure 6-4).

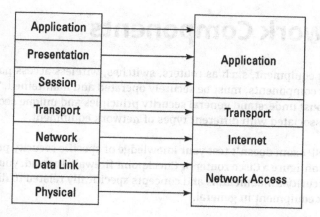

FIGURE 6-4:
Comparing the
OSI model and
the TCP/IP Model.

The OSI Model   **The TCP/IP Model**

>> **Application Layer:** Consists of network applications and processes, and loosely corresponds to the upper layers of the OSI model (Application, Presentation, and Session layers).

>> **Transport Layer:** Provides end-to-end delivery and corresponds to the OSI Transport Layer.

>> **Internet Layer:** Defines the IP datagram and routing, and corresponds to the OSI Network Layer.

>> **Network Access (or Link) Layer:** Contains routines for accessing physical networks and corresponds to the OSI Data Link and Physical layers.

Cryptography used to maintain communication security

Communication between devices often passes over networks that have varying risks of eavesdropping and interference by adversaries. While the endpoints involved in a communication session may be protected, the communication itself might not be. For this reason, cryptography is often employed to make communication unreadable by anyone (or any *thing*) that may be able to intercept them. Like the courier running an encrypted message through a battlefield in ancient times, an encrypted message in the modern context of computers and the Internet cannot be read by others.

Because there are so many different contexts and types of cryptography in data communication, cryptography is discussed throughout this chapter. Chapter 5 contains an extended section on cryptography.

Secure Network Components

Network equipment, such as routers, switches, wireless access points, and other network components, must be securely operated and maintained. The CISSP candidate must understand general security principles and unique security considerations associated with different types of network equipment.

TIP

The CISSP exam doesn't test your knowledge of specific security products, such as how to configure a Cisco router or Checkpoint firewall. Instead, you need to understand security fundamentals and concepts specifically related to different types of network equipment in general.

Operation of hardware

Network equipment, such as routers and switches (discussed earlier in this chapter), as well as firewalls, intrusion detection systems, wireless access points and other components (discussed in the following sections) must be securely deployed, operated, and maintained. Aspects of proper operation of hardware include

- >> **Training.** Personnel who deploy and manage hardware devices should receive proper training on the management of those devices.

- >> **Procedures.** Routine actions taken on hardware devices should be formally documented, so personnel will perform them consistently.

- >> **Standards.** The organization should establish standards for the secure and consistent configuration of hardware devices. This will ensure that multiple devices will be similarly (if not identically) configured, and that such configuration will not compromise the security of the organization's environment.

- >> **Monitoring.** The organization should monitor its hardware devices so that appropriate personnel are informed of security incidents, malfunctions, and other notable events.

- >> **Managed change.** Configuration changes, software updates, and security patching on hardware devices should be made through the organization's change management processes.

Transmission media

Network transmission media includes wired (for example, copper and fiber) and wireless. Wired transmission media is defined at the Physical Layer of the OSI model (discussed previously in this chapter). Wireless transmission media is defined at the Data Link Layer of the OSI model (discussed previously in this chapter). Additionally, the CISSP candidate must understand Wi-Fi security techniques and protocols.

Protecting wired networks

Aside from the use of encryption to render any intercepted communications unreadable by unauthorized parties, it's also important to protect communication media from eavesdropping and sabotage. Techniques available to protect wired network media include

>> **Conduit.** Running communications cabling through conduit is a great way to make wiring more difficult to access.

>> **Physical access control.** Where communications cabling passes through rooms and corridors, to the greatest extent possible, physical access controls should be used so that only authorized personnel are permitted to get near any cabling. Controls may include key card access systems, locking cabinets, and video surveillance.

Protecting Wi-Fi networks

Security on wireless networks, as with all security, is best implemented by using a defense-in-depth approach. Security techniques and protocols include broadcast of SSIDs, authentication, and encryption using WEP, WPA, and WPA2.

SERVICE SET IDENTIFIER (SSID)

An SSID is a name (up to 32 characters) that uniquely identifies a wireless network. A wireless client must know the SSID to connect to the WLAN. However, most APs broadcast their SSID (or the SSID can be easily sniffed), so the security provided by an SSID is largely inconsequential.

WIRED EQUIVALENT PRIVACY (WEP)

As its name implies, WEP was originally conceived as a security protocol to provide the same level of confidentiality that wired networks have. However, significant weaknesses were quickly uncovered in the WEP protocol.

WEP uses an RC4 stream cipher for confidentiality and a CRC-32 checksum for integrity. WEP uses either a 40-bit or 104-bit key with a 24-bit initialization vector (IV) to form a 64-bit or 128-bit key. Because of the relatively short initialization vector used (and other flaws), WEP keys can be easily cracked by readily available software in a matter of minutes.

WEP supports two methods of authentication:

>> **Open System authentication:** Doesn't require a wireless client to present credentials during authentication. After the client associates with the access point, WEP encrypts the data that's transmitted over the wireless network.

>> **Shared Key authentication:** Uses a four-way handshake to authenticate and associate the wireless client with the access point, then encrypts the data.

Despite its many security flaws, WEP is still used in both residential and business networks as the default security protocol. WEP security can be enhanced by using tunneling protocols such as IPsec and SSH, but other security protocols are available to enhance WLAN security, as discussed in the following section.

WI-FI PROTECTED ACCESS (WPA AND WPA2)

WPA and WPA2 provide significant security enhancements over WEP and were introduced as a quick fix to address the flaws in WEP while the 802.11i wireless security standard was being developed.

WPA uses the Temporal Key Integrity Protocol (TKIP) to address some of the encryption problems in WEP. TKIP combines a secret root key with the initialization vector by using a key-mixing function. WPA also implements a sequence counter to prevent replay attacks and a 64-bit message integrity check. Despite these improvements, WPA that uses TKIP is now considered insufficient because of some well-known attacks.

WPA and WPA2 also support various EAP extensions (see the section "Remote access," later in this chapter) to further enhance WLAN security. These extensions include EAP-TLS (Transport Layer Security), EAP-TTLS (Tunneled Transport Layer Security), and Protected EAP (PEAPv0 and v1).

Further security enhancements were introduced in WPA2. WPA2 uses the AES-based algorithm Counter Mode with Cipher Block Chaining Message Authentication Code Protocol (CCMP), which replaces TKIP and WEP to produce a WLAN protocol that is far more secure.

TIP

For more information on the topic of wireless network security, pick up a copy of *Hacking Wireless Networks For Dummies* by our friends Kevin Beaver and Peter T. Davis.

Network access control devices

Network access control (NAC) devices include firewalls (and proxies), intrusion detection systems (IDSs) and intrusion prevention systems (IPSs).

Firewalls

A *firewall* controls traffic flow between a trusted network (such as a home network or corporate LAN) and an untrusted or public network (such as the Internet). A firewall can comprise hardware, software, or a combination of both hardware and software.

FIREWALL TYPES

There are three basic classifications of firewalls: packet-filtering, circuit-level gateway, and application-level gateway.

REMEMBER

Three basic types of firewalls are packet-filtering, circuit-level gateway, and application-level gateway.

Packet-filtering

A packet-filtering firewall (or *screening router*), one of the most basic (and inexpensive) types of firewalls, is ideally suited for a low-risk environment. A *packet-filtering firewall* permits or denies traffic based solely on the TCP, UDP, ICMP, and IP headers of the individual packets. It examines the traffic direction (inbound or outbound), the source and destination IP addresses, and the source and destination TCP or UDP port numbers. This information is compared with predefined rules that have been configured in an access control list (ACL) to determine whether each packet should be permitted or denied. A packet-filtering firewall typically operates at the Network Layer or Transport Layer of the OSI model. Some advantages of a packet-filtering firewall are

- ➤➤ It's inexpensive. (It can be implemented as a router ACL, which is free — the ACL, not the router!)
- ➤➤ It's fast and flexible.
- ➤➤ It's transparent to users.

Disadvantages of packet-filtering firewalls are

- ➤➤ Access decisions are based only on address and port information, rather than more sophisticated information such as the packet's content, context, or application.
- ➤➤ It has no protection from IP or DNS address spoofing (forged addresses).
- ➤➤ It doesn't support strong user authentication.
- ➤➤ Configuring and maintaining ACLs can be difficult.
- ➤➤ Logging information may be limited.

A more advanced variation of the packet-filtering firewall is the *dynamic packet-filtering firewall*. This type of firewall supports dynamic modification of the firewall rule base by using context-based access control (CBAC) or reflexive ACLs — both of which create dynamic access list rules for individual sessions as they are established. For example, an ACL might be automatically created to allow a user working from the corporate network (inside the firewall) to connect to an FTP server outside the firewall in order to upload and download files between her PC and the FTP server. When the file transfer is completed, the ACL is automatically deleted from the firewall.

Circuit-level gateway

A circuit-level gateway controls access by maintaining state information about established connections. When a permitted connection is established between two hosts, a *tunnel* (or virtual circuit) is created for the session, allowing packets to flow freely between the two hosts without the need for further inspection of individual packets. This type of firewall operates at the Session Layer (Layer 5) of the OSI model.

Advantages of this type of firewall include

>> Speed (After a connection is established, individual packets aren't analyzed.)

>> Support for many protocols

>> Easy maintenance

Disadvantages of this type of firewall include

>> Dependence on the trustworthiness of the communicating users or hosts. (After a connection is established, individual packets aren't analyzed.)

>> Limited logging information about individual data packets is available after the initial connection is established.

A *stateful inspection firewall* is a type of circuit-level gateway that captures data packets at the Network Layer and then queues and *analyzes* (examines the state and context of) these packets at the upper layers of the OSI model.

Application-level gateway

An application-level (or Application Layer) gateway operates at the Application Layer of the OSI model, processing data packets for specific IP applications. This type of firewall is generally considered the most secure and is commonly implemented as a proxy server. In a *proxy server*, no direct communication between two hosts is permitted. Instead, data packets are intercepted by the proxy server, which analyzes the packet's contents and — if permitted by the firewall rules — sends a copy of the original packet to the intended host.

Advantages of this type of firewall include

>> Data packets aren't transmitted directly to communicating hosts, a tactic that masks the internal network's design and prevents direct access to services on internal hosts.

>> It can be used to implement strong user authentication in applications.

Disadvantages of this type of firewall include

>> It reduces network performance because packets must be passed up to the Application Layer of the OSI model to be analyzed.

>> It must be tailored to specific applications. (Such customization can be difficult to maintain or update for new or changing protocols.)

Web application firewall

A *web application firewall* (WAF) is used to protect a web server (or group of web servers) from various types of web application attacks such as script injection and buffer overflow attacks. A WAF examines the contents of each packet being sent to a web server and employs rules to determine whether each packet is considered routine and friendly, or hostile.

FIREWALL ARCHITECTURES

The basic firewall *types* that we discuss in the preceding sections may be implemented by using one of the firewall *architectures* described in the following sections. The four basic types of firewall architectures are screening router, dual-homed gateway, screened-host gateway, and screened-subnet.

Screening router

A *screening router* is the most basic type of firewall architecture employed. An external router is placed between the untrusted and trusted networks, and a security policy is implemented by using ACLs. Although a router functions as a choke point between a trusted network and an untrusted network, an attacker — after gaining access to a host on the trusted network — may potentially be able to compromise the entire network.

Advantages of a screening router architecture include these:

>> It's completely transparent.

>> It's relatively simple to use and inexpensive.

Disadvantages of the screening router architecture include these:

>> It may have difficulty handling certain traffic.

>> It has limited or no logging available.

>> It doesn't employ user authentication.

>> It makes masking the internal network structure difficult.

>> It has a single point of failure.

>> It doesn't truly implement a firewall choke-point strategy because it isn't truly a firewall or a choke-point — it's a router that passes traffic between two networks (the "private" and "public" network).

Still, using a screening router architecture is better than using nothing.

Dual-homed gateways

Another common firewall architecture is the dual-homed gateway. A *dual-homed gateway* (or bastion host) is a system that has two network interfaces (NICs) and sits between an untrusted network and a trusted network. A *bastion host* is a general term often used to refer to proxies, gateways, firewalls, or any server that provides applications or services directly to an untrusted network. Because it's often the target of attackers, a bastion host is sometimes referred to as a *sacrificial lamb*.

However, this term is misleading because a bastion host is typically a hardened system that employs robust security mechanisms. A dual-homed gateway is often connected to the untrusted network via an external screening router. The dual-homed gateway functions as a proxy server for the trusted network and may be configured to require user authentication. A dual-homed gateway offers a more fail-safe operation than a screening router does because, by default, data isn't normally forwarded across the two interfaces. Advantages of the dual-homed gateway architecture include

>> It operates in a *fail-safe mode* — if it fails, it allows no access, rather than allowing full access for everyone.

>> Internal network structure is masked.

Disadvantages of the dual-homed gateway architecture include

>> Its use may inconvenience users by requiring them to authenticate to a proxy server or by introducing latency in the network.

>> Proxies may not be available for some services.

>> Its use may cause slower network performance.

>> It increases cost (adding a device to the architecture).

Screened-host gateways

A *screened-host gateway* architecture employs an external screening router and an internal bastion host. The screening router is configured so that the bastion host is the only host accessible from the untrusted network (such as the Internet). The bastion host provides any required web services to the untrusted network, such as HTTP and FTP, as permitted by the security policy. Connections to the Internet from the trusted network are routed via an application proxy on the bastion host or directly through the screening router.

Here are some of the advantages of the screened-host gateway:

>> It provides distributed security between two devices, rather than relying on a single device to perform all security functions.

>> It has transparent outbound access.

>> It has restricted inbound access.

Here are some disadvantages of the screened-host gateway:

>> It's considered less secure because the screening router can bypass the bastion host for certain trusted services.

>> Masking the internal network structure is difficult.

>> It can have multiple single points of failure (the router or bastion host).

>> It increases cost (adding a device to the architecture).

Screened-subnet

The screened-subnet is perhaps the most secure of the currently designed firewall architectures. The screened-subnet employs an external screening router, a dual-homed (or multi-homed) host, and a second internal screening router. This implements the concept of a network DMZ (or *demilitarized zone*). Publicly available services are placed on bastion hosts in the DMZ.

Advantages of the screened-subnet architecture include these:

>> It's transparent to end-users.

>> It's flexible.

>> Internal network structure can be masked.

>> It provides *defense in depth* instead of relying on a single device to provide security for the entire network.

Disadvantages of a screened-subnet architecture, compared to other firewall architectures, include these:

>> It's more expensive.

>> It's more difficult to configure and maintain.

>> It can be more difficult to troubleshoot.

Next-generation firewalls and unified threat management devices

Next-generation firewalls (often termed *next-gen firewalls* or NGFWs) and unified threat management devices (often called UTMs) are similar terms describing firewalls with multiple functions, including combinations of the following security devices:

>> **Firewall** (of course!)

>> **IDS/IPS** (discussed in the following section)

>> **VPN** (discussed earlier in this chapter)

>> **Web content filtering** (discussed later in this chapter)

>> **Cloud access security broker (CASB)** (discussed later in this chapter)

>> **Web application firewall (WAF)** (discussed earlier in this chapter)

>> **DLP** (discussed later in this chapter)

The main advantage of next-gen firewalls and UTM is greater simplicity. Rather than having to manage many separate security systems, all of these security functions are performed within a single device.

Intrusion detection and prevention systems (IDSs, IPSs, and IDPSs)

Intrusion detection is defined as real-time monitoring and analysis of network activity and data for potential vulnerabilities and attacks in progress. One major limitation of current intrusion-detection-system (IDS) technologies is the requirement to filter false alarms to prevent the operator (the system or security administrator) from being overwhelmed with data. IDSs are classified in many different ways, including active and passive, network-based and host-based, and knowledge-based and behavior-based.

TIP

Intrusion detection systems (IDS) and intrusion prevention systems (IPS) are sometimes referred to as intrusion detection and prevention systems (IDPS).

ACTIVE AND PASSIVE IDS

Commonly known as an *intrusion prevention system* (IPS) or as an *intrusion detection and prevention system* (IDPS), an *active IDS* is a system that's configured to automatically block suspected attacks in progress without requiring any intervention by an operator. IPS has the advantage of providing real-time corrective action in response to an attack, but it has many disadvantages as well. An IPS must be placed inline along a network boundary; thus the IPS itself is susceptible to attack. Also, if false alarms and legitimate traffic haven't been properly identified and filtered, authorized users and applications may be improperly denied access. Finally, the IPS itself may be used to effect a *Denial of Service* (DoS) attack, which involves intentionally flooding the system with alarms that cause it to block connections until no connection or bandwidth is available.

A *passive* IDS is a system that's configured to monitor and analyze network traffic activity and alert an operator to potential vulnerabilities and attacks. It can't perform any protective or corrective functions on its own. The major advantages of passive IDS are that these systems can be easily and rapidly deployed and aren't normally susceptible to attack themselves. Passive IDS is usually connected to a network segment via a tap (physical or virtual) or switched port analyzer (SPAN) port.

An *IDS* is a passive system that monitors, analyzes, and alerts. *IPS* is an active system that monitors, analyzes, and acts (such as alert, block, or drop).

REMEMBER

NETWORK-BASED AND HOST-BASED IDS

A *network-based IDS* (NIDS) usually consists of a network appliance (or sensor) that includes a Network Interface Card (NIC) operating in *Promiscuous* mode (meaning it listens to, or "sniffs," all traffic on the network, not just traffic addressed to a specific host) and a separate management interface. The IDS is placed along a network segment or boundary, and it monitors all traffic on that segment.

A *host-based IDS* (HIDS) requires small programs (or *agents*) to be installed on the individual systems that are to be monitored. The agents monitor the operating system and write data to log files and/or trigger alarms. A host-based IDS can monitor only the individual host systems on which the agents are installed; it doesn't monitor the entire network.

KNOWLEDGE-BASED AND BEHAVIOR-BASED IDS

A *knowledge-based* (or *signature-based*) IDS references a database of previous attack profiles and known system vulnerabilities to identify active intrusion attempts.

Knowledge-based IDSs are currently more common than behavior-based IDSs. Advantages of knowledge-based systems include

>> They have lower false-alarm rates than behavior-based IDSs.

>> Alarms are more standardized and more easily understood than behavior-based IDS alarms.

Disadvantages of knowledge-based systems include

>> The signature database must be continually updated and maintained.

>> New, unique, or original attacks may not be detected or may be improperly classified.

A *behavior-based* (or *statistical anomaly-based*) IDS references a baseline or learned pattern of normal system activity to identify active intrusion attempts. Deviations from this baseline or pattern cause an alarm to be triggered. Advantages of behavior-based systems include that they

>> Dynamically adapt to new, unique, or original attacks.

>> Are less dependent on identifying specific operating system vulnerabilities than knowledge-based IDSs are.

Disadvantages of behavior-based systems include

>> Higher false alarm rates than knowledge-based IDSs.

>> An inability to adapt to legitimate usage patterns that may change often and therefore aren't static enough to implement an effective behavior-based IDS.

Web content filters

A web content filter is typically an inline device that monitors and controls internal users' access to Internet web sites. Web content filters can be configured to block access to both specific web sites and categories of web sites (for example, blocking access to sites that discuss polka music).

Organizations that use web content filters to block access to categories of web sites are often trying to keep employees from accessing sites that are not related to work. The use of web content filters also helps to enforce policies and protect the organization from potential liability. (For example, blocking access to pornographic and hate-related websites helps to enforce sexual harassment and racial discrimination/safe working environment policies, and can help to demonstrate due diligence).

Web content filters typically employ large databases of websites that are constantly being evaluated and updated by the security vendor of the content filtering software. These databases often contain errors in classification, which will require policies and procedures for employees to request access to legitimate websites or access to blocked websites for legitimate work purposes. These processes often can be frustrating for employees, particularly if it takes more than a few minutes for the security team to respond to the request. An alternate policy used by many organizations is "trust but verify". Websites are not blocked, but users are warned prior to navigating to a potentially suspicious, dangerous, offensive, or otherwise inappropriate website; the individual user must positively acknowledge that they understand the risk and that they are visiting the site for a legitimate purpose. The website visit is logged and reported; typically, appropriate security or human resources personnel will follow up with the employee, if necessary.

Tech savvy users often use various proxy software programs in an attempt to circumvent web content filters. Proxy software is a significant risk to enterprise security and should be explicitly forbidden by policy. Next-generation firewalls and certain advanced web content filters are capable of detecting proxy software in the enterprise.

Data loss prevention

Data loss prevention (DLP) refers to a class of security products that are designed to detect and (optionally) prevent the exfiltration of sensitive data over an organization's network connections. DLP systems work by performing pattern matching (for example, XXX–XX–XXXX representing a Social Security Number, or XXXX XXXX XXXX XXXX representing a credit card number) against data transmitted over the network. Depending on the type of DLP system and its configuration, the DLP system can either generate an alert describing the suspected data exfiltration or block the transmission altogether.

There is another class of DLP products that are used to scan file servers and database management systems in search of sensitive data. The idea is that people sometimes extract sensitive data from sanctioned repositories and then make copies of that data and store it in less secure locations.

Cloud access security brokers

Cloud access security broker (CASB) systems are used to monitor and control end-user access to cloud-based services. For instance, if an organization uses Box.com for unstructured file storage, a CASB system can be configured to block end-user access to alternative storage services such as Dropbox and Skydrive.

Organizations generally use CASB systems to limit the exfiltration of sensitive information and steer personnel to officially sanctioned applications. They can be thought of as security policy enforcement points.

Endpoint security

It's often said that security is only as strong as its weakest link. And that weakest link often is the endpoint. Endpoints, including desktop and laptop computers, smartphones, tablets, and other mobile equipment (such as medical devices, bar-code scanners, and other so-called "smart" devices), have become very attractive targets for cybercriminals. Endpoints are particularly vulnerable to attack for many reasons, including:

>> **Number and variety.** The sheer number and variety of endpoints on the network creates numerous opportunities for an attacker to exploit vulnerabilities in different operating systems and applications. Keeping all endpoints properly patched in a timely manner is also a challenge.

>> **End users.** Endpoints are operated by end users with varying computer skill levels and awareness of security and privacy issues. End users are susceptible to social engineering, and many end users willingly circumvent security measures on endpoints for the sake of convenience (for example, rooting a smartphone to install free or unauthorized apps).

>> **Privilege.** In some organizations, end-user accounts have the role of "local administrator." This means that any action carried out by an end user is executed at the highest level of privilege on the system. This can make malware attacks on endpoints far more potent.

>> **Prioritization.** Endpoints are often treated as "lower value" assets on the network. For this reason, security efforts are typically focused on the data center and higher value assets, such as servers and databases.

At its most basic level, endpoint security consists of anti-malware (or antivirus) software. *Signature-based* software is the most common type of antivirus software used on endpoints. Signature-based antivirus software scans an endpoint's hard drive and memory in real time and at scheduled times. If a known malware signature is detected, the software performs an action, such as:

>> **Quarantine:** Isolates the infected file on the endpoint so that it can't infect other files.

>> **Delete:** Removes the infected file.

>> **Alert:** Notifies the user (and/or security administrator) that malware has been detected.

Signature-based antivirus software must be kept up to date to be effective, and it can only detect known threats. The endpoint is vulnerable to any new "zero-day" malware threats until a signature is created by the software vendor and uploaded to the endpoint.

Application whitelisting is another common anti-malware approach used for endpoint protection. This approach requires a positive control model on the endpoint — only applications that have been explicitly authorized can be run on the endpoint. Trends such as "bring your own device" (BYOD) that allow end users to use their personal devices for work-related purposes make application whitelisting approaches difficult to implement in the enterprise. Another limitation of application whitelisting is that an application (such as Microsoft Word or Adobe Acrobat) that has already been whitelisted can be run on an endpoint, even if that application is exploited (for example, with a malicious Word document or Adobe PDF).

Behavior-based (also known as *heuristics-based* or *anomaly-based*) endpoint protection attempts to create a baseline of "normal" activity on the endpoint. Any unusual activity (as determined by the baseline) is detected and stopped. Unfortunately, behavior-based software is prone to high false positives and typically requires significant computing resources.

Container-based endpoint protection isolates any vulnerable processes running on an endpoint by creating virtual barriers around individual processes. If a malicious process is detected, the software kills the process before the malicious process can infect any legitimate processes on the endpoint. Container-based approaches typically require significant computing resources and extensive knowledge of any applications running on the endpoint.

In addition to anti-malware prevention, endpoint protection should include

>> **Access controls.** Access controls should be enabled and enforced on all endpoints, including smartphones and tablets (such as PINs, passwords, passphrases, swipe patterns, and biometrics such as fingerprint and facial recognition).

>> **Automatic lockout.** Endpoints should be configured to automatically lock after a few minutes of non-activity, so that others will not be able to use them.

>> **Encryption.** Drive encryption should be enabled to protect data on the endpoint device.

>> **Firewalls.** An OS-based or third-party firewall should be installed and configured on each endpoint.

>> **Patch management.** Applications and the endpoint OS must be kept patched and up-to-date.

- » **Host-based intrusion prevention systems (HIPS).** Some organizations deploy HIPS on endpoints to provide additional protection.

- » **Network controls.** Network controls include next-generation firewalls (that can identify and authenticate endpoints and users), virtual private networks (VPNs), intrusion prevention systems (IPS), and network segmentation.

- » **Administrative control.** Endpoints should be configured so that any firmware settings and boot control is password protected. Endpoint operating systems should be configured so users are not local administrators.

- » **Physical security.** Endpoints should be protected from unauthorized access and theft. Endpoints should not be left unattended; they should be locked so that they cannot be accessed by unauthorized personnel and physically tethered or locked so that they cannot be stolen.

Content distribution networks

Content distribution (or delivery) networks (*CDNs*) are large distributed networks of servers that cache web content, such as static web pages, downloadable objects, on-demand and streaming music and video, and web applications for subscriber organizations, and serve that content to Internet users over the most optimal network path available.

CDNs offload much of the performance demand on Internet-facing systems for subscriber organizations and many offer optional security services, such as distributed denial-of-service (DDoS) attack mitigation.

CDNs operate data centers throughout a large geographic region, or worldwide, and must ensure the security of their data center systems and networks for their customers. Service-level agreements (SLAs) and applicable regulatory compliance must be addressed when evaluating CDN providers.

Some CDN providers include optional web application firewall (WAF) capabilities that protect web servers from application layer attacks.

Physical devices

It's often said in the information security profession: If an adversary obtains physical access to a target system, it's *game over*. In other words, an adversary with physical access to a device is often able to take complete control of the device, to the detriment of its owner.

HERE COMES THE INTERNET OF THINGS (IoT)

The "Internet of things" (IoT) promises to keep security professionals busy for years to come. The Internet of Things refers to the proliferation of Internet-connected devices of every kind, including appliances, gadgets, and automobiles. While this tsunami of Internet-connected devices promises new connectivity, features, and convenience, there will inevitably be security issues galore.

Many (if not most) IoT devices do not have security integrated by design. This means that many of these devices can be easily hacked by intruders and used to steal information, or used as a springboard to access other systems on the same internal networks. Based on how long it took computer and network device manufacturers to start getting security right, it will be many years before IoT devices are sufficiently resistant to attacks and compromise.

More than that, an adversary who gains physical access to a device can also use that device as a means to access other devices, systems, and data in an organization's network.

The topic of physical access security is discussed in several areas of this book:

>> **Endpoints.** Covered in the "Endpoint Security" section in this chapter.

>> **Servers and Data Centers.** Covered in Chapter 5.

Design and Establish Secure Communication Channels

The CISSP exam requires knowledge of secure design principles and implementation of various communication technologies, including voice, email, Web, fax, multimedia collaboration, remote access, data, and virtualized networks.

Voice

PBX (Private Branch Exchange) switches, POTS (Plain Old Telephone Systems), and VoIP (Voice over Internet Protocol) switches are some of the most overlooked and costly aspects of a corporate telecommunications infrastructure. Many employees don't think twice about using a company telephone system for extended personal use, including long-distance calls. Personal use of company-supplied mobile phones is another area of widespread abuse. Perhaps the simplest and most effective countermeasure against internal abuse is to publish and enforce a corporate telephone-use policy. Regular auditing of telephone records is also effective for deterring and detecting telephone abuse. Similarly, as both voice communications and the global workforce have become increasingly mobile, organizations need to define and implement appropriate bring your own device (BYOD), choose your own device (CYOD), or corporate owned personally enabled (COPE) mobile device policies.

In recent years, cloud communications (also known as Unified Communications as a Service, or UCaaS) has become a viable alternative to PBX and on-premises VoIP systems for many organizations, from small and midsize businesses to large enterprises. Many cloud communications providers offer the same advanced features and functionality of on-premises PBX and VoIP systems, with all the business and technical benefits of the cloud.

Similarly, over-the-top (OTT) services, such as Skype, Jabber, Vonage, Vimeo, and Zoom, are increasingly common in business communications.

Finally, mobile operators are introducing innovations such as Voice over Long-Term Evolution (VoLTE), Voice over Wi-Fi (VoWiFi), and Wi-Fi Calling. 5G networks will begin to be made commercially available in the U.S. beginning in 2019, enabling new opportunities — and security challenges — in mobile communications, the Internet of Things (IoT), and machine-to-machine (M2M) communications, among other applications.

Types of attacks on voice communications systems include

>> **Identify fraud,** such as caller ID spoofing, eavesdropping, and vishing.

>> **Toll fraud,** such as number harvesting, call hijacking, spam over Internet telephony (SPIT), and spam over instant messaging (SPIM), and voice over misconfigured Internet telephones (VOMIT).

>> **Eavesdropping,** whereby an attacker uses techniques to intercept and monitor communications messages.

>> **Denial of service (DoS),** such as distributed denial of service (DDoS) attacks and telephony denial of service (TDoS) attacks.

Email

Email has emerged as one of the most important communication mediums in our global economy, with over 50 billion email messages sent worldwide every day.

Unfortunately, spam and phishing account for as much as 85 percent of that email volume. Spam is more than a minor nuisance — it's a serious security threat to all organizations worldwide.

The Simple Mail Transfer Protocol (SMTP) is used to send and receive email across the Internet. It operates on TCP/UDP port 25 and contains many well-known vulnerabilities. Most SMTP mail servers are configured by default to forward (or *relay*) all mail, regardless of whether the sender's or recipient's address is valid.

Failing to secure your organization's mail servers may allow spammers to misuse your servers and bandwidth as an *open relay* to propagate their spam. The bad news is that you'll eventually (it usually doesn't take more than a few days) get blacklisted by a large number of organizations that maintain real-time blackhole lists (RBLs) against open relays, effectively preventing most (if not all) email communications from your organization reaching their intended recipients. It usually takes several months to get removed from those RBLs after you've been blacklisted, and it does significant damage to your organization's communications infrastructure and credibility.

REMEMBER

Using RBLs is only one method to combat spam, and it's generally not even the most effective or reliable method, at that. The organizations that maintain these massive lists aren't perfect and do make mistakes. If a mistake is made with your domain or IP addresses, you'll curse their existence — it's a case in which the cure is sometimes worse than the disease.

Failure to make a reasonable effort towards spam prevention in your organization is a failure of due diligence. An organization that fails to implement appropriate countermeasures may find itself a defendant in a sexual harassment lawsuit from an employee inundated with pornographic emails sent by a spammer to his or her corporate email address. Plus, the failure to block spam and phishing exposes an organization to attack. Over 90 percent of security breaches begin with phishing messages, so it makes good sense to block spam and phishing by any means available.

Other risks associated with spam email include

>> **Missing or deleting important emails:** Your boss might inadvertently delete that email authorizing your promotion and pay raise because her inbox is flooded with spam and she gets trigger-happy with the Delete button — at least it's a convenient excuse!

>> **Viruses and other "mail-icious" code:** Although you seem to hear less about viruses in recent years, they're still prevalent, and email remains the favored medium for propagating them.

>> **Phishing and pharming scams:** *Phishing* and *pharming* attacks, in which victims are lured to an apparently legitimate website (typically online banking or auctions) ostensibly to validate their personal account information, are usually perpetrated through mass mailings. It's a complex scam increasingly perpetrated by organized criminals. Ultimately, phishing and pharming scams cost the victim his or her moolah — and possibly his or her identity. *Spear phishing* is a targeted phishing attack against a specific organization, and *whaling* is a targeted attack against a specific individual — usually someone wealthy, powerful, or prominent.

Countering these threats requires an arsenal of technical solutions and user-awareness efforts and is — at least, for now — a never-ending battle. Begin by securing your servers, end-user PCs, mobile devices, and IoT devices. Mail servers should always be placed in a DMZ or outsourced, and unnecessary or unused services should be disabled — and change that default relay setting! Most other servers, and almost all client PCs, should have port 25 disabled. Implement a spam filter or other secure mail gateway. Also, consider the following user-awareness tips:

TIP

>> **Never unsubscribe or reply to spam email.** Unsubscribe links in spam emails are often used to confirm the legitimacy of your email address, which can then be added to mass-mailing lists that are sold to other spammers. And, as tempting as it is to tell a spammer what you really think of his or her irresistible offer to enhance your social life or improve your financial portfolio, most spammers don't actually read your replies and (unfortunately) aren't likely to follow your suggestion that they jump off a cliff.

REMEMBER

Although legitimate offers from well-known retailers or newsletters from professional organizations may be thought of as spam by many people, it's likely that, at some point, a recipient of such a mass mailing actually signed up for that stuff — so it's technically not spam. Everyone seems to want your email address whenever you fill out an application for something, and providing your email address often translates to an open invitation for them to tell you about every sale from here to eternity. In such cases, senders are required by U.S. law to provide an Unsubscribe hyperlink in their mass mailings, and clicking it does remove the recipient from future mailings.

>> **Don't send auto-reply messages to Internet email addresses (if possible).** Mail servers can be configured not to send auto-reply messages (such as out-of-office messages) to Internet email addresses. However, this setting may not be (and probably isn't) practical in your organization. Be aware of the implications — auto-reply rules don't discriminate against spammers, so the spammers know when you're on vacation, too!

>> **Get a firewall for your home computer *before* you connect it to the Internet.** This admonishment is particularly true if you have an always-on, high-speed Internet connection such as cable, DSL, or fiber. Typically, a home

computer that has high-speed access will be scanned and attacked within minutes of being connected to the Internet. And if it isn't protected by a firewall, this computer will almost certainly be compromised and become an unsuspecting zombie in some spammer's bot-net army (over 250,000 new zombies are added to the Internet every day!). Then, you'll become part of the problem because your home computer and Internet bandwidth are used to send spam and phishing emails to thousands of other victims around the world, and you'll be left wondering why your brand-new state-of-the-art home computer is suddenly so slow and your blazing new high-speed Internet connection isn't so high-speed just two weeks after you got it.

REMEMBER

Your end users don't have to be CISSP-certified to secure their home computers. A simple firewall software package that has a basic configuration is usually enough to deter the majority of today's hackers — most are using automated tools to scan the Internet and don't bother to slow down for a computer that presents even the slightest challenge. Size matters in these bot-net armies, and far too many unprotected computers are out there to waste time (even a few minutes) defeating your firewall.

Spam is only the tip of the iceberg. Cryptocurrency (such as Bitcoin) mining has become an enormous blight requiring vast amounts of computing power to verify cryptocurrency transactions and issue new cryptocurrency. Compromised computers and networks provide attackers with a free source of distributed computing power (as well as free electricity) to solve computationally complex cryptocurrency block chains and earn transaction fees and new cryptocurrency.

TIP

Several protocols exist for secure email, including SMTP over TLS (also known as opportunistic TLS), S/MIME, PEM, and PGP. We discuss several of these protocols in the section "Application Layer (Layer 7)," earlier in this chapter.

Other email security considerations include malicious code contained in attachments, lack of privacy, and lack of authentication. These considerations can be countered by implementing antivirus scanning software, encryption, and digital signatures, respectively.

Several applications employing various cryptographic techniques have been developed to provide confidentiality, integrity, authentication, non-repudiation, and access control for email communications. For example, Microsoft Office 365 Message Encryption (OME) is a popular solution for many organizations.

» **SMTP over TLS:** This is a method used to encapsulate SMTP traffic with TLS so that eavesdroppers can't alter or read the contents of email being transmitted from one email server to another. SMTP over TLS can be configured in two ways:

   • **Opportunistic:** A TLS connection will be established if both email servers have TLS capabilities.

- **Mandatory:** An email server will only communicate with other email servers if they also have TLS capabilities.

>> **Secure Multipurpose Internet Mail Extensions (S/MIME):** S/MIME is a secure method of sending email incorporated into several popular browsers and email applications. S/MIME provides confidentiality and authentication by using the RSA asymmetric key system, digital signatures, and X.509 digital certificates. S/MIME complies with the Public Key Cryptography Standard (PKCS) #7 format, and an IETF specification.

>> **MIME Object Security Services (MOSS):** MOSS provides confidentiality, integrity, identification and authentication, and non-repudiation by using MD5 and RSA asymmetric keys. MOSS has never been widely implemented or used, primarily because of the popularity of PGP.

>> **Privacy Enhanced Mail (PEM):** PEM was proposed as a PKCS-compliant standard by the IETF, but has never been widely implemented or used. It provides confidentiality and authentication by using 3DES for encryption, MD5 message digests, X.509 digital certificates, and the RSA asymmetric system for digital signatures and secure key distribution.

>> **Pretty Good Privacy (PGP):** PGP is a popular email encryption application. It provides confidentiality and authentication by using the IDEA Cipher for encryption and the RSA asymmetric system for digital signatures and secure key distribution. Instead of a central Certificate Authority (CA), PGP uses a decentralized *trust model* (in which the communicating parties implicitly trust each other) which is ideally suited for smaller groups to validate user identity (instead of using PKI infrastructure, which can be costly and difficult to maintain).

Today, two basic versions of PGP software are available: a commercial version from Symantec Corporation (www.symantec.com), and an open-source version, GPG (www.gnupg.org).

REMEMBER

PGP is a freeware email security application (free to individuals, not organizations) that uses the IDEA algorithm (symmetric) for encryption and the RSA algorithm (asymmetric) for key distribution and digital signatures.

Web

The two principal technologies that make up the World Wide Web are the Hyper-Text Transport Protocol (HTTP) and the HyperText Markup Language (HTML). HTTP is the command-and-response language used by browsers to communicate with web servers, and HTML is the display language that defines the appearance of web pages.

HyperText Transport Protocol Secure (HTTPS) is the secure version of HTTP, which includes protocols for authenticating users (not used often) and web servers (used quite often) as well as for encrypting web traffic between web servers and end users' browsers.

HTTP, HTTPS, and HTML5 are the means used to facilitate all sorts of high-value activities, such as online banking and business applications. It should be of no surprise, then, to know that these protocols are under constant attack by hackers. Some of the types of attacks are

>> **Script injection:** Hackers attempt to inject scripting language commands into form fields on web pages in an attempt to fool the web server into sending the contents of back-end databases to the hacker.

>> **Buffer overflow:** Hackers try to send machine language instructions as parts of queries to web servers in an attempt to run those instructions. If successful, the hacker can execute commands of his or her own choosing on the server, with potentially disastrous results.

>> **Denial of Service (DoS):** Hackers can send specially crafted queries to a web server in order to cause it to malfunction and stop working. Another form of Denial of Service involves merely sending huge volumes of queries to the web server in an attempt to clog its inputs and make it unavailable for legitimate use.

>> **Man in the Middle (MITM):** Hackers attack the establishment of an HTTPS secure channel in an attempt to gain the ability to easily decrypt the otherwise secure traffic between web server and browser.

>> **Cross-site scripting (XSS):** This is an attack where the attacker attempts to inject a client-side script into web pages viewed by other intended victims.

>> **Cross-site request forgery (CSRF):** An attacker attempts to trick a victim into clicking a link that will perform an action the victim would not otherwise approve.

>> **Watering hole attacks:** Here, attackers compromise websites visited by individuals in a target organization, infecting them with malware that will be downloaded to unsuspecting victims.

>> **Man in the Browser (MITB):** Hackers attempt to trick users into installing browser helper objects (BHOs) that act as proxies between users' browsers and the web sites they are communicating with. MITB attacks eavesdrop on web communications and can even alter traffic.

These and other types of attacks have made web security testing a necessity. Many organizations that have web applications, especially ones that facilitate high-value activities (such as banking, travel, and information management), employ tools and other methods to make sure that no vulnerabilities exist that could permit malicious attacks to expose sensitive information or cause the application to malfunction.

Facsimile

Facsimile transmissions are often taken for granted, but they definitely present major security issues. Many organizations still use fax machines to regularly conduct business (including attorneys, Realtors, and pizza delivery restaurants, to name a few!), and multifunction printers often have built-in fax machines. Even if you don't configure the fax capability on a multifunction printer, it can still be a security risk.

In many organizations, email-based fax services have replaced traditional fax machines. Email security concepts (discussed in the preceding section) should be applied in such cases.

A fax transmission, like any other electronic transmission, can be easily intercepted or re-created. General administrative and technical controls for fax security include

- >> Using cover pages (that include appropriate routing and classification markings)
- >> Placing fax machines in secure areas
- >> Using preprogrammed numbers
- >> Using secure phone lines
- >> Encrypting fax data
- >> Using centralized fax servers

TIP

Many faxes are lost in situations in which the recipient doesn't know a fax is coming, and someone else in the office takes too many pages from the fax machine, including the fax destined for the unaware recipient! If you're sending a fax that contains sensitive information, inform the recipient in advance so that he or she can be sure to grab it from the fax machine!

Multimedia collaboration

Multimedia collaboration includes remote meeting software, certain voice over Internet Protocol (VoIP) applications (see the earlier section, "Voice"), and instant messaging, among others.

Remote meeting (Skype, WebEx, Zoom, and GoToMeeting) software has become immensely popular and enables rich collaboration over the Internet. Potential security issues associated with remote meeting software include downloading and installing potentially vulnerable add-on components or other required software. Other security issues arise from the capabilities inherent to remote meeting software, such as remote desktop control, file sharing, sound, and video. An unauthorized user that connects to an endpoint via remote meeting software could potentially have access to all of these capabilities.

Instant messaging (IM) applications enable simple and convenient communications within an organization and can significantly boost productivity. However, IM has long been a favorite attack vector for cybercriminals. Users need to be aware that IM is no more secure than any other communication method. Communications can be intercepted (IMs are rarely encrypted) and malware can be spread via instant messages.

Remote access

Remote access to corporate networks has become more ubiquitous over the past decade. Such trends such as telecommuting and mobile computing blur the distinction between work lives and personal lives for many people today. Safely enabling ubiquitous access to corporate network resources from any device requires extensive knowledge of various remote access security methods, protocols, and technologies.

Remote access security methods

Remote access security methods include restricted allowed addresses, geolocation, caller ID, callback, and multi-factor authentication.

>> **Restricted address:** The restricted address method blocks access to the network based on allowed IP addresses, essentially performing rudimentary *node* authentication, but not *user* authentication.

>> **Geolocation:** This method blocks access based on the geographic location of the user. This method is a useful countermeasure in the case of theft of remote access credentials.

>> **Caller ID:** The caller ID method restricts access to the network based on allowed phone numbers, thus performing a slightly more secure form of node authentication because phone numbers are more difficult to spoof than IP addresses. However, this method can be difficult to administer for road warriors that routinely travel to different cities.

>> **Callback:** The callback method restricts access to the network by requiring a remote user to first authenticate to the remote access service (RAS) server. The RAS server then disconnects and calls the user back at a preconfigured phone number. As with caller ID, this method can be difficult to administer for road warriors.

>> **Multi-factor authentication:** Requiring users to authenticate with a userid and password, plus an additional factor such as a one-time passcode (for example sent to a mobile device via SMS text message), token, or biometric, reduces the risk of compromised login credentials.

REMEMBER

One limitation of callback is that it can be easily defeated by using call forwarding.

Remote access security

Remote access security technologies include RAS servers that utilize various authentication protocols associated with PPP, RADIUS, and TACACS.

>> **RAS:** Remote access service (RAS) servers utilize the Point-to-Point Protocol (PPP) to encapsulate IP packets and establish dial-in connections over serial and ISDN links. PPP incorporates the following three authentication protocols:

- **PAP:** The Password Authentication Protocol (PAP) uses a two-way handshake to authenticate a peer to a server when a link is initially established. PAP transmits passwords in cleartext, and provides no protection from replay or brute force attacks.

- **CHAP:** The Challenge Handshake Protocol (CHAP) uses a three-way handshake to authenticate both a peer and a server when a link is initially established and, optionally, at regular intervals throughout the session. CHAP requires both the peer and the server to be preconfigured with a shared secret that must be stored in cleartext. The peer uses the secret to calculate the response to a server challenge by using an MD5 one-way hash function. MS-CHAP, a Microsoft enhancement to CHAP, allows the shared secret to be stored in an encrypted form.

- **EAP:** The Extensible Authentication Protocol (EAP) adds flexibility to PPP authentication by implementing various authentication mechanisms, including MD5-challenge, S/Key, generic token card, digital certificates, and so on. EAP is implemented in many wireless networks.

>> **RADIUS:** The Remote Authentication Dial-In User Service (RADIUS) protocol is an open-source, UDP-based (usually ports 1812 and 1813, and sometimes ports 1645 and 1646), client-server protocol, which provides authentication and accountability. A user provides username/password information to a RADIUS client by using PAP or CHAP.

The RADIUS client encrypts the password and sends the username and encrypted password to the RADIUS server for authentication.

Note: Passwords exchanged between the RADIUS client and the RADIUS server are encrypted, but passwords exchanged between the PC client and the RADIUS client aren't necessarily encrypted — if using PAP authentication, for example. However, if the PC client happens to also be the RADIUS client, all password exchanges are encrypted, regardless of the authentication protocol being used.

TECHNICAL STUFF

RADIUS is an AAA (authentication, authorization, and accounting) protocol that manages access in an AAA transaction.

>> **Diameter:** The Diameter protocol is the next-generation RADIUS protocol. Diameter overcomes several RADIUS shortcomings. For instance, it uses TCP rather than UDP, supports IPsec or TLS, and has a larger address space than RADIUS.

>> **TACACS:** The Terminal Access Controller Access Control System (TACACS) is a UDP-based access control protocol (originally developed for the MILNET), which provides authentication, authorization, and accountability (AAA). The original TACACS protocol has been significantly enhanced, primarily by Cisco, as XTACACS (no longer used) and TACACS+ (the most common implementation of TACACS). TACACS+ is TCP-based (port 49) and supports practically any authentication mechanism (PAP, CHAP, MS-CHAP, EAP, token cards, Kerberos, and so on). The basic operation of TACACS+ is similar to RADIUS, including the caveat about encrypted passwords between client and server. The major advantages of TACACS+ are its wide support of various authentication mechanisms and granular control of authorization parameters.

A *Virtual Private Network* (VPN) creates a secure tunnel over a public network, such as the Internet. Encrypting the data as it's transmitted across the VPN creates a secure tunnel. The two ends of a VPN are commonly implemented by using one of the following methods:

>> Client-to-VPN-Concentrator (or Device)

>> Client-to-Firewall

>> Firewall-to-Firewall

>> Router-to-Router

REMEMBER

Common VPN protocol standards include Point-to-Point Tunneling Protocol (PPTP), Layer 2 Forwarding Protocol (L2F), Layer 2 Tunneling Protocol (L2TP), Internet Protocol Security (IPsec), and Secure Sockets Layer (SSL).

POINT-TO-POINT TUNNELING PROTOCOL (PPTP)

The Point-to-Point Tunneling Protocol (PPTP) was developed by Microsoft to enable the Point-to-Point Protocol (PPP) to be tunneled through a public network. PPTP uses native PPP authentication and encryption services (such as PAP, CHAP, and EAP). PPTP is commonly used for dial-up connections. PPTP operates at the Data Link Layer (Layer 2) of the OSI model and is designed for individual client-server connections.

LAYER 2 FORWARDING PROTOCOL (L2F)

The Layer 2 Forwarding Protocol (L2F) was developed by Cisco and provides similar functionality to PPTP. Like its name implies, L2F operates at the Data Link Layer of the OSI model and permits tunneling of Layer 2 WAN protocols such as HDLC and SLIP.

LAYER 2 TUNNELING PROTOCOL (L2TP)

The Layer 2 Tunneling Protocol (L2TP) is an IETF standard that combines Microsoft (and others') PPTP and Cisco L2F protocols. Like PPTP and L2F, L2TP operates at the Data Link Layer of the OSI model to create secure VPN connections for individual client-server connections. The L2TP addresses the following end-user requirements:

>> **Transparency:** Requires no additional software.

>> **Robust authentication:** Supports PPP authentication protocols, Remote Authentication Dial-In User Service (RADIUS), Terminal Access Controller Access Control System (TACACS), smart cards, and one-time passwords.

>> **Local addressing:** The VPN entities, rather than the ISP, assign IP addresses.

>> **Authorization:** Authorization is managed by the VPN server-side, similar to direct dial-up connections.

>> **Accounting:** Both the ISP and the user perform AAA accounting.

IPsec

Internet Protocol Security (IPsec) is an IETF open standard for VPNs that operates at the Network Layer (Layer 3) of the OSI model. It's the most popular and robust VPN protocol in use today. IPsec ensures confidentiality, integrity, and authenticity by using Layer 3 encryption and authentication to provide an end-to-end solution. IPsec operates in two modes:

>> **Transport mode:** Only the data is encrypted.

>> **Tunnel mode:** The entire packet is encrypted.

The two modes of IPsec are Transport mode (on the LAN) and Tunnel mode (on the WAN).

The two main protocols used in IPsec are

>> **Authentication Header (AH):** Provides integrity, authentication, and non-repudiation.

>> **Encapsulating Security Payload (ESP):** Provides confidentiality (encryption) and limited authentication.

Each pair of hosts communicating in an IPsec session must establish a security association.

A *security association* (SA) is a one-way connection between two communicating parties; thus, two SAs are required for each pair of communicating hosts. Additionally, each SA supports only a single protocol (AH or ESP). Therefore, using both an AH and an ESP between two communicating hosts will require a total of four SAs. An SA has three parameters that uniquely identify it in an IPsec session:

>> **Security Parameter Index (SPI):** The SPI is a 32-bit string used by the receiving station to differentiate between SAs terminating on that station. The SPI is located within the AH or ESP header.

>> **Destination IP address:** The destination address could be the end station or an intermediate gateway or firewall, but it must be a unicast address.

>> **Security Protocol ID:** The Security Protocol ID must be either an AH or ESP association.

In IPsec, a security association (SA) is a one-way connection. You need a minimum of two SAs for two-way communications.

Key management is provided in IPsec by using the Internet Key Exchange (IKE). *IKE* is actually a combination of three complementary protocols: the Internet Security Association and Key Management Protocol (ISAKMP), the Secure Key Exchange Mechanism (SKEME), and the Oakley Key Exchange Protocol. IKE operates in three modes: Main mode, Aggressive mode, and Quick mode.

SSL

The *Secure Sockets Layer* (SSL) protocol, developed by Netscape Communications in 1994, provides session-based encryption and authentication for secure communication between clients and servers on the Internet. SSL operates at the Transport Layer (Layer 4) of the OSI model. SSL VPNs (using TLS 1.0 through 1.2) have rapidly gained widespread popularity and acceptance in recent years because of their ease of use and low cost. An SSL VPN requires no special client hardware or software (other than a web browser), and little or no client configuration. SSL VPNs provide secure access to web-enabled applications and thus are somewhat more granular in control — a user is granted access to a specific application, rather than to the entire private network. This granularity can also be considered a limitation of SSL VPNs; not all applications will work over an SSL VPN, and many convenient network functions (file and print sharing) may not be available over an SSL VPN.

REMEMBER

All versions of SSL are now considered inadequate for protecting communications. TLS 1.2 or newer is now recommended instead of SSL.

SSL uses the RSA asymmetric key system; IDEA, DES, and 3DES symmetric key systems; and the MD5 hash function. The current version (published in 1996) is SSL 3.0. In 2014, a vulnerability that affects all block ciphers in SSL was discovered. The RC4 stream cipher used in SSL 3.0 is also vulnerable to attack. RFC 6176, published in 2011, deprecates and prohibits the use of SSL 2.0. Similarly, RFC 7568, published in 2015 deprecates and prohibits the use of SSL 3.0.

SSL 3.0 was standardized by the IETF in Transport Layer Security (TLS) 1.0 and released in 1999 with only minor modifications to the original SSL 3.0 specification. TLS 1.2 is the most current version of TLS, and TLS 1.3 at the time of this writing remains a draft standard, although the final specification is expected in 2018.

Data communications

Network data communications are secured using a number of technologies and protocols.

Virtual LANs (VLANs) are used to logically segment a network, for example by department or resource. VLANs (see the sidebar "Fill-in-the-blank area networks (___AN)" earlier in this chapter) are configured on network switches and restrict VLAN access to devices that are connected to ports that are configured on the switch as VLAN members.

The Transport Layer Security/Secure Sockets Layer (TLS/SSL) protocol (discussed in the preceding section) is commonly used to encrypt network communications.

Virtualized networks

Virtualized networks are a big part of the cloud computing revolution that is sweeping the world. The earlier form of virtualized networks came in the form of virtual local area networks (VLANs), discussed earlier in this chapter. But the big advancement is in software-defined networking (SDN), software-defined security (SD-S), and network functions virtualization (NFV), in which network components such as routers, switches, firewalls, intrusion detection systems (IDSs), and more are no longer hardware appliances but virtual machines that live in virtual environments (see the next section).

Virtualization

Virtualization has been one of the hottest and most disruptive computing trends of the past decade, and is a key enabling technology in cloud computing. Virtualization technology emulates physical computing resources, such as desktop computers and servers, processors, memory, storage, networking, and individual applications. The core component of virtualization technology is the hypervisor which runs between a hardware kernel and an OS, and enables multiple "guest" virtual machines (VMs) to run on a single physical "host" machine.

Two commonly defined types of hypervisors are Type 1 (*native* or *bare metal*) hypervisors that run directly on host hardware, and Type 2 (*hosted*) hypervisors that run within an operating system environment (OSE).

In additional to virtualized servers, virtualization technology is increasingly being used for

>> **Desktop and application virtualization.** Desktop virtualization is increasingly popular for remote desktop applications used in conjunction with VPN software. Application virtualization allows various use cases such as legacy applications that can't run on newer operating systems, multiple versions of the same application running on a desktop, and multiple versions of software components (such as Java) running on a desktop. Application virtualization is also used for softphone software installed on endpoints.

>> **Storage virtualization.** Block (SAN) and file (NAS) virtualization enables storage administrators to manage enterprise storage space that uses commodity or standard off-the-shelf compute and storage hardware components with storage management functions performed in the virtual software.

>> **Network virtualization.** Network virtualization abstracts network functions (such as routing, switching, and traffic management) from the underlying hardware. Popular network virtualization technologies and capabilities include software-defined networks (SDN), micro-segmentation, and network functions virtualization (NFV).

Security in virtualized environments begins with the hypervisor. A compromised hypervisor can potentially give an attacker access to and control of an entire virtualized environment.

Operational security issues associated with virtualized environments include

>> **VM sprawl.** Virtualization technology enables organizations to deploy VMs in minutes rather than days or weeks. This has caused VMs to proliferate in many data centers.

>> **Guest operating systems.** All of the various OSes and OS versions that exist in a virtualized environment need to be regularly patched and kept updated.

>> **Dormant VMs.** VMs that are no longer needed are often turned off rather than de-provisioned. If a dormant VM is later turned on, it will be missing critical security patches and may therefore be vulnerable to attack.

>> **Network visibility.** Most organizations begin their virtualization journey with virtualized servers. This often means multiple NICs are installed in a single physical server and all network traffic flowing to and from the VMs on that server runs over the NICs. Without network virtualization, network administrators have limited visibility into this traffic for troubleshooting and security monitoring purposes.

A recent innovation in virtualization is known as *containerization*. In the same manner in which a hypervisor can facilitate the use of multiple operating system instances, containerization facilitates the use of multiple application instances within a single operating system. Each application executes in a *container*, which is isolated from other containers. Containerization is useful in environments where applications are designed to be run by themselves in a running operating system. Popular software containers include Docker and Kubernetes.

Prevent or Mitigate Network Attacks

Most attacks against networks are Denial of Service (DoS) or Distributed Denial of Service (DDoS) attacks in which the objective is to consume a network's bandwidth so that network services become unavailable. But several other types of attacks exist, some of which are discussed in the following sections.

Bluejacking and bluesnarfing

With Bluetooth technology becoming wildly popular, several attack methods have evolved, including *bluejacking* (sending anonymous, unsolicited messages to

Bluetooth-enabled devices) and *bluesnarfing* (stealing personal data, such as contacts, pictures, and calendar information from a Bluetooth-enabled phone). Even worse, in a bluesnarfing attack, information about your cellular phone (such as its serial number) can be downloaded, then used to clone your phone.

ICMP flood

In an *ICMP flood* attack, large numbers of ICMP packets (usually Echo Request) are sent to the target network to consume available bandwidth and/or system resources. Because ICMP isn't required for normal network operations, the easiest defense is to drop ICMP packets at the router or filter them at the firewall.

Smurf

A *Smurf* attack is a variation of the ICMP flood attack. In a Smurf attack, ICMP Echo Request packets are sent to the broadcast address of a target network by using a spoofed IP address on the target network. The target, or *bounce site,* then transmits the ICMP Echo Request to all hosts on the network. Each host then responds with an Echo Reply packet, overwhelming the available bandwidth and/ or system resources. Countermeasures against Smurf attacks include dropping ICMP packets at the router.

Fraggle

A *Fraggle* attack is a variant of a Smurf attack that uses UDP Echo packets (UDP port 7) rather than ICMP packets. Cisco routers can be configured to disable the TCP and UDP services (known as *TCP and UDP small servers*) that are most commonly used in Fraggle attacks.

DNS Server Attacks

There are various attacks that can be carried out against DNS servers, which are designed to cause targeted DNS servers to provide erroneous responses to end users, resulting in end users being sent to imposter systems (usually web sites). Defenses against DNS server attacks include DNS server hardening (including Domain Name System Security Extensions, or DNSSEC) and application firewalls.

Man-in-the-Middle

A *man-in-the-middle* (MITM) attack consists of an attacker that attempts to alter communications between two parties through impersonation. A common MITM technique attacks the establishment of a TLS session, so that the attacker will be able to easily decrypt encrypted communications between the two endpoints (for example, on a coffee shop Wi-Fi network).

Defenses against MITM attacks include stronger authentication, implementation of DNSSEC, latency examination, and out-of-band verification.

Session hijacking (spoofing)

IP *spoofing* involves altering a TCP packet so that it appears to be coming from a known, trusted source, thus giving the attacker access to the network.

Session hijacking (session token interception)

Session hijacking typically involves a Wi-Fi network without encryption, where an attacker is able to intercept another user's HTTP session cookie. The attacker then uses the same cookie to take over the victim user's HTTP session. This has been demonstrated with the Firesheep Firefox extension.

SYN flood

In a *SYN flood* attack, TCP packets with a spoofed source address request a connection (SYN bit set) to the target network. The target responds with a SYN-ACK packet, but the spoofed source never replies. *Half-open connections* are incomplete communication sessions awaiting completion of the TCP three-way handshake. These connections can quickly overwhelm a system's resources while the system waits for the half-open connections to time out, which causes the system to crash or otherwise become unusable.

SYN floods are countered on Cisco routers by using two features: *TCP Intercept*, which effectively proxies for the half-open connections; and *Committed Access Rate* (CAR), which limits the bandwidth available to certain types of traffic. Checkpoint's FW-1 firewall has a feature known as *SYN Defender* that functions in way similar to the Cisco TCP Intercept feature. Other defenses include changing the default maximum number of TCP half-open connections and reducing the timeout period on networked systems.

Teardrop

In a *Teardrop* attack, the Length and Fragmentation offset fields of sequential IP packets are modified, causing some target systems to become confused and crash.

UDP flood

In a *UDP flood* attack, large numbers of UDP packets are sent to the target network to consume available bandwidth and/or system resources. UDP floods can generally be countered by dropping unnecessary UDP packets at the router. However, if the attack uses a required UDP port (such as DNS port 53), other countermeasures need to be employed.

Eavesdropping

Eavesdropping is the act of listening to network traffic, which is generally performed because an attacker wants to learn something about the communications session or its content. The attacker may be looking for login credentials being passed in cleartext, or other sensitive information of interest using SIPVicious, for example, to listen to VoIP traffic. Whatever the reason, we need to reduce attackers' ability to learn from network traffic: Eavesdropping can be defeated through encryption (to protect sensitive content), as well as encapsulation (to conceal additional information about the communication).

Chapter **7**

Identity and Access Management

Identity and access management (IAM) is often the first — and sometimes the *only* — line of defense between adversaries and sensitive information. In fact, in the modern cloud era with ubiquitous mobile computing and anywhere, anytime access to applications and data, many security practitioners now refer to identity as "the new perimeter." Security professionals must have a thorough understanding of the concepts and technologies involved. This domain represents 13 percent of the CISSP certification exam.

Identity and access management is a collection of processes and technologies that are used to control the access to critical assets. Together with other critical controls, IAM is a part of the core of information security: When implemented correctly, unauthorized persons are not permitted to access critical assets. Breaches and other abuses of information and assets are less likely to occur.

Security professionals must fully *understand identity and access management concepts* (including control types and authentication, authorization, and accounting), *system access controls* (including identification and authentication techniques, methodologies and implementation, and methods of attack), and *data access controls* (including access control techniques and models) within centralized, decentralized, and cloud-based computing environments. We must also understand the techniques that attackers use to compromise or bypass access management controls, and know how to strengthen those controls.

Control Physical and Logical Access to Assets

The purpose of identity and access management systems and processes is the management of access to information, systems, devices, and facilities. A variety of controls are used for this purpose in several contexts that are discussed in this section. Chapter 3 contains a discussion of the types and categories of controls.

Information

Controlling access to information assets is primarily achieved through logical controls that determine which persons or systems (known as *subjects*) are permitted to access which files, directories, databases, tables, records, or fields (known as *objects*). The mechanisms used to control access to information include

>> **File and directory level permissions.** This is typically managed at the operating system level or within a file sharing system (such as a file server, SharePoint, or Box).

>> **Database table, view, field, and row permissions.** Usually managed within a database management system or a third party tool, permissions can be granted at various levels.

Systems and devices

Controlling access to systems and devices is achieved mainly through mechanisms built into those systems, including:

>> **Port level access control.** At the network level, a system can be configured to accept incoming connection requests based upon their origin (such as IP address, IP network, or geographic region), as well as the port number.

- » **Console login.** A physical or logical console controls access to the system, generally based upon the proven identity of the subject who wants to connect.

- » **Remote console login.** A system can be accessed via a remote console connection, which has the general appearance of a local, physical console, but is accessed via a network. Again, access permission is based upon the proven identity of the subject who wishes to connect.

- » **Application programming interfaces (APIs).** A system or application can be accessed programmatically through an API that typically is used by an application that needs to access data or functions.

Systems and devices are far more than servers and routers. Many kinds of business and consumer products are marketed as "smart" devices and equipped with Ethernet, Wi-Fi, and Bluetooth connectivity. When pondering systems and devices, be sure to include the vast array of things that are connected to networks, including the following:

- » **Industrial control systems:** This includes remote monitoring and control of utility infrastructure including electric power and distribution, water supplies, and sewage treatment. And don't forget automated manufacturing, 3-D printing, building environmental systems, and voting machines.

- » **Medical devices:** Equipment in hospitals such as patient monitoring and IV pumps, as well as things on or in our bodies, including insulin pumps and pacemakers.

- » **Wearables:** This consists of watches, fitness devices, video glasses, and the like.

- » **Transportation:** Automobiles, self-driving cars, drones, and satellites. Also, GPS navigation, auto-pilots, air traffic control, and more.

Facilities

The purpose of controlling access to facilities is to ensure the safety of personnel who work in those facilities, as well as the protection of information systems and other assets located there. Controlling access to facilities is accomplished by different means, including:

- » **Key card access systems.** With optional biometric readers and/or PIN pads, these systems control which persons are permitted to access which buildings and rooms. These systems are used in both preventive (by restricting access to sensitive areas) and detective (by recording subjects' movement) contexts.

>> **Escorts.** Visitors and subjects with lower security clearances may be escorted by other personnel.

>> **Guards and guard dogs.** Security personnel with their optional canine assistants ensure that only authorized personnel and properly escorted personnel are able to enter a building.

>> **Visitor logs.** Although they serve as an administrative control, visitor logs provide a business record of guests and visitors who enter and leave a facility. This control is improved somewhat through the verification of visitor identity by examining a government-issued photo identification.

>> **Fences, walls, and gates.** These help to establish a secure physical perimeter and controlled entry/exit points around a building or facility.

>> **Mantraps and sally ports.** Combinations of passageways and entryways that restrict access to an area, for example, with a set of interlocking doors that require one set of doors to be closed before the next set can open.

>> **Bollards and crash gates.** These control vehicle flow approaching and near facilities.

Many other aspects of physical security are discussed in Chapter 5.

Life safety

We are all witness to a staggering variety of devices that are now embedded with TCP/IP, complete with the addition of "smart" to the device itself. We now have "smart" automobiles, "smart" televisions, and "smart" appliances. This revolution has progressed into wearable and life safety products, such as vital signs (heart rate, respiration, and so on) monitoring, as well as insulin pumps, IV pumps, patient monitoring, pacemakers, as well as automobiles and aircraft navigation and control.

Security experts have observed that many of these new "smart" products have security capabilities that range from well designed to poorly designed to outright absent. But never has identity and access management been so important: Exceptionally good authentication and authorization are needed for all of these new types of devices, to prevent unauthorized access to them. The consequences of doing this wrong can literally cost someone his or her life.

Manage Identification and Authentication of People, Devices, and Services

The core activity within identity and access management (IAM) is the management of identities, including people, devices, and services. In this section, we describe the processes and technologies in use today.

Identity management implementation

Implementing identity management begins with a plan. An identity and access management (IAM) system in an organization is a complex, distributed system that touches systems, networks, and applications, and also controls access to assets. An IAM system also includes the business processes that work together with IAM technologies and personnel to get the job done.

An IAM system probably is the most important function that an organization will ever implement. Next to the network itself, the IAM system typically is the most critical in an environment, because the IAM system controls access to all systems and applications.

Single sign-on (SSO)

The concept of single sign-on (SSO) addresses a common problem for both users and security administrators. Every account that exists in a system, network, or application is a potential point of unauthorized access. Multiple accounts that belong to a single user represent an even greater risk:

>> Users who need access to multiple systems or applications often must maintain numerous sets of credentials. Inevitably, this leads to shortcuts in creating and recalling passwords. Left to their own devices, users create weak passwords that have only slight variations, or worse yet, they'll use the same passwords everywhere they can. When they have multiple sets of credentials to manage, users are more likely to write them down. It doesn't stop at the organization's boundary: Users often use the same passwords at work that they do for their personal accounts.

>> Multiple accounts also affect user productivity (and sanity!) because the user must stop to log in to different systems. Someone must also create and maintain accounts, which involves unlocking accounts and supporting, removing, resetting, and disabling multiple sets of userids and passwords.

At first glance (alas), SSO seems the "perfect" solution that users and security administrators seek. SSO allows a user to present a single set of logon credentials, typically to an authentication server, which then transparently logs the user into *all* other enterprise systems and applications for which that user is authorized. Of course, SSO does have some disadvantages, which include

>> **Woo-hoo!:** After you're authenticated, you have the keys to the kingdom. Read that as *access to all authorized resources!* It's the security professional's nightmare. If login credentials for a user's accounts are compromised, an intruder can access everything the end user was authorized to access.

>> **Complexity:** Implementing SSO can be difficult and time-consuming. You have to address interoperability issues between different systems and applications. But, hey — that's why you get paid (or should get paid) the big bucks!

SSO is commonly implemented by various protocols and solutions, including the following.

SECURITY ASSERTION MARKUP LANGUAGE (SAML)

The de facto protocol for authentication, SAML is used for facilitating user authentication across systems and among organizations, through the exchange of authentication and authorization information between organizations. SAML is the glue that is used to make most single sign-on (SSO) systems work.

As its full name suggests, SAML is an XML markup language. XML is becoming a standard method for exchanging information between dissimilar systems.

KERBEROS

Kerberos, commonly used in the Sun Network File System (NFS) and Microsoft Windows, is perhaps the most popular ticket-based symmetric key authentication protocol in use today.

TECHNICAL STUFF

Kerberos is named for the fierce, three-headed dog that guards the gates of Hades in Greek mythology. (Not to be confused with *Ker-beer-os*, the fuzzy, six-headed dog sitting at the bar that keeps looking better and better!) Researchers at the Massachusetts Institute of Technology (MIT, also known as *Millionaires in Training*) developed this open-systems protocol in the mid-1980s.

The CISSP exam requires a general understanding of Kerberos operation. Unfortunately, Kerberos is a complex protocol that has many different implementations and no simple explanation. The following step-by-step discussion is a basic description of Kerberos operation:

1. The client prompts the subject (such as a user) for an identifier and a credential (for example, username and password). Using the authentication information (password), the client temporarily generates and stores a secret key for the subject by using a one-way hash function and then sends only the subject's identification (username) to the Key Distribution Center's (KDC) Authentication Server (AS). The password/secret key *isn't* sent to the KDC. See Figure 7-1.

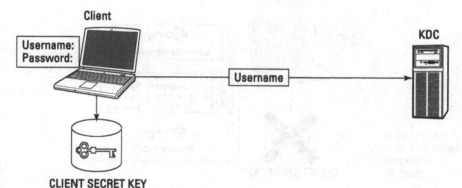

FIGURE 7-1:
Kerberos: Logon
initiation (Step 1).

2. The AS on the KDC verifies that the subject (known as a *principal*) exists in the KDC database. The KDC Ticket Granting Service (TGS) then generates a Client/TGS Session Key encrypted with the subject's secret key, which only the TGS and the client know. The TGS also generates a Ticket Granting Ticket (TGT), consisting of the subject's identification, the client network address, the valid period of the ticket, and the Client/TGS Session Key. The TGS encrypts the TGT by using its secret key, which only the TGS knows, then sends the Client/TGS Session Key and TGT back to the client. See Figure 7-2.

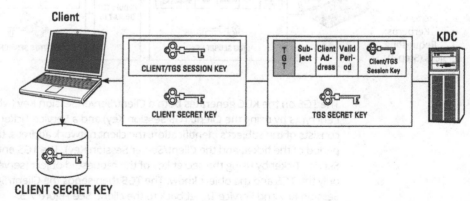

FIGURE 7-2:
Kerberos: Client/
TGS Session Key
and TGT
generation
(Step 2).

3. The client decrypts the Client/TGS Session Key — using the stored secret key that it generated by using the subject's password — authenticates the subject (user), and then erases the stored secret key to avoid possible compromise. The client can't decrypt the TGT, which the TGS encrypted by using the TGS secret key. See Figure 7-3.

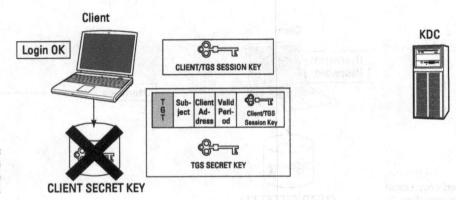

FIGURE 7-3: Kerberos: Logon completion (Step 3).

4. When the subject requests access to a specific object (such as a server, also known as a *principal*), it sends the TGT, the object identifier (such as a server name), and an authenticator to the TGS on the KDC. (The *authenticator* is a separate message that contains the client ID and a timestamp, and uses the Client/TGS Session Key to encrypt itself.) See Figure 7-4.

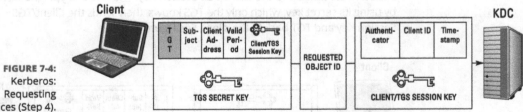

FIGURE 7-4: Kerberos: Requesting services (Step 4).

5. The TGS on the KDC generates both a Client/Server Session Key (which it encrypts by using the Client/TGS Session Key) and a Service Ticket (which consists of the subject's identification, the client network address, the valid period of the ticket, and the Client/Server Session Key). The TGS encrypts the Service Ticket by using the secret key of the requested object (server), which only the TGS and the object know. The TGS then sends the Client/Server Session Key and Service Ticket back to the client. See Figure 7-5.

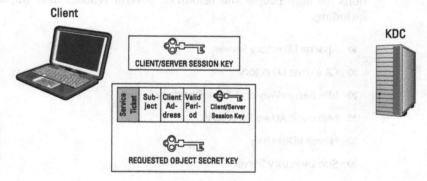

FIGURE 7-5:
Kerberos: Client/
Server Session
Key and Service
Ticket generation
(Step 5).

Client

CLIENT/SERVER SESSION KEY

CLIENT/TGS SESSION KEY

KDC

Service Ticket | Sub-ject | Client Ad-dress | Valid Peri-od | Client/Server Session Key

REQUESTED OBJECT SECRET KEY

6. The client decrypts the Client/Server Session Key by using the Client/TGS Session Key. The client can't decrypt the Service Ticket, which the TGS encrypted by using the secret key of the requested object. See Figure 7-6.

Client

CLIENT/SERVER SESSION KEY

Service Ticket | Sub-ject | Client Ad-dress | Valid Peri-od | Client/Server Session Key

REQUESTED OBJECT SECRET KEY

KDC

FIGURE 7-6:
Kerberos: Decrypt
Client/Server
Session Key
(Step 6).

7. The client can then communicate directly with the requested object (server). The client sends the Service Ticket and an authenticator to the requested object (server). The client encrypts the authenticator (comprising the subject's identification and a timestamp) by using the Client/Server Session Key that the TGS generated. The object (server) decrypts the Service Ticket by using its secret key. The Service Ticket contains the Client/Server Session Key, which allows the object (server) to then decrypt the authenticator. If the subject identification and timestamp are valid (according to the subject identification, client network address, and valid period specified in the Service Ticket), then communication between the client and server is established. The Client/Server Session Key is then used for secure communications between the subject and object. See Figure 7-7.

See Chapter 5 for more information about symmetric key cryptography.

REMEMBER

In Kerberos, a *session key* is a dynamic key that is generated when needed, shared between two principals, then destroyed when it is no longer needed. A *secret* key is a static key that is used to encrypt a session key.

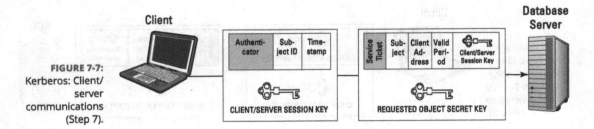

FIGURE 7-7:
Kerberos: Client/
server
communications
(Step 7).

LDAP

Lightweight Directory Access Protocol (LDAP) is both an IP protocol and a data model. LDAP (pronounced *EL-dap*) is used to support authentication and directory functions for both people and resources. Several vendors have implemented LDAP, including:

>> Apache Directory Server

>> CA eTrust Directory

>> IBM SecureWay and Tivoli Directory Server

>> Microsoft Active Directory

>> Novell eDirectory

>> Sun Directory Server

You can also find several open-source versions of LDAP available, including Open-LDAP and tinyldap.

RADIUS

The *Remote Authentication Dial-In User Service* (RADIUS) protocol is an open-source, client-server networking protocol — defined in more than 25 current IETF (Internet Engineering Task Force) RFCs (Request For Comments) — that provides authentication, authorization, and accounting (AAA) services. RADIUS is an Application Layer protocol that utilizes User Datagram Protocol (UDP) packets for transport. UDP is a connection-less protocol, which means it's fast but not as reliable as other transport protocols.

RADIUS is commonly implemented in network service provider (NSP) networks, as well as corporate remote access service (RAS) and virtual private networks (VPNs). RADIUS is also becoming increasingly popular in corporate wireless networks. A user provides username/password information to a RADIUS client by using PAP or CHAP. The RADIUS client encrypts the password and sends the username and encrypted password to the RADIUS server for authentication.

Note: Passwords exchanged between the RADIUS client and RADIUS server are encrypted, but passwords exchanged between the workstation client and the RADIUS client are not necessarily encrypted — if using PAP authentication, for example. If the workstation client happens to also be a RADIUS client, all password exchanges are encrypted, regardless of the authentication protocol used.

RAS

Remote Access Service (RAS) servers utilize the Point-to-Point Protocol (PPP) to encapsulate IP packets and establish dial-in connections over serial and ISDN links. PPP incorporates the following three authentication protocols:

TECHNICAL STUFF

>> **PAP:** The *Password Authentication Protocol* (PAP) uses a two-way handshake to authenticate a peer to a server when a link is initially established. PAP transmits passwords in clear text and provides no protection from replay attacks (in which part of a session is captured or recorded, then played back to the system) or brute force attacks.

A *two-way handshake* refers to a communications session in which the communicating devices, for example a remote workstation and a remote access server. The connection is established whereby one device sends an initial TCP SYN (Synchronize) packet to the other, and the other responds by sending an ACK (Acknowledgment) packet to indicate that the connection has been accepted.

>> **CHAP:** The *Challenge Handshake Authentication Protocol* (CHAP) uses a three-way handshake to authenticate both a peer and server when a link is initially established and, optionally, at regular intervals throughout the session. CHAP requires both the peer and server to be preconfigured with a shared secret that must be stored in plain text. The peer uses the secret to calculate the response to a server challenge by using an MD5 one-way hash function. *MS-CHAP,* a Microsoft enhancement to CHAP, allows the shared secret to be stored in an encrypted form.

>> **EAP:** The *Extensible Authentication Protocol* (EAP) adds flexibility to PPP authentication by implementing various authentication mechanisms, including MD5-challenge, S/Key, generic token card, digital certificates, and so on. Many wireless networks implement EAP.

TACACS

The *Terminal Access Controller Access Control System* (TACACS) is a remote authentication control protocol, originally developed for the MILNET (U.S. Military Network), which provides AAA services. The original TACACS protocol has been significantly enhanced, as XTACACS (no longer used) and TACACS+ (which is the most common implementation of TACACS). However, TACACS+ is a completely new protocol and therefore isn't backward-compatible with either TACACS or XTACACS. TACACS+ is TCP based on (port 49) and supports practically any authentication mechanism (PAP, CHAP, MS-CHAP, EAP, token cards, Kerberos, and so on). The major advantages of TACACS+ are its wide support of various authentication mechanisms and granular control of authorization parameters. TACACS+ can also use dynamic passwords; TACACS uses static passwords only.

The original TACACS protocol is often used in organizations for simplifying administrative access to network devices such as firewalls and routers. TACACS facilitates the use of centralized authentication credentials that are managed centrally, so that organizations don't need to manage user accounts on every device.

DIAMETER

This next-generation RADIUS protocol was developed to overcome some of RADIUS's deficiencies, but it has yet to overcome RADIUS's popularity, so it's not yet widely implemented.

Like RADIUS, Diameter provides AAA services and is an open protocol standard defined in 11 current RFCs.

Unlike RADIUS, Diameter utilizes Transmission Control Protocol (TCP) and Stream Control Transmission Protocol (SCTP) packets to provide a more reliable, connection-oriented transport mechanism. Also, Diameter uses Internet Protocol Security (IPsec) or Transport Layer Security (TLS) to provide network security or transport layer security (respectively) — rather than PAP or CHAP (used in RADIUS) — to provide a more secure connection. See Chapter 6 for a complete discussion of TCP and SCTP, IPsec and TLS, and the OSI model.

Diameter isn't fully backward-compatible with RADIUS, but it does provide an upgrade path for RADIUS-based environments. Diameter isn't an acronym, but a pun on the term RADIUS. (In geometry, the diameter of a circle is twice its radius.)

SESAME

The *Secure European System and Applications in a Multi-vendor Environment* (SESAME) project, developed by the European Computer Manufacturers Association (ECMA), is a ticket-based system, like Kerberos, with some additional functionality. It uses both symmetric and asymmetric cryptography to distribute secret keys and securely transmit data. By using public key cryptography, SESAME can securely communicate between different organizations or security domains. It incorporates a trusted authentication server at each host (known as a *Privileged Attribute Server*, or PAS), employs MD5 and CRC-32 one-way hash functions, and uses two separate certificates (known as a *Privileged Attribute Certificates*, or PACs) to provide authentication and define access privileges. However, SESAME also has some serious security flaws in its basic implementation, including these:

>> It uses an XOR function for encryption.

>> It performs authentication based on a small segment of the message rather than on the entire message.

>> Its key generation is not really very random.

>> It's vulnerable to password-guessing attacks. (Want to bet that somebody thought "open" was a pretty clever password?)

See Chapter 5 for more information on one-way hash functions, XOR functions, and key generation.

KryptoKnight

Developed by IBM, *KryptoKnight* is another example of a ticket-based SSO authentication and key distribution system that establishes peer-to-peer relationships between the Key Distribution Center (KDC) and its principals. In addition to user authentication with SSO, KryptoKnight provides two-party authentication, key distribution, and data integrity services. KryptoKnight is an extremely compact and flexible protocol that can be easily exported to other systems and applications, and it can function at any layer of the OSI model. Unlike Kerberos, KryptoKnight doesn't require clock synchronization (it uses nonces instead).

A *nonce* is literally a *number used once*. Similar in concept to an initialization vector (see Chapter 5), a nonce is a randomly generated value (usually based on a time-stamp) that can be used only once to authenticate a session.

REMEMBER

Kerberos, SESAME, and KryptoKnight are three examples of ticket-based authentication technologies that provide SSO services.

REMEMBER

LDAP, RAS (PAP and CHAP), RADIUS, Diameter, and TACACS are examples of centralized access control for remote access.

Cloud-based access controls

As organizations move their infrastructure and applications to cloud-based service providers, organizations are opting to employ cloud-based authentication as well.

The protocols that are used for cloud-based access management such as SAML, RADIUS, and TACACS are still used. The primary difference with cloud-based access is that the directory servers are in the cloud — either in an organization's cloud-based infrastructure, or through a cloud-based authentication service.

Decentralized access controls

Decentralized access control systems keep user account information in separate locations, maintained by the same or different administrators, throughout an organization or enterprise. This type of system makes sense in extremely large organizations or in situations where very granular control of complex user access rights and relationships is necessary. In such a system, administrators typically have a more thorough understanding of their users' needs and can apply the appropriate permissions — say, in a research and development lab or a manufacturing facility. However, decentralized access control systems also have various potential disadvantages. For example, organizations may apply security policies inconsistently across various systems, resulting in the wrong level of access (too much or not enough) for particular users; and if you need to disable numerous accounts for an individual user, the process becomes much more labor-intensive and error-prone.

Single/multi-factor authentication

Authentication is a two-step process that consists of identification and authentication (I&A). *Identification* is the means by which a user or system (subject) presents a specific identity (such as a username) to a system (object). *Authentication* is the process of verifying that identity. For example, a username/password combination is one common technique (albeit a weak one) that demonstrates the concepts of identification (username) and authentication (password).

Authentication is based on any of these factors:

>> *Something you know,* such as a password or a personal identification number (PIN): This concept is based on the assumption that only the owner of the account knows the secret password or PIN needed to access the account. Username and password combinations are the simplest, least expensive, and therefore most common authentication mechanism implemented today. Of course, passwords are often shared, stolen, guessed, or otherwise compromised — thus, they're also one of the weakest authentication mechanisms.

>> *Something you have,* such as a smart card, security token, or smartphone: This concept is based on the assumption that only the owner of the account has the necessary key to unlock the account. Smart cards, USB tokens, smartphones, and key fobs are becoming more common, particularly in relatively secure

organizations, such as government or financial institutions. A lot of online applications such as LinkedIn and Twitter have implemented multi-factor authentication as well. Although smart cards and tokens are somewhat more expensive and complex than other, less-secure authentication mechanisms, they're not (usually) prohibitively expensive or overly complicated to implement, administer, and use. Smartphones that can receive text messages or run soft token apps such as Google Authenticator or Microsoft Authenticator are increasingly popular because of their lower cost and convenience. Regardless of the method chosen, all forms of multi-factor authentication provide a *significant* boost to authentication security. Of course, tokens, smartcards, and smartphones are sometimes lost, stolen, or damaged.

WARNING

Because of the risks associated with text messages (such as mobile phone porting scams), the U.S. National Institute of Standards and Technology (NIST) has deprecated the use of text messages for multi-factor authentication.

» **Something you are,** such as fingerprint, face, voice, retina, or iris characteristics: This concept is based on the assumption that the face, finger, or eyeball attached to your body is actually yours and uniquely identifies you (of course, fingers and eyes can be lost, or worse). Actually, the major drawback with this authentication mechanism is acceptance — people are sometimes uneasy about using these systems. There is also the issue of spoofing: Some biometric systems, such as fingerprint and facial recognition, are not immune to spoofing attacks. Software-based biometric systems such as facial recognition are generally inexpensive, but hardware-based biometric systems are more costly to deploy.

REMEMBER

Authentication is based on something you *know*, something you *have*, or something you *are*.

The various identification and authentication (I&A) techniques that we discuss in the following sections include passwords/passphrases and PINs (knowledge-based); biometrics and behavior (characteristic–based); and one-time passwords, tokens, and single sign-on (SSO).

The identification component is normally a relatively simple mechanism based on a username or, in the case of a system or process, based on a computer or process name, Media Access Control (MAC) address, Internet Protocol (IP) address, or Process ID (PID). Identification requirements include only that it must uniquely identify the user (or system/process) and shouldn't identify that user's role or relative importance in the organization (the identification shouldn't include labels such as *accounting* or *CEO*). Common, shared, and group accounts, such as *root*, *admin*, or *system* should not be permitted. Such accounts provide no accountability and are prime targets for malicious beings.

REMEMBER

Identification is the act of claiming a specific identity. Authentication is the act of verifying that identity.

Single factor authentication

Single factor authentication requires only one of the three preceding factors discussed above (something you *know*, something you *have*, or something you *are*) for authentication. Common single factor authentication mechanisms include passwords and passphrases, one-time passwords, and personal identification numbers (PINs).

PASSWORDS AND PASSPHRASES

"A password should be like a toothbrush. Use it every day; change it regularly; and DON'T share it with friends." –USENET

Passwords are easily the most common — and weakest — authentication credentials in use today. Although there are more advanced and secure authentication technologies available, including tokens and biometrics, organizations typically use those technologies as supplements to or in combination with — rather than as replacements for — traditional usernames and passwords.

A *passphrase* is a variation on a password; it uses a sequence of characters or words, rather than a single password. Generally, attackers have more difficulty breaking passphrases than breaking regular passwords because longer passphrases are generally more difficult to break than shorter, complex passwords. Passphrases also have the following advantages:

>> Users frequently use the same passwords to access numerous accounts; their corporate networks, their home PCs, their Gmail or Yahoo! email accounts, their eBay accounts, and their Amazon.com accounts, for example. So an attacker who targets a specific user may be able to gain access to his or her work account by going after a less secure system, such as his or her home PC, or by compromising an Internet account (because the user has passwords conveniently stored in that bastion of security — Internet Explorer!). Internet sites and home PCs typically don't use passphrases, so you improve the chances that your users have to use different passwords/passphrases to access their work accounts.

>> Users can actually remember and type passphrases more easily than they can remember and type a much shorter, cryptic password that requires contorted finger acrobatics to type on a keyboard.

However, passphrases also have a downside:

- Users can find passphrases inconvenient, so you may find passphrases difficult to implement. ("You mean I need to have a 20-character password now?!")

- Not all systems support passphrases. Such systems ignore anything longer than the system limit (for example, eight characters).

- Many command-line interfaces and tools don't support the space character that separates words in a passphrase.

- Ultimately, a passphrase is still just a password (albeit, a much longer and better one) and thus shares some of the same problems associated with passwords.

You, as a CISSP candidate, should understand the general problems associated with passwords, as well as common password controls and management features.

Password/passphrase problems include that they're

- **Insecure:** Passwords are generally insecure for several reasons, including:

    - **Human nature:** In the case of user-generated passwords, users often choose passwords that they can easily remember and consequently attackers can easily guess (such as a spouse's or pet's name, birthday, anniversary, or hobby). Users may also be inclined to write down passwords (particularly complex, system-generated passwords) or share their passwords with others.

    - **Transmission and storage:** Many applications and protocols (such as file transfer protocol [FTP] and password authentication protocol [PAP]) transmit passwords in clear text. These applications and protocols may also store passwords in plaintext files, or in a security database that uses a weak hashing algorithm.

- **Easily broken:** Passwords are susceptible to brute-force and dictionary attacks (which we discuss in the section "Methods of attack," later in this chapter) by readily available programs such as John the Ripper and L0phtCrack (pronounced *loft-crack*).

- **Easily stolen:** From phishing scams to watering hole attacks and key loggers, users can be tricked into giving up passwords, and malware can steal them as they type them. Some organizations store their users' passwords unencrypted, hashed without salting, or encrypted with an easily discovered key; any of these methods make it relatively easy for an intruder to obtain passwords from a poorly protected system.

>> **Inconvenient:** Easily agitated users can find entering passwords tiresome. In an attempt to bypass these controls, users may select an easily typed, weak password; they may automate logons (for instance, a keyboard macro, or selecting the Remember My Password check box in a browser); and they can neglect to lock their workstations or log out when they leave their desks.

>> **Refutable:** Transactions authenticated with only a password don't necessarily provide absolute proof of a user's identity. Authentication mechanisms must guarantee non-repudiation, which is a critical component of accountability. (For more on non-repudiation, see the section "Accountability," earlier in this chapter.)

Passwords have the following login controls and management features that you should configure in accordance with an organization's security policy and security best practices:

>> **Length:** Generally, the longer the better. A password is, in effect, an encryption key. Just as larger encryption keys (such as 1024-bit or 2048-bit) are more difficult to crack, so too are longer passwords. You should configure systems to require a minimum password length of ten to fifteen characters. Of course, users can easily forget long passwords or simply find them too inconvenient, leading to some of the human-nature problems discussed earlier in this section.

>> **Complexity:** Strong passwords contain a mix of upper- and lowercase letters, numbers, and special characters such as # and $. Be aware that some systems may not accept certain special characters, or those characters may perform special functions (for example, in terminal emulation software).

>> **Expiration (or maximum password aging):** You should set maximum password aging to require password changes at regular intervals: 30-, 60-, or 90-day periods are common.

>> **Minimum password aging:** This prevents a user from changing his or her password too frequently. The recommended setting is one to ten days to prevent a user from easily circumventing password history controls (for example, by changing their password five times within a few minutes, then setting it back to their original password).

>> **Re-use:** Password re-use settings (five to ten is common) allow a system to remember previously used passwords (or, more appropriately, their hashes) for a specific account. This security setting prevents users from circumventing maximum password expiration by alternating between two or three familiar passwords when they're required to change their passwords.

>> **Limited attempts:** This control limits the number of unsuccessful logon attempts and consists of two components: counter threshold (for example,

three or five) and counter reset (for example, 5 or 30 minutes). The *counter threshold* is the maximum number of consecutive unsuccessful attempts permitted before some action occurs (such as automatically disabling the account). The *counter reset* is the amount of time between unsuccessful attempts. For example, three unsuccessful logon attempts within a 30-minute period may result in an account lockout for a set period (for example, 24 hours); but two unsuccessful attempts in 25 minutes, and then a third unsuccessful attempt 10 minutes later, wouldn't result in an account lockout. A successful logon attempt also resets the counter.

» **Lockout duration (or intruder lockout):** When a user exceeds the counter threshold that we describe in the preceding bullet, the account is locked out. Organizations commonly set the lockout duration to 30-minutes, but you can set it for any duration. If you set the duration to forever, an administrator must unlock the account. Some systems don't notify the user when it locks out an account, instead quietly alerting the system administrator to a possible break-in attempt. Of course, an attacker can use the lockout duration as a simple means to perform a *Denial of Service attack* (intentionally making repeated bad logon attempts to keep the user's account locked).

» **Limited time periods:** This control restricts the time of day that a user can log in. For example, you can effectively reduce the period of time that attackers can compromise your systems by limiting users' access to business hours only. However, this type of control is becoming less common in the modern age of the workaholic and the global economy, both of which require users to legitimately perform work at all hours of the day.

» **System messages:** System messages include the following:

- **Login banner:** Welcome messages literally invite criminals to access your systems. Disable any "welcome" message and replace it with a legal warning instead that requires the user to click OK to acknowledge the warning and accept the legal terms of use.

- **Last username:** Many popular operating systems display the username of the last successful account logon. Users (who only need to type in their password) find this feature convenient — and so do attackers (who only need to crack the password without worrying about matching it to a valid user account). Disable this feature.

- **Last successful logon time:** After successfully logging on to the system, this message tells the user the last time that he or she logged on. If the system shows that the last successful logon for a user was Saturday morning at 2:00 a.m. and the user knows that he couldn't possibly have logged in at that time because he has a life, he knows that someone has compromised his account, and he can report the incident accordingly.

- **Last successful login location:** After successfully logging in to the system, this message tells the user the last geographical location used when he or she logged in. If the system reports that the user last logged in from some obscure, far-away country, this can be a clue that the user's account has been compromised.

We're sure that you know many of the following widely available and well-known guidelines for creating more secure passwords, but just in case, here's a recap:

» Use a mix of upper- and lowercase letters, numbers, and special characters (for example, !@#$%).

» Do not include your name or other personal information (such as spouse, street address, school, birthdays, and anniversaries).

» Replace some letters with numbers (for example, replace e with 3). This technique of modifying spelling is known as leet or leetspeak.

» Use nonsense phrases, misspellings, substitutions, or before-and-after words and phrases (combining two unrelated words or phrases, such as "Wheel of Fortune Cookies").

» Combine multiple words by using special characters (for example, sALT&pEPPER or W3'r3-n0t-in-K4ns4s-4nym0r3).

» Create a longer password that is actually a pass phrase. For instance, "I Love Green Bananas."

» Use a combination of all the other tips in this list (for example, "Snow White and the Seven Habits of Highly Effective People" becomes SW&t7HoH3P!).

» Do not use repeating patterns between changes (for example, password1, password2, password3).

» Do not use the same passwords for work and personal accounts.

» Do not use passwords that are too difficult to remember.

» Do not use any passwords you see in a published book, including this one. (But you knew that.)

The problem with these guidelines is that they're *widely available and well known*! In fact, attackers use some of these same guidelines to create their aliases or handles: *super-geek* becomes *5up3rg33k*. Also, a password such as *Qwerty12!* technically satisfies these guidelines, but it's not really a good password because it's a relatively simple and obvious pattern (the first row on your keyboard). Many dictionary attacks include not only word lists, but also patterns such as this one.

TIP

You can use a software tool that helps users evaluate the quality of their passwords when they create them. These tools are commonly known as *password/passphrase generators* or *password appraisers*.

ONE-TIME PASSWORDS

A *one-time password* is a password that's valid for one logon session only. After a single logon session, the password is no longer valid. Thus, if an attacker obtains a one-time password that someone has already used, that password has no value. A one-time password is a *dynamic password*, meaning it changes at some regular interval or event. Conversely, a *static password* is a password that remains the same for each logon. Similar to the concept of a one-time pad in cryptography (which we discuss in Chapter 5), a one-time password provides maximum security for access control.

Security professionals should be sure to distinguish one-time passwords from passwords that are valid for a short period of time. Often, what is considered a one-time password is actually a password that is valid for several minutes. Limited-time passwords are a big improvement in security, but they're subject to replay attacks if the attacker acts quickly.

PERSONAL IDENTIFICATION NUMBERS (PINs)

A PIN in itself is a relatively weak authentication mechanism because you have only 10,000 possible combinations for a four-digit numeric PIN. Therefore, organizations usually use some other safeguard in combination with a PIN. For example, a PIN used with a one-time token password and an account lockout policy is also very effective, allowing a user to attempt only one PIN/password combination per minute and then locking the account after three or five failed attempts as determined by the security policy.

REMEMBER

Two examples of one-time password implementations are tokens (which we discuss in the following section) and the S/Key protocol. The *S/Key protocol*, developed by Bell Communications Research and defined in Internet Engineering Task Force (IETF) Request For Comment (RFC) 1760, is client/server based and uses MD4 and MD5 to generate one-time passwords. *MD4* and *MD5* are algorithms used to verify data integrity by creating a 128-bit message digest from data input.

Multi-factor authentication

Multi-factor authentication involves two or more of *what you know*, *what you have*, and *what you are*. Multi-factor authentication is more challenging for an adversary to attack, since a successful attack of multi-factor authentication requires the attacker possess the user's token, or the ability to trick a biometric reader. Types of multi-factor authentication are discussed in this section and include tokens, certificates, and biometrics.

TOKENS

Tokens are access control devices such as key fobs, dongles, smart cards, magnetic cards, software (known as *soft tokens* and installed on a tablet, mobile device, smartphone, laptop, or PC), and keypad or calculator-type cards that store static passwords (or digital certificates) or that generate dynamic passwords. The three general types of tokens are

>> **Static password tokens:** Store a static password or digital certificate.

>> **Synchronous dynamic password tokens:** Continuously generate a new password or passcode at a fixed time interval (for example, 60 seconds) or in response to an event (such as every time you press a button). Typically, the passcode is valid only during a fixed time window (say, one minute) and only for a single logon (so, if you want to log on to more than one system, you must wait for the next passcode).

>> **Asynchronous (or *challenge-response*) dynamic password tokens:** Generate a new password or passcode asynchronously by calculating the correct response to a system-generated random challenge string (known as a *nonce*) that the owner manually enters.

Tokens provide two-factor authentication (something you have and something you know) by either requiring the owner to authenticate to the token first or by requiring that the owner enters a secret PIN along with the generated password. Both RADIUS and Terminal Access Controller Access Control System (TACACS+; which we discuss in the section "Centralized access controls," earlier in this chapter) support various token products.

WARNING

A soft token that's installed on a laptop or PC doesn't provide strong (two-factor) authentication because the "something you have" is the computer you're trying to log on to! However, a soft token such as Google Authenticator and Microsoft Authenticator on a smartphone would provide adequate two-factor authentication, provided the user is not trying to log in to an application from a smartphone.

You can use tokens to generate one-time passwords and provide two-factor authentication.

SMARTPHONE / SMS PASSWORDS

When a user attempts to log on to a system, a one-time or short-duration password can be sent to a smartphone or mobile device via a text message or other messaging mechanism. Upon receiving this password, the user would then enter it into the system's password field and complete the logon procedure.

DIGITAL CERTIFICATES

A digital certificate can be installed on the user's device. When the user attempts to authenticate to a system, the system will query the user's device for the digital certificate to confirm the user's identity. If the digital certificate can be obtained and if it is confirmed to be genuine, the user is permitted to log on.

Digital certificate authentication also helps to enforce users logging in using only company-provisioned devices. This presupposes the fact that the user is unable to copy the digital certificate to another, perhaps personally owned, device, or that an intruder is unable to copy the certificate to his own device.

WARNING

When implementing digital certificates on devices such as laptop computers, administrators need to be sure they implement a per-device or per-user certificate on each laptop computer, not a general company certificate.

BIOMETRICS

The only absolute method for positively identifying an individual is to base authentication on some unique physical or behavioral characteristic of that individual. Biometric identification uses physical characteristics, including fingerprints, hand geometry, and facial features such as retina and iris patterns. Behavioral biometrics are based on measurements and data derived from an action, and they indirectly measure characteristics of the human body. Behavioral characteristics include voice, signature, and keystroke patterns.

Biometrics are based on the third factor of authentication — something you are. Biometric access control systems apply the concept of identification and authentication (I&A) slightly differently, depending on their use:

>> **Physical access controls:** The individual presents the required biometric characteristic and the system attempts to *identify* the individual by matching the input characteristic to its database of authorized personnel. This type of control is also known as a *one-to-many* search.

>> **Logical access controls:** The user enters a username or PIN (or inserts a smart card), and then presents the required biometric characteristic for verification. The system attempts to *authenticate* the user by matching the claimed identity and the stored biometric image file for that account. This type of control is also known as a *one-to-one* search.

WARNING

Biometric authentication, in and of itself, doesn't provide *strong* authentication because it's based on only one of the three authentication requirements — something you *are*. To be considered a truly strong authentication mechanism, biometric authentication must include either something you *know* or something you *have*. (Although you might argue that your hand or eye is both something you have *and* something you are, for the purposes of the CISSP exam you'd be wrong!)

The necessary factors for an effective biometrics access control system include

>> **Accuracy:** The most important characteristic of any biometric system. The *uniqueness* of the body organ or characteristic that the system measures to guarantee positive identification is an important element of accuracy. In common biometric systems today, the only organs that satisfy this requirement are the fingers/hands and the eyes.

Another important element of accuracy is the system's ability to detect and reject forged or counterfeit input data. The accuracy of a biometric system is normally stated as a percentage, in the following terms:

- **False Reject Rate (FRR) or Type I error:** Authorized users to whom the system incorrectly denies access, stated as a percentage. Reducing a system's sensitivity reduces the FRR but increases the False Accept Rate (FAR).

REMEMBER

The False Reject Rate (or Type I error) is the percentage of authorized users to whom the system incorrectly denies access.

- **False Accept Rate (FAR) or Type II error:** Unauthorized users to whom the system incorrectly grants access, stated as a percentage. Increasing a system's sensitivity reduces the FAR but increases the FRR.

REMEMBER

The False Accept Rate (or Type II error) is the percentage of unauthorized users to whom the system incorrectly grants access.

- **Crossover Error Rate (CER):** The point at which the FRR equals the FAR, stated as a percentage. (See Figure 7-8.) Because you can adjust the FAR and FRR by changing a system's sensitivity, the CER is considered the most important measure of biometric system accuracy.

- The Crossover Error Rate is the point at which the FRR equals the FAR, stated as a percentage.

REMEMBER

>> **Speed and throughput:** The length of time required to complete the entire authentication procedure. This time measurement includes stepping up to the system, inputting a card or PIN (if required), entering biometric data (such as inserting a finger or hand in a reader, pressing a sensor, aligning an eye with a camera or scanner, speaking a phrase, or signing a name), processing the input data, and opening and closing an access door (in the case of a physical access control system). Another important measure is the initial enrollment time required to create a biometric file for a user account. Generally accepted standards are a speed of less than five seconds, a throughput rate of six to ten per minute, and enrollment time of less than two minutes.

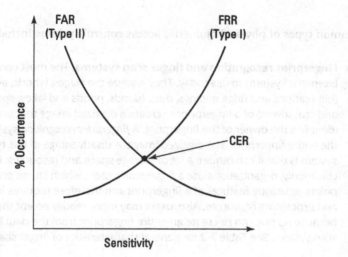

FIGURE 7-8:
Use CER to
compare FAR
and FRR.

>> **Data storage requirements:** The size of a biometric system's input files can be as small as 9 bytes or as large as 10,000 bytes, the normal range being 256 to 1,000 bytes.

>> **Reliability:** Reliability is an important factor in any system. The system must operate continuously and accurately without frequent maintenance outages.

>> **Acceptability:** Getting users to accept a biometric system is the biggest hurdle to widespread implementation. Certain privacy and ethics issues arise with the prospect of organizations using these systems to collect medical or other physical data about employees. Other factors that might potentially alarm users include intrusiveness of the data collection procedure and undesirable physical contact with common system components, such as pressing an eye against a plastic cup or placing lips close to a microphone for voice recognition.

REMEMBER

Gaining user acceptance is the most common difficulty with biometric systems.

Table 7-1 summarizes the generally accepted standards for the factors described in the preceding list.

TABLE 7-1

Generally Accepted Standards for Biometric Systems

Characteristic	Standard
Accuracy	CER < 10%
Speed	5 seconds
Throughput	6–10 per minute
Enrollment time	< 2 minutes

Common types of physical biometric access control systems include

>> **Fingerprint recognition and finger scan systems:** The most common biometric systems in use today. They analyze the ridges, whorls, and minutiae (bifurcations and ridge endings, dots, islands, ponds and lakes, spurs, bridges, and crossovers) of a fingerprint to create a digitized image that uniquely identifies the owner of the fingerprint. A *fingerprint recognition* system stores the entire fingerprint as a digitized image. A disadvantage of this type of system is that it can require a lot of storage space and resources. More commonly, organizations use a *finger scan system,* which stores only sample points or unique features of a fingerprint and therefore requires less storage and processing resources. Also, users may more readily accept the technology because no one can re-create an entire fingerprint from the data in a finger scan system. See Table 7-2 for general characteristics of finger scan systems.

TABLE 7-2   **General Characteristics of Finger Scan and Hand Geometry Systems**

Characteristic	Finger Scan	Hand Geometry
Accuracy	< 1%–5% (CER)	< 1%–2% (CER)
Speed	1–7 seconds	3–5 seconds
File size	~250–1500 bytes	~10 bytes
Advantages	Nonintrusive, inexpensive	Small file size
Disadvantages	Sensor wear and tear; accuracy may be affected by swelling, injury, or wearing rings	Sensor wear and tear; accuracy may be affected by swelling, injury, or wearing rings

REMEMBER

Finger scan systems, unlike fingerprint recognition systems, don't store an image of the entire fingerprint — only a digitized file describing its unique characteristics. This fact should allay the privacy concerns of most users.

>> **Facial recognition systems:** Fast becoming a popular authentication method used by Apple, Microsoft, and others, facial recognition works through recognition of the unique geometry of the user's facial features. Facial recognition software examines the face as the user looks into the device's camera and decides whether the person looking into the camera is the same person who is authorized to use the device.

» **Hand geometry systems:** Like finger scan systems, *hand geometry systems* are also nonintrusive and therefore generally more easily accepted than other biometric systems. These systems generally can more accurately uniquely identify an individual than finger scan systems, and they have some of the smallest file sizes compared with other biometric system types. A digital camera simultaneously captures a vertical and a horizontal image of the subject's hand, acquiring the three-dimensional hand geometry data. The digitized image records the length, width, height, and other unique characteristics of the hand and fingers. See Table 7-2 for general characteristics of hand geometry systems.

» **Retina pattern:** These systems record unique elements in the vascular pattern of the retina. Major concerns with this type of system are fears of eye damage from a laser (which is actually only a camera with a focused low-intensity light) directed at the eye and, more feasibly, privacy concerns. Certain health conditions, such as diabetes and heart disease, can cause changes in the retinal pattern, which these types of systems may detect. See Table 7-3 for general characteristics of retina pattern systems.

TABLE 7-3   **General Characteristics of Retina and Iris Pattern Systems**

Characteristic	Retina Pattern	Iris Pattern
Accuracy	1.5% (CER)	< 0.5% (CER)
Speed	4–7 seconds	2.5–4 seconds
File size	~96 bytes	~256–512 bytes
Advantages	Overall accuracy	Best overall accuracy
Disadvantages	Perceived intrusiveness; sanitation and privacy concerns	Subject must remain absolutely still; subject can't wear colored contact lenses or glasses (clear contacts are generally okay)

» **Iris pattern:** By far the most accurate of any type of biometric system. The *iris* is the colored portion of the eye surrounding the pupil. The complex patterns of the iris include unique features such as coronas, filaments, freckles, pits, radial furrows, rifts, and striations. The characteristics of the iris, formed shortly before birth, remain stable throughout life. The iris is so unique that even the two eyes of a single individual have different patterns. A camera directed at an aperture mirror scans the iris pattern. The subject must glance at the mirror from a distance of approximately 3 to 10 inches. It's technically feasible — but perhaps prohibitively expensive — to perform an iris scan from a distance of several feet. See Table 7-3 for general characteristics of iris pattern systems.

Common types of behavioral biometric systems include

>> **Voice recognition:** These systems capture unique characteristics of a subject's voice and may also analyze phonetic or linguistic patterns. Most voice recognition systems are text-dependent, requiring the subject to repeat a specific phrase. This functional requirement of voice recognition systems also helps improve their security by providing two-factor authentication: something you know (a phrase) and something you are (your voice). More advanced voice recognition systems may present a random phrase or group of words, which prevents an attacker from recording a voice authentication session and later replaying the recording to gain unauthorized access. See Table 7-4 for general characteristics of voice recognition systems.

TABLE 7-4 **General Characteristics of Voice Recognition and Signature Dynamics Systems**

Characteristic	Voice Recognition	Signature Dynamics
Accuracy	< 10% (CER)	1% (CER)
Speed	10–14 seconds	5–10 seconds
File size	~1,000–10,000 bytes	~1,000–1,500 bytes
Advantages	Inexpensive; nonintrusive	Nonintrusive
Disadvantages	Accuracy, speed, file size; affected by background noise, voice changes; can be fooled by voice imitation	Signature tablet wear and tear; speed; can be fooled by a forged signature

>> **Signature dynamics:** These systems typically require the subject to sign his or her name on a signature tablet. The enrollment process for a signature dynamics system captures numerous characteristics, including the signature pattern itself, the pressure applied to the signature pad, and the speed of the signature. Of course, signatures commonly exhibit some slight changes because of different factors, and they can be forged (although the signature dynamics are difficult to forge). See Table 7-4 for general characteristics of signature dynamics systems.

>> **Keystroke or typing dynamics:** These systems typically require the subject to type a password or phrase. The keystroke dynamic identification is based on unique characteristics such as how long a user holds down a key on the keyboard (dwell time) and how long it takes a user to get to and press a key (seek or flight time). These characteristics are measured by the system to form a series of mathematical data representing a user's unique typing pattern or signature, which is then used to authenticate the user.

WARNING

Digital signatures and *electronic signatures* — which are electronic copies of people's signatures — are not the same as the signatures used in biometric systems. These terms are *not* related and are *not* interchangeable.

TIP

In general, the CISSP candidate doesn't need to know the specific characteristics and specifications of the different biometric systems, but you should know how they compare with each other. For example, know that iris pattern systems are more accurate than retina pattern systems, and be familiar with the concepts of false reject rate, false accept rate, and crossover error rate.

Accountability

The concept of *accountability* refers to the capability of a system to associate users and processes with their actions (what they did). Audit trails and system logs are components of accountability.

Systems use audit logs and audit trails primarily as a means of troubleshooting problems and verifying events. Users should not view audit logs and audit trails as a threat or as "big brother" watching over them because they cannot be trusted. As a matter of fact, astute users consider these mechanisms as protective, because they not only prove what they did, but they also help to prove what they did not do. Still, it's wise for users to be mindful of the fact that the systems they use are recording their actions.

An important security concept that's closely related to accountability is non-repudiation. *Non-repudiation* means that a user (username Madame X) can't deny an action because her identity is positively associated with her actions. Non-repudiation is an important legal concept. If a system permits users to log in using a generic user account, or a user account that has a widely known password, or no user account at all, then you can't absolutely associate any user with a given (malicious) action or (unauthorized) access on that system, which makes it extremely difficult to prosecute or otherwise discipline that user.

REMEMBER

Accounting in AAA (authentication, authorization and accounting) services records what a subject did.

REMEMBER

Non-repudiation means that a user can't deny an action because you can irrefutably associate him or her with that action.

Session management

A *session* is a formal term referring to an individual user's dialogue, or series of interactions, with an information system. Information systems need to track individual users' sessions in order to properly distinguish one user's actions from another's.

In order to protect the confidentiality and integrity of data accessible through a session, information systems generally utilize session or activity timeouts, to prevent an unauthorized user from continuing a session that has been idle or otherwise inactive for a specified period of time.

Two primary means of session timeouts are utilized:

>> **Screen savers.** Implemented by the operating system, a screen saver locks the workstation or mobile device itself and requires the user to log back into the system after a period of inactivity. The workstation's or mobile device's screen saver protects all application sessions. Make sure that this actually locks the screen or device, as some systems can be configured to *not* require a PIN or password to unlock them.

>> **Inactivity timeouts.** Individual software applications may utilize an auto-locking or auto-logout feature if a user has been inactive for a specific period of time.

For example, if an authorized user leaves a computer terminal unlocked or a browser window on a workstation unattended, an unauthorized user can simply sit down at the workstation and continue the session.

TIP

Workstation inactivity timeouts were originally called "screen savers," to prevent a static image on a cathode ray tube (CRT) display from being burned into the display. While today's monitors do not require this protection, the term "screen saver" is still in common use.

Registration and proofing of identity

Formal user registration processes are important for secure account provisioning, particularly in large organizations where it is not practical or possible to know all of the workers. This is particularly critical in SSO, Federated, and PKI environments (see Chapter 5), where users will have access to multiple systems and applications.

Proof of identity often begins at the time of hire, when new workers are usually required to show government-issued identification and legal right-to-work status. These procedures should form the basis for initial user registration to information systems.

Organizations need to take several precautions when registering and provisioning users:

>> **User identity.** The organization must ensure that new user accounts are provisioned for, and given to, the correct user.

>> **Protection of privacy.** The organization should not use Social Security number, date of birth, or other sensitive private information to authenticate the user. Instead, other values should be used, such as employee number (or others that cannot be obtained by other employees).

>> **Temporary credentials.** The organization must ensure that temporary login credentials are assigned to the correct person. Others should not be able to easily guess temporary credentials. Finally, temporary credentials should be set to expire in a short period of time.

>> **Birthright access.** The organization should periodically review what birthright access is granted to new workers, following the principles of *need to know* and *least privilege*.

Additional considerations about user identity occur when a user is attempting to log on to a system. These are

>> **Geographic location.** This can be derived from the IP address of the user. This is not absolutely reliable, but can be helpful to determine the user's location. Many devices, particularly smartphones and tablet computers, utilize GPS technology for location information, which is generally more reliable than IP address.

>> **Workstation in use.** The organization may have policies about whether a user is permitted to log on with a personally owned or from a public kiosk workstation.

>> **Elapsed time since last logon.** How long it has been since the user last logged on to the system or application.

>> **Logon attempt after failed attempts.** Whether there have been recent unsuccessful logon attempts.

Depending on the preceding conditions, the system may be configured to present additional challenges to the user. These challenges ensure that the person attempting to log in actually is the authorized user, not another person or machine. This is known as *risk-based authentication*.

Federated identity management

Federated identity management (FIM) enables multiple organizations to use each other's user identification and authentication systems to access their networks and systems. Federation of identity (FIdM) comprises the standards, technologies, and tools used to facilitate the portability of identity across separately managed organizations.

FIdM permits organizations that want to facilitate easier user access to their systems without having to create custom solutions. Instead, they need only configure existing tools and occasionally add "connectors" to facilitate inter-organization identity management.

Technologies in common use in federated environments include

>> Single sign-on (SSO)

>> Security Assertion Markup Language (SAML)

>> OAuth

>> OpenID

Credential management systems

Credential management systems enable an organization to centrally organize and control userids and passwords for users. This should not be confused with systems used to store and manage users' professional credentials (such as the CISSP certification).

Credential management systems are available as commercial software products that can be implemented either on-premises or in the cloud.

Credential management systems create user accounts for subjects, and provision those credentials as required into both individual systems and centralized identity management systems (such as LDAP or Microsoft Active Directory). Credential management systems can be either separate applications (as explained previously) or an integral part of an identity and access management system.

Integrate Identity-as-a-Service

Most organizations have a variety of business applications, some of which run on-premises while others are in the cloud. In order to avoid the issue of users having to manage multiple sets of user credentials, many organizations have implemented some form of cloud-based identity management service. The benefits to organizations are twofold:

>> **Increased convenience.** Users have fewer (as few as one) sets of logon credentials for access to business systems.

>> **Reduced risk.** Users are apt to use stronger passwords, and are less likely to handle credentials unsafely (such as using sticky notes on monitors). Many organizations employ multi-factor authentication, further reducing risk.

The manner in which organizations implement a centralized identity and access management system depends on several factors, including:

>> **Integration effort.** Newer applications have one or more interfaces available to facilitate automated account provisioning and single sign-on. Older applications usually lack these interfaces.

>> **Available resources.** Even for easily integrated applications, there is still some effort required to perform and maintain integrations over time.

>> **Efficiency tolerance.** If the organization is intolerant of inefficiencies, such as users having to log on to business applications many times each day, they may be more likely to pursue an IAM solution.

>> **Risk tolerance.** If an organization as averse to the risks associated with users possessing multiple sets of logon credentials for critical business systems, it will be more apt to implement an IAM solution.

Because most organizations' newer business systems are cloud based, many are opting to implement cloud based identity management and/or single sign-on systems. While each IAM platform has its own unique capabilities and architecture, generally an IAM system will resemble the architecture depicted in Figure 7-9.

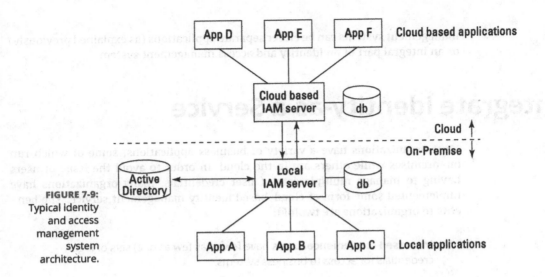

App D | App E | App F Cloud based applications

Cloud based IAM server — db

Cloud ↑
On-Premise ↓

Active Directory — Local IAM server — db

App A | App B | App C Local applications

FIGURE 7-9: Typical identity and access management system architecture.

Integrate Third-Party Identity Services

Organizations with on-premises systems often purchase and integrate identity management tools into their environments in order to reduce the burden of identity management, as well as improve end user experience. Where Microsoft servers are used, organizations can integrate their systems and applications with Active Directory, which is included with Microsoft server operating systems. In organizations without Microsoft servers, open source tools that use LDAP (lightweight directory access protocol) are a preferred choice. There are also several commercial on-premises identity service products that can be installed and integrated with systems, devices, and software applications.

On-premises identity management tools generally have the same features as their cloud-based counterparts. Some of these tools can be either implemented on-premises or cloud-based, and a few offer solutions that employ cloud-based and on-premises working together as a single identity access solution.

Implement and Manage Authorization Mechanisms

Authorization mechanisms are the portions of operating systems and applications that determine which data and functions a user is permitted to access, based upon the user's identity. *Authorization* (also referred to as *establishment*) defines the rights and permissions granted to a user account or process (what the user can do and/or what data the user can access)). After a system or application authenticates a user, authorization determines what that user (subject) can do with a system or resource (object).

Data access controls protect systems and information by restricting access to system files and user data based on user identity. Data access controls also provide authorization and accountability, relying on system access controls to provide identification and authentication.

Access control techniques

Data access control techniques are generally categorized as either discretionary or mandatory. You, as a CISSP candidate, must fully understand the concept of discretionary and mandatory access controls and be able to describe specific access control methods that fall under each category.

Role-based access control

Role-based access control (RBAC) is a method for managing user access controls. Role-based access control assigns group membership according to organizational or functional roles. Individuals may belong to one or many groups (either acquiring cumulative permissions or limited to the most restrictive set of permissions for all assigned groups); a group may contain only a single individual (corresponding to a specific organizational role assigned to one person). Access rights and permissions for objects are assigned to groups, rather than (or in addition to) individuals. RBAC greatly simplifies the management of access rights and permissions, particularly in organizations that have large functional groups or departments, and organizations that routinely rotate personnel through various positions or otherwise experience high turnover.

The advantages of role-based access control include

>> User access tends to be more uniform.

>> Changing many users' access often involves just changing the access rights for one or more roles.

Many systems that employ RBAC still permit access rights to be granted to individual end users. Still, many organizations tend to stick with the use of roles, even if there are instances where only one member is a member of a role.

The concept of role based access control is depicted in Figure 7-10.

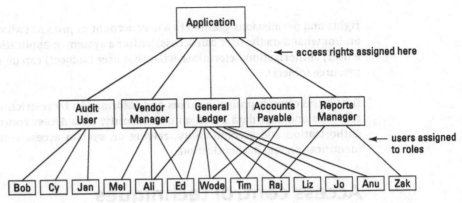

FIGURE 7-10:
Role based
access control.

Role based access control

Rule-based access control

Rule-based access control (not to be confused with role-based access control in the preceding section) is one method of applying mandatory access control. Actually, all MAC-based systems (discussed next) implement a simple form of rule-based access control by matching an object's sensitivity label and a subject's sensitivity label to determine whether the system should grant or deny access. You can apply additional rules by using rule-based access control to further define specific conditions for access to a requested object. Other types of rules to govern access include

>> Time of day

>> Workstation or terminal in use

>> User geographical location

>> Contents of data being accessed

Mandatory access control

A *mandatory access control* (MAC) is an access policy determined by the system, rather than by the owner. Organizations use MAC in multilevel systems that process highly sensitive data, such as classified government and military information. A *multilevel system* is a single computer system that handles multiple classification levels between subjects and objects. Two important concepts in MAC are

>> **Sensitivity labels:** In a MAC-based system, all subjects and objects must have assigned labels. A subject's sensitivity label specifies its level of trust. An object's sensitivity label specifies the level of trust required for access. In order to access

a given object, the subject must have a sensitivity level equal to or higher than the requested object. For example, a user (subject) with a Top Secret clearance (sensitivity label) is permitted to access a file (object) that has a Secret classification level (sensitivity label) because his or her clearance level exceeds the minimum required for access. We discuss classification systems in Chapter 4.

>> **Data import and export:** Controlling the import of information from other systems and the export to other systems (including printers) is a critical function of MAC-based systems, which must ensure that the system properly maintains and implements sensitivity labels so that sensitive information is appropriately protected at all times.

Lattice-based access controls are another method of implementing mandatory access controls. A *lattice model* is a mathematical structure that defines greatest lower-bound and least upper-bound values for a pair of elements, such as a subject and an object. Organizations can use this model for complex access control decisions involving multiple objects and/or subjects. For example, given a set of files that have multiple classification levels, the lattice model determines the minimum clearance level that a user requires to access all the files.

Major disadvantages of mandatory access control techniques include

>> Lack of flexibility

>> Difficulty in implementing and programming

>> User frustration

REMEMBER

In MAC, the system determines the access policy.

Discretionary access control

A *discretionary access control* (DAC) is an access policy determined by the owner of a file (or other resource). The owner decides who's allowed access to the file and what privileges they have.

REMEMBER

In DAC, the owner determines the access policy.

Two important concepts in DAC are

>> **File and data ownership:** Because the owner of the resource (which may consist of files, directories, data, system resources, and devices) determines the access policy, every object in a system must have an owner. Theoretically, an object without an owner is left unprotected, or without a user who can

determine who or what can access it. Normally, the *owner* of a resource is the person who created the resource (such as a file or directory), but in certain cases, you may need to explicitly identify the owner.

>> **Access rights and permissions:** The controls that an owner can assign to individual users or groups for specific resources. Various systems (Windows-based or UNIX-based) define different sets of permissions that are essentially variations or extensions of three basic types of access:

- **Read (R):** The subject can read contents of a file or list contents of a directory.

- **Write (W):** The subject can change the contents of a file or directory (including add, rename, create, and delete).

- **Execute (X):** If the file is a program, the subject can run the program.

Access control lists (ACLs) provide a flexible method for applying discretionary access controls. An ACL lists the specific rights and permissions that are assigned to a subject for a given object.

Major disadvantages of discretionary access control techniques such as ACLs or role-based access control include

>> Lack of centralized administration.

>> Dependence on security-conscious resource owners.

>> Many popular operating systems defaulting to full access for everyone if the owner doesn't explicitly set permissions.

>> Difficult, if not impossible, auditing because of the large volume of individual permissions, as well as log entries that can be generated.

REMEMBER

Various operating systems implement ACLs differently. Although the CISSP exam doesn't directly test your knowledge of specific operating systems or products, you should be aware of this fact. Also, understand that ACLs in this context are different from ACLs used on routers (see Chapter 5), which have nothing to do with DAC.

Attribute-based access control

Attribute-based access control (ABAC) is an access policy determined by the attributes of a subject and object, as well as environmental factors. In an ABAC-based system, the ability for a subject to access an object is based on one or more attributes about the subject (such as the subject's position title, department, or project assignment), as well as attributes about the object itself (such as its name, project name, owner, or location). Further, environmental factors are used to determine whether access will be granted; example environmental factors include the location of the subject, the time of day, and other conditions.

In an ABAC-based system, the access decision is made by the Policy Decision Point (PDP) and enforced by the Policy Enforcement Point (PEP).

TIP
ABAC is defined in NIST SP-162, Guide to Attribute Based Access Control (ABAC) Definition and Considerations, which is available at www.nist.gov.

Prevent or Mitigate Access Control Attacks

Gaining access to a system or network is often on an attacker's list of objectives. Attackers commonly use several methods of attack against access control systems, including:

>> **Brute-force attack:** The attacker attempts every possible combination of letters, numbers, and characters to crack a password, passphrase, or PIN.

>> **Dictionary attack:** A *dictionary attack* is essentially a more focused type of brute force attack in which the attacker uses a predefined word list. You can find such word lists or dictionaries, including foreign language and special-interest dictionaries, widely available on the Internet for use in password-cracking utilities such as L0phtCrack and John the Ripper. Attackers typically run these password-cracking utilities against a copy of the target system's (or network's) security accounts database or password file. The utility creates hashes of passwords contained in its dictionary or word list, and then compares the resulting hash to the password file. These types of programs work very quickly and effectively (see the sidebar "How much brute force does it take to crack your passwords?" in this chapter), even when organizations use complex passwords, so the key to defending against a brute-force or dictionary attack is to protect your security accounts databases and password files.

>> **Rainbow table:** Here, an attacker steals the file or database containing hashed passwords from a target system, and then looks up the hashes in a large database called a *rainbow table*. This is essentially a list of all possible hashes and the original plaintext for each hash. If an organization has not "salted" its hashes, this type of attack is relatively easy to carry out.

>> **Buffer or stack overflow:** *Buffer or stack overflows* constitute the most common and successful type of computer attacks today. Although often used in Denial of Service attacks, buffer overflows in certain systems or applications may enable an attacker to bypass authentication controls and gain unauthorized access to a

system or directory. An overflow occurs when an application or protocol attempts to store more information than the allotted resources will allow. This causes previously entered data to become corrupted, the protocol or application to crash, or other unexpected or erratic behavior to occur. A *teardrop attack* is a type of stack overflow attack that exploits vulnerabilities in the IP protocol. The best defense against buffer or stack overflow attacks is to identify and patch vulnerabilities in the system, network, and applications as quickly as possible after each vulnerability is identified (and, ideally, before the affected code or application is used in a production environment).

» **Man-in-the-Middle attacks:** Here, an attacker intercepts messages between two parties and forwards a modified version of the original message to the intended recipient. For example, an attacker may substitute his or her own public key during a public-key exchange between two parties. The two parties believe that they're still communicating only with each other and unknowingly encrypt messages by using the attacker's public key, rather than the intended recipient's public key. The attacker can then decrypt secret messages between the two parties, modify their contents as desired, and send them on to the unwary recipient.

» **Packet (or password) sniffing:** An attacker uses an application or device, known as a *sniffer*, to capture network packets and analyze their contents, such as usernames and passwords, and shared keys.

» **Session hijacking:** Similar to a Man-in-the-Middle attack, except that the attacker impersonates the intended recipient, instead of modifying messages in transit.

» **Social engineering:** This low-tech method is one of the most effective and easily perpetrated forms of attack. Common techniques involve phishing, dumpster diving, shoulder surfing, raiding cubicles (looking for passwords on monitors, under keyboards, and under mouse pads), and plain ol' asking. This latter brazen technique can simply involve the attacker calling a user, pretending to be a system administrator and asking for the user's password, or calling a help desk pretending to be a user and asking to have the password reset.

Organizations should employ various tactics and processes to counter access control attacks, including:

» **Threat modeling.** Ensures that security is a key design consideration early in the application development lifecycle. A security specification is created and tested during the design phase to identify likely threats, vulnerabilities and countermeasures for a specific application and its uses.

- **Asset valuation.** The process of assigning a financial value to an organization's information assets, thereby enabling an objective measure of the systems and data that require various levels of protection.

- **Vulnerability analysis.** This is the process of identifying, defining, and prioritizing a system's vulnerabilities.

- **Source code review.** Developers examine the source code for an application, to see whether software defects that could permit a successful attack exist in the system.

- **Access aggregation.** Simplify access controls by combining all of a user's access rights, privileges, and permissions across a single or multiple systems (for example, using reduced sign-on or single sign-on).

Manage the Identity and Access Provisioning Lifecycle

Organizations must adopt formal policies and procedures to address account provisioning, review, and revocation. The phases in the IAM provisioning lifecycle are

- **Role design, creation, and review.** During development, customization, or configuration of a system, each of the user roles is designed. These designs are subjected to a review process to ensure they are appropriate.

- **Access provisioning.** When new or temporary employees, contractors, partners, auditors, and third parties require access to an organization's systems and networks, the organization must have a formal methodology for requesting access. The steps in access provisioning are:

  - **Access request.** A requestor, typically but not always the end user, makes a formal request to access specific data or a specific role in a system.

  - **Request review.** The request is reviewed by a designated person or group for appropriateness. Sometimes the reviewer may ask questions of the requestor to better understand the reason for the request.

  - **Access approval.** The request is approved by a designated person or group.

  - **Access provisioning.** The requested and approved access is provisioned in the system.

REMEMBER

New accounts must be provisioned correctly and in a timely manner to ensure access is ready and available when the user needs it, but not too soon (so as to ensure that new accounts not yet in active use are not compromised by an attacker).

>> **Account access review.** User and system accounts, along with their assigned privileges, should be reviewed on a regular basis to ensure that they are still appropriate. For example, an employee may no longer require the same privilege levels due to rotation of duties (see Chapter 9) or a transfer or promotion.

>> **Role review.** Periodically, designated personnel examine the roles in a system to determine whether the access rights defined in each role are appropriate.

>> **Inactivity review.** Periodically, designated personnel will examine a system to see whether users are accessing it. Users who have not accessed a system (or a role in the system) for a given period of time (for example, 90 days) may have their access revoked.

>> **Access termination.** Finally, when access is no longer required, accounts must be promptly disabled and deprovisioned. Deprovisioning should be automated when possible and should include moving the disabled account to a protected organizational unit (in Active Directory) or other restricted group, as well as removing the disabled account from all group memberships.

TIP

User accounts are typically locked within 24 hours of termination. In the case of dismissal, user accounts are typically locked immediately prior to the employee being notified.

Chapter **8**

Security Assessment and Testing

I n this chapter, you learn about the various tools and techniques that security professionals use to continually assess and validate an organization's security environment. This domain represents 12 percent of the CISSP certification exam.

Design and Validate Assessment and Test Strategies

Modern security threats are rapidly and constantly evolving. Likewise, an organization's systems, applications, networks, services, and users are frequently changing. Thus, it is critical that organizations develop an effective strategy to regularly test, evaluate, and adapt their business and technology environment to reduce the probability and impact of successful attacks, as well as achieve compliance with applicable laws, regulations, and contractual obligations.

Organizations need to implement a proactive assessment and test strategy for both existing and new information systems and assets. The strategy should be an integral part of the risk management process to help the organization identify new and changing risks that are important enough to warrant analysis, decisions, and action.

Security personnel must identify all applicable laws, regulations, and other legal obligations such as contracts to understand what assessments, testing, and auditing are required. Further, security personnel should examine their organization's risk management framework and control framework to see what assessments, control testing, and audits are suggested or required. The combination of these would then become a part of the organization's overall strategy for assuring that all its security-related tools, systems, and processes are operating properly.

There are three main perspectives that come into play when planning for an organization's assessments, testing, and auditing:

>> **Internal:** This represents assessments, testing, and auditing performed by personnel who are a part of the organization. The advantages of using internal resources for assessments, tests, and audits include lower cost and greater familiarity with the organization's practices and systems. However, internal personnel may not be as objective as external parties.

>> **External:** This represents assessments, testing, and audits performed by people from an external organization or agency. Some laws and regulations, as well as contractual obligations, may require external assessments, test, and audits of certain systems and processes. The greatest advantage of using external personnel is that they're objective. However, they're often more expensive, particularly for activities requiring higher skill levels or specialized tools.

>> **Third parties:** This is all about audits of critical business activities that have been outsourced to external service providers, or third parties. Here, the systems and personnel being examined belong to an external service provider. Depending upon requirements in applicable laws, regulations, and contracts, these assessments of third parties may be performed by internal personnel, or in some cases external personnel may be required.

TIP

Many third-party service providers will commission external audits whose audit reports can be distributed to their customers. This can help service providers avoid multiple audits by its customers. Examples of such audits include SSAE 18, SOC-1, and SOC-2. Service providers also commission security consulting firms to conduct penetration tests on systems and applications, which helps them to reduce the number of customers who would want to do this themselves.

Conduct Security Control Testing

Security control testing employs various tools and techniques, including vulnerability assessments, penetration (or *pen*) testing, synthetic transactions, interfaces testing, and more. You learn about these and other tools and techniques in the following sections.

Vulnerability assessments

A vulnerability assessment is performed to identify, evaluate, quantify, and prioritize security weaknesses in an application or system. Additionally, a vulnerability assessment provides remediation steps to mitigate specific vulnerabilities that are identified in the environment.

There are three general types of vulnerability assessments:

>> Port scan (not intensive)

>> Vulnerability scan (more intensive)

>> Penetration test (most intensive)

Generally, automated network-based scanning tools are used to identify vulnerabilities in applications, systems, and network devices in a network. Sometimes, system-based scanning tools are used to examine configuration settings to identify exploitable vulnerabilities. Often, network- and system-based tools are used together to build a more complete picture of vulnerabilities in an environment.

Port scanning

A *port scan* uses a tool that communicates over the network with one or more target systems on various Transmission Control Protocol/Internet Protocol (TCP/IP) ports. A port scan can discover the presence of ports that should probably be disabled (because they serve no useful or necessary purpose on a particular system).

Vulnerability scans

Network-based vulnerability scanning tools send network messages to systems in a network to identify any utilities, programs, or tools that may be configured to communicate over the network. These tools attempt to identify the version of any utilities, programs, and tools; often, it is enough to know the versions of the programs that are running, because scanning tools often contain a database of known vulnerabilities associated with program versions. Scanning tools may also send specially crafted messages to running programs to see if those programs contain any exploitable vulnerabilities.

Tools are also used to identify vulnerabilities in software applications. Generally, these tools are divided into two types: dynamic application security testing (DAST) and static application security testing (SAST). DAST will execute an application and then use techniques such as fuzzing to attempt to identify exploitable vulnerabilities that could permit an attacker to successfully compromise a software application; this would permit an attacker to alter or steal data or take over control of the system. SAST examine an application's source code and look for exploitable vulnerabilities. Neither DAST nor SAST can find all vulnerabilities, but when used together by skilled personnel, many exploitable vulnerabilities can be found.

Examples of network-based vulnerability scanning tools include Nessus, Rapid7, and Qualys. Examples of system-based vulnerability scanning tools include Microsoft Baseline Security Analyzer (MBSA) and Flexera (formerly Secunia) PSI. Examples of application scanning tools include IBM AppScan, HP WebInspect, HP Fortify, Accunetix, and Burp Suite.

Unauthenticated and authenticated scans

Vulnerability scanning tools (both those used to examine systems and network devices, as well as those that examine applications) generally perform two types of scans: unauthenticated scans and authenticated scans. In an *authenticated scan*, the scanning tool will be configured with login credentials and will attempt to log in to the device, system, or application to identify vulnerabilities not discoverable otherwise. In an *unauthenticated scan*, the scanning tool will not attempt to log in; hence, it can only discover vulnerabilities that would be exploitable by someone who does not possess valid login credentials.

Vulnerability scan reports

Generally, all the types of scanning tools discussed in this section create some sort of a report that contains summary and detailed information about the scan that was performed and vulnerabilities that were identified. Many of these tools produce a good amount of detail, including steps used to identify each vulnerability, the severity of each vulnerability, and steps that can be taken to remediate each vulnerability.

Some vulnerability scanning tools employ a proprietary methodology for vulnerability identification, but most scanning tools include a common vulnerability scoring system (CVSS) score for each identified vulnerability. Application security is discussed in more detail in Chapter 10.

Vulnerability assessments are a key part of risk management (discussed in Chapter 3).

Penetration testing

Penetration testing (*pen testing* for short) is the most rigorous form of vulnerability assessment. The level of effort required to perform a penetration test is far higher than for a port scan or vulnerability scan. Typically, an organization will employ a penetration test on a target system or environment when it wants to simulate an actual attack by an adversary.

Network penetration testing

A *network penetration test* of systems and network devices generally begins with a port scan and/or a vulnerability scan. This gives the pen tester an inventory of the attack surface of the network and the systems and devices connected to the network. The pen test will continue with extensive use of manual techniques used to identify and/or exploit vulnerabilities. In other words, the pen tester uses both automated as well as manual techniques to identify and confirm vulnerabilities.

Occasionally, a pen tester will exploit vulnerabilities during a penetration test. Pen testers generally tread carefully here because they must be acutely aware of the target environment. For instance, if a pen tester is testing a live production environment, exploiting vulnerabilities could result in malfunctions or outages in the target environment. In some cases, data corruption or data loss could also result.

When performing a penetration test, the pen tester will often take screen shots showing the exploited system or device. Often, a pen tester does this because system/device owners sometimes don't believe that their environments contain exploitable vulnerabilities. By including screen shots in the final report, the pen tester is "proving" that vulnerabilities exist and are exploitable.

Pen testers often include details for reproducing exploits in their reports. This is helpful for system or network engineers who often want to reproduce the exploit, so that they can "see for themselves" that the vulnerability does, in fact, exist. It's also helpful when engineers or developers make changes to mitigate the vulnerabilities; they can use the same techniques to see whether their fixes closed the vulnerabilities.

In addition to scanning networks, some other techniques are generally included in the topic of network penetration testing, including the following:

>> **War dialing:** Hackers use war dialing to sequentially dial all phone numbers in a range to discover any active modems. The hacker then attempts to compromise any connected systems or networks via the modem connection. This is old school, but it's still used occasionally.

THE COMMON VULNERABILITY SCORING SYSTEM

The common vulnerability scoring system (CVSS) is an industry-standard method that has been used to numerically score vulnerabilities according to their severity. Numeric scores for vulnerabilities help security personnel prioritize remediation, generally by fixing vulnerabilities with higher scores before tackling those with lower scores.

The formula for arriving at a CVSS score for a given vulnerability is fairly complicated. All you need to understand is its basic structure. A CVSS score examines several aspects of a vulnerability, including the following:

- **Access vector:** How a vulnerability is exploited.

- **Access complexity:** How easy or difficult it is to exploit a vulnerability.

- **Authentication:** Whether an attacker must authenticate to a target system to exploit it.

- **Confidentiality:** The potential impact on the confidentiality of data on the target system if it is exploited.

- **Integrity:** The potential impact on the integrity of data on the target system if it is exploited.

- **Availability:** The potential impact on the availability of data or applications on the target system if it is exploited.

Generally speaking, the higher a CVSS score, the easier it is to exploit a given vulnerability, and with more impact on the target systems.

- **» War driving:** War driving is the 21st-century version of war dialing. Someone uses a laptop computer and literally drives around a densely populated area, looking to discover unprotected (or poorly protected) wireless access points.

- **» Radiation monitoring:** *Radio frequency* (RF) *emanations* are the electromagnetic radiation emitted by computers and network devices. *Radiation monitoring* is similar to packet sniffing and war driving in that someone uses sophisticated equipment to try to determine what data is being displayed on monitors, transmitted on local area networks (LANs), or processed in computers.

- **» Eavesdropping:** Eavesdropping is as low-tech as dumpster diving, but a little less (physically) dirty. Basically, an *eavesdropper* takes advantage of one or more persons who are talking or using a computer — and paying little attention to whether someone else is listening to their conversations or watching them work with discreet over-the-shoulder glances. (The technical term for the latter is *shoulder surfing*.)

» **Packet sniffing:** A *packet sniffer* is a tool that captures all TCP/IP packets on a network, not just those being sent to the system or device doing the sniffing. An Ethernet network is a shared-media network (see Chapter 6), which means that any or all devices on the LAN can (theoretically) view all packets. However, switched-media LANs are more prevalent today and sniffers on switched-media LANs generally pick up only packets intended for the device running the sniffer.

TIP

A network adapter that operates in *promiscuous mode* accepts all packets, not just the packets destined for the system and sends them to the operating system.

Application penetration testing

An *application penetration test* is used to identify vulnerabilities in a software application. Although the principles of an application penetration test are the same as a network penetration test, the tools and skills are somewhat different. Someone performing an application penetration test generally will have an extensive background in software development. Indeed, the best application pen testers are often former software developers or software engineers.

Physical penetration testing

Penetration tests are also performed on the controls protecting physical premises, to see whether it is possible for an intruder to bypass security controls such as locked doors and keycard-controlled entrances. Sometimes pen testers will employ various social engineering techniques to gain unauthorized access to work centers and sensitive areas within work centers such as computer rooms and file storage rooms. Often, they plant evidence, such as a business card or other object to prove they were successful.

PACKET SNIFFING ISN'T ALL BAD

Packet sniffing isn't just a tool used by hackers to pick up user IDs and passwords from the LAN. Packet sniffing has legitimate uses, as well. Primarily, you can use it as a diagnostic tool to troubleshoot network devices, such as a firewall (to see whether the desired packets get through), routers, switches, and virtual LANs (VLANs).

The obvious danger of the packet sniffer falling into the wrong hands is that it provides the capability to capture sensitive data, including user IDs and passwords. Equally perilous is the fact that packet sniffers can be difficult to detect on a network.

TIP

Hacking for Dummies, 6th Edition, explores penetration testing and other techniques in more detail.

In addition to breaking into facilities, another popular technique used by physical pen testers is dumpster diving. Dumpster diving is low-tech penetration testing at its best (or worst), and is exactly what it sounds like. Dumpster diving can sometimes be an extraordinarily fruitful way to obtain information about an organization. Organizations in highly competitive environments also need to be concerned about where their trash and recycled paper goes.

Social engineering

Social engineering is any testing technique that employs some means for tricking individuals into performing some action or providing some information that provides the pen tester with the ability to break in to an application, system, or network. Social engineering involves such low-tech tactics as an attacker pretending to be a support technician, then calling an employee and asking for their password. You'd think most people would be smart enough not to fall for this, but people are people (and Soylent Green is people)! Some of the ruses used in social engineering tests include the following:

>> **Phishing messages:** Email messages purporting to be something they're not, in an attempt to lure someone into opening a file or clicking a link. Test phishing messages are, of course, harmless but are used to see how many personnel fall for the ruse.

PHISHING AND ITS VARIANTS

Phishing messages pretend to be something they're not. There are several specific forms of phishing, including:

- **Pharming.** This is an attack that results in users visiting an imposter website instead of the site they intend to visit. This can be accomplished through an attack on a system's *hosts* file, an organization's DNS, or a domain homograph attack.

- **Spear phishing.** These are phishing messages that specifically target a single organization (or part of an organization) with highly customized messaging.

- **Whaling.** These are phishing messages that target executes.

- **Smishing.** These are phishing messages that are delivered through SMS (short message service), also known as texting.

- **Lishing.** These are messages created using fraudulent LinkedIn user profiles.

>> **Telephone calls:** Calls to various workers inside an organization can be made to trick them into performing tasks. For instance, a call to the service desk might attempt to reset a user's account (possibly enabling the pen tester to log in using that user's account), a call to any employee claiming to be from the IT service desk to see whether the user will give up login credentials or perform a task, or a call to any employee claiming to be someone in need of assistance.

>> **Tailgating:** Attempts to enter a restricted work area by following legitimate personnel as they pass through a controlled doorway. Sometimes the tester will be carrying boxes in the hopes that an employee will hold the door open for them, or they may pose as a delivery or equipment repair person.

Log reviews

Reviewing your various security logs on a regular basis (daily, ideally) is a critical step in security control testing. Unfortunately, this important task often ranks only slightly higher than "updating documentation" on many administrators' "to-do" list. Log reviews often happen only after an incident has already occurred. But that's not the time to discover that your logging is incomplete or insufficient.

Logging requirements (including any regulatory or legal mandates) need to be clearly defined in an organization's security policy, including:

>> What gets logged, such as

- Events in network devices, such as firewalls, intrusion prevention systems (IPS), web filters, and data loss prevention (DLP) systems
- Events in server and workstation operating systems
- Events in subsystems, such as web servers, database management systems, and application gateways
- Events in applications

>> What's in the logs, such as

- Date/time of event
- Source (and destination, if applicable), protocol, and IP addresses
- Device, System and/or User ID
- Event ID and category
- Event details

>> When and how often the logs are reviewed.

>> The level of logging (how verbose the logs are)

>> How and where the logs are transmitted, stored, and protected; for example:

- Are the logs stored on a centralized log server or on the local system hard drives?
- Which secure transmission protocol is used to ensure the integrity of the logging data in transit?
- How are date and timestamps synchronized (such as an NTP server)?
- Is encryption of the logs required?
- Who is authorized access to the logs?
- Which safeguards are in place to protect the integrity of the logs?
- How is access to the logs logged?

>> How long the logs are retained.

>> Which events in logs are triggered to generate alerts, and to whom alerts are sent.

TIP

Various log management tools, such as *security information and event management* (SIEM) systems (discussed in Chapter 9), often are used to help with real-time monitoring, parsing, anomaly detection, and generation of alerts to key personnel.

Synthetic transactions

Synthetic transactions are real-time actions or events that automatically execute on monitored objects. For example, a tool may be used to regularly perform a series of scripted steps on an e-commerce website to measure performance, identify impending performance issues, and simulate the user experience. Thus, synthetic transactions can help an organization proactively test, monitor, and ensure availability (refer to the C–I–A triad in Chapter 3) for critical systems and monitor service-level agreement (SLA) guarantees.

Application performance monitoring tools traditionally have produced such metrics as system uptime, correct processing, and transaction latency. While uptime certainly is an important aspect of availability, it is only one component. Increasingly, reachability (which is a more user- or application-centric metric) is becoming the preferred metric for organizations that focus on customer experience. After all, it doesn't do your customers much good if your web servers are up 99.999 percent of the time, but Internet connections from their region of the world are slow, DNS doesn't resolve quickly, or web pages take 5 or 6 seconds to load in an online world that measures responsiveness in milliseconds! Hence, other key metrics for applications are correct processing (perhaps expressed as a percentage, which should be pretty close to 100 percent!) and *transaction latency* (the length of time it takes for specific types of transactions to complete). These metrics help operations personnel spot application problems.

Code review and testing

Code review and testing (sometimes known as *peer review*) involves systematically examining application source code to identify bugs, mistakes, inefficiencies, and security vulnerabilities in software programs. Online software repositories, such as Mercurial and Git, enable software developers to manage source code in a collaborative development environment. A code review can be accomplished either manually by carefully examining code changes visually, or by using automated code reviewing software (such as IBM AppScan Source, HP Fortify, and CA Veracode). Different types of code review and testing techniques include

>> **Pair programming.** *Pair* (or *peer*) *programming* is a technique commonly used in agile software development and extreme programming (both discussed in Chapter 10), in which two developers work together and alternate between writing and reviewing code, line by line.

>> **Lightweight code review.** Often performed as part of the development process, consisting of informal walkthroughs, e-mail pass-around, tool-assisted, and/or over-the-shoulder (not recommended for the rare introverted or paranoid developer!) reviews.

>> **Formal inspections.** Structured processes, such as the *Fagan inspection*, used to identify defects in design documents, requirements specifications, test plans and source code, throughout the development process.

TIP

Code review and testing can be invaluable in helping to identify software vulnerabilities such as buffer overflows, script injection vulnerabilities, memory leaks, and race conditions (see Chapter 10 to learn more).

Misuse case testing

The opposite of *use case testing* (in which normal or expected behavior in a system or application is defined and tested), *abuse/misuse case testing* is the process of performing unintended and malicious actions in a system or application in order to produce abnormal or unexpected behavior, and thereby identify potential vulnerabilities.

After misuse case testing identifies a potential vulnerability, a use case can be developed to define new requirements for eliminating or mitigating similar vulnerabilities in other programs and applications.

A common technique used in misuse case testing is known as *fuzzing*. Fuzzing involves the use of automated tools that can produce dozens (or hundreds, or even more) of combinations of input strings to be fed to a program's data input fields in order to elicit unexpected behavior. Fuzzing is used, for example, in an attempt to successfully attack a program using *script injection*. Script injection is a technique where a program is tricked into executing commands in various languages, mainly JavaScript and SQL. Tools such as HP WebInspect, IBM AppScan, Acunetix, and Burp Suite have built-in fuzzing and script injection tools that are pretty good at identifying script injection vulnerabilities in software applications.

WHY WOULD SOMEONE TYPE *THAT?*

Since time immemorial, when writing programs that interfaced with people, programmers would think of all the valid use cases when programming input fields. For example, an input field asking for an amount of currency would be programmed to accept proper numeric input. The program would expect, and accept, a numeric value in that field and process it accordingly. Programmers' mind-sets were focused on valid input, and that was that.

Fast-forward to the web with HTML, and programs with their input fields exposed to the world. Hackers soon found that interesting things could be typed into input fields that would provide interesting results. We know these today as SQL injection, JavaScript injection, cross-site scripting, cross-site request forgery, and buffer overflow.

These attacks caught nearly the entire programming community off guard. Simply put, the mind-set from a programmer's perspective was: Why would someone type binary code into a numeric field? Abuse simply had not occurred to many. Fortunately, today a multitude of code libraries "sanitize" input to make sure that only proper characters are input, thereby blunting the effects of SQL injection and other attacks. And there are organizations like the Open Web Application Security Project (OWASP) that produce learning content so that programmers can more easily write better, secure programs that are less susceptible to input field attacks.

Test coverage analysis

Test (or *code*) *coverage analysis* measures the percentage of source code that is tested by a given test (or validation) suite. Basic coverage criteria typically include

» **Branch coverage** (for example, every branch at a decision point is executed as TRUE or FALSE)

» **Condition (or predicate) coverage** (for example, each Boolean expression is evaluated to both TRUE and FALSE)

» **Function coverage** (for example, every function or subroutine is called)

» **Statement coverage** (for example, every statement is executed at least once)

For example, a security engineer might use a dynamic application security testing tool (DAST), such as AppScan or WebInspect, to test a travel booking program to determine whether the program has any exploitable security defects. Tools such as these are powerful, and they use a variety of methods to "fuzz" input fields in attempts to discover flaws. But the other thing these tools need to do is fill out forms in every conceivable combination, so that all the program's code will be executed. In this example of a travel booking tool, these combinations would involve every way in which flights, hotels, or cars could be searched, queried, examined, and finally booked. In a complex program, this can be really daunting. Highly systematic analysis would be needed, to make sure that every possibly combination of conditions is tested so that all of a program's code is tested.

Interface testing

Interface testing focuses on the interface between different systems and components. It ensures that functions (such as data transfer and control between systems or components) perform correctly and as expected. Interface testing also verifies that any execution errors are properly handled and do not expose any potential security vulnerabilities. Examples of interfaces tested include

» Application programming interfaces (APIs)

» Web services

» Transaction processing gateways

» Physical interfaces, such as keypads, keyboard/mouse/display, and device switches and indicators

TIP APIs, web services, and transaction gateways can often be tested with automated tools such as HP WebInspect, IBM AppScan, and Acunetix, which are also used to test the human-input portion of web applications.

Collect Security Process Data

Assessment of security management processes and systems helps an organization determine the efficacy of its key processes and controls. Periodic testing of key activities is an important part of management and regulatory oversight, to confirm the proper functioning of key processes, as well as identification of improvement areas.

Several factors must be considered when determining who will perform this testing, including:

>> **Regulations.** Various regulations specify which parties must perform testing, whether qualified internal staff or outside consultants.

>> **Staff resources and qualifications.** Regulations and other conditions permitting, an organization may have adequately skilled and qualified staff that can perform some or all of its testing.

>> **Organizational integrity.** While an organization may have the resources and expertise to test its management processes, often an organization will elect to have an outside, qualified organization perform testing. Independent outside testing helps avoid bias.

These factors will also determine required testing methods, including the tools used, testing criteria, sampling, and reporting. For example, in a U.S. public company, an organization is required to self-evaluate its information security controls in specific ways and with specific auditing standards, under the auspices of the Sarbanes–Oxley (SOX) Act of 2002, also known as the Public Company Accounting Reform and Investor Protection Act.

Account management

Management must regularly review user and system accounts and related business processes and records to ensure that privileges are provisioned and de-provisioned appropriately and with proper approvals. The types of reviews include

>> All user account provisioning was properly requested, reviewed, approved, and executed.

>> All internal personnel transfers result in timely termination of access that is no longer needed.

>> All personnel terminations result in timely termination of all access.

>> All users holding privileged account access still require it, and their administrative actions are logged.

>> All user accounts can be traced back to a proper request, review, and approval.

>> All unused user accounts are evaluated to see whether they can be deactivated.

>> All users' access privileges are certified regularly as necessary.

Account management processes are discussed in more detail in Chapter 9.

Management review

Management provides resources and strategic direction for all aspects of an organization, including its information security program. As a part of its overall governance, management will need to review key aspects of the security program. There is no single way that this is done; instead, in the style and with the rigor that management reviews other key activities in an organization, management will review the security program. In larger organizations, this review will likely be quite formal, with executive–level reports created periodically for senior management, including key activities, events, and metrics (think *eye candy* here). In smaller organizations, this review will probably be a lot less formal. In the smallest organizations, as well as organizations lower security maturity levels, there may not be any management review at all. Management review often includes these activities:

>> Review of recent security incidents

>> Review of security-related spending

>> Review (and ratification) of recent policy changes

>> Review (and ratification) of risk treatment decisions

>> Review (and ratification) of major changes to security-related processes, and the security-related components of other business processes

>> Review of operational- and management-level metrics and risk indicators

The internationally recognized standard, ISO/IEC 27001, "Information technology — Security techniques — Information security management systems — Requirements," requires that an organization's management determine what activities and elements in the information security program need to be monitored, the methods to be used, and the individuals or teams that will review them.

Key performance and risk indicators

Key performance and risk indicators are meaningful measurements of key activities in an information security program that can be used to help management at every level better understand how well the security program and its components are performing.

This is easier said than done; here are a few reasons why:

>> There is no single set of universal metrics that are applicable to every organization.

>> There are different ways to measure performance and risk.

>> Executives will want key activities measured in specific ways.

>> Maturity levels vary from organization to organization.

Organizations will typically develop metrics and key risk indicators (KRIs) around its key security-related activities to ensure that security processes are operating as expected. Metrics help identify improvement areas by alerting management through unexpected trends.

Some of the focus areas for security metrics include the following:

>> **Vulnerability management:** Operational metrics will include numbers of scans performed, numbers of vulnerabilities identified (and by severity), and numbers of patches applied. Key risk indicators will focus on the elapsed time between the public release of a vulnerability and the completion of patching.

>> **Incident response:** Operational metrics will focus on the numbers and categories of incidents, and whether trends suggest new weaknesses in defenses. Key risk indicators will focus on the time required to realize an incident is in progress (known as *dwell time*) and the time required to contain and resolve the incident.

>> **Security awareness training:** Operational metrics and key risk indicators generally focus on the completion rate over time.

>> **Logging and monitoring:** Operational metrics generally focus on the numbers and types of events that occur. Key risk indicators focus on the proportion of assets whose logs are being monitored, and the elapsed time between the start of an incident and the time when personnel begin to take action.

Key risk indicators are so-called because they are harbingers of information risk in an organization. Although the development of operational metrics is not all that difficult, security managers often struggle with the problem of developing key risk indicators that make sense to executive management. For example, the vulnerability management process involves the use of one or more vulnerability scanning tools and subsequent remediation efforts. Here, some good operational metrics include numbers of scans performed, numbers of vulnerabilities identified, and the time required to remediate identified vulnerabilities. These metrics, however, will make no sense to management, because they're lacking business context. However, one or more good key risk indicators can be derived from data in the vulnerability management process. For instance, "percentage of servers supporting manufacturing whose critical security defects are not remediated within ten days" is a great key risk indicator. This metric directly helps management understand how well the vulnerability management process is performing in a specific business context. This is also a good leading indicator of the risk of a potential breach (which exploits an unpatched, vulnerable server) that could impact business operations (manufacturing, in this case).

Backup verification data

Organizations need to routinely review and test system and data backups, and recovery procedures, to ensure they are accurate, complete, and readable. Organizations need to regularly test the ability to actually recover data from backup media, to ensure that they can do so in the event of a hardware malfunction or disaster.

On the surface, this seems easy enough. But, as they say, the devil's in the details. There are several gotchas and considerations including the following:

>> **Data recovery versus disaster recovery:** There are two main reasons for backing up data:

- **Data recovery:** When various circumstances require the recovery of data from a past state.

- **Disaster recovery:** When an event has resulted in damage to primary processing systems, necessitating recovery of data onto alternate processing systems.

For data recovery, you want your backup media (in whatever form) logically and physically near your production systems, so that the logistics of data recovery are simple. However, disaster recovery requires backup media to be far away from the primary processing site so that it is not involved in the same natural disaster. These two are at odds with one another; organizations sometimes solve this by creating two sets of backup media: One stays in the primary processing center, while the other is stored at a secure, offsite storage facility.

» **Data integrity:** For requests to "roll back" data to an earlier date and time, it is vital to know exactly what data needs to be recovered. Database management systems enforce a rule known as *referential integrity*. This means that a database cannot be recovered to a state where relationships between indexes, tables, and foreign keys would be broken. This issue often comes into play in larger, distributed systems with multiple databases on different servers, sometimes owned by different organizations.

» **Version control:** For requests to recover data to an earlier state, personnel also need to be mindful of all changes to programs and database design that are dependent on one another. For instance, rolling data back to a point in time last week may also require that associated computer programs be rolled back, if there were changes in the application that involved both code and data changes. Further, rolling back to an earlier point in time could also involve other components such as run-time libraries, subsystems such as Java, and even operating system versions and patches.

» **Staging environments:** Depending upon the reason for recovering data from a point in time in the past, it may be appropriate to recover data onto a separate environment. For instance, if certain transactions in an e-commerce environment were lost, it may make sense to recover data including the lost transactions onto a test server, so that those transactions can be found. If older data was recovered onto the primary production environment, this would effectively wipe out transactions from that point in time up to the present.

Training and awareness

Organizations need to measure the participation in and effectiveness of security training and awareness programs. This will ensure that individuals at all levels in the organization understand how to respond to new and evolving threats and vulnerabilities. Security awareness training is discussed in Chapter 3.

Disaster recovery and business continuity

Organizations need to periodically review and test their disaster recovery (DR) and business continuity (BC) plans, to determine whether recovery plans are up-to-date and will result in the successful continuation of critical business processes in the event of a disaster. Disaster recovery and business continuity plan development and testing are discussed in Chapters 3 and 9.

TIP

Information security continuous monitoring (ISCM) is defined in NIST SP 800-137 as "maintaining ongoing awareness of information security, vulnerabilities, and threats to support organizational risk management decisions." An ISCM strategy helps the organization to systematically maintain an effective security management program in a dynamic environment.

Analyze Test Output and Generate Reports

Various systems and tools are capable of producing volumes of log and testing data. Without proper analysis and interpretation, these reports are useless or may be used out of context. Security professionals must be able to analyze log and test data, and report this information in meaningful ways, so that senior management can understand organizational risks and make informed security decisions.

Often this requires that test output and reports be developed for different audiences with information in a form that is useful to them. For example, the output of a vulnerability scan report with its lists of IP addresses, DNS names, and vulnerabilities with their respective common vulnerabilities and exposures codes (CVEs) and CVSSs would be useful to system engineers and network engineers who would use such reports as lists of individual defects to be fixed. But give that report to a senior executive, and he'll have little idea what it's about or what it means in business terms. For senior executives, vulnerability scan data would be rolled up into meaningful business metrics and key risk indicators to inform senior management of any appreciable changes in risk levels.

The key here for information security professionals is knowing the meaning of data and transforming it for various purposes and different audiences. Security professionals who do this well are more easily able to obtain funding for additional tools and staff. This is because they're able to articulate the need for resources in business terms.

Conduct or Facilitate Security Audits

Auditing is the process of examining systems and/or business processes to ensure that they've been properly designed, are being properly used, and are considered effective. Audits are frequently performed by an independent third-party or an independent group within an organization. This helps to ensure that the audit results are accurate and are not biased because of organizational politics or other circumstances.

Audits are frequently performed to ensure an organization is in compliance with business or security policies and other requirements that the business may be subject to. These policies and requirements can include government laws and regulations, legal contracts, and industry or trade group standards and best practices.

The major factors in play for internal and external audits include

>> **Purpose and scope.** The reason for an internal or external audit, and the scope of the audit, need to be fully understood by both management in the audited organization and those performing the audit. Scope may include one or more of the following factors:

- Organization business units and departments

- Geographic locations

- Business processes, systems, and networks

- Time periods

>> **Applicable standards or regulations.** Often, an audit is performed under the auspices of a law, regulation, or standard. Often, this will determine such matters as who may perform the auditing, auditor qualifications, the type of auditing, scope of audits, and obligations of the audited organization at the conclusion of the audit.

>> **Qualifications of auditors.** The personnel performing audits often are required to have specific work experience, possess specific training and/or certifications, or work in certain types of firms.

>> **Types of auditing.** There are several types of audit activities that comprise an audit, including:

- **Observation.** Auditors passively observe activities performed by personnel and/or information systems.

- **Inquiry.** Auditors ask questions of control or process owners to understand how key activities are performed.

- **Inspection.** Auditors inspect documents, records, and systems to verify that key controls or processes are operating properly.

- **Reperformance.** Auditors perform tasks or transactions on their own to see whether the results are correct.

>> **Sampling.** The process of selecting items in a large population is known as *sampling*. Regulations and standards often specify the types and rates of sampling that are required for an audit.

>> **Management response.** In some types of audits, management in the auditee organization are permitted to write a statement in response to an auditor's findings.

There are three main contexts for audits of information systems and related processes:

>> **Internal audit:** Personnel in the organization will conduct an audit on selected information systems and/or business processes.

>> **External audit:** Auditors from an outside firm will conduct an audit on one or more information systems and/or business processes.

>> **Third-party audit:** Auditors, internal or external, will perform an audit of a third-party service provider that is performing services on behalf of the organization. For example, an organization may outsource a part of its software development to another company. From time to time, the organization will audit the software development company, to ensure that its business processes and information systems are in compliance with applicable regulations and business requirements.

TIP

Security professionals who are interested in the information systems auditing profession may want to explore the Certified Information Systems Auditor (CISA) certification.

TIP

Business-critical systems need to be subject to regular audits as dictated by regulatory, contractual, or trade group requirements.

WARNING

For organizations that are subject to regulatory requirements, such as Sarbanes-Oxley (discussed in Chapter 3), it's all too easy and far too common to make the mistake of focusing on audits and compliance rather than on implementing a truly effective and comprehensive security strategy. Remember, compliance *does not* equal security. Compliance isn't optional, but neither is security. Don't assume that achieving compliance will automatically achieve effective security (or vice versa). Fortunately, security and compliance aren't mutually exclusive — but you need to ensure your efforts truly achieve both objectives.

IN THIS CHAPTER

» **Understanding investigations**

» **Applying security operations concepts and controls**

» **Responding to incidents**

» **Preparing for disasters**

» **Keeping facilities and personnel safe**

Chapter **9**

Security Operations

The Security Operations domain covers lots of essential security concepts and builds on many of the other security domains, including Security and Risk Management (Chapter 3), Asset Security (Chapter 4), Security Architecture and Engineering (Chapter 5), and Communication and Network Security (Chapter 6). Security operations represents routine operations that occur across many of the CISSP domains. This domain represents 13 percent of the CISSP certification exam.

Understand and Support Investigations

Conducting investigations for various purposes is an important function for security professionals. You must understand evidence collection and handling procedures, reporting and documentation requirements, various investigative processes, and digital forensics tools and techniques. Successful conclusions in investigations depend heavily on proficiency in these skills.

Evidence collection and handling

Evidence is information presented in a court of law to confirm or dispel a fact that's under contention, such as the commission of a crime, the violation of policy, or an ethics matter. A case can't be brought to trial or other legal proceeding without sufficient evidence to support the case. Thus, properly gathering and protecting evidence is one of the most important and most difficult tasks that an investigator must master.

Important evidence collection and handling topics covered on the CISSP exam include the types of evidence, rules of evidence, admissibility of evidence, chain of custody, and the evidence lifecycle.

Types of evidence

Sources of legal evidence that you can present in a court of law generally fall into one of four major categories:

>> **Direct evidence:** Oral testimony or a written statement based on information gathered through a witness's five senses (in other words, an eyewitness account) that proves or disproves a specific fact or issue.

>> **Real (or physical) evidence:** Tangible objects from the actual crime, such as the tools or weapons used and any stolen or damaged property. May also include visual or audio surveillance tapes generated during or after the event. Physical evidence from a computer crime is not always available.

>> **Documentary evidence:** Includes originals and copies of business records, computer-generated and computer-stored records, manuals, policies, standards, procedures, and log files. Most evidence presented in a computer crime case is documentary evidence. The *hearsay rule* (which we discuss in the section "Hearsay rule," later in this chapter) is an extremely important test of documentary evidence that must be understood and applied to this type of evidence.

>> **Demonstrative evidence:** Used to aid the court's understanding of a case. Opinions are considered demonstrative evidence and may be either *expert* (based on personal expertise and facts) or *non-expert* (based on facts only). Other examples of demonstrative evidence include models, simulations, charts, and illustrations.

Other types of evidence that may fall into one or more of the above major categories include

>> **Best evidence:** Original, unaltered evidence, which is preferred by the court over secondary evidence. Read more about this evidence in the section "Best evidence rule," later in this chapter.

>> **Secondary evidence:** A duplicate or copy of evidence, such as a tape backup, screen capture, or photograph.

>> **Corroborative evidence:** Supports or substantiates other evidence presented in a case.

>> **Conclusive evidence:** Incontrovertible and irrefutable — you know, the smoking gun.

>> **Circumstantial evidence:** Relevant facts that you can't directly or conclusively connect to other events, but about which a reasonable person can make a reasonable inference.

Rules of evidence

Important rules of evidence for computer crime cases include the *best evidence rule* and the *hearsay evidence rule*. The CISSP candidate must understand both of these rules and their applicability to evidence in computer crime cases.

BEST EVIDENCE RULE

The best evidence rule, defined in the Federal Rules of Evidence, states that "to prove the content of a writing, recording, or photograph, the original writing, recording, or photograph is [ordinarily] required."

However, the Federal Rules of Evidence define an exception to this rule as "[i]f data are stored in a computer or similar device, any printout or other output readable by sight, shown to reflect the data accurately, is an 'original'."

Thus, data extracted from a computer — if that data is a fair and accurate representation of the original data — satisfies the best evidence rule and may normally be introduced into court proceedings as such.

HEARSAY RULE

Hearsay evidence is evidence that's not based on personal, first-hand knowledge of a witness, but rather comes from other sources. Under the Federal Rules of Evidence, hearsay evidence is normally not admissible in court. This rule exists to prevent unreliable testimony from improperly influencing the outcome of a trial.

Business records, including computer records, have traditionally, and perhaps mistakenly, been considered hearsay evidence by most courts because these records cannot be proven accurate and reliable. One of the most significant obstacles for a prosecutor to overcome in a computer crime case is seeking the admission of computer records as evidence.

TIP

A prosecutor may be able to introduce computer records as best evidence, rather than hearsay evidence, which we discuss in the preceding section.

Several courts have acknowledged that the hearsay rules are applicable to *computer-stored* records containing human statements but are not applicable to *computer-generated* records untouched by human hands.

Perhaps the most successful and commonly applied test of admissibility for computer records, in general, has been the *business records exception*, established in the U.S. Federal Rules of Evidence, for records of regularly conducted activity, meeting the following criteria:

>> Made at or near the time (contemporaneously) that the act occurred.

>> Made by a person who has knowledge of the business process or from information transmitted by a person who has knowledge of the business process.

>> Made and relied on during the regular conduct of business or in the furtherance of the business, as verified by the custodian or other witness familiar with the records' use.

>> Kept for motives that tend to assure their accuracy.

>> In the custody of the witness on a regular basis (as required by the chain of evidence).

TIP

The chain of evidence establishes accountability for the handling of evidence throughout the evidence lifecycle. See the section "Chain of custody and the evidence lifecycle" later in this chapter.

Admissibility of evidence

Because computer-generated evidence can sometimes be easily manipulated, altered, or tampered with, and because it's not easily and commonly understood, this type of evidence is usually considered suspect in a court of law. In order to be admissible, evidence must be

>> **Relevant:** It must tend to prove or disprove facts that are relevant and material to the case.

>> **Reliable:** It must be reasonably proven that what is presented as evidence is what was originally collected and that the evidence itself is reliable. This is accomplished, in part, through proper evidence handling and the chain of custody. (We discuss this in the upcoming section "Chain of custody and the evidence lifecycle.")

>> **Legally permissible:** It must be obtained through legal means. Evidence that's not legally permissible may include evidence obtained through the following means:

- **Illegal search and seizure:** Law enforcement personnel must obtain a prior court order; however, non–law enforcement personnel, such as a supervisor or system administrator, may be able to conduct an authorized search under some circumstances.

- **Illegal wiretaps or phone taps:** Anyone conducting wiretaps or phone taps must obtain a prior court order.

- **Entrapment or enticement:** *Entrapment* encourages someone to commit a crime that the individual may have had no intention of committing. Conversely, *enticement* lures someone toward certain evidence (a honey pot, if you will) after that individual has already committed a crime. Enticement isn't necessarily illegal, but it does raise certain ethical arguments and may not be admissible in court.

- **Coercion:** Coerced testimony or confessions are not legally permissible. Coercion involves compelling a person to involuntarily provide evidence through the use of threats, violence (torture), bribery, trickery, or intimidation.

- **Unauthorized or improper monitoring:** Active monitoring must be properly authorized and conducted in a standard manner; users must be notified that they may be subject to monitoring.

Chain of custody and the evidence lifecycle

The *chain of custody* (or *chain of evidence*) provides accountability and protection for evidence throughout its entire lifecycle and includes the following information, which is normally kept in an evidence log:

>> **Persons involved (Who):** Identify any and all individual(s) who discovered, collected, seized, analyzed, stored, preserved, transported, or otherwise controlled the evidence. Also identify any witnesses or other individuals present during any of the above actions.

>> **Description of evidence (What):** Ensure that all evidence is completely and uniquely described.

>> **Location of evidence (Where):** Provide specific information about the evidence's location when it is discovered, analyzed, stored, or transported.

>> **Date/Time (When):** Record the date and time that evidence is discovered, collected, seized, analyzed, stored, or transported. Also, record date and time information for any evidence log entries associated with the evidence.

>> **Methods used (How):** Provide specific information about how evidence was discovered, collected, stored, preserved, or transported.

Any time that evidence changes possession or is transferred to a different media type, it must be properly recorded in the evidence log to maintain the chain of custody.

Law enforcement officials must strictly adhere to chain of custody requirements, and this adherence is highly recommended for anyone else involved in collecting or seizing evidence. Security professionals and incident response teams must fully understand and follow chain of custody principles and procedures, no matter how minor or insignificant a security incident may initially appear. In both cases, chain of custody serves to prove that digital evidence has not been modified at any point in the forensic examination and analysis.

Even properly trained law enforcement officials sometimes make crucial mistakes in evidence handling and safekeeping. Most attorneys won't understand the technical aspects of the evidence that you may present in a case, but they will definitely know evidence-handling rules and will most certainly scrutinize your actions in this area. Improperly handled evidence, no matter how conclusive or damaging, will likely be inadmissible in a court of law.

The *evidence lifecycle* describes the various phases of evidence, from its initial discovery to its final disposition.

The evidence lifecycle has the following five stages:

>> Collection and identification

>> Analysis

>> Storage, preservation, and transportation

>> Presentation in court

>> Final disposition — for example, return to owner or destroy (if it is a copy)

The following sections explain more about each stage.

COLLECTION AND IDENTIFICATION

Collecting evidence involves taking that evidence into custody. Unfortunately, evidence can't always be collected and must instead be seized. Many legal issues are involved in seizing computers and other electronic evidence. The publication *Searching and Seizing Computers and Obtaining Evidence in Criminal Investigations* (3rd edition, 2009), published by the U.S. Department of Justice (DOJ) Computer Crime and Intellectual Property Section (CCIPS), provides comprehensive guidance on this subject. Find this publication available for download at www.justice.gov/sites/default/files/criminal-ccips/legacy/2015/01/14/ssmanual2009.pdf.

In general, law enforcement officials can search and/or seize computers and other electronic evidence under any of four circumstances:

- >> **Voluntary or consensual:** The owner of the computer or electronic evidence can freely surrender the evidence.

- >> **Subpoena:** A court issues a subpoena to an individual, ordering that individual to deliver the evidence to the court.

- >> **Search warrant or Anton Piller order:** A *search warrant* is issued to a law enforcement official by the court, allowing that official to search and seize specific evidence. An *Anton Piller order* is a court order that allows the premises to be searched and evidence seized without prior warning, usually to prevent the possible destruction of evidence.

- >> **Exigent circumstances:** If probable cause exists and the destruction of evidence is imminent, that evidence may be searched or seized without a warrant.

When evidence is collected, it must be properly marked and identified. This ensures that it can later be properly presented in court as actual evidence gathered from the scene or incident. The collected evidence must be recorded in an evidence log with the following information:

- >> A **description** of the particular piece of evidence including any specific information, such as make, model, serial number, physical appearance, material condition, and preexisting damage.

- >> The **name(s)** of the person(s) who discovered and collected the evidence.

- >> The exact **date and time, specific location, and circumstances** of the discovery/collection.

Additionally, the evidence must be marked, using the following guidelines:

- >> **Mark the evidence:** If possible without damaging the evidence, mark the actual piece of evidence with the collecting individual's initials, the date, and the case number (if known). Seal the evidence in an appropriate container and again mark the container with the same information (see the previous bullet).

- >> **Use an evidence tag:** If the actual evidence cannot be marked, attach an evidence tag with the same information as above, seal the evidence and tag in an appropriate container, and again mark the container with the same information.

- >> **Seal the evidence:** Seal the container with evidence tape and mark the tape in a manner that will clearly indicate any tampering.

- >> **Protect the evidence:** Use extreme caution when collecting and marking evidence to ensure that it's not damaged. If you're using plastic bags for evidence containers, be sure that they're static free to protect magnetic media.

Always collect and mark evidence in a consistent manner so that you can easily identify evidence and describe your collection and identification techniques to an opposing attorney in court, if necessary.

ANALYSIS

Analysis involves examining the evidence for information pertinent to the case. Analysis should be conducted with extreme caution, by properly trained and experienced personnel only, to ensure the evidence is not altered, damaged, or destroyed.

STORAGE, PRESERVATION, AND TRANSPORTATION

All evidence must be properly stored in a secure facility and preserved to prevent damage or contamination from various hazards, including intense heat or cold, extreme humidity, water, magnetic fields, and vibration. Evidence that's not properly protected may be inadmissible in court, and the party responsible for collection and storage may be liable. Care must also be exercised during transportation to ensure that evidence is not lost, temporarily misplaced, damaged, or destroyed.

PRESENTATION IN COURT

Evidence to be presented in court must continue to follow the chain of custody and be handled with the same care as at all other times in the evidence lifecycle. This process continues throughout the trial until all testimony related to the evidence is completed and the trial has concluded or the case is settled or dismissed.

FINAL DISPOSITION

After the conclusion of the trial or other disposition, evidence is normally returned to its proper owner. However, under some circumstances, certain evidence may be ordered destroyed, such as contraband, drugs, or drug paraphernalia. Any evidence obtained through a search warrant is legally under the control of the court, possibly requiring the original owner to petition the court for its return.

Reporting and documentation

As described in the preceding section, complete and accurate recordkeeping is critical to each investigation. An investigation's report is intended to be a complete record of an investigation, and usually includes the following:

>> Incident investigators, including their qualifications and contact information.

>> Names of parties interviewed, including their role, involvement, and contact information.

- List of all evidence collected, including chain(s) of custody.
- Tools used to examine or process evidence, including versions.
- Samples and sampling methodologies used, if applicable.
- Computers used to examine, process, or store evidence, including a description of configuration.
- Root-cause analysis of incident, if applicable.
- Conclusions and opinions of investigators.
- Hearings or proceedings.
- Parties to whom the report is delivered.

Investigative techniques

An investigation should begin immediately upon report of an alleged computer crime, policy violation, or incident. Any incident should be handled, at least initially, as a computer crime investigation or policy violation until a preliminary investigation determines otherwise. Different investigative techniques may be required, depending upon the goal of the investigation or applicable laws and regulations. For example, incident handling requires expediency to contain any potential damage as quickly as possible. A root cause analysis requires in-depth examination to determine what happened, how it happened, and how to prevent the same thing from happening again. However, in all cases, proper evidence collection and handling is essential. Even if a preliminary investigation determines that a security incident was not the result of criminal activity, you should always handle any potential evidence properly, in case either further legal proceedings are anticipated or a crime is later uncovered during the course of a full investigation. The CISSP candidate should be familiar with the general steps of the investigative process:

1. **Detect and contain an incident.**

Early detection is critical to a successful investigation. Unfortunately, computer-related incidents usually involve passive or reactive detection techniques (such as the review of audit trails and accidental discovery), which often leave a cold evidence trail. Containment minimizes further loss or damage. The computer incident response team (CIRT), which we discuss later in this chapter, is the team that is normally responsible for conducting an investigation. The CIRT should be notified (or activated) as quickly as possible after a computer crime is detected or suspected.

2. Notify management.

Management must be notified of any investigations as soon as possible. Knowledge of the investigations should be limited to as few people as possible, on a need-to-know basis. Out-of-band communication methods (reporting in person) should be used to ensure that an intruder does not intercept sensitive communications about the investigation.

3. Conduct a preliminary investigation.

This preliminary investigation determines whether an incident or crime actually occurred. Most incidents turn out to be honest mistakes rather than malicious conduct. This step includes reviewing the complaint or report, inspecting damage, interviewing witnesses, examining logs, and identifying further investigation requirements.

4. Determine whether the organization should disclose that the crime occurred.

First, and most importantly, determine whether laws or regulations require the organization to disclose a crime or incident. Next, by coordinating with a public relations or public affairs official of the organization, determine whether the organization wants to disclose this information.

5. Conduct the investigation.

Conducting the investigation involves three activities:

a. Identify potential suspects.

Potential suspects include insiders and outsiders to the organization. One standard discriminator to help determine or eliminate potential suspects is the MOM test: Did the suspect have the Motive, Opportunity, and Means? The Motive might relate to financial gain, revenge, or notoriety. A suspect had Opportunity if he or she had access, whether as an authorized user for an unauthorized purpose or as an unauthorized user — due to the existence of a security weakness or vulnerability — for an unauthorized purpose. And Means relates to whether the suspect had the necessary tools and skills to commit the crime.

b. Identify potential witnesses.

Determine whom you want interviewed and who conducts the interviews. Be careful not to alert any potential suspects to the investigation; focus on obtaining facts, not opinions, in witness statements.

c. Prepare for search and seizure.

Identify the types of systems and evidence that you plan to search or seize, designate and train the search and seizure team members (normally members of the Computer Incident Response Team, or CIRT), obtain and serve proper search warrants (if required), and determine potential risk to the system during a search and seizure effort.

6. **Report your findings.**

The results of the investigation, including evidence, should be reported to management and turned over to proper law enforcement officials or prosecutors, as appropriate.

REMEMBER

MOM stands for *Motive*, *Opportunity*, and *Means*.

Digital forensics tools, tactics, and procedures

Digital forensics is the science of conducting a computer incident investigation to determine what has happened and who is responsible, and to collect legally admissible evidence for use in subsequent legal proceedings, such as a criminal investigation, internal investigation, or lawsuit.

Proper forensic analysis and investigation requires in-depth knowledge of hardware (such as endpoint devices and networking equipment), operating systems (including desktop, server, mobile device, and other device operating systems, like routers, switches, and load balancers), applications, databases, and software programming languages, as well as knowledge and experience using sophisticated forensics tools and toolkits.

The types of forensic data-gathering techniques include

» **Hard drive forensics.** Here, specialized tools are used to create one or more forensically identical copies of a computer's hard drive. A device called a *write blocker* is typically used to prevent any possible alterations to the original drive. Cryptographic checksums can be used to verify that a forensic copy is an exact duplicate of the original.

Tools are then used to examine the contents of the hard drive in order to determine

- Last known state of the computer

- History of files accessed

- History of files created

- History of files deleted

- History of programs executed

- History of web sites visited by a browser

- History of attempts by the user to remove evidence

>> **Live forensics.** Here, specialized tools are used to examine a running system, including:

- Running processes
- Currently open files
- Contents of main storage (RAM)
- Keystrokes
- Communications traffic in/out of the computer

Live forensics are difficult to perform, because the tools used to collect information can also affect the system being examined.

Understand Requirements for Investigation Types

The purpose of an *investigation* is to determine what happened and who is responsible, and to collect evidence that supports this hypothesis. Closely related to, but distinctly different from, investigations is incident management (discussed in detail later in this chapter). Incident management determines what happened, contains and assesses damage, and restores normal operations.

Investigations and incident management must often be conducted simultaneously in a well-coordinated and controlled manner to ensure that the initial actions of either activity don't destroy evidence or cause further damage to the organization's assets. For this reason, it's important that Computer Incident (or Emergency) Response Teams (CIRT or CERT, or Computer Security Incident Response Teams - CSIRT, respectively) be properly trained and qualified to secure a computer-related crime scene or incident while preserving evidence. Ideally, the CIRT includes individuals who will actually be conducting the investigation.

An analogy to this would be an example of a police patrolman who discovers a murder victim. It's important that the patrolman quickly assesses the safety of the situation and secures the crime scene, but at the same time, he must be careful not to disturb or destroy any evidence. The homicide detective's job is to gather and analyze the evidence. Ideally, but rarely, the homicide detective would be the individual who discovers the murder victim, allowing her to assess the safety of the situation, secure the crime scene, and begin collecting evidence. Think of yourself as a *CSI*-SSP!

Different requirements for various investigation types include

>> **Operational.** After any damage from a security incident has been contained, operational investigations typically focus on root-cause analysis, lessons learned, and management reporting.

>> **Criminal.** Criminal investigations require strict adherence to proper evidence collection and handling procedures. The investigation is focused on discovering and preserving evidence for possible prosecution of any culpable parties.

>> **Civil.** A civil investigation may result from a data breach or regulatory violation, and typically will focus on quantifying any damage, and establishing due diligence or negligence.

>> **Regulatory.** Regulatory investigations often take the form of external, mandatory audits, and are focused on evaluating security controls and compliance.

Various industry standards and guidelines provide guidance for conducting investigations. These include the American Bar Association's (ABA) *Best Practices in Internal Investigations*, various best practice guidelines and toolkits published by the U.S. Department of Justice (DOJ), and ASTM International's *Standard Practice for Computer Forensics (ASTM E2763)*.

Conduct Logging and Monitoring Activities

Event logging is an essential part of an organization's IT operations. Increasingly, organizations are implementing centralized log collection systems that often serve as security information and event management (SIEM) platforms.

Intrusion detection and prevention

Intrusion detection is a passive technique used to detect unauthorized activity on a network. An intrusion detection system is frequently called an *IDS*. Three types of IDSs used today are

>> *Network-based* **intrusion detection (NIDS):** Consists of a separate device attached to a network that listens to all network traffic by using various methods (which we describe later in this section) to detect anomalous activity.

>> *Host-based* **intrusion detection (HIDS):** This is really a subset of network-based IDS, in which only the network traffic destined for a particular host is monitored.

>> **_Wireless_ intrusion detection (WIDS):** This is another type of network intrusion detection that focuses on wireless intrusion by scanning for rogue access points.

Both network- and host-based IDSs use a couple of methods:

>> **Signature-based:** A _signature-based_ IDS compares network traffic that is observed with a list of patterns in a signature file. A signature-based IDS detects any of a known set of attacks, but if an intruder is able to change the patterns that he uses in his attack, then his attack may be able to slip by the IDS without being detected. The other downside of signature-based IDS is that the signature file must be frequently updated.

>> **Reputation-based:** Closely akin to signature based, reputation-based alerting is all about detecting when communications and other activities involve known-malicious domains and IP networks. Some IDSs update themselves several times daily, including adding to a list of known-malicious domains and IP addresses. Then, when any activities are associated with a known-malicious domain or IP address, the IDS can create an alert that lets personnel know about the activity.

>> **Anomaly-based:** An _anomaly-based_ IDS monitors all the traffic over the network and builds traffic profiles. Over time, the IDS will report deviations from the profiles that it has built. The upside of anomaly-based IDSs is that there are no signature files to periodically update. The downside is that you may have a high volume of false-positives. Behavior-based and heuristics-based IDSs are similar to anomaly-based IDSs and share many of the same advantages. Rather than detecting anomalies to normal traffic patterns, behavior-based and heuristics-based systems attempt to recognize and learn potential attack patterns.

Intrusion detection doesn't stop intruders, but intrusion prevention does . . . or, at least, it slows them down. _Intrusion prevention systems_ (IPSs) are newer and more common systems than IDSs, and IPSs are designed to detect _and block_ intrusions. An intrusion prevention system is simply an IDS that can take action, such as dropping a connection or blocking a port, when an intrusion is detected.

REMEMBER

Intrusion detection looks for known attacks and/or anomalous behavior on a network or host.

See Chapter 6 for more on intrusion detection and intrusion prevention systems.

Security information and event management

Security information and event management (SIEM) solutions provide real-time collection, analysis, correlation, and presentation of security logs and alerts generated by various network sources (such as firewalls, IDS/IPS, routers, switches, servers, and workstations).

A SIEM solution can be software- or appliance-based, and may be hosted and managed either internally or by a managed security service provider.

A SIEM requires a lot of up-front configuration and tuning, so that only the most important, actionable events are brought to the attention of staff members in the organization. However, it's worth the effort: a SIEM combs through millions, or billions, of events daily, and presents only the most important few, actionable events so that security teams can take appropriate action.

Many SIEM platforms also have the ability to accept threat intelligence feeds from various vendors including the SIEM manufacturers. This permits the SIEM to automatically adjust its detection and blocking capabilities for the most up-to-date threats.

Continuous monitoring

Continuous monitoring technology collects and reports security data in near real time. Continuous monitoring components may include

- **Discovery:** Ongoing inventory of network and information assets, including hardware, software, and sensitive data.

- **Assessment:** Automatic scanning and baselining of information assets to identify and prioritize vulnerabilities.

- **Threat intelligence:** Feeds from one or more outside organizations that produce high-quality, actionable data.

- **Audit:** Nearly real-time evaluation of device configurations and compliance with established policies and regulatory requirements.

- **Patching:** Automatic security patch installation and software updating.

- **Reporting:** Aggregating, analyzing and correlating log information and alerts.

Egress monitoring

Egress monitoring (or extrusion detection) is the process of monitoring outbound traffic to discover potential data leakage (or loss). Modern cyberattacks employ various stealth techniques to avoid detection as long as possible for the purpose of data theft. These techniques may include the use of encryption (such as SSL/TLS) and steganography (discussed in Chapter 4).

Data loss prevention (DLP) systems are often used to detect the exfiltration of sensitive data, such as personally identifiable information (PII) or protected health information (PHI), in e-mail messages, data uploads, PNG or JPEG images, and other forms of communication. These technologies often perform deep packet inspection (DPI) to decrypt and inspect outbound traffic that is TLS encrypted.

DLP systems can also be used to disable removable media drive interfaces on servers and workstations, and also to encrypt data written onto removable media.

Static DLP tools are used to discover sensitive and proprietary data in databases, file servers, and other data storage systems.

Securely Provisioning Resources

An organization's information architecture is dynamic and constantly changing. As a result, its security posture is also dynamic and constantly changing. Provisioning (and decommissioning) of various information resources can have significant impacts (both direct and indirect) on the organization's security posture. For example, an application may either directly introduce new vulnerabilities into an environment or integrate with a database in a way that compromises the integrity of the database. For these reasons, security planning and analysis must be an integral part of every organization's resource provisioning processes, as well as throughout the lifecycle of all resources. Important security considerations include

>> **Asset inventory.** Maintaining a complete and accurate inventory is critical to ensure that all potential vulnerabilities and risks in an environment can be identified, assessed, and addressed. Indeed, so many other critical security processes are dependent upon sound asset inventory that asset inventory is one of the most important (but mundane) activities in IT organizations.

TIP

Asset inventory is the first control found in the well-known CIS 20 Controls. Asset inventory appears first because it is fundamental to most other security controls.

>> **Change management.** Change management processes are used to strictly control changes to systems in production environments, so that only duly requested and approved changes are made.

>> **Configuration management.** Configuration management processes need to be implemented and strictly enforced to ensure information resources are operated in a safe and secure manner. Organizations typically implement an automated configuration management database (CMDB) that is part of a system configuration management system used for managing asset inventory data. It's also often used to manage the configuration history of systems.

>> **Physical assets.** Physical assets must be protected against loss, damage, or theft. Valuable or sensitive data stored on a physical asset may far exceed the value of the asset itself.

>> **Virtual assets.** Virtual machine sprawl has increasingly become an issue for organizations with the popularity of virtualization technology and software defined networks (SDN). Virtual machines (VMs) can be (and often are) provisioned in a matter of minutes, but aren't always properly decommissioned when they are no longer needed. Dormant VMs often aren't backed up, and can go unpatched for many months This exposes the organization to increased risk from unpatched security vulnerabilities.

Of particular concern to security professionals is the implementation of VMs without proper review and approvals. This was not a problem before virtualization, as organizations had other checks and balances in place to prevent the implementation of unauthorized systems (namely, the purchasing process). But VM's can be implemented unilaterally, often without the knowledge or involvement of other personnel within the organization.

>> **Cloud assets.** As more organizations adopt cloud strategies that include software as a service (SaaS), platform as a service (PaaS), and infrastructure as a service (IaaS) solutions, it's important to keep track of these assets. Ultimately, an organization is responsible for the security and privacy of its applications and data — not the cloud service provider. Issues of data residency and trans-border data flow need to be considered.

A new class of security tools known as *cloud access security brokers* (CASB) can detect access to, and usage of, cloud-based services. These tools give the organization more visibility into its sanctioned and unsanctioned use of cloud services. Many CASB systems, in cooperation with cloud services, can be used to control the use of cloud services.

>> **Applications.** These include both commercial and custom applications, private clouds, web services, software as a service (SaaS), and the interfaces and integrations between application components. Securing the provisioning of these assets requires strict access controls; only designated administrators should be able to deploy and configure them.

Understand and Apply Foundational Security Operations Concepts

Fundamental security operations concepts that need to be well understood and managed include the principles of *need-to-know* and *least privilege*, *separation of duties and responsibilities*, *monitoring of special privileges*, *job rotation*, information lifecycle management and service-level agreements.

Need-to-know and least privilege

The concept of *need-to-know* states that only people with a valid business justification should have access to specific information or functions. In addition to having a need-to-know, an individual must have an appropriate security clearance level in order for access to be granted. Conversely, an individual with the appropriate security clearance level, but without a need-to-know, should not be granted access.

One of the most difficult challenges in managing need-to-know is the use of controls that enforce need-to-know. Also, information owners need to be able to distinguish *I need-to-know* from *I want-to-know*, *I-want-to-feel-important*, and *I'm-just-curious*.

Need-to-know is closely related to the concept of least privilege and can help organizations implement least privilege in a practical manner.

The principle of *least privilege* states that persons should have the capability to perform only the tasks (or have access to only the data) that are required to perform their primary jobs, and no more.

To give an individual more privileges and access than required invites trouble. Offering the capability to perform more than the job requires may become a temptation that results, sooner or later, in an abuse of privilege.

For example, giving a user full permissions on a network share, rather than just read and modify rights to a specific directory, opens the door not only for abuse of those privileges (for example, reading or copying other sensitive information on the network share) but also for costly mistakes (accidentally deleting a file — or the entire directory!). As a starting point, organizations should approach permissions with a "deny all" mentality, then add needed permissions as required.

TIP

Least privilege is also closely related to separation of duties and responsibilities, described in the following section. Distributing the duties and responsibilities for a given job function among several people means that those individuals require fewer privileges on a system or resource.

The principle of least privilege states that people should have the fewest privileges necessary to allow them to perform their tasks.

Several important concepts associated with need to know and least privilege include

>> **Entitlement.** When a new user account is provisioned in an organization, the permissions granted to that account must be appropriate for the level of access required by the user. In too many organizations, human resources simply instructs the IT department to give a new user "whatever so-and-so (another user in the same department) has access to". Instead, entitlement needs to be based on the principle of least privilege.

>> **Aggregation.** When people transfer between jobs and/or departments within an organization (see the section on job rotations later in this chapter), they often need different access and privileges to do their new jobs. Far too often, organizational security processes do not adequately ensure that access rights which are no longer required by an individual are actually revoked. Instead, individuals accumulate privileges, and over a period of many years an employee can have far more access and privileges than they actually need. This is known as *aggregation,* and it's the antithesis of least privilege!

   Privilege creep is another term commonly used here.

>> **Transitive trust.** Trust relationships (in the context of security domains) are often established within, and between, organizations to facilitate ease of access and collaboration. A trust relationship enables subjects (such as users or processes) in one security domain to access objects (such as servers or applications) in another security domain (see Chapter 5 and Chapter 7 to learn more about objects and subjects). A transitive trust extends access privileges to the subdomains of a security domain (analogous to inheriting permissions to subdirectories within a parent directory structure). Instead, a nontransitive trust should be implemented by requiring access to each subdomain to be explicitly granted based on the principle of least privilege, rather than inherited.

Separation of duties and responsibilities

The concept of *separation* (or *segregation*) *of duties and responsibilities* ensures that no single individual has complete authority and control of a critical system or process. This practice promotes security in the following ways:

>> **Reduces opportunities for fraud or abuse:** In order for fraud or abuse to occur, two or more individuals must collude or be complicit in the performance of their duties.

>> **Reduces mistakes:** Because two or more individuals perform the process, mistakes are less likely to occur or mistakes are more quickly detected and corrected.

>> **Reduces dependence on individuals:** Critical processes are accomplished by groups of individuals or teams. Multiple individuals should be trained on different parts of the process (for example, through job rotation, discussed in the following section) to help ensure that the absence of an individual doesn't unnecessarily delay or impede successful completion of a step in the process.

Here are some common examples of separation of duties and responsibilities within organizations:

>> A bank assigns the first three numbers of a six-number safe combination to one employee and the second three numbers to another employee. A single employee isn't permitted to have all six numbers, so a lone employee is unable to gain access to the safe and steal its contents.

>> An accounting department might separate record entry and internal auditing functions, or accounts payable and check disbursing functions.

>> A system administrator is responsible for setting up new accounts and assigning permissions, which a security administrator then verifies.

>> A programmer develops software code, but a separate individual is responsible for testing and validation, and yet another individual is responsible for loading the code on production systems.

>> Destruction of classified materials may require two individuals to complete or witness the destruction.

>> Disposal of assets may require an approval signature by the office manager and verification by building security.

In smaller organizations, separation of duties and responsibilities can be difficult to implement because of limited personnel and resources.

Privileged account management

Privileged entity controls are the mechanisms, generally built into computer operating systems and network devices, that give privileged access to hardware, software, and data. In UNIX and Windows, the controls that permit privileged functions reside in the operating system. Operating systems for servers, desktop computers, and many other devices use the concept of *modes* of execution to define privilege levels for various user accounts, applications, and processes that run on a system. For instance, the UNIX root account and Windows Server Enterprise, Domain, and Local Administrator account roles have elevated rights that allow those accounts to install software, view the entire file system and, in some cases, directly access the OS kernel and memory.

Specialized tools are used to monitor and record activities performed by privileged and administrative users. This helps to ensure accountability on the part of each administrator and aids in troubleshooting, through the ability to view actions performed by administrators.

System or network administrators typically use privileged accounts to perform operating system and utility management functions. Supervisor or Administrator mode should be used only for system administration purposes. Unfortunately, many organizations allow system and network administrators to use these privileged accounts or roles as their normal user accounts even when they aren't doing work which requires this level of access. Yet another horrible security practice is to allow administrators to share a single "administrator" or "root" account.

WARNING

System or network administrators occasionally grant root or administrator privileges to normal applications as a matter of convenience, rather than spending the time to figure out exactly what privileges the application actually requires, and then creating an account role for the application with only those privileges. Allowing a normal application these privileges is a serious mistake because applications that run in privileged mode bypass some or all security controls, which could lead to unexpected application behavior. For instance, any user of a payroll application could view or change anyone's data because the application running in privileged mode was never told *no* by the operating system. Further, if an application running in privileged mode is compromised by an attacker, the attacker may then inherit privileged access for the entire system.

TIP

Hackers specifically target Supervisor and other privileged modes, because those modes have a great deal of power over systems. The use of Supervisor mode should be limited wherever possible, especially on end-user workstations.

MONITORING — EVERYBODY'S SPECIAL!

Monitoring the activities of an organization's users, particularly those who have special (for example, administrator) privileges, is an important security operations practice.

User monitoring can include casual or direct observation, analysis of security logs, inspection of workstation hard drives, random drug testing (in certain job functions and in accordance with applicable laws), audits of attendance and building access records, review of call logs and transcripts, and other activities.

User monitoring, and its purposes, should be fully addressed in an organization's written policy manuals. Information systems should display a login warning that clearly informs the user that their activities may be monitored and for what purposes. The login warning should also clearly indicate who owns the information and information assets processed on the system or network, and that the user has *no expectation of privacy* with regard to information stored or processed on the system. The login process should require users to affirmatively acknowledge the login warning by clicking OK or I Agree in order to gain access to the system.

An organization should conduct user monitoring in accordance with its written policies and applicable laws. Also, only personnel authorized to do so (such as security, legal, or human resources) should perform this monitoring, and only for authorized purposes. User and entity behavior analytics (UEBA) is a process that is helpful in detecting potential breaches, intrusions, or other malicious activity using monitoring data to establish baselines of normal behavior or activity and analyzing anomalies.

Job rotation

Job rotation (or *rotation of duties*) is another effective security control that gives many benefits to an organization. Similar to the concept of separation of duties and responsibilities, job rotations involve regularly (or randomly) transferring key personnel into different positions or departments within an organization, with or without notice. Job rotations accomplish several important organizational objectives:

>> **Reduce opportunities for fraud or abuse.** Regular job rotations can accomplish this objective in the following two ways:

- People hesitate to set up the means for periodically or routinely stealing corporate information because they know that they could be moved to another shift or task at almost any time.

- People don't work with each other long enough to form collusive relationships that could damage the company.

>> **Eliminate single points of failure.** By ensuring that numerous people within an organization or department know how to perform several different job functions, an organization can reduce dependence on individuals and thereby eliminate single points of failure when an individual is absent, incapacitated, no longer employed with the organization, or otherwise unavailable to perform a critical job function.

>> **Promote professional growth.** Through cross-training opportunities, job rotations can help an individual's professional growth and career development, and reduce monotony and/or fatigue.

MANDATORY AND PERMANENT VACATIONS: JOB ROTATIONS OF A DIFFERENT SORT!

Mandatory vacations and termination of employment are two important security operations topics that warrant a few paragraphs! You might think of a mandatory vacation as a very short (one or two week) job rotation — and a termination as a permanent vacation!

Requiring employees to take one or more weeks of their vacation in a single block of time gives an organization an opportunity to uncover potential fraud or abuse. Employees engaging in illegal or prohibited activities are sometimes reluctant to be away from the office, concerned that these activities will be discovered in their absence. This may occur as a result of an actual audit or investigation, or when someone else performing that person's normal day-to-day functions in their absence uncovers an irregularity. Less ominously, mandatory vacations may help in other ways:

- Reduce individual stress and therefore reduce opportunities for mistakes or coercion by others.

- Discover inefficient processes when a substitute performs a job function more quickly or discovers a better way to get something done.

- Reveal single points of failure, shadow processes, and opportunities for job rotation (and separation of duties and responsibilities) when a process or job function idles because the only person who knows how to perform that function is lying on a beach somewhere.

Finally, it is vital to lock down or revoke local and remote access for a terminated employee as soon as possible, especially in cases where the employee is being fired or laid off. The potential consequences associated with continued access by an angry employee are serious enough to warrant emergency procedures for immediate termination of access.

Job rotations can also include changing workers' workstations and work locations, which can also keep would-be saboteurs off balance and less likely to commit.

As with the practice of separation of duties, small organizations can have difficulty implementing job rotations.

Information lifecycle

The information lifecycle refers to the activities related to the introduction, use, and disposal of information in an organization. The phases in the information lifecycle typically are

>> **Plan.** Development of formal plans on how to create and use information.

>> **Creation.** Information is created, collected, received, or captured in some way.

>> **Store.** Information is stored in an information system.

>> **Use.** Information is used, maintained, and perhaps disseminated.

>> **Protection.** Information is protected according to its criticality and sensitivity.

>> **Disposal.** Information at the end of its service life is discarded. Sensitive information will be erased using techniques to prevent its recovery.

TIP

The European Union's General Data Protection Regulation (GDPR) and other privacy regulations bring to light the steps in the information lifecycle, by giving data subjects legal rights regarding use of information about them.

Service-level agreements

Users of business- or mission-critical information systems need to know whether their systems or services will function when they need them, and users need to know more than "Is it up?" or "Is it down *again?*" Their customers, and others, hold users accountable for getting their work done in a timely and accurate manner, so consequently, those users need to know whether they can depend on their systems and services to help them deliver as promised.

The service-level agreement (SLA) is a quasi-legal document (it's a real legal document when it is included in or referenced by a contract) that pledges the system or service performs to a set of minimum standards, such as

>> **Hours of availability:** The wall-clock hours that the system or service will be available for users. This could be 24 x 7 (24 hours per day, 7 days per week) or something more limited, such as daily from 4:00 a.m. to 12:00 p.m. Availability specifications may also cite *maintenance windows* (for instance, Sundays from 2:00 a.m. to 4:00 a.m.) when users can expect the system or service to be down for testing, upgrades, and maintenance.

>> **Average and peak number of concurrent users:** The maximum number of users who can use the system or service at the same time.

>> **Transaction throughput:** The number of transactions that the system or service can perform or support in a given time period. Usually, *throughput* is expressed as transactions per second, per minute, or per hour.

>> **Transaction accuracy:** The accuracy of transactions that the system or service performs. Generally, this is related to complex calculations (such as calculating sales tax) and accuracy of location data.

>> **Data storage capacity:** The amount of data that the users can store in the system or service (such as cloud storage). Capacity may be expressed in raw terms (megabytes or gigabytes) or in numbers of transactions.

>> **Response times:** The maximum periods of time (in seconds) that key transactions take. Response times for long processes (such as nightly runs, batch jobs, and so on) also should be covered in the SLA.

>> **Service desk response and resolution times:** The amount of time (usually in hours) that a service desk (or help desk) will take to respond to requests for support and resolve any issues.

>> **Mean Time Between Failures (MTBF):** The amount of time, typically measured in (thousands of) hours, that a component (such as a server hard drive) or system is expected to continuously operate before experiencing a failure.

>> **Mean Time to Restore Service (MTRS):** The amount of time, typically measured in minutes or hours, that it is expected to take in order to restore a system or service to normal operation after a failure has occurred.

>> **Security incident response times:** The amount of time (usually in hours or days) between the realization of a security incident and any required notifications to data owners and other affected parties.

>> **Escalation process during times of failure:** When things go wrong, how quickly the service provider will contact the customer, as well as what steps the provider will take to restore service.

REMEMBER

Availability is one of the three tenets of information security (Confidentiality, Integrity, and Availability, discussed in Chapter 3). Therefore, SLAs are an important security document.

Because the SLA is a quantified statement, the service provider and the user alike can take measurements to see how well the service provider is meeting the SLA's standards. This measurement, which is sometimes accompanied by analysis, is frequently called a *scorecard*.

TIP

Operational-level agreements (OLAs) and underpinning contracts (UCs) are important SLA supporting documents. An OLA is essentially an SLA between the different interdependent groups that are responsible for the terms of the SLA, for example, a Service Desk and the Desktop Support team. UCs are used to manage third-party relationships with entities that help support the SLA, such as an external service provider or vendor.

Finally, for an SLA to be meaningful, it needs to have teeth! How will the SLA be enforced, and what will happen when violations occur? What are the escalation procedures? Will any penalties or service credits be paid in the event of a violation? If so, how will penalties or credits be calculated?

TIP

Internal SLAs (and OLAs), such as those between an IT department and their users, typically don't provide penalties or service credits for service violations. Internal SLAs are structured more as a commitment between IT and the user community, and are useful for managing service expectations. Clearly defined escalation procedures (who gets notified of a problem; when, how, and when it goes up the chain of command) are critical in an internal SLA.

TIP

SLAs rarely, if ever, provide meaningful financial penalties for service violations. For example, an hour of Internet downtime might legitimately cost an e-commerce company $10,000 of business. But most service providers will typically only provide a credit equivalent to the amount paid for the lost hour of Internet service (a few hundred dollars). This may seem incredibly disproportionate, but consider it from the service provider's perspective. That same credit has to be given to *all* of their customers that experienced the outage. Thus, an outage could potentially cost the service provider hundreds of thousands of dollars. If service providers were legally obligated to reimburse every customer for their actual losses, it's fair to guess that no one would be in the business of providing Internet service (or it would cost a few thousand dollars a month for a T-1 circuit). Instead, look for such penalties as an early termination clause that lets you get out of a long-term contract if your service provider repeatedly fails to meet its service level obligations.

Apply Resource Protection Techniques

Resource protection is the broad category of controls that protect information assets and information infrastructure. Resources that require protection include

>> **Communications hardware and software:** Routers, switches, firewalls, load balancers, intrusion prevention systems, fax machines, Virtual Private Network (VPN) servers, and so on, as well as the software that these devices use.

>> **Computers and their storage systems:** All corporate servers and client workstations, storage area networks (SANs), network-attached storage (NAS), direct-attached storage (DAS), near-line and offline storage systems, cloud-based storage, and backup devices.

>> **Business data:** All stored information, such as financial data, sales and marketing information, personnel and payroll data, customer and supplier data, proprietary product or process data, and intellectual property.

>> **System data:** Operating systems, utilities, user IDs and password files, audit trails, and configuration files.

>> **Backup media:** Tapes, tape cartridges, removable disks, and off-site replicated disk systems.

>> **Software:** Application source code, programs, tools, libraries, vendor software, and other proprietary software.

Media management

Media management refers to a broad category of controls that are used to manage information classification and physical media. *Data classification* refers to the tasks of marking information according to its sensitivity, as well as the subsequent handling, storage, transmission, and disposal procedures that accompany each classification level. Physical media is similarly marked; likewise, controls specify handling, storage, and disposal procedures. See Chapter 4 to learn more about data classification.

Sensitive information such as financial records, employee data, and information about customers must be clearly marked, properly handled and stored, and appropriately destroyed in accordance with established organizational policies, standards, and procedures:

>> **Marking:** How an organization identifies sensitive information, whether electronic or hard copy. For example, a marking might read PRIVILEGED AND CONFIDENTIAL. See Chapter 4 for a more detailed discussion of data classification.

>> **Handling:** The organization should have established procedures for handling sensitive information. These procedures detail how employees can transport, transmit, and use such information, as well as any applicable restrictions.

>> **Protection:** This involves two components:

- The physical protection of the actual media, such as locked cabinets and secured vehicles.

- The logical protection of information on media, such as encryption.

>> **Storage and Backup:** Similar to handling, the organization must have procedures and requirements specifying how sensitive information must be stored and backed up.

>> **Retention:** Most organizations are bound by various laws and regulations to collect and store certain information, as well as to keep it for minimum and/or maximum specified periods of time. An organization must be aware of legal requirements and ensure that it's in compliance with all applicable regulations. Records retention policies should cover any electronic records that may be located on file servers, document management systems, databases, e-mail systems, archives, and records management systems, as well as paper copies and backup media stored at off-site facilities. Organizations that want to retain information longer than required by law should firmly establish why such information should be kept longer. Nowadays, just having information can be a liability, so this should be the exception rather than the norm.

>> **Destruction:** Sooner or later, an organization must destroy sensitive information. The organization must have procedures detailing how to destroy sensitive information that has been previously retained, regardless of whether the data is in hard copy or saved as an electronic file.

WARNING

At the opposite end of the records retention spectrum, many organizations now destroy records (including backup media) as soon as legally permissible in order to limit the scope (and cost) of any *future* discovery requests or litigation. Before implementing any such draconian retention policies that severely restrict your organization's retention periods, you should fully understand the negative implications such a policy has for your disaster recovery capabilities. Also, consult with your organization's legal counsel to ensure that you're in full compliance with all applicable laws and regulations. Although extremely short retention policies and practices may be prudent for limiting future discovery requests or litigation, they're *illegal* for limiting *pending* discovery requests or litigation (or even records that you have a reasonable expectation may become the subject of future litigation). In such cases, don't destroy pertinent records — otherwise you go to jail. You go directly to jail! You don't pass Go, you don't collect $200, and (oh, yeah) you don't pass the CISSP exam, either — or even remain eligible for CISSP certification!

Hardware and software asset management

Maintaining a complete and accurate inventory with configuration information about all of an organization's hardware and software information assets is an important security operations function.

Without this information, managing vulnerabilities becomes a truly daunting challenge. With popular trends such as "bring your own device" becoming more commonplace in many organizations, it is critical that organizations work with their information security leaders and end users to ensure that all devices and applications that are used are known to — and appropriately managed by — the organization. This allows any inherent risks to be known — and addressed.

Conduct Incident Management

The formal process of detecting, responding to, and fixing a security problem is known as *incident management* (also known as *security incident management*).

WARNING

Do not confuse the concept of incident management, described herein, with the more general concept of incident management as defined by the Information Technology Infrastructure Library's (ITIL) Service Management best practices.

Incident management includes the following steps:

1. Preparation. Incident management begins before an incident actually occurs. Preparation is the key to quick and successful incident management. A well-documented and regularly practiced *incident management* (or *incident response*) *plan* ensures effective preparation. The plan should include:

- **Response procedures:** Include detailed procedures that address different contingencies and situations.

- **Response authority:** Clearly define roles, responsibilities, and levels of authority for all members of the Computer Incident Response Team (CIRT).

- **Available resources:** Identify people, tools, and external resources (consultants and law enforcement agents) that are available to the CIRT. Training should include use of these resources, when possible.

- **Legal review:** The incident response plan should be evaluated by appropriate legal counsel to determine compliance with applicable laws and to determine whether they're enforceable and defensible.

2. Detection. Detecting that a security incident or event has occurred is the first and, often, most difficult step in incident management. Detection may occur through automated monitoring and alerting systems, or as the result of a reported security incident (such as a lost or stolen mobile device). Under the best of circumstances, detection may occur in real-time as soon as a security incident occurs, such as malware that is discovered by anti-malware software on a computer. More often, a security incident may not be detected for quite some time (months or years), such as in the case of a sophisticated "low and slow" cyberattack. Determining whether a security incident has occurred is similar to the detection and containment step in the investigative process (discussed earlier in this chapter) and includes defining what constitutes a security incident for your organization.

3. Response. Upon determination that an incident has occurred, it's important to immediately begin detailed documentation of every action taken throughout the incident management process. You should also identify the appropriate alert level. (Ask questions such as "Is this an isolated incident or a system-wide event?" and "Has personal or sensitive data been compromised?" and "What laws may have been violated?") The answers will help you determine who to notify and whether or not to activate the entire incident response team or only certain members. Next, notify the appropriate people about the incident — both incident response team members and management. All contact information should be documented before an incident, and all notifications and contacts during an incident should be documented in the incident log.

4. Mitigation. The purpose of this step is to contain the incident and minimize further loss or damage. For example, you may need to eradicate a virus, deny access, or disable services in order to halt the incident in progress.

5. **Reporting.** This step requires assessing the incident and reporting the results to appropriate management personnel and authorities (if applicable). The assessment includes determining the scope and cause of damage, as well as the responsible (or liable) party.

6. **Recovery.** Recovering normal operations involves eradicating any components of the incident (for example, removing malware from a system or disabling e-mail service on a stolen mobile device). Think of recovery as returning a system to its pre-incident state.

7. **Remediation.** Remediation may include rebuilding systems, repairing vulnerabilities, improving safeguards, and restoring data and services. Do this step in accordance with a business continuity plan (BCP) that properly identifies recovery priorities.

8. **Lessons learned.** The final phase of incident management requires evaluating the effectiveness of your incident management plan and identifying any lessons learned — which should include not only what went wrong, but also what went right.

REMEMBER

Investigations and incident management follow similar steps but have different purposes: The distinguishing characteristic of an investigation is the gathering of evidence for possible prosecution, whereas incident management focuses on containing the damage and returning to normal operations.

Operate and Maintain Detective and Preventive Measures

Detective and preventive security measures include various security technologies and techniques, including:

>> **Firewalls.** Firewalls are typically deployed at the network or data center perimeter and at other network boundaries, such as between zones of trust. Increasingly, host-based firewalls are being deployed to protect endpoints and virtual servers throughout the data center. Firewalls are discussed in more detail in Chapter 6.

>> **Intrusion detection and prevention systems (IDS/IPS).** Intrusion detection systems passively monitor traffic in a network segment or to and from a host and provide alerts of suspicious activity. An intrusion prevention system (IPS) can detect and either block an attack or drop the network packets from the attack source. IDS and IPS are discussed earlier in this chapter and in Chapter 6.

» **Whitelisting and blacklisting.** Whitelisting involves explicitly allowing some action, such as email delivery from a known sender, traffic from a specific IP address range, or execution of a trusted application. Blacklisting explicitly blocks specific actions.

» **Third-party security services.** Third-party security services cover a wide spectrum of possible security services, such as

- **Managed security services (MSS),** which typically involves a service provider that monitors an organization's IT environment for malfunctions and incidents. Service providers can also perform management of infrastructure devices, such as network devices and servers.

- **Vulnerability management services,** where a service provider periodically scans internal and external networks, then reports vulnerabilities back to the customer organization for remediation.

- **Security information and event management** (SIEM, discussed earlier in this chapter).

- **IP reputation services,** usually in the form of a threat intelligence feed to an organization's IDSs, IPSs, and firewalls.

- **Web filtering,** where an on-premises appliance or a cloud-based service limits or blocks end-user access to banned categories of websites (think gambling or pornography), as well as websites known to contain malicious software.

- **Cloud-based malware detection,** offered as a service that provides real-time scanning of files in the cloud and leverages the speed and scale of the cloud to detect and prevent zero-day threats more quickly than traditional on-premises antimalware solutions.

- **Cloud-based spam filtering,** offered as a service that blocks or quarantines spam and phishing emails before it reaches the corporate network, thereby significantly reducing the volume of email traffic and performance overhead associated with transmitting and processing unwanted and potentially malicious email.

- **DDoS mitigation,** typically deployed in an upstream network to drop or reroute DDoS traffic before it impacts the customer's network, systems, and applications.

» **Sandboxing.** A sandbox enables untrusted or unknown programs to be executed in a separate, isolated operating environment, so any security threats or vulnerabilities can be safely analyzed. Sandboxing is used in many types of systems today, including anti-malware, web filtering, and intrusion prevention systems (IPS).

>> **Honeypots and honeynets.** A honeypot is a decoy system that is used to attract attackers, so their methods and techniques can be observed (somewhat like a trojan horse for the good guys!). A honeynet is a network of honeypots.

>> **Anti-malware.** Anti-malware (also known as *antivirus*) software intercepts operating system routines that store and open files. The anti-malware software compares the contents of the file being opened or stored against a database of malware signatures. If a malware signature is matched, the anti-malware software prevents the file from being opened or saved and (usually) alerts the user. Enterprise anti-malware software typically sends an alert to a central management console so that the organization's security team is alerted and can take the appropriate action. Advanced anti-malware tools use various advanced techniques such as machine learning to detect and block malware from executing on a system.

Implement and Support Patch and Vulnerability Management

Software bugs and flaws inevitably exist in operating systems, database management systems, and various applications, and are continually discovered by researchers. Many of these bugs and flaws are security vulnerabilities that could permit an attacker to control a target system and subsequently access sensitive data or critical functions. Patch and vulnerability management is the process of regularly assessing, testing, installing and verifying fixes and patches for software bugs and flaws as they are discovered.

To perform patch and vulnerability management, follow these basic steps:

1. Subscribe to security advisories from vendors and third-party organizations.

2. Perform periodic security scans of internal and external infrastructure to identify systems and applications with unsecure configuration and missing patches.

3. Perform risk analysis on each advisory and missing patch to determine its applicability and risk to your organization.

4. Develop a plan to either install the security patch or to perform another workaround, if any is available.

You should base your decision on which solution best eliminates the vulnerability or reduces risk to an acceptable level.

5. Test the security patch or workaround in a test environment.

   This process involves making sure that stated functions still work properly and that no unexpected side-effects arise as a result of installing the patch or workaround.

6. Install the security patch in the production environment.

7. Verify that the patch is properly installed and that systems still perform properly.

8. Update all relevant documentation to include any changes made or patches installed.

Understand and Participate in Change Management Processes

Change management is the business process used to control architectural and configuration changes in a production environment. Instead of just making changes to systems and the way that they relate to each other, change management is a formal process of request, design, review, approval, implementation, and recordkeeping.

Configuration Management is the closely related process of actively managing the configuration of every system, device, and application and then thoroughly documenting those configurations.

REMEMBER

>> **Change Management** is the approval-based process that ensures that only approved changes are implemented.

>> **Configuration Management** is the control that records all of the soft configuration (settings and parameters in the operating system, database, and application) and software changes that are performed with approval from the Change Management process.

Implement Recovery Strategies

Developing and implementing effective backup and recovery strategies are critical for ensuring the availability of systems and data. Other techniques and strategies are commonly implemented to ensure the availability of critical systems, even in the event of an outage or disaster.

Backup storage strategies

Backups are performed for a variety of reasons that center around a basic principle: sometimes things go wrong and we need to get our data back. In order to cover all reasonable scenarios, backup storage strategies often involve the following:

» **Secure offsite storage.** Store backup media at a remote location, far enough away so that the remote location is not directly affected by the same events (weather, natural disasters, man-made disasters), but close enough so that backup media can be retrieved in a reasonable period of time.

» **Transport via secure courier.** This can discourage or prevent theft of backup media while it is in transit to a remote location.

» **Backup media encryption.** This helps to prevent any unauthorized third party from being able to recover data from backup media.

» **Data replication.** Sending data to an offsite or remote data center, or cloud-based storage provider, in near real-time.

Recovery site strategies

These include hot sites (a fully functional data center or other facility that is always up and ready with near real-time replication of production systems and data), cold sites (a data center or facility that may have some recovery equipment available but not configured, and no backup data onsite), and warm sites (some hardware and connectivity is prepositioned and configured, plus an offsite copy of backup data).

Selecting a recovery site strategy has everything to do with cost and service level. The faster you want to recover data processing operations in a remote location, the more you will have to spend in order to build a site that is "ready to go" at the speed you require.

In a nutshell: *Speed costs.*

Multiple processing sites

Many large organizations operate multiple data centers for critical systems with real-time replication and load balancing between the various sites. This is the ultimate solution for large commercial sites that have little or no tolerance for downtime. Indeed, a well-engineered multi-site application can suffer even significant whole-data-center outages without customers even knowing anything is wrong.

System resilience, high availability, quality of service, and fault tolerance

System resilience, high availability, quality of service (QoS), and fault tolerance are similar characteristics that are engineered into a system to make it as reliable as possible:

>> **System resilience.** This includes eliminating *single points of failure* in system designs and building fail-safes into critical systems.

>> **High availability.** This typically consists of clustered systems and databases configured in an active-active (both systems are running and immediately available) or active-passive (one system is active, while the other is in standby but can become active, usually within a matter of seconds). Clusters in active-passive mode have the *failover* mechanism used to automatically switch the "active" role from one server in the cluster to another.

HOW VIRTUALIZATION MAKES HIGH-AVAILABILITY A REALITY

Server virtualization is a rapidly growing and popular trend that has come of age in recent years. Virtualization allows organizations to build more resilient, highly efficient, cost-effective technology infrastructures to better support their business-critical systems and applications. Popular virtualization solutions include VMware vSphere and Microsoft Hyper-V. Although virtualization has many, many benefits, here's a quick look at the high-availability benefit.

Virtual systems can be replicated or "moved" between separate physical systems, often without interrupting server operations or network connectivity. This can be accomplished over a local area network (LAN) when two physical servers (hosting multiple virtual servers) share common storage (a storage-area network [SAN]). For example, if Physical Server #1 fails, all the virtual servers on that physical server can be quickly "moved" to Physical Server #2. Or, in an alternate scenario, if a virtual server on Physical Server #1 reaches a pre-defined performance threshold (such as processor, memory, or bandwidth utilization), the virtual server can be "moved" — automatically and seamlessly — to Physical Server #2.

For business continuity or disaster recovery purposes (discussed in the next section and in Chapter 3), virtual servers can also be pre-staged in separate geographic locations, ready to be activated or "booted up" when needed. Using a third-party application, critical applications and data can be continuously replicated to a disaster recovery site or secondary datacenter in near real-time, so that normal business operations can be restored as quickly as possible.

>> **Quality of service.** Refers to a mechanism where systems that provide various services prioritize certain services to ensure they're always available or perform at a certain level. For example, Voice over Internet Protocol (VoIP) systems typically are prioritized to ensure sufficient network bandwidth is always available to avoid any traffic delay or degradation of voice quality. Other services that are not as sensitive to delays (such as web browsing or file downloads) will be prioritized at a lower level in such cases.

>> **Fault tolerance.** This includes engineered redundancies in critical components, such as multiple power supplies, multiple network interfaces, and RAID (redundant array of independent disks) configured storage systems.

Implement Disaster Recovery (DR) Processes

A variety of disasters can beset an organization's business operations. They fall into two main categories: natural and man-made.

In many cases, formal methodologies are used to predict the likelihood of a particular disaster. For example, *50-year flood plain* is a term that you've probably heard to describe the maximum physical limits of a river flood that's likely to occur once in a 50-year period. The likelihood of each of the following disasters depends greatly on local and regional geography:

>> Fires and explosions

>> Earthquakes

>> Storms (snow, ice, hail, prolonged rain, wind, dust, solar)

>> Floods

>> Hurricanes, typhoons, and cyclones

>> Volcanoes and lava flows

>> Tornadoes

>> Landslides

>> Avalanches

>> Tsunamis

>> Pandemics

Many of these occurrences may have secondary effects; often these secondary effects have a bigger impact on business operations, sometimes in a wider area than the initial disaster (for instance, a landslide in a rural area can topple power transmission lines, which results in a citywide blackout). Some of these effects are

>> **Utility outages:** Electric power, natural gas, water, and so on

>> **Communications outages:** Telephone, cable, wireless, TV, and radio

>> **Transportation outages:** Road, airport, train, and port closures

>> **Evacuations/unavailability of personnel:** From both home and work locations

As if natural disasters weren't enough, man-made disasters can also disrupt business operations, all as a result of deliberate and accidental acts:

>> **Accidents:** Hazardous materials spills, power outages, communications failures, and floods due to water supply accidents

>> **Crime and mischief:** Arson, vandalism, and burglary

>> **War and terrorism:** Bombings, sabotage, and other destructive acts

>> **Cyber attacks/cyber warfare:** Denial of Service (DoS) attacks, malware, data destruction, and similar acts

>> **Civil disturbances:** Riots, demonstrations, strikes, sickouts, and other such events

TIP

For a more complete reference on disaster recovery planning, we recommend *IT Disaster Recovery Planning For Dummies*.

Disasters can affect businesses in a lot of ways — some obvious, and others not so obvious.

>> **Damage to business buildings.** Disasters can damage or destroy a building or make it uninhabitable.

>> **Damage to business records.** Along with damaging a building, a disaster may damage a building's contents, including business records, whether they are in the form of paper, microfilm, or electronic.

>> **Damage to business equipment.** A disaster may be capable of damaging business equipment including computers, copiers, and all sorts of other machinery. Anything electrical or mechanical from calculators to nuclear reactors can be damaged in a disaster.

DISASTER RECOVERY PLANNING AND TERRORIST ATTACKS

The 2001 terrorist attacks in New York, Washington, D.C., and Pennsylvania — and the subsequent collapse of the World Trade Center buildings — had Disaster Recovery Planning and Business Continuity Planning officials all over the world scrambling to update their plans.

This kind of planning is still a highly relevant topic more than 15 years later. The attacks redefined the limits of extreme, deliberate acts of destruction. Previously, the most heinous attacks imaginable were large-scale bombings such as the 1993 attack on the World Trade Center or the 1995 bombing of the Alfred P. Murrah Federal Building in Oklahoma City.

The collapse of the World Trade Center towers resulted in the loss of life of 40 percent of the employees of the Sandler O'Neill & Partners investment bank. Bond broker Cantor Fitzgerald lost 658 employees in the attack — nearly its entire workforce. The sudden loss of a large number of employees had rarely been figured into BCP and DRP plans before. Businesses suddenly had to figure into contingency and recovery plans the previously unheard-of scenario, "What do we do if significant numbers of employees are suddenly lost?"

Traditional BCP and DRP plans nearly always assumed that a business still had plenty of workers around to keep the business rolling; those insiders might be delayed by weather or other events, but eventually they'd be back to continue running the business. The attacks on September 11, 2001, changed all that forever. Organizations need to include the possibility of the loss of a significant portion of their workforces into their business continuity plans. They owe this to their constituents and to their investors.

>> **Damage to communications.** Disasters can damage common carrier facilities including telephone networks (both landline and cellular), data networks, even wireless and satellite-based systems. Even if a business's buildings and equipment are untouched by a disaster, communications outages can be crippling. Further, damaged communications infrastructure in other cities can be capable of knocking out many businesses' voice and data networks (the September 11, 2001, attacks had an immediate impact on communications over a wide area of the northeastern U.S.; a number of telecommunications providers had strategic regional facilities there).

>> **Damage to public utilities.** Power, water, natural gas, and steam services can be damaged by a disaster. Even if a business's premises are undamaged, a utility outage can cause significant business disruption.

>> **Damage to transportation systems.** Freeways, roads, bridges, tunnels, railroads, and airports can all be damaged in a disaster. Damaged transportation infrastructure in other regions (where customers, partners, and suppliers are located, for instance) can cripple organizations dependent on the movement of materials, goods, or customers.

>> **Injuries and loss of life.** Violent disasters in populated areas often cause casualties. When employees, contractors, or customers are killed or injured, businesses are affected in negative ways: There may be fewer customers or fewer available employees to deliver goods and services. Losses don't need to be the employees or customers themselves; when family members are injured or in danger, employees will usually stay home to care for them and return to work only when those situations have stabilized.

>> **Indirect damage: suppliers and customers.** If a disaster strikes a region where key suppliers or customers are located, the effect on businesses can be almost as serious as if the business itself suffered damage.

PLANNING FOR PANDEMICS

In the last hundred years (and indeed, in all of recorded history before the 20th century), several pandemics have swept through the world. A *pandemic* is a rapid spread of a new disease for which few people have natural immunity. Large numbers of people may fall ill, resulting in high rates of absenteeism; supplier slowdowns; and shortages in materials, goods, and services. Some pandemics have a high mortality rate — many people die.

Contingency planning for a pandemic requires a different approach from that for other types of disasters. When a disaster such as an earthquake, hurricane, or volcano occurs, help in many forms soon comes pouring into the region to help repair transportation, communications, and other vital services. Organizations can rely on outsourced help or operations in other regions to keep critical operations running. But in a pandemic, no outside help may be available, and much larger regions may be affected. In general, a pandemic can induce a global slowdown in manpower, supplies, and services, as well as a depressed demand for most goods and services. Whole national economies can grind to a near-halt.

Businesses affected by a pandemic should expect high rates of absenteeism for extended periods of time. Local or regional municipalities may impose quarantines and travel restrictions, which slow the movement of customers and supplies. Schools may be closed for extended periods of time, which could require working parents to stay at home. Businesses should plan on operating only the most critical business processes, and they may have to rely on cross-trained staff because some of the usual staff members may be ill, or unwilling or unable to travel to work.

The list above isn't complete, but should help you think about all the ways a disaster can affect your organization.

Response

Emergency response teams must be prepared for every reasonably possible scenario. Members of these teams need a variety of specialized training to deal with such things as water and smoke damage, structural damage, flooding, and hazardous materials.

Organizations must document all the types of responses so that the response teams know what to do. The emergency response documentation consists of two major parts: how to respond to each type of incident, and the most up-to-date facts about the facilities and equipment that the organization uses.

In other words, you want your teams to know how to deal with water damage, smoke damage, structural damage, hazardous materials, and many other things. Your teams also need to know everything about every company facility: Where to find utility entrances, electrical equipment, HVAC equipment, fire control, elevators, communications, data closets, and so on; which vendors maintain and service them; and so on. And you need experts who know about the materials and construction of the buildings themselves. Those experts might be your own employees, outside consultants, or a little of both.

REMEMBER

It is the DRP team's responsibility to identify the experts needed for all phases of emergency response.

Responding to an emergency branches into two activities: salvage and recovery. Tangential to this is preparing financially for the costs associated with salvage and recovery.

Salvage

The salvage team is concerned with restoring full functionality to the damaged facility. This restoration includes several activities:

>> **Damage assessment:** Arrange a thorough examination of the facility to identify the full extent and nature of the damage. Frequently, outside experts, such as structural engineers, perform this inspection.

>> **Salvage assets:** Remove assets, such as computer equipment, records, furniture, inventory, and so on, from the facility.

- >> **Cleaning:** Thoroughly clean the facility to eliminate smoke damage, water damage, debris, and more. Outside companies that specialize in these services frequently perform this job.

- >> **Restoring the facility to operational readiness:** Complete repairs, and restock and reequip the facility to return it to pre-disaster readiness. At this point, the facility is ready for business functions to resume there.

REMEMBER

The salvage team is primarily concerned with the restoration of a facility and its return to operational readiness.

Recovery

Recovery comprises equipping the BCP team (yes, the BCP team — recovery involves both BCP and DRP) with any logistics, supplies, or coordination in order to get alternate functional sites up and running. This activity should be heavily scripted, with lots of procedures and checklists in order to ensure that every detail is handled.

Financial readiness

The salvage and recovery operations can cost a lot of money. The organization must prepare for potentially large expenses (at least several times the normal monthly operating cost) to restore operations to the original facility.

Financial readiness can take several forms, including:

- >> **Insurance:** An organization may purchase an insurance policy that pays for the replacement of damaged assets and perhaps even some of the other costs associated with conducting emergency operations.

- >> **Cash reserves:** An organization may set aside cash to purchase assets for emergency use, as well as to use for emergency operations costs.

- >> **Line of credit:** An organization may establish a line of credit, prior to a disaster, to be used to purchase assets or pay for emergency operations should a disaster occur.

- >> **Pre-purchased assets:** An organization may choose to purchase assets to be used for disaster recovery purposes in advance, and store those assets at or near a location where they will be utilized in the event of a disaster.

- >> **Letters of agreement:** An organization may wish to establish legal agreements that would be enacted in a disaster. These may range from use of emergency work locations (such as nearby hotels), use of fleet vehicles, appropriation of computers used by lower-priority systems, and so on.

>> **Standby assets:** An organization can use existing assets as items to be re-purposed in the event of a disaster. For example, a computer system that is used for software testing could be quickly re-used for production operations if a disaster strikes.

Personnel

People are the most important resource in any organization. As such, disaster response must place human life above all other considerations when developing disaster response plans and when emergency responders are taking action after a disaster strikes. In terms of life safety, organizations can do several things to ensure safety of personnel:

>> **Evacuation plans.** Personnel need to know how to safely evacuate a building or work center. Signs should be clearly posted, and drills routinely held, so that personnel can practice exiting the building or work center calmly and safely. For organizations with large numbers of customers or visitors, additional measures need to be taken so that persons unfamiliar with evacuation routes and procedures can safely exit the facilities.

>> **First aid.** Organizations need to have plenty of first aid supplies on hand, including longer-term supplies in the event a natural disaster prevents paramedics from being able to respond. Personnel need to be trained in first aid and CPR in the event of a disaster, especially when communications and/ or transportation facilities are cut.

>> **Emergency supplies.** For disasters that require personnel to shelter in place, organizations need to stock emergency water, food, blankets and other necessities in the event that personnel are stranded at work locations for more than a few hours.

REMEMBER

Personnel are the most important resource in any organization.

Communications

A critical component of the DRP is the communications plan. Employees need to be notified about closed facilities and any special work instructions (such as an alternate location to report for work). The planning team needs to realize that one or more of the usual means of communications may have also been adversely affected by the same event that damaged business facilities. For example, if a building has been damaged, the voice-mail system that people would try to call into so that they could check messages and get workplace status might not be working.

Organizations need to anticipate the effects of an event when considering emergency communications. For instance, you need to establish in advance two or more ways to locate each important staff member. These ways may include landlines, cell phones, spouses' cell phones, and alternate contact numbers (such as neighbors or relatives).

TIP Text messaging is often an effective means of communication, even when mobile communications systems are congested.

Many organizations' emergency operations plans include the use of audio conference bridges so that personnel can discuss operational issues hour by hour throughout the event. Instead of relying on a single provider (which you might not be able to reach because of communications problems or because it's affected by the same event), organizations should have a second (and maybe even a third) audio conference provider established. Emergency communications documentation needs to include dial-in information for both (or all three) conference systems.

In addition to internal communications, the DRP must address external communications to ensure that customers, investors, government, and media are provided with accurate and timely information.

Assessment

When a disaster strikes, an organization's DRP needs to include procedures to assess damage to buildings and equipment.

First, the response team needs to examine buildings and equipment, to determine which assets are a total loss, which are repairable, and which are still usable (although not necessarily in their current location).

For such events as floods, fires and earthquakes, a professional building inspector usually will need to examine a building to see whether it is fit for occupation. If not, then the next step is determining whether a limited number of personnel will be permitted to enter the building to retrieve needed assets.

Once assessment has been completed, assets can be divided into three categories:

>> **Salvage.** These are assets that are a total loss and cannot be repaired. In some cases, components can be removed to repair other assets.

>> **Repair.** Some assets can be repaired and returned to service.

>> **Reuse.** Undamaged assets can be placed back into service, although this may require them to be moved to an alternate work location if the building cannot be occupied.

Restoration

The ultimate objective of the disaster recovery team is the restoration of work facilities with their required assets, so that business may return to normal. Depending on the nature of the event, restoration may take the form of building repair, building replacement, or permanent relocation to a different building.

Similarly, assets used in each building may need to undergo their own restoration, whether that takes the form of replacement, repair, or simply placing it back into service in whatever location is chosen.

Prior to full restoration, business operations may be conducted in temporary facilities, possibly by alternate personnel who may be other employees or contractors hired to fill in and help out. These temporary facilities may be located either near the original facilities or some distance away. The circumstances of the event will dictate some of these matters, as well as the organization's plans for temporary business operations.

Training and awareness

An organization's ability to effectively respond to a disaster is highly dependent on its advance preparations. In addition to the development of high quality, workable disaster recovery and business continuity plans that are kept up to date, the next most important part is making sure that employees and other needed personnel are periodically trained in the actual response and continuity procedures. Training and practice helps to reinforce understanding of proper response procedures, giving the organization the best chance at surviving the disaster.

An important part of training is the participation in various types of testing, which is discussed in the following section.

Test Disaster Recovery Plans

By the time that an organization has created a DRP, it's probably spent hundreds of hours and possibly tens (or hundreds) of thousands of dollars on consulting fees. You'd think that after making such a big investment, they'd test the DRP to make sure that it really works when an actual disaster strikes!

The following sections outline DRP testing methods.

Read-through

A *read-through* (or *checklist*) *test* is a detailed review of DRP documents, performed by individuals on their own. The purpose of a read-through test is to identify inaccuracies, errors, and omissions in DRP documentation.

It's easy to coordinate this type of test, because each person who performs the test does it when his or her schedule permits (provided they complete it before any deadlines).

By itself, a document review is an insufficient way to test a DRP; however, it's a logical starting place. You should perform one or more of the other DR tests described in the following sections shortly after you do a read-through test.

Walkthrough or tabletop

A *walkthrough* (or *tabletop* or *structured walkthrough*) *test* is a team approach to the read-through test. Here, several business and technology experts in the organization gather to "walk" through the DRP. A moderator or facilitator leads participants to discuss each step in the DRP so that they can identify issues and opportunities for making the DRP more accurate and complete. Group discussions usually help to identify issues that people will not find when working on their own. Often the participants want to perform the review in a fancy mountain or oceanside retreat, where they can think much more clearly! (Yeah, right.)

During a walkthrough test, the facilitator writes down "parking lot" issues (items to be considered at a later time, written down now so they will not be forgotten) on a whiteboard or flipchart while the group identifies those issues. These are action items that will serve to make improvements to the DRP. Each action item needs to have an accountable person assigned, as well as a completion date, so that the action items will be completed in a reasonable time. Depending upon the extent of the changes, a follow-up walkthrough may need to be conducted at a later time.

TIP

A walkthrough test usually requires two or more hours to complete.

Simulation

In a *simulation test*, all the designated disaster recovery personnel practice going through the motions associated with a real recovery. In a simulation, the team doesn't actually perform any recovery or alternate processing.

An organization that plans to perform a simulation test appoints a facilitator who develops a disaster scenario, using a type of disaster that's likely to occur in the region. For instance, an organization in San Francisco might choose an earthquake scenario, and an organization in Miami could choose a hurricane.

In a simple simulation, the facilitator reads out announcements as if they're news briefs. Such announcements describe an unfolding scenario and can also include information about the organization's status at the time. An example announcement might read like this:

> It is 8:15 a.m. local time, and a magnitude 7.1 earthquake has just occurred, fifteen miles from company headquarters. Building One is heavily damaged and some people are seriously injured. Building Two (the one containing the organization's computer systems) is damaged and personnel are unable to enter the building. Electric power is out, and the generator has not started because of an unknown problem that may be earthquake related. Executives Jeff Johnson and Sarah Smith (CIO and CFO) are backpacking on the Appalachian Trail and cannot be reached.

The disaster-simulation team, meeting in a conference room, discusses emergency response procedures and how the response might unfold. They consider the conditions described to them and identify any issues that could impact an actual disaster response.

The simulation facilitator makes additional announcements throughout the simulation. Just like in a real disaster, the team doesn't know everything right away — instead, news trickles in. In the simulation, the facilitator reads scripted statements that, um, simulate the way that information flows in a real disaster.

A more realistic simulation can be held at the organization's emergency response center, where some resources that support emergency response may be available. Another idea is to hold the simulation on a day that is not announced ahead of time, so that responders will be genuinely surprised and possibly be less prepared to respond.

TIP Remember to test your backup media to make sure that you can actually restore data from backups!

Parallel

A *parallel test* involves performing all the steps of a real recovery, except that you keep the real, live production systems running. The actual production systems run in parallel with the disaster recovery systems. The parallel test is very time-consuming, but it does test the accuracy of the applications because analysts compare data on the test recovery systems with production data.

The technical architecture of the target application determines how a parallel test needs to be conducted. The general principle of a parallel test is that the *disaster recovery system* (meaning the system that remains on standby until a real disaster occurs, at which time, the organization presses it into production service) runs process work at the same time that the primary system continues its normal work.

Precisely *how* this is accomplished depends on technical details. For a system that operates on batches of data, those batches can be copied to the DR system for processing there, and results can be compared for accuracy and timeliness.

Highly interactive applications are more difficult to test in a strictly parallel test. Instead, it might be necessary to record user interactions on the live system and then "play back" those interactions using an application testing tool. Then responses, accuracy, and timing can be verified after the test to verify whether the DR system worked properly.

While a parallel test may be difficult to set up, its results can provide a good indication of whether disaster recovery systems will perform during a disaster. Also, the risks associated with a parallel test are low, since a failure of the DR system will not impact real business transactions.

REMEMBER

The parallel test includes loading data onto recovery systems without taking production systems down.

Full interruption (or cutover)

A *full interruption* (or *cutover*) *test* is similar to a parallel test except that in a full interruption test, a function's primary systems are actually shut off or disconnected. A full interruption test is the *ultimate* test of a disaster recovery plan because one or more of the business's critical functions actually depends upon the availability, integrity, and accuracy of the recovery systems.

A full interruption test should be performed only after successful walkthroughs and at least one parallel test. In a full interruption test, backup systems are processing the full production workload and all primary and ancillary functions including:

>> User access

>> Administrative access

>> Integrations to other applications

>> Support

>> Reporting

>> . . . And whatever else the main production environment needs to support

REMEMBER

A full interruption test is the ultimate test of the ability for a disaster recovery system to perform properly in a real disaster, but it's also the test with the highest risk and cost.

Participate in Business Continuity (BC) Planning and Exercises

Business continuity and disaster recovery planning are closely related but distinctly different activities. As described in Chapter 3, business continuity focuses on keeping a business running after a disaster or other event has occurred, while disaster recovery deals with restoring the organization and its affected processes and capabilities back to normal operations.

TIP

If you don't recall the similarities and differences between business continuity and disaster recovery planning, we strongly recommend that you refer back to Chapter 3!

Security professionals need to take an active role in their organization's business continuity planning activities and related exercises. As a CISSP, you'll be a recognized expert in the area of business continuity and disaster recovery, and you will need to contribute your specialized knowledge and experience to help your organization develop and implement effective and comprehensive business continuity and disaster recovery plans.

Implement and Manage Physical Security

Physical security is yet another important aspect of the security professional's responsibilities. Important physical security concepts and technologies are covered extensively in Chapter 5 and Chapter 7.

As with other information security concepts, ensuring physical security requires appropriate controls at the physical perimeter (this includes the building exterior, parking areas, and common grounds) and internal security controls to (most importantly) protect personnel, as well as to protect other physical and information assets from various threats, such as fire, flooding, severe weather, civil disturbances, terrorism, criminal activity, and workplace violence.

Address Personnel Safety and Security Concerns

Security professionals contribute to the safety and security of personnel by helping their organizations develop and implement effective personnel security policies (discussed in Chapter 3), and through physical security measures (discussed in the preceding section, as well as Chapter 5 and Chapter 7).

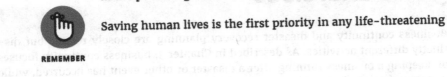

Saving human lives is the first priority in any life-threatening situation.

IN THIS CHAPTER

» Applying security throughout the software development lifecycle

» Enforcing security controls

» Protecting development environments

» Assessing software security

» Reducing risk by applying safe coding practices

» Sizing up the security impact of off-the-shelf software

Chapter **10**

Software Development Security

Y ou must understand the principles of software security controls, software development, and software vulnerabilities. Software and data are the foundation of information processing; software can't exist apart from software development. An understanding of the software development process is essential for the creation and maintenance of software that's appropriate, reliable, and secure. This domain represents 10 percent of the CISSP certification exam.

Understand and Integrate Security in the Software Development Lifecycle

The *software development lifecycle* (SDLC, also known as the *systems development lifecycle* and the *software development methodology* [SDM]) refers to all the steps required to develop software and systems from conception through implementation, support, and (ultimately) retirement. In other words, the entire life of software and systems, from birth to death, and everything in between (like adolescence, going off to college, getting married, and retirement)!

The lifecycle is a development process designed to achieve two objectives: software and systems that perform their intended functions correctly and securely, and a development or integration project that's completed on time and on budget.

TIP

As we point out numerous times in this chapter, the term *software development lifecycle* is giving way to *systems development lifecycle*. This is because the process applies to more than just software development; it more broadly applies to systems development. This can include networks, servers, database management systems, and more.

Development methodologies

Popular development methodologies include *waterfall* and *Agile*, as discussed in the following sections.

Waterfall

In the *waterfall model* of software (or system) development, each of the stages in the lifecycle progress like a series of waterfalls (see Figure 10-1). Each of the stages is performed sequentially, one at a time. Typically, these stages consist of the following:

>> **Conceptual definition.** This is a high-level description of the software or system deliverable. It generally contains no details — it's the sort of description that you want to give to the business and finance people (those folks who fund your projects and keep you employed). You don't want to scare them with details. And they probably don't understand them anyway!

>> **Functional requirements.** These are the required characteristics of the software or system deliverable. (Basically, a list.) Rather than a design, the functional requirements are a collection of things that the software or system must do. Although functional requirements don't give you design-level material, this description contains more details than the conceptual definition. Functional requirements usually include a *test plan,* which is a detailed list of software or system functions and features that must be tested. The test plan describes both how each test should be performed and the expected results. Generally, you have at least one test in the test plan for each requirement in the functional requirements. Functional requirements also must contain expected security requirements for the software or system.

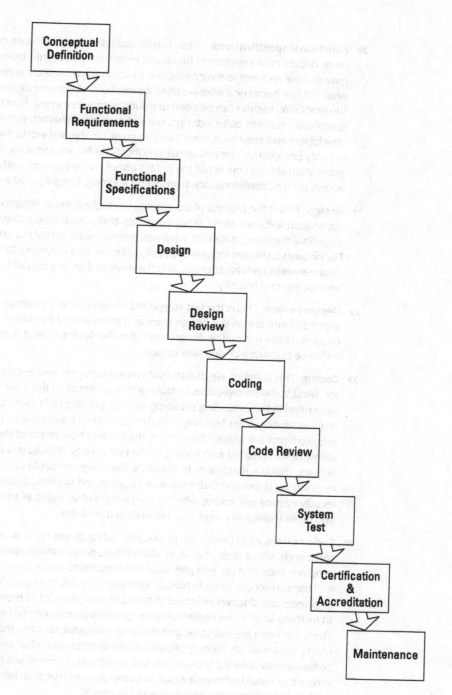

FIGURE 10-1:
A typical system
development
model takes a
project from start
to finish.

Conceptual
Definition

Functional
Requirements

Functional
Specifications

Design

Design
Review

Coding

Code Review

System
Test

Certification
&
Accreditation

Maintenance

» **Functional specifications.** These can be considered the software development department's version of functional requirements. Rather than a list of *have-to-have* and *nice-to-have* items, the functional specification is more of a *what-it-is* (we hope) or a *what-we-think-we-can-build* statement (to this point, the MoSCoW method can be used to prioritize requirements). Functional specifications aren't quite a design, but rather a list of characteristics that the developers and engineers think they can create in the real world. From a security perspective, the functional specifications for an operating system or application should contain all the details about authentication, authorization, access control, confidentiality, transaction auditing, integrity, and availability.

» **Design.** This is the process of developing the highest-detail designs. In the application software world, design includes entity-relationship diagrams, data-flow diagrams, database schemas, over-the-wire protocols, and more. For networks, this will include the design of local area networks (LANs), wide area networks (WANs), subnets, and the devices that tie them all together and provide needed security.

» **Design review.** This is the last step in the design process, in which a group of experts (some are on the design team and some aren't) examine the detailed designs. Those not on the design team give the design a set of fresh eyes and a chance to catch a design flaw or two.

» **Coding.** This is the phase that the software developers and engineers yearn for. Most software developers would prefer to skip all of the prior steps (described in the preceding sections) and start coding right away (and system or network engineers building their things) — even before the formal requirements are known! It's scary to think about how much of the world's software was created with coding as the first activity. (Would you fly in an airplane that the machinists built before the designers could produce engineering drawings? Didn't think so.) Coding and systems development usually include *unit testing*, which is the process of verifying all the modules and other individual pieces that are built in this phase.

» **Code review.** As in the design phase, the coding phase for software development ends with a code review, in which developers examine each other's program code and get into philosophical arguments about levels of indenting and the correct use of curly braces. Seriously, though, during code review, engineers can discover mistakes that would cost you a lot of money if you had to fix them later in the implementation process or in maintenance mode. There are several good static and dynamic code analysis tools that you can use to automatically identify security vulnerabilities and other errors in software code. Many organizations use these tools to ferret out programming errors that would otherwise result in vulnerabilities that attackers might exploit. You can review code review in Chapter 8!

>> **Configuration review.** For systems development, such as operating systems and networks, the configuration review phase involves the examination of system or device configuration checks and similar activities. This is an important step that helps to verify that individual components were built properly. This activity helps save time in the long run, because errors found at this stage ensure that subsequent steps will go more smoothly and that errors in subsequent steps will be somewhat easier to troubleshoot because the configuration of individual components will have already taken place.

>> **Unit test.** When portions of an application or other system have been developed, it's often possible to test the pieces separately. This is called *unit testing*. Unit testing allows a developer, engineer, or tester to verify the correct functioning of individual modules in an application or system. Unit testing is usually done during coding and other component development. It doesn't always show up as a separate step in process diagrams.

>> **System test.** A system test occurs when all the components of the entire system have been assembled, and the entire system is tested from *end to end*. The test plan that was developed in the functional requirements step is carried out here. Of course, the system test includes testing all the system's security functions, because the program's designers included those functions in the test plan (right?). You can find some great tools to rigorously test for vulnerabilities in software applications, as well as operating systems, database management systems, network devices, and other things. Many organizations consider the use of such tools a necessary step in system tests, so that they can ensure that the system has no exploitable vulnerabilities.

>> **Certification & accreditation.** *Certification* is the formal evaluation of the application or system: Every intended feature performs as planned, and the system is declared fully functional. *Accreditation* means that the powers that be have said that it's okay to put the system into production. That could mean to offer it for sale, build it and ship it, or whatever "put into production" means in your organization.

TIP

(ISC)² now offers the Certification and Accreditation Professional (CAP) certification. You might consider it, if you want to take accreditation to the next level in your career.

>> **Implementation.** When all testing and any required certifications and accreditations are completed, the software can be released to production. This usually involves a formal mechanism whereby the software developers create a "release package" to operations. The release package contains the new software, as well as any instructions for operations personnel so that they know how to implement it and verify that it was implemented correctly. An implementation plan usually also includes "backout" instructions used to revert the software (and any other changes) back to its pre-change state.

CIS SYSTEM AND DEVICE HARDENING STANDARDS

The systems development lifecycle generally has more to do with the design and development of information systems, which may include many components, including server operating systems, network devices, database management systems, embedded systems, and other components. Similar to OWASP (described earlier for software developers), there are many good system and device hardening standards available. Of particular note is the vast collection of hardening standards from the Center for Internet Security (CIS). No, we're not talking about criminal investigators, but an organization dedicated to the development of high-quality documents that provide detailed, step-by-step instructions on how to build and configure a system that will be highly resistant to attack. Best of all, these standards are all free! You can find out more at www.cisecurity.org.

WARNING

>> **Maintenance.** At this point, the software or system is fully functional, in production, and doing what it was designed to do. The maintenance phase is system's "golden years". Then, customers start putting in change requests because — well, because that's what people do! Change management and configuration management are the processes used to maintain control of (and document all changes to) the software or system over its lifetime. Change and configuration management are both discussed later in this chapter!

You need good documentation, in the form of those original specification and design documents, because the developers who wrote this software or built the system have probably moved on to some other cool project, or even another organization . . . and the new guys and gals are left to maintain it.

Agile

Agile development involves a more iterative, less formal approach to software and systems development than more traditional methodologies, such as the waterfall method (discussed in the preceding section). As its name implies, agile development focuses on speed in support of rapidly, and often constantly, evolving business requirements.

The Manifesto for Agile Software Development (www.agilemanifesto.org) describes the underlying philosophy of agile development as follows:

>> *Individuals and interactions* over processes and tools

>> *Working software* over comprehensive documentation

>> *Customer collaboration* over contract negotiation

>> *Responding to change* over following a plan

The manifesto doesn't disregard the importance of the items on the right (such as processes and tools), but it focuses more on the italicized items on the left.

Specific implementations of agile development take many forms. One common approach is the *Scrum* methodology. Typical activities and artifacts in the Scrum methodology include

>> **Product backlog.** This is a prioritized list of customer requirements, commonly known as *user stories*, that is maintained by the *product owner*. The product owner is a business (or customer) representative that communicates with the scrum team on behalf of the project stakeholders.

>> **User stories.** These are the formal requirements written as brief, customer-centric descriptions of the desired feature or function. User stories usually take the form "As a [role], I want to [feature/function] so that I can [purpose]". For example, "As a customer service representative, I want to be able to view full credit card information so that I can process customer refunds."

WARNING

The user story in the preceding example should be raising all sorts of red flags and sounding alarms in your head! This example illustrates why security professionals need to be involved in the development process (particularly when agile development methods are used, in which requirements are developed "on the fly" and may not be well thought out or part of a well-documented and comprehensive security strategy). The user in this example may simply be trying to perform a legitimate job function, and may have a limited understanding of the potential security risks this request introduces. If the developer is not security-focused and doesn't challenge the requirement, the feature may be delivered as requested. In the developer's mind, a feature was rapidly developed as requested and delivered to the customer error-free, but major security risks may have been unintentionally and unwittingly made an inherent part of the software! That may mean that someone in security (maybe you!) needs to attend development meetings to be sure risky features aren't being developed.

>> **Sprint planning.** During sprint planning, the entire team meets during the first two hours and selects the product backlog items they believe they can deliver during the upcoming *sprint* (also known as an *iteration*), typically a two-week time boxed cycle. During the next two hours of the sprint planning meeting (or event), the development team breaks down the product backlog items (selected during the first two hours) into discrete tasks and plans the work that will be required during the sprint (including who will do what).

>> **Daily standup.** The team members hold a daily 15-minute standup (or *scrum*) meeting throughout the two-week sprint during which each team member answers the following three questions:

- What did I accomplish yesterday?

- What will I accomplish today?

- What obstacles or issues exist that may prevent me from meeting the sprint goal?

The daily standup is run by the *scrum master*, who is responsible for tracking (and reporting) the sprint's progress and resolving any obstacles or issues that are identified during the daily standup.

>> **Sprint review and retrospective.** At the end of each two-week sprint, the team holds a *sprint review* meeting (typically, two hours) with the product owner and stakeholders to

- Present (or demonstrate) the work that was completed during the sprint.

- Review any work that was planned, but not completed, during the sprint.

The *sprint retrospective* is typically a 90-minute meeting. The team identifies what went well during the sprint, and what can be improved in the next sprint.

WARNING

The preceding scrum process is a very high-level overview of one possible Scrum methodology. There are as many iterations of agile software development methods as there are iterations of software development! For a more complete discussion of Agile and Scrum methodologies, we recommend *Agile Project Management For Dummies* and *Scrum For Dummies*, both by Mark Layton! Another thing you can do is perform an Internet search on "pigs and chickens" to learn about the folklore behind the Scrum methodology. You'll probably find it interesting. Make sure you find the accompanying joke about the pig and the chicken who discussed opening a restaurant together.

Security concerns to be addressed within any agile development process can include a lack of formal documentation or comprehensive planning. In more traditional development approaches, such as waterfall, extensive upfront planning is done before any actual development work begins. This planning can include creating formal test acceptance criteria, security standards, design and interface specifications, detailed frameworks and modeling, and certification and accreditation requirements. The general lack of such formal documentation and planning in the agile methodology isn't a security issue itself, but it does mean that security needs to be "front of mind" for everyone involved in the agile development process throughout the lifecycle of the project.

Maturity models

Organizations that need to understand the quality of their software and systems development processes and practices can benchmark their SDLC by measuring its maturity. There are models available for measuring software and systems development maturity, including:

» **Capability Maturity Model Integration (CMMI).** By far the most popular model for measuring software development maturity, the CMMI is required by many U.S. government agencies and contractors. The model defines five levels of maturity:

- **Initial.** Processes are chaotic and unpredictable, poorly controlled, and reactive.

- **Managed.** Processes are characterized for projects, but are still reactive.

- **Defined.** Processes are defined (written down) and more proactive.

- **Quantitatively managed.** Processes are defined and measured.

- **Optimizing.** Processes are measured and improved.

Information about the CMMI is available at http://isaca.org.

» **Software Assurance Maturity Model (SAMM).** This model is an open framework that is geared towards organizations that want to ensure that development projects include security features.

More information about SAMM is available at www.opensamm.org.

» **Building Security In Maturity Model (BSIMM).** This model is used to measure the extent to which security is included in software development processes. This model has four domains:

- Governance

- Intelligence

- Secure Software Development Lifecycle (SSDL) Touchpoints

- Deployment

Information is available from www.bsimm.com.

» **Agile Maturity Model (AMM).** This is a software process improvement framework for organizations that use Agile software development processes. More information about AMM is available here: www.researchgate.net/publication/45227382_Agile_Maturity_Model_(AMM)_A_Software_Process_Improvement_framework_for_Agile_Software_Development_Practices.

Organizations can either perform self-assessments or employ outside experts to measure their development maturity. Some opt for outside experts as a way of instilling confidence for customers.

Operation and maintenance

Software and systems that have been released to operations become a part of IT operations and its processes. Several operational aspects come into play, including:

>> **Access management.** If the application or system uses its own user access management, then the person or team that fulfills access requests will do so for the application.

>> **Event management.** The application or system will be writing entries to one or more audit logs or audit logging systems. Either personnel will review these logs, or (better) these logs will be tied to a security information and event management (SIEM) system to notify personnel of actionable events.

>> **Vulnerability management.** Periodically, personnel will test the application or system to see whether it contains security defects that could lead to a security breach. The types of tests that may be employed include security scans, vulnerability assessments, and penetration tests. For software applications, tests could also include static and dynamic code reviews.

>> **Performance management.** The application or system may be writing performance-related entries into a logging system, or external tools may be used to measure the response time of key system functions. This helps ensure that the system is healthy, usable, and not consuming excessive or inappropriate resources.

>> **Audits.** To the extent that an application or system is in scope for security or privacy audits, operational aspects of an application or system will be examined by internal or external auditors to ensure that the application or system is being properly managed and that it is operating correctly. This topic is expanded later in this chapter.

From the time that a software application or system is placed into production, development will continue, but typically at a slower pace. During this phase, additional development tasks may be needed, such as

>> Minor feature updates

>> Bug fixes

>> Security patching and updating

>> Custom modifications

Finally, at the end of a system's service life, it will be decommissioned. This typically involves one of three outcomes:

>> **Migration to a replacement system.** Here, data in the old system may be migrated to a replacement system to preserve business records so that transaction history during the era of the old system may be viewed in its replacement.

>> **Co-existence with replacement system.** Here, the old system may be modified so that it operates in a "read only" mode, permitting users to view data and records in the old system. Organizations that take this path will keep an old system for a period of a few months to a year or longer. This option usually is taken when the cost of migrating data to the new system exceeds the cost of keeping the old system running.

>> **Shutdown.** In some instances, an organization will discontinue use of the system. Here, the business records may be archived for long-term storage if requirements or regulations dictate.

TIP

The operations and maintenance activities here may be a part of an organization's DevOps processes. We discuss this later in this chapter.

Change management

Change management is the formal business process that ensures all changes made to a system receive formal review and approval from all stakeholders before implementation. Change management gives everyone a chance to voice their opinions and concerns about any proposed change, so that the change goes as smoothly as possible, with no surprises or interruptions in service.

Change management is discussed in greater detail in Chapter 9.

REMEMBER

The process of approving modifications to a production environment is called *change management*.

WARNING

Don't confuse the concept of *change management* with *configuration management* (discussed later in this chapter). The two are distinctly different from one another.

Integrated product team

DevOps is a popular trend that represents the fusion of Development and Operations. It extends Agile development practices to the entire IT organization. Perhaps not as exciting as an Asian-Italian fusion restaurant serving up a gourmet sushi calzone, but hey, this is software and systems development, not fine dining! (Sorry.)

The goal of DevOps is to improve communication and collaboration between software/systems developers and IT operations teams, in order to facilitate the rapid and efficient deployment of software and infrastructure.

However, as with Agile development methodologies, there are inherent security challenges that must be addressed in a DevOps environment. Traditional IT organizations and security best practices have maintained strict separation between development and production environments. While these distinctions remain in a DevOps environment, they are a little less absolute. Therefore, this situation can introduce additional risks to the production environment that must be adequately addressed with proper controls and accountability throughout the IT organization.

To learn more about DevOps, pick up a copy of either *The Phoenix Project* or *The Visible Ops Handbook*, both written by Kevin Behr, Gene Kim, and George Spafford. They are considered must-reads for many IT organizations.

Identify and Apply Security Controls in Development Environments

Development environments are the collection of systems and tools used to develop and test software and systems prior to their release to production. Particular care is required in securing development environments, to ensure that security vulnerabilities and back doors are not introduced into the software that is created there. These safeguards also protect source code from being stolen by adversaries.

Security of the software environments

To ensure the security of the software programs produced by developers and development teams, the software development environment itself must be protected. Controls to be considered include

» **Separate systems for development, testing, quality assurance (QA), and user acceptance testing (UAT).** These activities should take place in separate environments, so that various activities will not interfere with each other. In some cases, there may be restrictions on which developers (as well as testers and users) are permitted to access which environments. Also, the workstations used for writing and testing code should not be the same ones used for routine office functions, such as email and accessing internal and Internet applications.

» **Don't use live production data in development, test, or QA environments.** In many applications, production instances contain sensitive data such as personally identifiable information (PII) and other sensitive or personal information. Instead, tools to anonymize such data can be used to provide realistic data in test environments without risking exposing such data.

» **Isolate from the Internet.** Because development systems aren't used for web access or email, there should be little objection to this. Security patches can be pushed from internal systems, instead of retrieving them from the Internet (that's the preferred practice anyway).

» **Event logging.** Logging of events at the OS level, as well as at the development level, is used to troubleshoot problems, as well as to give auditors a running history of developer actions.

» **Source code version control.** All changes to source code need to be managed through a modern source code management system that has check-out, check-in, rollback, locking, access control, and logging functions. This helps to ensure that all access to, and modification of, source code is logged. These systems are also used to restrict access to highly sensitive code, such as that used for authentication and session management, so that it is accessible by as few developers as feasible.

» **Remove administrative privileges.** The user account used for coding and testing should not be a local or domain administrator.

Some developers may bristle at this one; they argue that they can't perform testing like software installation and OS level debugging. No problem. Give them another machine (or virtual machine) with admin privileges for that. But then, don't let them use that system for routine office tasks such as email and Internet access.

» **Use standard development tools.** All developers on the same team or project should be using the same IDE (integrated development environment) or whatever coding, testing, and compiling tools they use. Developers should not be permitted to "do their own thing", as this may introduce compromised tools or libraries that could leak or inject back doors into the software they're developing.

» **Use only company-owned systems.** Developers should not be developing on BYOD (bring your own device) systems. Instead, they should be using company-acquired and -supported systems, to ensure that these systems are fully protected from malware and tampering.

KEEP DEVELOPERS OUT OF PRODUCTION ENVIRONMENTS

Software developers should not have access to production environments in an organization. This practice is required by regulations and standards, including PCI DSS, NIST SP800-53, and ISO/IEC 27002.

Different personnel should be installing updated software into production environments. Developers can put installable software on a staging system for trained operations personnel to install and verify proper operation.

Developers may, on occasion, require read-only access to production environments so that they can troubleshoot problems. However, even this read-only access should be disabled, except during actual support cases.

These safeguards should be applied to both developer workstations and centralized build and test systems.

Configuration management as an aspect of secure coding

Configuration management is often confused with change management, but actually has little to do with approvals and *everything* to do with recording all the facts about the change. Configuration management captures actual changes to software code, end-user documentation, operations documentation, developer tools and settings, program build tools and settings, disaster recovery planning documentation, and other details of the change. Configuration management archives technical details for each change and release of the system, as well as for each instance of the software, if more than one instance exists.

Configuration management is also entirely relevant and applicable to system environments, including but not limited to operating systems, database management systems, middleware, and all types of network devices. When changes are made via the change management process, the details of all configuration changes are recorded in a configuration management database (CMDB). This can help engineers troubleshoot problems later by giving them the ability to easily know both current (expected) and prior configuration settings in all these types of systems and devices.

REMEMBER

Change management and configuration management address two different aspects of change in a system's maintenance mode:

>> Change management is the *why*.

>> Configuration management is the *what*.

REMEMBER

The process of managing the changes being made to systems is called change management. The process of recording modifications to a production environment is called configuration management.

Security of code repositories

During and after development, program source code resides in a central source code repository. Source code must be protected from both unauthorized access and unauthorized changes. Controls to enforce this protection include

>> **System hardening.** Intruders must be kept out of the OS itself. This includes all of the usual system hardening techniques and principles for servers, as discussed in Chapter 5.

>> **System isolation.** The system should be reachable by only authorized personnel, and no other persons. It should not be reachable from the Internet, nor should it be able to access the Internet, for any reason. The system should function only as a source code repository and not for other purposes.

>> **Restricted developer access.** Only authorized developers and any other personnel should have access to source code.

>> **Restricted administrator access.** Only authorized personnel (ideally *not* developers!) should have administrative access to the source code repository software, as well as the underlying operating system, and other components such as database management systems.

>> **No direct source code access.** No one should be able to access source code directly. Instead, everyone should be accessing it through the management software.

>> **Limited, controlled checkout.** Developers should only be able to check out modules when specifically authorized. This can be automated through integration with a software defect tracking system.

>> **Restricted access to critical code.** Few developers should have access to the most critical code, including code used for security functions such as authentication, session management, and encryption.

>> **No bulk access.** Developers should not, under any circumstances, be able to check out all modules. (This is primarily for preventing intellectual property theft.)

>> **Retention of all versions.** The source code repository should maintain copies of all previous versions of source code, so modules can be "rolled back" as needed.

>> **Check-in approval.** All check-ins should require approval of another person. This prevents a developer from unilaterally introducing defects or back doors into a program.

>> **Activity reviews.** The activity logs for a source code repository should be periodically reviewed to make sure that there are no unauthorized check-outs or check-ins, and all check-ins represent only authorized changes to source code.

Assess the Effectiveness of Software Security

Former U.S. President Ronald Reagan was well known for his phrase *trust but verify*. We take this a little further by saying *don't trust until verified*. This credo applies to many aspects of information security, including the security of software.

Initial and periodic security testing of software is an essential part of the process of developing (or acquiring) and managing software throughout its entire lifespan. The reason for periodic testing is that researchers (both white hat and black hat) are always finding new ways of exploiting software programs that were once considered secure.

Other facets of security testing are explored in lurid detail in Chapter 8.

Auditing and logging of changes

Logging changes is an essential aspect of system and software behavior. The presence of logs facilitates troubleshooting, verification, and reconstruction of events.

There are two facets of changes that are important here:

>> **Changes performed *by* the software.** Mainly, this means changes made to data. As such, a log entry will include "before" and "after" values, as well as other essentials, including user, date, time, and transaction ID. This also includes configuration changes that alter software behavior.

>> **Changes made *to* the software.** This generally means changes to the actual software code. In most organizations, this involves change management and configuration management processes. However, while investigating system problems, you shouldn't discount the possibility of unauthorized changes. The absence of change management records is not evidence of the absence of changes.

Log data for these categories may be stored either locally or in a central repository, such as a SIEM (security information and event management) system. Appropriate personnel should be notified in a timely manner when actionable events take place. This is discussed more fully in Chapter 9.

Risk analysis and mitigation

Risk analysis of software programs and systems is an essential means for identifying and analyzing risks. The types of risks that will likely be included are

>> **Known vulnerabilities.** What vulnerabilities can be identified, how they can be exploited, and whether the software has any means of being aware of attempted exploitation and defending itself.

>> **Unknown vulnerabilities.** Here, we're talking about vulnerabilities that have yet to be discovered. If you're unsure of what we mean, just imagine any of several widely available programs that seem to be plagued with new vulnerabilities month after month. Software with that kind of track record certainly has more undisclosed vulnerabilities. We won't shame them by listing them here.

>> **Transaction integrity.** In other words, does the software work properly and produce the correct results in all cases, including unintentional and deliberate misuse and abuse? Manual or automated auditing of software programs can be used to identify transaction calculation and processing problems, but humans often spot them, too.

Tools that are used to assess the vulnerability of software include

>> **Security scanners.** These are tools, such as WebInspect, AppScan, and Acunetix Web Vulnerability Scanner, that scan an entire web site or web application. They examine form variables, hidden variables, cookies, and other web page features to identify vulnerabilities.

>> **Web site security tools.** These are tools like Burp, Nikto, Tamper Data, and Paros Proxy that are used to manually examine web pages to look for vulnerabilities that scanners often can't find.

» **Source code scanning tools.** These are such tools as Veracode, AppScan Static, and HP Fortify. These tools examine program source code and identify vulnerabilities that security scanners often cannot see.

Another approach to discovering vulnerabilities and design defects uses a technique known as *threat modeling*. This involves a systematic and detailed analysis of all of a program's interfaces, including user interfaces, APIs, and interaction with the underlying database management and operating systems. The analysis involves a study of these elements to understand all the ways in which they could be used, misused, and abused by insiders and adversaries. A popular tool for this is the Microsoft Threat Modeling Tool.

The STRIDE threat classification model is also handy for threat modeling. STRIDE stands for the following:

» Spoofing of user identity

» Tampering

» Repudiation

» Information disclosure

» Denial of service

» Elevation of privilege

Mitigation of software vulnerabilities generally means updating source code (if you have it!) or applying security patches. However, patches often cannot be obtained and applied right away, which means either implementing temporary workarounds, or relying on security in other layers, such as a web application firewall.

Mitigation of transaction integrity issues may require either manual adjustments to affected data, or workarounds in associated programs.

Acceptance testing

Acceptance testing is the formal process of verifying that a software program performs as expected in all scenarios. Acceptance testing is usually performed when a program or system is first acquired, prior to placing it into production use, and whenever configuration changes or code changes are made to the program or system throughout its service life.

Acceptance testing is most often associated with business end-user testing, where it's called user acceptance testing (UAT). However, acceptance testing is (or should be!) performed in other aspects that are not necessarily visible or obvious to end users, including:

- » **Malicious and erroneous input.** Users may be satisfied to test programs using reasonable, acceptable input, but security professionals know that this is only the beginning. Inputs of all types, including malicious and erroneous, must be included in testing, to ensure that the system behaves properly and cannot be compromised.

- » **Secure data storage.** All instances of data storage must be secure, commensurate with the sensitivity of the data. Testing needs to include checks for data remanence, to make sure that programs do not leave sensitive data behind that could be discovered by others.

- » **Secure data transport.** All instances of data transmitted to another program or system must be performed using means that are commensurate with the sensitivity of the data. Over the public Internet, this almost always means using encryption.

- » **Authentication and authorization.** These mechanisms must be proven to work properly and not be vulnerable to attacks or abuse.

- » **Session management.** This mechanism is used to track each individual user of a system or application. Weaknesses in session management can permit an attacker to take over control of an existing user's session. Years ago, the Firefox browser extension Firesheep was an excellent proof-of-concept tool that could be used to steal another user's web application session.

Assess Security Impact of Acquired Software

Every organization acquires some (or all) of its software from other entities. Any acquired software that is related to the storage or processing of sensitive data needs to be understood from a security perspective, so that an organization is aware of the risks associated with its use.

There are some use cases that bear further discussion:

- » **Open source.** Many security professionals fondly recall those blissful days when we all trusted open source software, under the belief that many caring and talented individuals' examination of the source code would surely root out security defects. However, security vulnerabilities in OpenSSL, jQuery, and MongoDB and others have burst that bubble. It is now obvious that we need to examine open source software with as much scrutiny as any other software.

>> **Commercial.** Confirming the security of commercial tools is usually more difficult than open source, because the source code usually is not available to examine. Depending on the type of software, automated scanning tools may help, but testing is often a manual effort. Some vendors voluntarily permit security consulting firms to examine their software for vulnerabilities and permit customers to view test results (sometimes just in summary form).

>> **Software libraries.** Here, we are talking about collections of software modules that by themselves are not programs, but are used to build programs or used by programs while they're running. Think of them as pre-assembled pieces created by others. Careful scrutiny of all such libraries is essential, as there are many that are not secure, and more that do not always function correctly — particularly under stress and abuse. Further, software libraries should be checked for vulnerabilities — trust and verify!

>> **Operating systems.** Open source or not, we generally are satisfied with the use of good hardening guidelines, effective patch management, and scanning with such tools as Nessus, Rapid7, and Qualys to find vulnerabilities.

Define and Apply Secure Coding Guidelines and Standards

Organizations that develop software, whether for their own use only or as products for use by other organizations, need to develop policies and standards regarding the development of source code to reduce the number of vulnerabilities that could lead to errors, incidents, and security breaches. Even organizations that use tools to discover vulnerabilities in source code (and at run-time) would benefit from such practices, for two reasons:

>> The time to fix code vulnerabilities is reduced.

>> Some code vulnerabilities may not be discovered by tools or code reviews but could still be exploited by an adversary, leading to an error, incident, or breach.

Security weaknesses and vulnerabilities at the source-code level

Software development organizations must have standards, processes, and tools in place to ensure that all developed software is free of defects, including security vulnerabilities that could lead to system compromise and data tampering or theft. The types of defects that need to be identified include

>> **Buffer overflow.** This is an attack where a program's input field is deliberately overflowed in an attempt to corrupt the running software program in a way that would permit the attacker to force the program to run arbitrary instructions. A buffer overflow attack permits an attacker to have partial or complete control of the target system, thereby enabling him or her to access, tamper with, destroy, or steal sensitive data.

>> **Injection attacks.** An attacker may be able to manipulate the application through a SQL injection or script injection attack, with a variety of results, including access to sensitive data.

>> **Escalation of privileges.** An attacker may be able to trick the target application or system into raising the attacker's level of privilege, allowing him or her to either access sensitive data or take control of the target system.

>> **Improper authentication.** Authentication that is not air-tight may be exploited by an attacker who may be able to compromise or bypass authentication altogether. Doing authentication correctly means writing resilient code as well as avoiding features that would give an attacker an advantage (such as telling the user that the userid is correct but the password is not).

>> **Improper session management.** Session management that is not programmed and configured correctly may be exploited by intruders, which could lead to session hijacking through a session replay attack.

>> **Improper use of encryption.** Strong encryption algorithms can be ineffective if they are not properly implemented. This could make it easy for an attacker to attack the cryptosystem and access sensitive data. This includes not only proper use of encryption algorithms, but also proper encryption key management.

>> **Gaming.** This is a general term referring to faulty application or system design that may permit a user or intruder to use the application or system in ways not intended by its owners or designers. For example, an image-sharing service may be used by criminals to pass messages using steganography.

>> **Memory leaks.** This type of defect occurs when a program fails to release unneeded memory, resulting in the memory requirements of a running program growing steadily over time, until available resources are exhausted.

>> **Race conditions.** This type of defect involves two (or more) programs, processes, or threads that each access and manipulate a resource as though they had exclusive access to the resource. This can cause an unexpected result with one or more of the programs, processes, or threads.

These weaknesses, and others, are addressed in detail by the Open Web Application Security Project (OWASP) at www.owasp.org.

Security of application programming interfaces

Application programming interfaces, or APIs, are components of software programs used for data input and data output. An API will have an accompanying specification (whether documented or not) that defines functionalities, input and/or output fields, data types, and other details. Typically, an API is used for non-human interaction between programs. Although you would consider a web interface as a human-readable interface, an API is considered a machine-readable interface.

APIs exist in many places: operating systems, subsystems (such as web servers and database management systems), utilities, and application programs. APIs also are implemented in computer hardware for components, such as memory, as well as peripheral devices, such as disk drives, network interfaces, keyboards, and display devices.

In software development, a developer can either create his or her own API from scratch (not recommended), or acquire an API by obtaining source code modules or libraries with APIs built in, such as RESTful. An API can be a part of an application that is used to transfer data back and forth to other applications, in bulk or transaction by transaction.

APIs need to be secure so that they do not become the means through which an intruder is able to either covertly obtain sensitive data or cause the target system to malfunction or crash. Three primary means of ensuring an API is secure include

>> **Secure design.** Each API needs to be implemented so that it carefully examines and sanitizes all input data, to defeat any attempts at injection or buffer overflow attacks, as well as program malfunctions. Output data must also be examined so that the API does not output any non-compliant or malicious data.

>> **Security testing.** Each API needs to be thoroughly tested to be sure that it functions correctly and resists attacks.

>> **External protection.** In the case of a Web Services API, a web application firewall may be able to protect an API from attack. However, such an option may not be available if the API uses other protocols. Packet filtering firewalls do not protect APIs from logical attacks —firewalls do not examine the contents of packets, only their source and destination IP addresses and ports.

Secure coding practices

The purpose of secure coding practices is the reduction of exploitable vulnerabilities in tools, utilities, and applications. The practice of secure coding isn't just about secure coding, but many other considerations and activities. Here are some of the factors related to secure coding:

>> **Tools.** From the selection and configuration of integrated development environments, to the use of static and dynamic code testing tools (SAST and DAST, respectively), tools can be used to detect the presence of source code defects including security vulnerabilities. The earlier such defects are found, the less effort it takes to correct them.

>> **Processes.** As discussed earlier in this chapter, software development processes need to be designed and managed with security in mind. Processes define the sequence of events; in the context of software and systems development, security-related steps such as peer reviews and the use of vulnerability scanning tools will ensure that all the right steps are taken to make sure that source code is reasonably free of defects.

>> **Training.** Software developers and engineers are more likely to write good, safe code when they know how to. Training in secure development is essential. Very few universities include secure development in their undergraduate computer science programs. Secure coding is not a part of university training, so organizations must fill the gap.

>> **Incentives.** Money talks. Providing incidents of some form will help software developers pay more attention to whether they're producing code with security vulnerabilities. We like the carrot more than the stick, so perhaps rewards for the fewest defects per calendar quarter or year is a good start.

>> **Selection of source code languages.** The selection of source code languages and policies about the use of open-source code comes into play. Some coding languages by design are more secure (or we might say "safe") than others. For example, the C language, as powerful as it is, has no protective features, which requires software developers to be more skilled and knowledgeable about writing safe and secure code. Developed in the 1970s, the C language was created during an era when there was more trust. However, Brian Kernigan or Dennis Ritchie, the co-creators of C, are allegedly attributed with the saying, "We (Unix and C) won't prevent you from doing something stupid, as that restriction might also prevent you from doing something cool." We have been unable to confirm whether either one said this or not. It might have been in a book (such as *The C Programming Language*), in a lecture, or in a pub after quaffing a few pints of ale. The point is, some languages are, by design, safer than others. We're sorry for the rabbit hole. Well, mostly sorry.

THE OPEN WEB APPLICATION SECURITY PROJECT

The Open Web Application Security Project, or OWASP, has published a short list of security standards that organizations have adopted, most notably the Payment Card Industry Data Security Standard (PCI DSS). The top ten software risks cited by OWASP are

- Injection
- Broken authentication
- Sensitive data exposure
- XML external entities (XXE)
- Broken access control
- Security misconfiguration
- Cross-site scripting (XSS)
- Insecure deserialization
- The use of components with known vulnerabilities
- Insufficient logging and monitoring

Earlier versions of the OWASP top ten software vulnerabilities included missing function level access control, cross site request forgery (CSRF), malicious file execution, information leakage and improper error handling, and insecure communications. These are also important security considerations for any software development project.

Removal of these risks makes a software application more robust, reliable, and secure. You can find out more about OWASP — and even join or form a local chapter — by visiting the organization's website at www.owasp.org.

3

The Part of Tens

IN THIS PART . . .

Plan your test preparation strategy.

Get ready for your test day.

Chapter **11**

Ten Test-Planning Tips

So much information, so little time! In this chapter, we recommend nine (mostly) long-term planning tips for helping you prepare for that special day. (No, not *that* special day; read *Wedding Planning For Dummies*, by Marcy Blum and Laura F. Kaiser [Wiley], for that one.) We're talking about the CISSP exam here.

Know Your Learning Style

As you mentally anticipate your study and preparation for the CISSP exam, it's important for you to understand your personal learning style. For example, you might prefer a long-term study plan as opposed to a one-week boot-camp style training course. And you may learn better in a study group, or by studying and reading alone in a quiet room. Your studying time might be more fruitful if you do it in short, frequent sessions (say, 30 minutes, a couple of times a day), or in less frequent and longer marathons (for example, four hours, a few nights a week).

To make the most of the tips in this chapter, you need to know in advance what works best for you, so you can customize your study plan and pass the CISSP exam with flying colors!

Get a Networking Certification First

The Communication and Network Security domain is the most comprehensive domain tested on the CISSP exam. Although its purpose is to test your security knowledge, you must have a strong understanding of communications and networking. For this reason, we strongly advise that you earn a networking certification, such as the CompTIA Network+ or the Cisco Certified Network Associate (CCNA), before attempting the CISSP exam, especially if you don't have at least a few years of experience with networking equipment including routers, switches, firewalls, and more. (For more information on these certifications, see www.comptia.org and www.cisco.com, respectively.) An additional benefit is that you then have another valuable technical certification in high demand within the computer industry.

If you already have one of these certifications, you should find most of the information in the Communication and Network Security domain to be very basic. In this case, a quick review that focuses on security concepts (particularly the methods of attack) should be sufficient for this domain. We dedicate Chapter 6 of this book to the Communication and Network Security domain.

TIP

If you haven't taken a computer-based examination before, getting a networking certification first will also help familiarize you with the testing center location and environment, as well as the general format of computer-based exams. You can take a generic practice computer-based exam to get used to how they work at www.pearsonvue.com.

Register Now!

Go online and register for the CISSP exam at www.pearsonvue.com/isc2 — *now!*

Committing yourself to a test date is the best cure for procrastination, especially because the test costs $699 (U.S.)! Setting your date can help you plan and focus your study efforts.

Make a 60-Day Study Plan

After you register for the CISSP exam, commit yourself to a 60-day study plan. Of course, your work experience and professional reading should span a much greater period, but for your final preparations leading up to the CISSP exam, plan on a 60-day period of intense study and review.

Exactly how intensely you study depends on your personal experience and learning ability, but plan on a minimum of 2 hours a day for 60 days. If you're a slow learner or reader, or perhaps find yourself weak in many areas, plan on 4 to 6 hours a day and more on the weekends. Regardless, try to stick to the 60-day plan. If you feel that you need 360 hours of study, you might be tempted to spread this out over a 6-month period for 2 hours a day. But committing to 6 months of intense study is much harder (on you, as well as your family and friends) than committing to 2 months. In the end, you'll likely find yourself studying only as much as you would have in a 60-day period.

Get Organized and Read!

A wealth of security information is available for the CISSP candidate. However, studying *everything* is impractical. Instead, get organized, determine your strengths and weaknesses, and then *read!*

Begin by downloading the free, official *CISSP Exam Outline* from the (ISC)² website (www.isc2.org) to get an idea of the subjects on which you'll be tested.

Next, read this book, use the online practice at www.dummies.com (see the Introduction for more information). *CISSP For Dummies*, 6th Edition, is written to provide the CISSP candidate with an excellent overview of all the broad topics covered on the CISSP exam.

Next, focus on the areas that you identify as your weakest. Read or review the respective chapters in this book. If needed, obtain additional references on specific topics as needed.

Finally, in the last week before your exam, go through all your selected study materials at least once. Review or read *CISSP For Dummies*, 6th Edition, one more time, as well as your personal study notes, and complete as many practice questions as you can.

TIP

You can download the free (ISC)² *Official CISSP Flash Cards* on the (ISC)² website at www.isc2.org/Training/Self-Study-Resources. You can also purchase the (ISC)² *Official CISSP Study App* in the App Store or Google Play.

Join a Study Group

You can find strength in numbers. Joining a study group or creating your own can help you stay focused and provide a wealth of information from the broad perspectives and experiences of other IT and security professionals. You can find a study group, discussion forums, and many other helpful resources at www.cccure.org.

Also, your local (ISC)² chapter or a chapter of the Information Systems Security Association (ISSA) may be sponsoring CISSP study groups. You can find their contact information at www.issa.org.

Take Practice Exams

No practice exams are available that exactly duplicate the CISSP exam. And forget about brain dumps (actual test questions and answers that others have unscrupulously posted on the Internet) — in addition to possibly being wrong, brain dumps violate the CISSP exam's non-disclosure agreement. However, many resources are available for practice questions. You may find some practice questions too hard, others too easy, and some just plain irrelevant. Despite that, the repetition of practice questions can help reinforce important information that you need to know in order to successfully answer questions on the CISSP exam. For this reason, we recommend taking as many practice exams as possible and using the results to help you focus on your weak areas. Try the CISSP Quizzes on the CISSP Open Study Group website (www.cccure.org).

Take a CISSP Training Seminar

You can take an official (ISC)² CISSP Training Seminar. The in-person training seminar (classroom-based or private on-site) is an intense, five-day session that definitely has you eating, drinking, and sleeping CISSP. The online training seminar gives you the same benefits of the in-person training seminar on a computer with a more flexible schedule, including options for weekday, weekend, evening, and self-paced courses. Schedules and additional information are available at www.isc2.org in the "Training Methods" section under "Education & Training."

Adopt an Exam-Taking Strategy

It'll be difficult to assess whether you're going too fast or too slow as you work through the exam questions because the test is now adaptive. You'll have a minimum of 100 questions and a maximum of 150 questions.

If you're going too slow on the exam — perhaps two-and-a-half hours have gone by and you've only answered 50 questions — rushing through the remaining questions could make matters worse. If you start making careless mistakes and getting more wrong answers, it's more likely you'll get more questions rather than fewer, so the test and the clock will both be working against you!

On the other hand, if you rush through the exam — perhaps you're 30 minutes into the exam and you've already answered 80 questions — you can't go back to check or change your answers.

With an adaptive exam, you need to develop a more in-depth strategy than simply "managing the clock." Think about what you'll do when you don't know the answer to a question. How will you eliminate answer choices to make a better guess? What will you do if you start feeling overwhelmed with panic or anxiety? What if you find yourself losing focus or second-guessing yourself? Have a strategy to deal with these and other possible scenarios during the exam.

Take a Breather

The day before the exam, relax and plan for a comfortable night's rest. If you've been cramming for the exam, set your study materials aside the day before the exam. At that point, you either know the material or you don't!

Chapter 12

Ten Test-Day Tips

Well, your big day has finally arrived. After months of study and mind-numbing stress, you cram all night before the exam, skip breakfast because you're running late, and then forget everything you know because you have a splitting headache for the next three hours (six hours if you're taking the non-English, form-based exam) while sitting for your exam! That isn't exactly a recipe for success — but the following ten test day tips can definitely get you on the right track.

Get a Good Night's Rest

The night before the exam isn't the time to do any last-minute cramming. Studies have proven that a good night's rest is essential to doing well on an exam. Have a nice dinner (we recommend going for some carbohydrates and avoiding anything spicy), and then get to bed early. Save the all-night party for the day after the exam.

Dress Comfortably

You should dress in attire that's comfortable — remember, this is a *three-hour* exam. It's also a good idea to dress in layers — the exam room could be warmer or cooler than you're used to.

Consider wearing loafers or other shoes that you can easily slip off (but please be considerate of others and wear clean socks!)

Eat a Good Meal

Try to get *something* down before sitting for the CISSP exam. Three hours can feel like an eternity on an empty stomach.

Arrive Early

Absolutely, *under no circumstances,* do you want to arrive late for this exam. Make sure that you know where the testing center is located, what the traffic is like at that time of the day, and where you can park. You may even want to do a dry run before the test day to be sure you know what delays you might encounter (particularly if you're not familiar with the area where the exam is being administered).

Bring a Photo ID

The testing center will verify your identity when you arrive for your exam. You need to bring your driver's license, government-issued ID, or passport — these are the only forms of ID that are accepted — and the name on your ID must *exactly* match the name you used to register for your exam.

Bring Snacks and Drinks

Check with your testing center (http://pearsonvue.com/isc2/) regarding their rules about consuming snacks and drinks in the testing area. If they are permitted, bring a small bag that holds enough food and drink to get you through the exam. A *big* bottle of water is essential. Also, consider bringing a soda and some snacks, a sandwich, energy bars — whatever you like to snack on that replenishes and renews you without making you too thirsty.

Bring Prescription and Over-the-Counter Medications

Again, check with your testing center and notify the test administrator if you're taking any prescription medication that must be taken during the exam. Nothing can ruin your chances of succeeding on the CISSP exam like a medical emergency! Also, if you're taking any over-the-counter meds, such as acetaminophen, nasal spray, or antacids to eliminate any annoying inconveniences such as headaches, heartburn, or a gastrointestinal malady, be sure to take them before you start the exam. A box of tissues might also be appropriate — if you have a cold or you feel like crying when you see the exam!

Leave Your Mobile Devices Behind

This is the one day that your office and family members will have to do without you. Turn off your mobile phone and anything else that goes beep or buzz. Even better, leave it locked and hidden in your car or at home. Most test centers have lockers that you can use to store personal belongings, but you should confirm this is the case before your exam. You don't want to rush through your exam worried that your mobile phone has left you for a new owner.

Take Frequent Breaks

Three hours is a long time. Be sure to get up and walk around during the exam, if permitted. If not, at least stretch your legs, curl your toes, crack your knuckles, rest your eyes (but don't fall asleep!), and roll your neck — or whatever you need to do (within reason) to keep the blood flowing throughout your body. We recommend taking short, frequent breaks throughout the exam. . . and then getting back to the task at hand. You might even incorporate breaks into your test-taking strategy. For example, answer 30 or 40 questions and then take a short break. At the very least, close your eyes and take a big breath — just don't fall asleep!

Also, if you find your mind wandering or you have trouble focusing, take a break. Burnout and fatigue can lead to careless mistakes or indifference. If you feel these symptoms coming on, take a break.

But be careful not to overdo your breaks. Stick to frequent but short breaks, and you'll be fine.

Guess — as a Last Resort

Guessing is a desperate approach to test-taking, but it can be effective when all else fails. An unanswered question is definitely wrong, so don't leave any questions unanswered. If you must guess, try to eliminate as many obviously wrong answers as possible. If you can eliminate two possible choices that are definitely wrong, you have a 50/50 chance of getting the answer right.

When all else fails, go with your gut feeling! Research has shown time and again that your first guess is often correct. So unless you find that you misread a question — for example you missed a key word like *NOT* or *ALL* in the question — avoid the temptation to change an answer without a compelling reason.

Glossary

3DES (Triple DES): An enhancement to the original DES algorithm that uses multiple keys to encrypt plaintext. Officially known as the Triple Data Encryption Algorithm (TDEA or Triple DEA). *See also* Data Encryption Standard (DES).

AAA: Shorthand for authentication, authorization, and accountability controls.

abstraction: A process that involves viewing an application from its highest-level functions, which makes lower-level functions abstract.

acceptance testing: The human verification of proper functionality of a software program or system.

access control: The capability to permit or deny the use of an *object* (a passive entity, such as a system or file) by a *subject* (an active entity, such as a person or process).

access control list (ACL): Lists the specific rights and permissions assigned to a subject for a given object.

Access Matrix Model: Provides object access rights (read/write/execute or R/W/X) to subjects in a DAC system. An access matrix consists of ACLs and capability lists. *See also* access control list (ACL) *and* discretionary access control (DAC).

accountability: The capability of a system to associate users and processes with their actions.

accreditation: An official, written approval for the operation of a specific system in a specific environment, as documented in a certification report.

acquisition: (1) The process of purchasing another organization. (2) The process of purchasing information systems hardware or software.

active-active: A clustered configuration in which all of the nodes in a system or network are load balanced, synchronized, and active. If one node fails, the other node(s) continue providing services seamlessly.

active-passive: A clustered configuration in which only one node in a system or network is active. If the primary node fails, a passive node becomes active and continues providing services, usually after a short delay.

ActiveX: A software framework created by Microsoft that adapts its earlier COM and OLE technologies for content downloaded from a network, such as the Internet. *See also* Component Object Model (COM) *and* Object Linking and Embedding (OLE).

Address Resolution Protocol (ARP): The network protocol used to query and discover the MAC address of a device on a LAN.

address space: A range of discrete addresses allocated to a network host, device, disk sector, or memory cell.

administrative controls: The policies and procedures that an organization implements as part of its overall information security strategy.

administrative laws: Legal requirements passed by government institutions that define standards of performance and conduct for major industries (such as banking, energy, and healthcare), organizations, and officials.

Advanced Encryption Standard (AES): A block cipher based on the Rijndael cipher, which replaced DES. *See also* Data Encryption Standard (DES).

adware: Software that's commonly installed with a freeware or shareware program. It provides a source of revenue for the software developer and runs only when you're using the associated program or until you purchase the program (in the case of shareware). *See also* malware.

agent: A software component that performs a particular service.

aggregation: (1) A database security issue that describes the act of obtaining information classified at a high sensitivity level by combining other items of low-sensitivity information. (2) The unintended accumulation of access privileges by persons who transfer from role to role in an organization over time.

Agile: A software development methodology known for its iterative approach to the development of a system.

Agile Maturity Model (AMM): A framework for measuring the maturity of agile software development processes and practices. *See also* Agile.

Annualized Loss Expectancy (ALE): A standard, quantifiable measure of the impact that a realized threat will have on an organization's assets. ALE is determined by the formula Single Loss Expectancy (SLE) × Annualized Rate of Occurrence (ARO) = ALE. *See also* Single Loss Expectancy (SLE) *and* Annualized Rate of Occurrence (ARO).

Annualized Rate of Occurrence (ARO): The estimated annual frequency of occurrence for a specific threat or event.

antivirus software: Software that's designed to detect and prevent computer viruses and other malware from entering and harming a system.

applet: A component in a distributed environment (various components are located on separate systems) that's downloaded into and executed by another program, such as a web browser.

application firewall: A firewall that inspects OSI Layer 7 content in order to block malicious content from reaching or leaving an application server. *See also* web application firewall (WAF).

Application Layer (OSI model): Layer 7 of the OSI model. *See also* Open Systems Interconnection (OSI) model.

Application Layer (TCP/IP model): Layer 4 of the TCP/IP model. *See also* TCP/IP model.

application penetration test: A penetration test of a software application. *See also* penetration test.

application scan: An automated test used to identify weaknesses in a software application.

application software: Computer software that a person uses to accomplish a specific task.

application-level firewall: *See* application firewall.

application programming interface (API): A specification for input data and output data for a system.

application whitelisting: A mechanism used to control which applications are permitted to execute on a system. *See also* whitelisting.

archive: In a public key infrastructure (PKI), an archive is responsible for long-term storage of archived information from the CA. *See also* Certification Authority (CA) *and* public key infrastructure (PKI).

artificial intelligence (AI): The ability of a computer to interact with and learn from its environment, and automatically perform actions without being explicitly programmed.

asset: A resource, process, product, system, or program that has some value to an organization and must therefore be protected. Assets can be hard goods, such as computers and equipment, but can also be information, programs, and intellectual property.

asset inventory: The process of tracking assets in an organization.

asset valuation: The process of assigning a financial or relative value to an organization's information assets.

asymmetric key system (or asymmetric algorithm; public key): A cryptographic system that uses two separate keys — one key to encrypt information and a different key to decrypt information. These key pairs are known as *public* and *private keys*.

Asynchronous Transfer Mode (ATM): A very high-speed, low-latency, packet-switched communications protocol.

attribute-based access control (ABAC): An access control model where a subject is granted access to an object based on subject attributes, object attributes, and environmental considerations.

audit: The independent verification of any activity or process.

audit trail: The auxiliary records that document transactions and other events.

augmented reality (AR): Technology that produces a composite view by superimposing high-resolution (even 3D) images on a real-world view.

authenticated scan: A vulnerability scan that attempts to log in to a device, system, or application during its search for exploitable vulnerabilities.

authentication: The process of verifying a subject's claimed identity in an access control system.

Authentication Header (AH): In IPsec, a protocol that provides integrity, authentication, and non-repudiation. *See also* Internet Protocol Security (IPsec).

authorization (or establishment): The process of defining and granting the rights and permissions granted to a subject (what you can do).

automatic controls: Controls that are not performed manually.

availability: The process of ensuring that systems and data are accessible to authorized users when they need it.

backdoor: Malware that enables an individual to bypass normal authentication to gain access to a compromised system. *See also* malware.

background check: The process of verifying a person's professional, financial, and legal history, usually in connection with employment.

baseline: A process that identifies a consistent basis for an organization's security architecture, taking into account system-specific parameters, such as different operating systems.

Bell-LaPadula model: A formal confidentiality model that defines two basic properties: the simple security property (ss property) and star property (* property). *See also* simple security property (ss property) *and* star property (* property).

best evidence: Original, unaltered evidence, which is preferred by the court over secondary evidence. *See also* best evidence rule *and* evidence.

best evidence rule: Defined in the Federal Rules of Evidence; states that "to prove the content of a writing, recording, or photograph, the original writing, recording, or photograph is (ordinarily) required." *See also* evidence.

Biba model: A formal integrity model that defines two basic properties: the simple integrity property and star integrity property (*-integrity property). *See also* simple integrity property *and* star integrity property (*-integrity property).

biometrics: Any of various means used, as part of an authentication mechanism, to verify the identity of a person. Types of biometrics used include fingerprints, palm prints, signatures, retinal scans, voice scans, and keystroke patterns.

birthday attack: A type of attack that attempts to exploit the probability of two messages using the same hash function and producing the same message digest. *See also* hash function.

black-box testing: A security test wherein the tester has no prior knowledge of the system being tested.

blacklisting: A mechanism that explicitly blocks access based on the presence of an item in a list. *See also* whitelisting.

blackout: Total loss of electric power.

block cipher: An encryption algorithm that divides plaintext into fixed-size blocks of characters or bits, and then uses the same key on each fixed-size block to produce corresponding ciphertext.

Bluetooth: A wireless technology standard for data exchange over short distances between fixed and mobile devices.

bollard: A post used to divert traffic from a building, area, or road.

bootkit: A kernel-mode malware variant of a rootkit, commonly used to attack computers that are protected by full-disk encryption. *See also* malware *and* rootkit.

bot: A target computer that is infected by malware and is part of a botnet. *See also* botnet *and* malware.

botnet: A broad network of malware-infected bots working together and controlled by an attacker through command-and-control (C2) servers. *See also* bot *and* malware.

breach: An action resulting in unauthorized disclosure of confidential information or damage to a system.

bridge: A network device that forwards packets to other networks.

bring your own device (BYOD): A mobile device policy that permits employees to use their personal mobile devices in the workplace for work-related and personal business.

broadcast: A type of network protocol whereby packets are sent from a source to every node on a network.

brownout: Prolonged drop in voltage from an electric power source, such as a public utility.

brute-force attack: A type of attack in which the attacker attempts every possible combination of letters, numbers, and characters to crack a password, passphrase, or PIN.

buffer (or stack) overflow attack: A type of attack in which the attacker enters an out-of-range parameter or intentionally exceeds the buffer capacity of a system or application to effect a Denial of Service (DoS) or exploit a vulnerability.

Building Security In Maturity Model (BSIMM): A maturity model for benchmarking software development processes.

bus (computer architecture): The logical interconnection between basic components in a computer system, including Central Processing Unit (CPU), memory, and peripherals.

bus (network topology): A network topology in which all devices are connected to a single cable.

business impact analysis (BIA): A risk analysis that, as part of a Business Continuity Plan, describes the impact to business operations that the loss of various IT systems would impose.

caller ID: The protocol used to transmit the calling party's telephone number to the called party's telephone equipment during the establishment of a telephone call.

caller ID spoofing: The use of a device or service to alter the caller ID of an outgoing call, used by callers to impersonate others for the purpose of perpetrating fraud. *See also* caller ID.

Capability Maturity Model Integration (CMMI): A maturity model for software development and other IT practices, including information security.

central processing unit (CPU): The electronic circuitry that performs a computer's arithmetic, logic, and computing functions.

certification: A formal methodology that uses established evaluation criteria to conduct comprehensive testing and documentation of information system security safeguards, both technical and nontechnical, in a given environment.

Certificate Authority (CA): In a PKI, the CA issues certificates, maintains and publishes status information and Certificate Revocation Lists (CRLs), and maintains archives. *See also* public key infrastructure (PKI).

chain of custody (or chain of evidence): Provides accountability and protection for evidence throughout that evidence's entire lifecycle.

Challenge-Handshake Authentication Protocol (CHAP): A remote access control protocol that uses a three-way handshake to authenticate both a peer and a server. *See also* three-way handshake.

change management: The formal business process that ensures all changes made to a system are properly requested, reviewed, approved, tested, and implemented.

choose your own device (CYOD): A mobile device policy that permits employees to select their preferred mobile device from a list of devices that have been approved by the organization.

chosen plaintext attack: An attack technique in which the cryptanalyst selects the plaintext to be encrypted and then analyzes the resulting ciphertext.

C-I-A: Confidentiality, integrity, and availability.

cipher: A cryptographic transformation.

Cipher Block Chaining (CBC): One of four operating modes for DES. Operates on 64-bit blocks of plaintext to produce 64-bit blocks of ciphertext. Each block is XORed with the ciphertext of the preceding block, creating a dependency (or chain), thereby producing a more random ciphertext result. CBC is the most common mode of DES operation. *See also* Cipher Feedback (CFB), Data Encryption Standard (DES), Electronic Code Book (ECB), Exclusive Or (XOR), *and* Output Feedback (OFB).

Cipher Feedback (CFB): One of four operating modes for DES. CFB is a stream cipher most often used to encrypt individual characters. In this mode, previously generated ciphertext is used as feedback for key generation in the next keystream, and the resulting ciphertext is chained together. *See also* Cipher Block Chaining (CBC), Data Encryption Standard (DES), Electronic Code Book (ECB), *and* Output Feedback (OFB).

ciphertext: A plaintext message that has been transformed (encrypted) into a scrambled message that's unintelligible.

circuit-switched network: Any of several telecommunications network designs that provide a dedicated physical circuit path between endpoints.

circumstantial evidence: Relevant facts that can't be directly or conclusively connected to other events, but about which a reasonable inference can be made. *See also* evidence.

civil (or tort) law: Legal codes that address wrongful acts committed against an individual or business, either willfully or negligently, resulting in damage, loss, injury, or death. Unlike criminal law, U.S. civil law cases are determined based on a preponderance of evidence, and punishments are limited to fines.

Clark-Wilson model: A formal integrity model that addresses all three goals of integrity (preventing unauthorized users from making any changes, preventing authorized users from making unauthorized changes, and maintaining internal and external consistency) and identifies special requirements for inputting data.

classification: The process of assigning to a document a security label that defines how the document should be handled.

closed system: A system that uses proprietary hardware and/or software that may not be compatible with other systems or components. *See also* open system.

cloud: Internet-based network, computing, and application infrastructure available on demand.

cloud access security broker (CASB): Systems used to enforce policy regarding the use of cloud-based resources.

cluster: A system or network configuration containing multiple redundant nodes for resiliency. *See also* active-active *and* active passive.

clustering (or key clustering): When identical ciphertext messages are generated from a plaintext message by using the same encryption algorithm but different encryption keys.

coaxial cable: A network medium consisting of a single, solid wire core that is surrounded by an insulation layer and a metal foil wrap.

collision domain: A portion of a network that would receive broadcast packets sent from one of its nodes.

common vulnerability scoring system (CVSS): An industry-standard method for determining the severity of a vulnerability identified by a vulnerability scan, penetration test, or other means.

container: A lightweight, standalone, executable package of a piece of software that includes everything it needs to run.

containerization: A virtualization technology in which multiple, isolated application instances (called *containers*) can exist in a single operating system instance.

COBIT: Formerly Control Objective for Information and Related Technologies. An IT controls and process framework developed by ISACA (formerly Information Systems Audit and Control Association).

code of ethics: A formal statement that defines ethical behavior in a given organization or profession.

code review: The examination of source code in order to identify defects.

cold site: An alternative computer facility that has electricity and HVAC, but no computer equipment located onsite. *See also* hot site, HVAC, *and* warm site.

Common Criteria: An international effort to standardize and improve existing European and North American information systems security evaluation criteria.

common law: A legal system, originating in medieval England, based on custom and judicial precedent.

community cloud: As defined by NIST, a cloud infrastructure "provisioned for exclusive use by a specific community of consumers from organizations that have shared concerns". *See also* cloud.

compensating controls: Controls that are implemented as an alternative to other preventive, detective, corrective, deterrent, or recovery controls.

compensatory damages: Actual damages to the victim including attorney/legal fees, lost profits, investigative costs, and so on.

Complex-Instruction-Set-Computing (CISC): A microprocessor instruction set architecture in which each instruction can execute several low-level operations. *See also* Reduced-Instruction-Set-Computing (RISC).

compliance: Conformance to rules including laws, regulations, standards, and legal agreements.

Component Object Model (COM): A platform-independent, distributed, object-oriented system for creating binary software components that can interact. COM is the foundation technology for Microsoft OLE and ActiveX. *See also* Object Linking and Embedding *and* ActiveX.

Computer Incident Response Team (CIRT) or Computer Emergency Response Team (CERT): A team that comprises individuals who are properly trained in incident response and investigation.

concealment cipher: A technique of hiding a message in plain sight. The key is knowing where the message lies.

concentrator: *See* hub.

conclusive evidence: Incontrovertible and irrefutable . . . you know, the *smoking gun*. *See also* evidence.

confidentiality: The concept of limiting access to information to subjects (users and machines) that require it.

confidentiality agreement: *See* non-disclosure agreement (NDA).

configuration management: The process of recording all changes to information systems.

content-distribution network (CDN): A system of distributed servers that delivers cached web pages and other static content to a user from the nearest geographic location to the user. Also known as a *content delivery network*.

continuing professional education (CPE): Training classes and other activities that further a person's skills and knowledge in a profession.

Continuity of Operations Planning (COOP): A blending of Disaster Recovery Planning (DRP) and Business Continuity Planning (BCP) into a single coordinated activity.

continual improvement: Practices that result in the gradual improvement of people, processes, and technology.

continuous monitoring: Real-time or near real-time examination of a process or system. *See also* monitoring.

control: A safeguard or countermeasure that helps avoid or mitigate a security risk.

control assessment: An examination of a control to determine its effectiveness.

control framework: An organized collection of controls.

copyright: A form of legal protection granted to the author(s) of "original works of authorship," both published and unpublished.

corrective controls: Controls that remedy violations and incidents or improve existing preventive and detective controls.

corroborative evidence: Evidence that supports or substantiates other evidence presented in a legal case. *See also* evidence.

countermeasure: A device, control, or action required to reduce the impact or probability of a security incident.

covert channel: An unintended communications path; it may be a covert storage channel or a covert timing channel.

criminal law: Defines those crimes committed against society, even when the actual victim is a business or individual(s). Criminal laws are enacted to protect the general public. Unlike civil law, U.S. criminal cases are decided when a party is guilty beyond a reasonable doubt and punishments may include fines, incarceration, and even execution.

criticality assessment: The part of a BIA that ranks the criticality of business processes and IT systems. *See also* Business Impact Analysis (BIA).

cross-frame scripting (XFS): *See* frame injection.

Crossover Error Rate (CER): In biometric access control systems, the point at which the FRR equals the FAR, stated as a percentage. *See also* False Accept Rate (FAR; or Type II Error) *and* False Reject Rate (FRR; or Type I Error).

cross-site request forgery (CSRF): An attack where an attacker is attempting to trick a victim into clicking a link that will perform an action the victim would not otherwise approve.

cross-site scripting (XSS): An attack where an attacker is attempting to inject client-side script into web pages viewed by other intended victims.

cryptanalysis: The science of deciphering ciphertext without using the cryptographic key.

cryptocurrency: A form of digital currency, such as Bitcoin, that uses encryption to control the creation of currency and verify the transfer of funds independent of a central bank or authority.

cryptography: The science of encrypting and decrypting information, such as a private message, to protect its confidentiality, integrity, and/or authenticity.

cryptology: The science that encompasses both cryptography and cryptanalysis.

cryptosystem: The hardware or software implementation that transforms plaintext into ciphertext (encrypts) and back into plaintext (decrypts).

cryptovariable (or key): A secret value applied to a cryptographic algorithm. The strength and effectiveness of the cryptosystem is largely dependent on the secrecy and strength of the cryptovariable.

culpable negligence: A legal term that may describe an organization's failure to follow a standard of due care in the protection of its assets and thereby expose the organization to a legal claim. *See also* due care.

custodian: An individual who has day-to-day responsibility for protecting information assets.

data classification: Policy that defines sensitivity levels and proper handling procedures for data at each level and in various handling scenarios.

data controller: An organization that directs the storage and processing of information, as defined by the European General Data Privacy Directive (GDPR) and other privacy laws.

data destruction: Any means used to remove data from a storage medium.

data dictionary: A centralized repository of information about data such as meaning, relationships to other data, origin, usage, and format.

data encapsulation: In networking, the wrapping of protocol information from the OSI layer immediately above in the data section of the layer immediately below. *See also* Open Systems Interconnection (OSI) model.

data encryption key (DEK): An encryption key used to encrypt and decrypt data. *See also* key encryption key (KEK).

Data Encryption Standard (DES): A commonly used symmetric key algorithm that uses a 56-bit key and operates on 64-bit blocks. *See also* Advanced Encryption Standard (AES).

Data Link Layer: Layer 2 of the OSI network model. *See also* Open Systems Interconnection (OSI) model.

data loss prevention (DLP): An application or device used to detect the unauthorized storage or transmission of sensitive data.

Data Over Cable Service Interface Specification (DOCSIS): A communications protocol for transmitting high-speed data over an existing TV cable system.

data remanence: Residual data that remains on storage media or in memory after the data has been deleted.

data retention: The activities supporting an organization's effort to retain data for minimum and/or maximum periods of time.

data warehouse: A special-purpose database used for decision support or research purposes.

database management system (DBMS): Restricts access by different subjects to various objects in a database.

data carrier equipment (DCE): A device used to establish, maintain, and terminate communications between a data source and its destination in a network. *See also* data terminal equipment (DTE).

data processor: An organization that processes information on behalf of a data controller, as defined by the European General Data Privacy Regulation (GDPR) and other privacy laws. *See also* General Data Protection Regulation (GDPR).

data protection officer (DPO): An individual responsible for the development and management of a data privacy program, as directed by the European General Data Privacy Regulation (GDPR) and other privacy laws. *See also* General Data Protection Regulation (GDPR).

data terminal equipment (DTE): A device that communicates with a DCE in a network. *See also* data carrier equipment (DCE).

decryption: The process of transforming ciphertext into plaintext.

deep packet inspection (DPI): An advanced method of examining and managing network traffic.

defense in depth: The principle of protecting assets by using layers of dissimilar mechanisms.

Defense Information Technology Security Certification and Accreditation Process (DITSCAP): A program that formalizes the certification and accreditation process for U.S. Department of Defense information systems.

demonstrative evidence: Evidence that is used to aid the court's understanding of a legal case. *See also* **evidence**.

denial of service (DoS): An attack on a system or network with the intention of making the system or network unavailable for use.

destructware: Malware that functions similar to ransomware, except that the attacker has no intention of extracting a ransom payment and, therefore, no decryption key is available to recover the encrypted data.

detective controls: Controls that identify violations and incidents.

deterrent controls: Controls that discourage violations.

DevOps: The culture and practice of improved collaboration between software developers and IT operations.

DevSecOps: The integration of security practices within DevOps. *See also* DevOps.

Diameter: The next-generation RADIUS protocol. *See also* Remote Authentication Dial-In User Service (RADIUS).

dictionary attack: A focused type of brute-force attack in which a predefined word list is used. *See also* brute-force attack.

Diffie-Hellman: A key-agreement algorithm based on discrete logarithms.

digital certificate: A certificate that binds an identity with a public encryption key.

Digital Signature Standard (DSS): Published by NIST in Federal Information Processing Standard (FIPS) 186-1, DSS specifies two acceptable algorithms in its standard: The RSA Digital Signature Algorithm and the Digital Signature Algorithm (DSA). *See also* NIST *and* Rivest, Shamir, Adleman (RSA).

digital subscriber line (xDSL): A high-bandwidth communications protocol delivered over analog telecommunications voice lines.

direct evidence: Oral testimony or a written statement based on information gathered through the witness's five senses that proves or disproves a specific fact or issue. *See also* evidence.

directory harvest attack (DHA): A brute-force technique used by spammers in an attempt to find valid email addresses in a domain.

discretionary access control (DAC): An access policy determined by the owner of a file or other resource. *See also* mandatory access control (MAC) system.

disk mirroring (RAID Level 1): When a duplicate copy of all data is written to another disk or set of disks.

disk striping (RAID Level 0): When data is written across multiple disks but doesn't provide redundancy or fault tolerance.

disk striping with parity (RAID Level 5): When data is written across multiple disks, along with parity data that provides fault tolerance if one disk fails.

distributed application: A software application whose components reside in several systems or locations.

distributed denial of service (DDoS): An attack where the attacker initiates simultaneous denial of service attacks from many systems.

Distributed Network Protocol (DNP3): A set of communications protocols used between components in process automation systems (for example public utilities).

DNS cache poisoning: A type of attack, also known as DNS spoofing that exploits vulnerabilities in DNS to divert Internet traffic away from legitimate destination servers to fake servers. *See also* domain name system (DNS).

DNS hijacking: An attack technique used to redirect DNS queries away from legitimate DNS servers. *See also* domain name system (DNS).

documentary evidence: Evidence that is used in legal proceedings, including originals and copies of business records, computer-generated and computer-stored records, manuals, policies, standards, procedures, and log files. *See also* evidence.

domain: A collection of users, computers, and resources that have a common security policy and single administration.

domain homograph attack: A type of spoofing attack in which the attacker uses similar looking keyboard characters to deceive computer users about the actual remote system they are communicating with, for example, by replacing a Latin O with a Cyrillic O in a website address.

domain name system (DNS): A hierarchical, decentralized directory service database that converts domain names to IP addresses for computers, services, and other computing resources connected to a network or the Internet.

domain name system security extensions (DNSSEC): Specifications for securing certain kinds of information provided by DNS as used on IP networks.

drive-by-download: Software, often malware, downloaded onto a computer from the Internet without the user's knowledge or permission. *See also* malware.

drug screen: A test for the presence of drugs and controlled substances, usually as a part of pre-employment screening. *See also* background check.

due care: The steps that an organization takes to implement security best practices.

due diligence: The prudent management and execution of due care.

dumpster diving: The process of examining garbage with the intention of finding valuable goods or information.

dwell time: The elapsed time between the onset of a security incident and the organization's realization that an incident has occurred (or is occurring).

dynamic application scanning tool (DAST): A tool used to identify vulnerabilities in a software application that works by executing the application and attempts various means to compromise the application.

dynamic link library (DLL): A type of file used in Microsoft operating systems that enables multiple programs to simultaneously share programming instructions contained in a single file to perform specific functions.

dynamic password: A password that changes at some regular interval or event.

eavesdropping: Listening to network traffic to obtain content or learn more about communications.

ECMAScript: A trademarked scripting-language specification standardized by Ecma International in ECMA-262 and ISO/IEC 16262.

edge computing: A method used to optimize cloud computing by processing data at the edge of the network, near the source of the data.

eDiscovery: *See* electronic discovery.

electromagnetic interference (EMI): Electrical noise generated by the different charges between the three electrical wires (hot, neutral, and ground) and can be *common-mode noise* (caused by hot and ground) or *traverse-mode noise* (caused by hot and neutral).

Electronic Code Book (ECB): One of four operating modes for DES. ECB operates on 64-bit blocks of plaintext independently and produces 64-bit blocks of ciphertext, and it's the native mode for DES operation. *See also* Cipher Block Chaining (CBC), Cipher Feedback (CFB), Data Encryption Standard (DES), *and* Output Feedback (OFB).

electronic discovery: A legal or investigative process in which a party produces relevant electronic data that is stored on its systems.

electronic protected healthcare information (ePHI): Any patient related health information as defined by HIPAA. *See also* Health Insurance Portability and Accountability Act (HIPAA).

electrostatic discharge (ESD): A sudden flow of electricity between two objects.

employment agreement: A legal agreement between an employer and employee that stipulates the terms and conditions of employment.

employment candidate screening: *See* background check.

employment termination: The cessation of employment for one or more employees in an organization.

encapsulation: The process of layering protocol information at different levels of a protocol stack.

Encapsulating Security Payload (ESP): In IPsec, a protocol that provides confidentiality (encryption) and limited authentication. *See also* Internet Protocol Security (IPsec).

encryption: The process of transforming plaintext into ciphertext.

end-to-end encryption: A process by which packets are encrypted once at the original encryption source and then decrypted only at the final decryption destination.

endpoint: A general term referring to a desktop computer, laptop or notebook computer, or mobile device.

enticement: Luring someone toward certain evidence after that individual has already committed a crime.

entitlement: Access rights assigned to employees based on job title, department, or other established criteria.

entrapment: Encouraging someone to commit a crime that the individual may have had no intention of committing.

escalation of privilege: An attack technique where the attacker uses some means to bypass security controls in order to attain a higher privilege level on the target system.

Escrowed Encryption Standard (EES): Divides a secret key into two parts, and places those two parts into escrow with two separate, trusted organizations. Published by NIST in FIPS PUB 185 (1994). *See also* NIST.

espionage: The practice of spying or using spies to obtain proprietary or confidential information.

Ethernet: A common bus-topology network transport protocol.

ethics: Professional principles and duties that guide decisions and behavior. *See also* code of ethics.

European Information Technology Security Evaluation Criteria (ITSEC): Formal evaluation criteria that address confidentiality, integrity, and availability for an entire system.

evidence: Information obtained in support of an investigation or incident.

evidence lifecycle: The various phases of evidence, from its initial discovery to its final disposition. The evidence lifecycle has the following five stages: collection and identification; analysis; storage, preservation, and transportation; presentation in court; and return to victim (owner).

Exclusive Or (XOR): A binary operation applied to two input bits. If the two bits are equal, the result is zero. If the two bits are not equal, the result is one.

exigent circumstances: If probable cause exists and the destruction of evidence is imminent, property or people may be searched and/or evidence may be seized by law enforcement personnel without a search warrant.

expert system: A type of artificial intelligence system based on an inference engine (a program that attempts to derive answers) and knowledge base.

exploit: (1) Software or code that takes advantage of a vulnerability in an operating system (OS) or application and causes unintended behavior in the OS or application, such as privilege escalation, remote control, or a denial-of-service; (2) Action taken by a subject, system, or program that uses a vulnerability to gain illicit access to an object.

Exposure Factor (EF): A measure, expressed as a percentage, of the negative effect or impact that a realized threat or event would have on a specific asset.

Extensible Authentication Protocol (EAP): A remote access control protocol that implements various authentication mechanisms, including MD5, S/Key, generic token cards, and digital certificates. Often used in wireless networks.

extranet: An intranet that has been extended to include external parties, such as customers, partners, and suppliers. *See also* intranet.

Fagan inspection: A structured process that is used to find defects in design documents, specifications, and source code.

fail closed: A control failure that results in all accesses being blocked.

fail open: A control failure that results in all accesses being permitted.

failover: A failure mode in which the system automatically transfers processing to a hot backup component, such as a clustered server, if a hardware or software failure is detected.

fail-safe: A failure mode in which program execution is terminated, and the system is protected from compromise, if a hardware or software failure is detected.

fail-soft (or resilient): A failure mode in which certain, noncritical processing is terminated, and the computer or network continues to function in a degraded mode, if a hardware or software failure is detected.

False Accept Rate (FAR; or Type II Error): In biometric access control systems, the percentage of unauthorized users who are incorrectly granted access. *See also* Crossover Error Rate (CER) *and* False Reject Rate (FRR; or Type I Error).

False Reject Rate (FRR; or Type I Error): In biometric access control systems, the percentage of authorized users who are incorrectly denied access. *See also* Crossover Error Rate (CER) *and* False Accept Rate (FAR; or Type II Error).

fault: Momentary loss of electric power.

fault-tolerant: A system that continues to operate after the failure of a computer or network component.

Federal Information Processing Standard (FIPS): Standards and guidelines published by the U.S. National Institute of Standards and Technology (NIST) for federal computer systems. *See also* NIST.

federated identity management: A system whereby multiple organizations share a common identity management system.

FedRAMP: The required process for U.S. federal government agencies when procuring cloud-based services.

Fiber Distributed Data Interface (FDDI): A star topology, token-passing, network transport protocol.

fiber optic cable: A network medium consisting of glass or plastic strands that carry light signals.

Fibre Channel over Ethernet (FCoE): A communications protocol that encapsulates Fibre Channel frames over 10 Gigabit Ethernet (or faster) networks.

firewall: A device or program that controls traffic flow between networks.

firmware: A program or code that's stored in ROM memory.

first aid: Techniques used to treat injuries to personnel prior to receiving medical care.

forensics (or computer forensics): The science of conducting a computer crime investigation in order to determine what's happened and who's responsible for what's happened. One major component of computer forensics involves collecting legally admissible evidence for use in a computer crime case.

frame injection: An attack where the attacker is attempting to load arbitrary code into a browser in order to steal data from other frames in the browser session.

frame relay (FR): A packet-switched network protocol used to transport WAN communications.

fraud: Any deceptive or misrepresented activity that results in illicit personal gain.

fuzzing: A software testing technique in which many different combinations of input strings are fed to a program in an attempt to elicit unexpected behavior.

fuzzy logic: An artificial intelligence method that's used to address uncertain situations to determine whether a given condition is true or false.

gateway: A system, connected to a network, which performs any real-time translation or interface function; for example, a system that converts Exchange email to Lotus Notes email.

General Data Protection Regulation (GDPR): Strengthens data protection for European Union (EU) citizens and addresses the export of personal data outside the EU.

global positioning system (GPS): A U.S. government-owned global system of satellites that provide geolocation and time information to GPS receivers anywhere on or near Earth where there is an unobstructed line of sight to four or more GPS satellites.

goals: Specific milestones that an organization hopes to accomplish.

governance: Policies and processes that ensure that executive management is fully informed and in control of some aspect of an organization.

gray-box testing: A security test wherein the tester has some prior knowledge of the system being tested.

guest: (1) An instantiation of an operating system within a virtual environment. *See also* virtualization; (2) A visitor in a commercial work facility.

guidelines: Similar to standards, but considered recommendations, rather than compulsory requirements.

hacktivist: An individual who attacks organizations' systems based on ideological motivations.

hardening standard: A written document describing security configuration settings for applicable systems.

hardware: The physical components in a computer system.

hardware segmentation: The practice of isolating functions by placing them on separate hardware platforms.

hash function: A mathematical function that creates a unique representation of a larger set of data (such as a digest). Hash functions are often used in cryptographic algorithms and to produce checksums and message digests. *See also* message digest.

Health Insurance Portability and Accountability Act (HIPAA): A federal act that addresses security and privacy requirements for medical systems and information.

hearsay evidence: Evidence that isn't based on the witness's personal, first-hand knowledge, but was instead obtained through other sources.

hearsay rule: Under the Federal Rules of Evidence, hearsay evidence is normally not admissible in court. Computer evidence is an exception to the hearsay rule.

heterogeneous environment: A systems environment that consists of a variety of types of systems. *See also* homogeneous environment.

hidden code: An attack in which secret (and usually malicious) computer code is embedded within another program.

High-Speed Serial Interface (HSSI): A point-to-point WAN connection protocol.

homogeneous environment: A systems environment that consists largely of one type of system. *See also* heterogeneous environment.

honeynet: A large deployment of honeypots. Also referred to as a *honeyfarm*. *See also* honeypot.

honeypot: A decoy system deployed by a security administrator to discover the attack methods of potential hackers.

host-based intrusion detection system (HIDS): An intrusion detection system designed to detect intrusions through examination of activities on a host system. *See also* intrusion detection system.

hot site: A fully configured alternative computer facility that has electrical power, HVAC, and functioning file/print servers and workstations. *See also* cold site, HVAC, *and* warm site.

hub: A network device used to connect several LAN devices together. Also known as a *concentrator*.

hybrid cloud: As defined by NIST, a cloud infrastructure composed of "two or more distinct cloud infrastructures (private, community, or public)".

hypertext transfer protocol (HTTP): An application protocol used to transfer data between web servers and web browsers.

hypertext transfer protocol secure (HTTPS): The HTTP protocol encrypted with SSL or TLS. *See also* hypertext transfer protocol.

hypervisor: In a virtualized environment, the supervisory program that controls allocation of resources and access to communications and peripheral devices. *See also* virtualization.

Infrastructure-as-a-Service (IaaS): As defined by NIST, "the capability provided to the consumer to provision processing, storage, networks, and other fundamental computing resources where the consumer is able to deploy and run arbitrary software, which can include operating systems and applications."

identification: The means by which a user claims a specific, unproven identity to a system. *See also* authentication.

identity and access management (IAM): The processes and procedures that support the lifecycle of people's identities and access privileges in an organization.

identity as a service: A centralized, usually external, service provider that provides tools for user identification.

identity management: The processes and procedures that support the lifecycle of people's identities in an organization.

inactivity timeout: A mechanism that locks, suspends, or logs off a user after a pre-determined period of inactivity.

indicators of compromise (IOCs): An artifact observed on a network or in an operating system that is likely to be associated with a breach attempt.

industrial control system (ICS): Systems and devices used to monitor and/or control industrial machinery.

inference: The ability of users to figure out information about data at a sensitivity level for which they're not authorized.

inference channel: A link that allows inference to occur.

inference engine: An artificial intelligence system that derives answers from a knowledge base.

information custodian (or custodian): The individual who has the day-to-day responsibility of protecting information assets.

information flow model: A lattice-based model in which each object is assigned a security class and value, and their direction of flow is controlled by a security policy.

information owner (or owner): The individual who decides who's allowed access to a file and what privileges are granted.

information security management system (ISMS): A set of processes and activities used to manage an information security program in an organization. ISMS is defined in ISO/IEC 27001.

injection attack: An attack against a system involving the use of malicious input.

inrush: Initial electric power surge experienced when electrical equipment is turned on.

Institute of Electrical and Electronics Engineers (IEEE): A technical professional organization that promotes the advancement of technology.

Integrated Services Digital Network (ISDN): A low-bandwidth communications protocol that operates over analog telecommunications voice lines.

integrity: Safeguards the accuracy and completeness of information and processing methods, and ensures that

>> Modifications to data aren't made by unauthorized users or processes.

>> Unauthorized modifications to data aren't made by authorized users or processes.

>> Data is internally and externally consistent, meaning a given input produces an expected output.

intellectual property: Includes patents, trademarks, copyrights, and trade secrets.

International Electrotechnical Commission (IEC): A standards organization that defines and publishes international standards for electrical, electronic, and related technologies.

International Organization for Standardization (ISO): An international body for creating standards. ISO is derived from the Greek word *isos,* meaning "equal."

International Telecommunications Union (ITU): A United Nations agency responsible for coordinating worldwide telecommunications operations and services.

Internet: The worldwide, publicly accessible network that connects the networks of organizations.

Internet Control Message Protocol (ICMP): An Internet Protocol used to transmit diagnostic messages.

Internet Engineering Task Force (IETF): An international, membership-based, nonprofit organization that develops and promotes voluntary Internet standards.

Internet Layer: Layer 2 of the TCP/IP model. *See also* TCP/IP model.

Internet of Things (IoT): The network of physical smart, connected objects that are embedded with electronics, software, sensors, and network connectivity.

Internet Protocol (IP): The Open Systems Interconnection (OSI) Layer 3 protocol that's the basis of the modern Internet.

Internet Protocol Security (IPsec): An IETF open-standard Virtual Private Network (VPN) protocol for secure communications over local area networks (LANs), wide area networks (WANs), and public IP-based networks.

Internet Relay Chat (IRC): An application layer protocol that facilitates communication in text form using a client-server network.

Internet Small Computer Systems Interface (iSCSI): A communications protocol that enables SCSI commands to be sent over LANs, WANs, or the Internet.

Internetwork Packet Exchange (IPX): A network packet-oriented protocol that's the basis for Novell Netware networks. IPX is analogous to IP.

intranet: An organization's private network that's used to securely share information among the organization's employees.

intrusion detection system (IDS): A hardware or software application that detects and reports on suspected network or host intrusions.

intrusion prevention system (IPS): A hardware or software application that both detects and blocks suspected network or host intrusions.

IT Infrastructure Library (ITIL): An industry standard of IT service management processes.

JavaScript: A high-level, dynamic, lightweight interpreted programming language used to make web pages interactive and provide online programs.

JScript: Microsoft's dialect of the ECMAScript standard that is used in Microsoft's Internet Explorer. *See also* ECMAScript.

job description: A formal description of a position's roles and responsibilities.

job rotation: The practice of moving employees from one position to another, for cross-training and security reasons.

Kerberos: A ticket-based authentication protocol, in which "tickets" are used to identify users, developed at the Massachusetts Institute of Technology (MIT).

key encryption key (KEK): An encryption key used to encrypt and decrypt a data encryption key (DEK). *See also* data encryption key (DEK).

key logging: The practice of recording keystrokes, usually for illicit purposes, such as acquiring user IDs, passwords, and other confidential information.

key performance indicator (KPI): A measurable value that evaluates how successful an organization is in achieving a specific objective or activity.

key risk indicator (KRI): A metric used to indicate the level of risk associated with a particular activity or course of action.

known-plaintext attack: An attack technique in which the cryptanalyst has a given plaintext message and the resulting ciphertext.

KryptoKnight: A ticket-based single sign-on (SSO) authentication system, in which "tickets" are used to identify users, developed by IBM.

lattice-based access controls: A method for implementing mandatory access controls in which a mathematical structure defines greatest lower-bound and least upper-bound values for a pair of elements: for example, subject and object.

Layer 2 Forwarding Protocol (L2F): A Virtual Private Network (VPN) protocol similar to Point-to-Point Tunneling Protocol (PPTP).

Layer 2 Tunneling Protocol (L2TP): A Virtual Private Network (VPN) protocol similar to Point-to-Point Tunneling Protocol (PPTP) and Layer 2 Forwarding Protocol (L2F).

least privilege: A principle requiring that a subject is granted only the minimum privileges necessary to perform an assigned task.

Lightweight Directory Access Protocol (LDAP): An Internet Protocol (IP) and data storage model that supports authentication and directory functions.

link encryption: Packet encryption and decryption at every node along the network path; requires each node to have separate key pairs for its upstream and downstream neighbors.

Link Layer: Layer 1 of the TCP/IP model. *See also* TCP/IP model.

live forensics: Techniques used to gather forensic information from a running system.

log review: The examination of a system or event log.

logic bomb: A program, or portion thereof, designed to perform some malicious function when a predetermined circumstance occurs. *See also* malware.

machine learning (ML): A method of data analysis that enables computers to analyze a data set and automatically perform actions based on the results without being explicitly programmed.

maintenance hook: A backdoor that allows a software developer or vendor to bypass access control mechanisms in order to perform maintenance. These backdoors are often well known and pose a significant security threat if not properly secured.

malware: Malicious software that typically damages, takes control of, or collects information from a computer. This classification of software broadly includes viruses, worms, ransomware Trojan horses, logic bombs, spyware, and (to a lesser extent) adware.

managed security service (MSS): Security-related services provided by a service provider, typically involving monitoring or management of information systems.

management review: Activities whereby management reviews a program or process.

mandatory access control (MAC) system: A type of access control system in which the access policy is determined by the system, rather than by the owner. *See also* discretionary access control (DAC).

man-in-the-browser attack: A type of attack in which an attacker tricks a user into installing a browser helper object that acts as a proxy to eavesdrop on traffic or alter it.

man-in-the-middle attack: A type of attack in which an attacker intercepts messages between two parties and forwards a modified version of the original message.

mantrap: A physical access control method consisting of a double set of locked doors or turnstiles, to prevent tailgating. *See also* bollard *and* sally port.

manual controls: Controls that are not performed automatically and, therefore, require human action.

maturity model: A technique used to assess the maturity of an organization and the capability of its processes.

maximum tolerable downtime (MTD): An extension of a Criticality Assessment that specifies the maximum period of time that a given business process can be inoperative before experiencing unacceptable consequences. *See also* criticality assessment.

maximum tolerable outage (MTO): The maximum period of time that a given business process can be operating in emergency or alternate processing mode.

maximum tolerable period of disruption (MTPD): *See* maximum tolerable downtime (MTD).

media controls: Controls that are used to manage information classification and physical media.

meet-in-the-middle attack: A type of attack in which an attacker encrypts known plaintext with each possible key on one end, decrypts the corresponding ciphertext with each possible key, and then compares the results *in the middle*.

memory addressing: The method used by the Central Processing Unit (CPU) to access the contents of memory.

memory leak: A software defect that results in a program continuing to allocate memory.

memory space: The amount of memory available in a computer system.

message digest: A condensed representation of a message that is produced by using a one-way hash function. *See also* **hash function.**

metadata: "Data about data" that may present a security risk by revealing private information about a document or its history.

metamorphism: A technique used in a virus to change its appearance in host programs without necessarily depending on encryption. The difference in appearance comes from changes made by the virus to its own body. *See also* polymorphism.

metropolitan area network (MAN): A network that extends across a large area, such as a city.

MIME Object Security Services (MOSS): Provides confidentiality, integrity, identification and authentication, and non-repudiation by using MD2 or MD5, RSA asymmetric keys, and DES. *See also* Data Encryption Standard (DES), Multipurpose Internet Mail Extensions (MIME), *and* Rivest, Shamir, Adleman (RSA).

mission statement: A statement that defines an organization's (or organizational unit's) reason for existence.

mobile app: An application that runs on a mobile device and has the capability to interact with the user, communicate over the Internet, and store data locally.

mobile device: A general term encompassing all smaller devices such as smartphones, phablets, and tablet computers, which run operating systems such as iOS, Android, and Windows 10.

mobile device management (MDM): Software used to manage the administration of mobile devices such as smartphones, phablets, and tablets.

monitoring: Activities that verify processes, procedures, and systems.

monoalphabetic substitution: A cryptographic system that uses a single alphabet to encrypt and decrypt an entire message.

multicast: A type of network protocol whereby packets are sent from a source to multiple destinations.

multi-factor authentication: Any authentication mechanism that requires two or more of the following factors: *something you know, something you have, something you are.*

multi-level system: A single computer system that handles multiple classification levels between subjects and objects.

multiprocessing: A system that executes multiple programs on multiple processors simultaneously.

multiprogramming: A system that alternates execution of multiple programs on a single processor.

multi-protocol label switching (MPLS): An extremely fast method of forwarding packets through a network by using labels inserted between Layer 2 and Layer 3 headers in the packet.

Multipurpose Internet Mail Extensions (MIME): An IETF standard that defines the format for messages that are exchanged between email systems over the Internet. *See also* IETF.

multitasking: A system that alternates execution of multiple subprograms or tasks on a single processor.

National Computer Security Center (NCSC): A U.S. government organization, within the National Security Agency (NSA), that is responsible for evaluating computing equipment and applications that are used to process classified data.

National Information Assurance Certification and Accreditation Process (NIACAP): Formalizes the certification and accreditation process for U.S. government national security information systems.

National Institute of Standards and Technology (NIST): A federal agency, within the U.S. Department of Commerce, that is responsible for promoting innovation and competitiveness through standards, measurement science, and technology.

near-field communications (NFC): A wireless communications protocol that operates over distances of up to 10 centimeters.

need-to-know: A status, granted to an individual, that defines the essential information needed to perform his or her assigned job function.

Network Access Layer: Layer 1 of the TCP/IP model. *See also* TCP/IP model.

network address translation (NAT): The process of converting internal, privately used addresses in a network to external, public addresses.

network-based intrusion detection system (NIDS): An intrusion detection system designed to detect intrusions through examination of network traffic. *See also* intrusion detection system.

network interface card (NIC): An adapter that permits a computer or other system to be connected to a network.

Network Layer: Layer 3 of the OSI model. *See also* Open Systems Interconnection (OSI) model.

network penetration test: A penetration test that targets systems and network devices on a network. *See also* penetration test.

network sprawl: A phenomenon where virtual network elements are created, generally without approval or with limited planning and control, in an environment such as the cloud.

neural network: A type of artificial intelligence system that approximates the function of the human nervous system.

next-generation firewall (NGFW): A network security platform that fully integrates traditional firewall and network intrusion prevention capabilities with other advanced security functions that provide deep packet inspection (DPI) for complete visibility, accurate application, content, and user identification, and granular policy-based control. *See also* deep packet inspection (DPI) *and* intrusion prevention system (IPS).

non-compete agreement: A legal agreement in which an employee agrees not to accept employment in a competing organization.

non-disclosure agreement (NDA): A legal agreement in which one or more parties agrees to refrain from disseminating confidential information related to other parties.

non-interference model: Ensures that the actions of different objects and subjects aren't seen by, and don't interfere with, other objects and subjects on the same system.

non-repudiation: The inability for a user to deny an action; his or her identity is positively associated with that action.

object: A passive entity, such as a system or file.

Object Linking and Embedding (OLE): A proprietary Microsoft technology that allows embedding and linking to documents and other objects.

object reuse: The process of protecting the confidentiality of objects that are reassigned after initial use. *See also* Trusted Computer System Evaluation Criteria (TCSEC).

objectives: Specific milestones that an organization wants to perform in order to meet its goals. *See also* goals.

on-premises: Information systems, applications and data that is physically located in an organization's own information processing center.

one-time pad: A cryptographic keystream that can be used only once.

one-time password: A password that's valid for only one log-on session.

one-way function: A problem that's easy to compute in one direction but not in the reverse direction.

open message format: A message encrypted in an asymmetric key system by using the sender's private key. The sender's public key, which is available to anyone, is used to decrypt the message. This format guarantees the message's authenticity. *See also* secure and signed message format *and* secure message format.

open relay: A misconfigured Internet email server that permits cybercriminals to use it for relaying spam and phishing email.

open source: A software licensing methodology wherein source code is freely available.

open system: A vendor-independent system that complies with an accepted standard, which promotes interoperability between systems and components made by different vendors. *See also* closed system.

Open Systems Interconnection (OSI) model: The seven-layer reference model for networks. The layers are Physical, Data Link, Network, Transport, Session, Presentation, and Application.

operating system (OS): Software that controls computer hardware and resources and facilitates the operation of application software. *See also* application software.

Orange Book: *See* Trusted Computer System Evaluation Criteria (TCSEC).

Output Feedback (OFB): One of four operating modes for DES. OFB is a stream cipher often used to encrypt satellite communications. In this mode, previous plaintext is used as feedback for key generation in the next keystream; however, the resulting ciphertext isn't chained together (unlike with CFB). *See also* Cipher Block Chaining (CBC), Cipher Feedback (CFB), *and* Data Encryption Standard (DES).

outsourcing: The use of an external organization (third party) to perform some aspect of business operations.

Open Web Application Security Project (OWASP): An online community dedicated to web application security.

owner: An individual in an organization who's responsible for management of an asset, including classification, handling, and access policy.

Platform-as-a-Service (PaaS): As defined by NIST, "the capability provided to the consumer to deploy onto the cloud infrastructure consumer-created or acquired applications created using programming languages, libraries, services, and tools supported by the provider."

packet sniffing: A type of attack in which an attacker uses a sniffer to capture network packets and analyze their contents.

packet-filtering firewall: A type of firewall that examines the source and destination addresses of an incoming packet, and then either permits or denies the packet based on an ACL. *See also* access control list (ACL).

packet-switched network: Any of several telecommunications network technologies where packets transport data between sender and receiver.

passphrase: A string of characters consisting of multiple words, that a subject provides to an authentication mechanism in order to authenticate to a system. *See also* password.

password: A string of characters (a word or phrase) that a subject provides to an authentication mechanism in order to authenticate to a system.

Password Authentication Protocol (PAP): A remote access control protocol that uses a two-way handshake to authenticate a peer to a server when a link is initially established.

patch: A corrective fix for a program or system to correct a defect.

patch management: The use of procedures and tools to apply patches to target systems.

patent: As defined by the U.S. Patent and Trademark Office (PTO), a patent is "the grant of a property right to the inventor."

Payment Card Industry Data Security Standard (PCI DSS): Protects personal data related to credit, debit, and cash card transactions.

penetration test: A test involving automated and manual techniques that is used to identify potential software vulnerabilities. Also known as *pen testing*.

personal identification number (PIN): A numeric-only passcode, usually used when only a numeric keypad (versus an alphanumeric keyboard) is available. *See also* password.

Personal Information Protection and Electronic Documents Act (PIPEDA): Applicable to organizations that do business with Canadian citizens. Protects the privacy of personal information for Canadian citizens.

personally identifiable information (PII): Information (such as name, address, Social Security number, birthdate, place of employment, and so on) that can be used on its own or with other information to identify, contact, or locate a person.

pharming: A phishing attack that's targeted towards a specific organization. *See also* phishing.

phishing: A social-engineering cyber-attack technique widely used in identity-theft crimes. An email, purportedly from a known legitimate business (typically financial institutions, online auctions, retail stores, and so on), requests the recipient to verify personal information online at a forged or hijacked website. *See also* pharming *and* spear phishing.

physical controls: Controls that ensure the safety and security of the physical environment.

physical evidence: *See* real evidence.

Physical Layer: Layer 1 of the OSI model. *See also* Open Systems Interconnection (OSI) model.

plaintext: A message in its original readable format or a ciphertext message that's been properly decrypted (unscrambled) to produce the original readable plaintext message.

Point-to-Point Protocol (PPP): A protocol used in remote access service (RAS) servers to encapsulate Internet Protocol (IP) packets and establish dial-in connections over serial and Integrated Services Digital Network (ISDN) links.

Point-to-Point Tunneling Protocol (PPTP): A virtual private network (VPN) protocol designed for individual client-server connections.

policy: A formal high-level statement of an organization's objectives, responsibilities, ethics and beliefs, and general requirements and controls.

polyinstantiation: Allows different versions of the same data to exist at different sensitivity levels.

polymorphism: A technique used in a virus to change its appearance in host programs. For instance, it encrypts its body with a different key each time and prepends a decryption routine to itself. The decryption routine (known as the *decryptor*) is mutated randomly across virus instances, so as to be not easily recognizable. *See also* metamorphism.

port hopping: A technique used by applications to improve accessibility, but also used in cyberattacks to dynamically switch TCP ports to evade detection. *See also* Transmission Control Protocol (TCP).

port scan: A test used to determine which Transmission Control Protocol/Internet Protocol (TCP/IP) and User Datagram Protocol (UDP) service ports on a system are active. *See also* Transmission Control Protocol (TCP), Internet Protocol (IP), *and* User Datagram Protocol (UDP.

PowerShell: A task-based command-line shell and scripting language built on the Microsoft .NET framework.

prepared statement: A canned database command that can be called by an application.

Presentation Layer: Layer 6 of the OSI model. *See also* Open Systems Interconnection (OSI) model.

Pretty Good Privacy (PGP): A freely available, open-source email application that provides confidentiality and authentication by using the International Data Encryption Algorithm (IDEA) cipher for encryption and the RSA asymmetric system for digital signatures and secure key distribution. *See also* Rivest, Shamir, Adleman (RSA).

preventive controls: Controls that prevent unwanted events.

privacy: In information security, the protection and proper handling of personal information.

Privacy Enhanced Mail (PEM): A protocol that provides confidentiality and authentication by using 3DES for encryption, MD2 or MD5 message digests, X.509 digital certificates, and the RSA asymmetric system for digital signatures and secure key distribution. *See also* 3DES (Triple DES) *and* Rivest, Shamir, Adleman (RSA).

private cloud: As defined by NIST, a cloud infrastructure "provisioned for exclusive use by a single organization comprising multiple consumers". *See also* cloud.

private network address: Addresses on TCP/IP networks that are not routable on the Internet and are used for private, internal networks.

privilege creep: *See* aggregation (2).

privilege escalation: See escalation of privilege.

procedures: Detailed instructions about how to implement specific policies and meet the criteria defined in standards.

process isolation: An operating system feature whereby different user processes are unable to view or modify information related to other processes.

process table: The collection of processes that are active in an operating system.

promiscuous mode: A setting on a network adapter that passes all network traffic to the associated device for processing, not just traffic that is specifically addressed to that device. *See also* sniffing.

Protected Extensible Authentication Protocol (PEAP): An open standard used to transmit authentication information in a protected manner.

protected health information (PHI): Any information about a health status, provisioning of healthcare, or payment for healthcare collected by a covered entity (such as a healthcare provider or insurance company) that can be linked to a specific individual.

protection domain: Prevents other programs or processes from accessing and modifying the contents of an address space that has already been assigned to an active program or process.

protection rings: A security architecture concept that implements multiple domains that have increasing levels of trust near the center.

protocol data unit (PDU): The unit of data used at a particular layer of a communications protocol.

proximate causation: An action taken or not taken as part of a sequence of events that result in negative consequences.

proxy server: A system that transfers data packets from one network to another.

prudent man rule: Under the Federal Sentencing Guidelines, senior corporate officers are required to perform their duties in good faith, in the best interests of the enterprise, and with the care and diligence that ordinary, prudent people in a similar position would exercise in similar circumstances.

pseudo flaw: A form of social engineering in which the attacker attempts to trick people into performing certain actions to remedy a supposed security situation.

public cloud: As defined by NIST, a cloud infrastructure "provisioned for open use by the general public." *See also* cloud.

public key cryptography: A cryptographic method that permits parties to communicate with each other without exchanging a secret key in advance.

public key infrastructure (PKI): A system that enables secure e-commerce through the integration of digital signatures, digital certificates, processes, procedures, and other services necessary to ensure confidentiality, integrity, authentication, non-repudiation, and access control.

punitive damages: Determined by a jury and intended to punish the offender.

qualitative risk analysis: A risk analysis that expresses risks and costs in qualitative terms versus quantitative terms (such as high, medium, and low). *See also* risk analysis.

Quality of Service (QoS): The ability to prioritize various types of voice and data traffic based on operational needs such as response time, packet loss and jitter.

quantitative risk analysis: A risk analysis that includes estimated costs. *See also* risk analysis.

quarantine: A general term referring to the process of isolating a resource for security reasons.

race condition: A situation where two programs, processes, or threads are accessing or manipulating a resource as though they are doing so exclusively, thereby leading to an unexpected outcome.

radio frequency interference (RFI): Electrical noise caused by electrical components, such as fluorescent lighting and electric cables.

rainbow table: A database of hashes and their corresponding passwords.

ransomware: Malware that encrypts files on an infected server or endpoint and demands a ransom payment, usually cryptocurrency, to retrieve the key to decrypt the files. *See also* malware *and* cryptocurrency.

real (or physical) evidence: Tangible objects from the actual crime, such as the tools or weapons used and any stolen or damaged property. *See also* evidence.

recovery controls: Controls that restore systems and information.

recovery point objective (RPO): The maximum period of time in which data may be lost if a disaster occurs.

recovery time objective (RTO): The period of time in which a business process must be recovered (during a disaster) in order to ensure the survival of the organization.

Reduced-Instruction-Set-Computing (RISC): A microprocessor instruction set architecture that utilizes a smaller and simpler instruction set than CISC, which makes RISC more efficient than CISC. *See also* Complex-Instruction-Set-Computing (CISC).

reduction analysis: A step in threat modeling designed to reduce duplication of effort.

redundancy: Multiple systems, nodes, or network paths that provide the same functionality for resiliency and availability in the event of failure.

redundant array of independent disks (RAID): A collection of one or more hard drives in a system for purposes of improved performance or reliability.

reference monitor: An abstract machine (a theoretical model for a computer system or software program) that mediates all access to an object by a subject.

referential integrity: A property of a database management system in which all data relationships such as indexes, primary keys, and foreign keys are sound.

Registration Authority (RA): In a PKI, the RA is responsible for verifying certificate contents for the CA. *See also* Certification Authority (CA) *and* public key infrastructure (PKI).

remote access service (RAS): A remote access protocol typically used over dial-up facilities.

remote access trojan (RAT): A type of malware that controls a system via a remote network connection for criminal, malicious, or unauthorized purposes. *See also* malware.

Remote Authentication Dial-In User Service (RADIUS): An open-source, User Datagram Protocol (UDP)–based client-server protocol used to authenticate remote users.

remote backup: A backup operation where the target backup media is located in a remote location.

remote desktop protocol (RDP): A proprietary Microsoft protocol used to connect to another computer over a network connection.

repeater: A device that boosts or re-transmits a signal, in order to physically extend the range of a wired or wireless network.

replication: The process of copying data transactions from one system to another.

repository: In a PKI infrastructure, a repository is a system that accepts certificates and Certificate Revocation Lists (CRLs) from a CA and distributes them to authorized parties. *See also* Certification Authority (CA) *and* public key infrastructure (PKI).

Reverse Address Resolution Protocol (RARP): A protocol used by diskless workstations to query and discover their own IP addresses using machine addresses (known as a media access control, or MAC, address).

Rijndael: The encryption algorithm used by the AES. *See also* Advanced Encryption Standard (AES).

ring: A network topology in which all devices are connected to a closed loop.

risk acceptance: Accepting a risk or residual risk as-is, without mitigating or transferring it.

risk analysis: A method used to identify and assess threats and vulnerabilities in a business, process, system, or activity as part of a risk assessment. *See also* risk assessment.

risk assessment: A study of risks associated with a business process, information system, work facility, or other object of study.

risk assignment (or transference): Transferring the potential loss associated with a risk to a third party, such as an insurance company.

risk avoidance: Eliminating risk through discontinuation of the activity related to the risk.

risk-based authentication: A process where an information system presents authentication challenges that are commensurate with the user's security profile (for example, geo-location, device type, and so on).

risk management: The process lifecycle that includes risk assessment and risk treatment.

risk mitigation: Reducing risk to a level that's acceptable to an organization.

risk reduction: Mitigating risk by implementing the necessary security controls, policies, and procedures to protect an asset.

risk tolerance: The explicit or implicit level of risk that an organization is willing to accept.

risk transfer: *See* risk assignment.

risk treatment: The formal decision-making process for the management of identified risks.:

Rivest, Shamir, Adleman (RSA): A key transport algorithm based on the difficulty of factoring a number that's the product of two large prime numbers.

role-based access control (RBAC): A method for implementing discretionary access controls in which access decisions are based on group membership, according to organizational or functional roles.

rootkit: Malware that provides privileged (root-level) access to a computer. *See also* malware.

rotation of duties (or job rotation): Regularly transferring key personnel into different positions or departments within an organization.

router: A network device that forwards packets between separate networks.

routing protocol: A network protocol used by routers to communicate information about internetwork connections.

RSA: *See* Rivest, Shamir, Adleman

rule-based access control: A method for applying mandatory access control by matching an object's sensitivity label and a subject's sensitivity label to determine whether access should be granted or denied.

safeguard: A control or countermeasure implemented to reduce the risk or damage associated with a specific threat.

sag: A short drop in voltage.

sally port: A secure, controlled entrance to a facility.

sandbox: A mechanism for isolating a program or system.

Sarbanes-Oxley (SOX): Attempts to prevent fraudulent accounting practices and errors in U.S. public corporations and mandates data retention requirements.

scan: A technique used to identify vulnerabilities in a system or network, usually by transmitting data to it and observing its response.

scareware: A type of social engineering attack wherein a Trojan horse program or a browser popup is intended to trick the user into thinking that there is a security problem in their computer. The intended victim is asked or tricked to click a button or link to fix a security problem; in reality the consenting user is enabling malware to run on the computer.

screen saver: An image or pattern that appears on a display, usually as part of an inactivity timeout. *See also* inactivity timeout.

screening router: A firewall architecture that consists of a router that controls packet flow through the use of ACLs. *See also* access control list (ACL) *and* firewall.

script injection: An attack in which the attacker injects script code, in hopes that the code will be executed on a target system.

script kiddie: An individual that does not have any programming or hacking skills, but instead uses scripts, malware, exploits, and other hacking tools developed by others to attack an endpoint or network.

Scrum: A common implementation of the Agile systems development methodology.

secondary evidence: A duplicate or copy of evidence, such as a tape backup, screen capture, or photograph. *See also* evidence.

secure and signed message format: A message encrypted in an asymmetric key system by using the recipient's public key and the sender's private key. This encryption method protects the message's confidentiality and guarantees the message's authenticity. *See also* open message format *and* secure message format.

Secure Electronic Transaction (SET): A now obsolete protocol, developed by MasterCard and Visa to provide secure e-commerce transactions by implementing authentication mechanisms while protecting the confidentiality and integrity of cardholder data.

Secure European System and Applications in a Multivendor Environment (SESAME): A ticket-based authentication protocol similar to Kerberos, with additional security enhancements. *See also* Kerberos.

Secure HyperText Transfer Protocol (S-HTTP): An Internet protocol that provides a method for secure communications with a webserver. S-HTTP is now considered obsolete. *See also* hypertext transfer protocol (HTTP) *and* hypertext transfer protocol secure (HTTPS).

secure message format: A message encrypted in an asymmetric key system by using the recipient's public key. Only the recipient's private key can decrypt the message. This encryption method protects the message's confidentiality. *See also* open message format *and* secure and signed message format.

Secure Multipurpose Internet Mail Extensions (S/MIME): Provides confidentiality and authentication for email by using the RSA asymmetric key system, digital signatures, and X.509 digital certificates. *See also* Rivest, Shamir, Adleman (RSA).

secure shell (SSH): A secure character-oriented protocol that's a secure alternative to *telnet* and *rsh*. *See also* telnet.

Secure Sockets Layer (SSL): A deprecated transport layer protocol that provided session-based encryption and authentication for secure communication between clients and servers on the Internet. *See also* Transport Layer Security (TLS).

Security Assertion Markup Language (SAML): An XML-based, open-standard data format for exchanging authentication and authorization credentials between organizations.

security awareness: The process of providing basic security information to users in an organization to help them make prudent decisions regarding the protection of the organization's assets.

security control assessment (SCA): An examination of one or more security controls in an organization.

security engineering: A sub-specialty of engineering that focuses on security design and operations.

security information and event management (SIEM): A system that provides real-time collection, analysis, correlation, and presentation of security logs and alerts.

security kernel: The combination of hardware, firmware, and software elements in a TCB that implements the reference monitor concept. *See also* Trusted Computing Base (TCB).

security modes of operation: Designations for U.S. military and government computer systems based on the need to protect secrets stored within them. The modes are *Dedicated, System High, Multi-Level,* and *Limited Access.*

security operation center (SOC): A facility that provides information security monitoring, assessment, defense, and remediation for enterprise compute and network resources, including on-premises and cloud environments.

security perimeter: The boundary that separates the TCB from the rest of the system. *See also* Trusted Computing Base (TCB).

security posture: The level of risk in an organization based on its security practices.

segregation of duties: *See* separation of duties and responsibilities.

Sensitive but Unclassified (SBU): A U.S. government data classification level for information that's not classified but requires protection, such as private or personal information.

sensitivity label: In a MAC-based system, a subject's sensitivity label specifies that subject's level of trust, whereas an object's sensitivity label specifies the level of trust required for access to that object. *See also* mandatory access control (MAC) system.

separation of duties and responsibilities: A concept that ensures no single individual has complete authority and control of a critical system or process.

Serial Line Internet Protocol (SLIP): An early Point-to-Point Protocol (PPP) used to transport Internet Protocol (IP) over dial-up modems. PPP is more commonly used for this purpose.

service level agreement (SLA): Formal minimum performance standards for systems, applications, networks, or services.

service set identifier (SSID): The name used to uniquely identify a WiFi network.

session hijacking: Similar to a man-in-the-middle attack, except that the attacker impersonates the intended recipient instead of modifying messages in transit. *See also* man-in-the-middle attack.

Session Layer: Layer 5 of the OSI model. *See also* Open Systems Interconnection (OSI) model.

shoulder surfing: A social engineering technique that involves looking over someone's shoulder to obtain information such as passwords or account numbers.

simple integrity property: A subject can't read information from an object that has a lower integrity level than the subject (no read down, or NRD). *See also* Biba model.

Simple Key Management for Internet Protocols (SKIP): A protocol used to share encryption keys.

Simple Mail Transport Protocol (SMTP): A protocol used to transport email messages between email servers.

Simple Mail Transport Protocol over TLS: A protocol used to transport email messages between email servers with encryption. *See also* Secure Sockets Layer/Transport Layer Security (SSL/TLS).

simple security property (ss property): A subject can't read information from an object that has a higher sensitivity label than the subject (no read up, or NRU). *See also* Bell-LaPadula model.

single factor authentication: Authentication using only one of the following factors to gain access to a system: *what you know, what you have,* or *what you are.*

Single Loss Expectancy (SLE): Asset Value × Exposure Factor (EF). A measure of the loss incurred from a single realized threat or event, expressed in dollars. *See also* Exposure Factor (EF).

single sign-on (SSO): A system that allows a user to present a single set of log-on credentials, typically to an authentication server, which then transparently logs the user on to all other enterprise systems and applications for which that user is authorized.

SKIP: *See* Simple Key Management for Internet Protocols (SKIP).

smartphone: *See* mobile device.

smurf: A denial of service attack in which the attacker sends forged Internet Control Message Protocol (ICMP) echo request packets into a network with the intention of having large numbers of nodes on the network sending ICMP echo replies to the target system. *See also* denial of service (DoS).

sniffing: The practice of intercepting communications for usually covert purposes.

social engineering: A low-tech attack method that employs techniques such as dumpster diving and shoulder surfing.

socket: A logical endpoint on a system or device used to communicate over a network to another system or device (or even on the same device).

software: Computer instructions that enable the computer to accomplish tasks. *See also* application software *and* operating system (OS).

Software-as-a-Service (SaaS): As defined by NIST, "the capability provided to the consumer to use the provider's applications running on a cloud infrastructure."

Software Assurance Maturity Model (SAMM): A maturity model for software development.

software-defined networking (SDN): A computer networking approach that abstracts higher-level network functionality from the underlying physical infrastructure.

software development lifecycle (SDLC): The business-level process used to develop and maintain software. *See also* systems development lifecycle (SDLC).

software escrow agreement: A legal agreement between a software manufacturer and its customer(s) wherein the software manufacturer will maintain a copy of its original software source code with a third-party software escrow company. In the event the software manufacturer ceases to operate as a going concern (or other events defined in the software escrow agreement), the software escrow company will release the original source code to the customers that are a party to the software escrow agreement.

source code: Human-readable machine instructions that are the basis of system and application software.

source code repository: A system used to store, manage, and protect application or system software source code.

source code review: *See* code review.

spam (or Unsolicited Commercial Email [UCE]): Junk email, which currently constitutes about 85 percent of all worldwide email.

spear phishing: A phishing attack that's highly targeted; for example, at a particular organization or part of an organization. *See also* phishing.

spike: A momentary rush of electric power.

SPIM: Spam that is delivered via instant messaging.

SPIT: Spam that is delivered via Internet telephony.

spoofing: A technique used to forge TCP/IP packet information or email header information. In network attacks, IP spoofing is used to gain access to systems by impersonating the IP address of a trusted host. In email spoofing, the sender address is forged to trick an email user into opening or responding to an email (which usually contains a virus or spam).

sprint: A short interval, usually two weeks, during which a development team develops features during a systems development project.

spyware: A form of malware that's installed on a user's computer, usually without his or her knowledge, often for the purpose of collecting information about a user's Internet usage or for taking control of his or her computer. Spyware increasingly includes keystroke loggers and Trojan horses. *See also* malware.

SQL injection: A type of attack where the attacker injects SQL commands into a computer input field, in hopes that the SQL command will be passed to the database management system.

SSL hiding: A technique that uses SSL encryption to hide the contents of network traffic, for example, to evade detection by network defenses while stealing sensitive data (known as data exfiltration). *See also* Secure Sockets Layer/Transport Layer Security (SSL/TLS)

standalone power system (SPS): An off-the-grid electricity system for generation, storage, and regulation, which is used in facilities that are not equipped with an electricity distribution system.

standards: Specific, mandatory requirements that further define and support high-level policies.

star: A network topology in which all devices are directly connected to a central hub or concentrator.

star integrity property (*-integrity property): A subject can't write information to an object that has a higher integrity level than the subject (no write up, or NWU). *See also* Biba model.

star property (* property): A subject can't write information to an object that has a lower sensitivity label than the subject (no write down, or NWD). *See also* Bell-LaPadula model.

state attack: An attack where the attacker is attempting to steal other users' session identifiers, in order to access a system using the stolen session identifier.

state machine model: An abstract model in which a secure state is defined and maintained during transitions between secure states.

stateful inspection firewall: A type of firewall that captures and analyzes data packets at all levels of the Open Systems Interconnection (OSI) model to determine the state and context of the data packet and whether it's to be permitted access to the network.

static application scanning tool (SAST): A tool used to identify vulnerabilities in a software application that works by examining the application's source code in search for exploitable vulnerabilities.

static password: A password that's the same for each log-on.

statutory damages: Mandatory damages determined by law and assessed for violating the law.

steganography: The art of hiding the very existence of a message; for example, in a picture.

stored procedure: A subroutine that is accessible by software programs, and which is stored in a relational database management system.

stream cipher: An encryption algorithm that operates on a continuous stream of data, typically bit-by-bit.

strong authentication: A means of authentication that requires two or more independent means of identification. *See also* two-factor authentication.

Structured Query Language (SQL): A computer language used to manipulate data in a database management system.

subject: An active entity, such as an individual or a process.

substitution cipher: Ciphers that replace bits, characters, or character blocks in plaintext with alternate bits, characters, or character blocks to produce ciphertext.

supervisor mode: A level of elevated privilege, usually intended for only system administration use. *See also* User mode.

Supervisory Control and Data Acquisition (SCADA): An industrial automation system that operates with coded signals over communication channels to provide remote control of equipment. *See also* industrial control system (ICS).

surge: A prolonged rush of electric power.

switch: An intelligent hub that transmits data to only individual devices on a network, rather than all devices (in the way that hubs do). *See also* hub.

Switched Multimegabit Data Service (SMDS): A high-speed, packet-switched, connectionless-oriented, datagram-based technology available over public switched networks.

symmetric key system (or symmetric algorithm, secret key, single key, private key): A cryptographic system that uses a single key to both encrypt and decrypt information.

SYN flood: An attack in which the attacker sends large volumes of Transmission Control Protocol (TCP) SYN (synchronize) packets to a target system. A SYN flood is a type of Denial of Service attack. *See also* Denial of Service (DoS).

Synchronous Optical Networking (SONET): A telecommunications carrier-class protocol used to communicate digital information over optical fiber.

synthetic transaction: A mechanized transaction executed on a system or application to determine its ability to perform transactions properly.

system access control: A control that prevents a subject from accessing a system unless the subject can present valid credentials.

system high mode: A state in which a system operates at the highest level of information classification.

system test (software development): A test of all of the modules of an application or program. *See also* unit test.

systems development lifecycle (SDLC): The business-level process used to develop and maintain information systems. *See also* software development lifecycle (SDLC).

tactics, techniques, and procedures (TTPs): An approach to cyber threat intelligence that analyzes the patterns and methods of a threat actor or group of threat actors to develop more effective security responses.

Take-Grant model: A security model that specifies the rights that a subject can transfer to or from another subject or object.

TCP/IP model: A four-layer networking model, originally developed by the U.S. Department of Defense.

teardrop attack: A type of stack overflow attack that exploits vulnerabilities in the Internet Protocol (IP).

technical (or logical) controls: Hardware and software technology used to implement access control.

telnet: A network protocol used to establish a command line interface on another system over a network. *See also* Secure Shell (SSH).

Terminal Access Controller Access Control System (TACACS): A User Datagram Protocol (UDP)–based access control protocol that provides authentication, authorization, and accounting.

termination: See employment termination.

third-party: An organization to which some portion of business operations are out-sourced. *See also* outsourcing.

threat: Any natural or man-made circumstance or event that can have an adverse or undesirable impact, whether minor or major, on an organizational asset.

threat modeling: A systematic process used to identify likely threats, vulnerabilities, and countermeasures for a specific application and its potential abuses during the design phase of the application (or software) development lifecycle.

three-way handshake: The method used to establish and tear down network connections in the Transmission Control Protocol (TCP).

token: A hardware device used in two-factor authentication.

token ring: A star-topology network transport protocol.

trade secret: Proprietary or business-related information that a company or individual uses and has exclusive rights to.

trademark: As defined by the U.S. Patent and Trademark Office (PTO), a trademark is "any word, name, symbol, or device, or any combination, used, or intended to be used, in commerce to identify and distinguish the goods of one manufacturer or seller from goods manufactured or sold by others."

traffic analysis: A method of attack in which an attacker observes network traffic patterns in order to make deductions about network utilization, architecture, behavior, or other discernible characteristics.

trans-border data flow: The transfer of electronic data across national borders.

transient: A momentary electrical line noise disturbance.

transitive trust: The phenomenon where a user inherits access privileges established in a domain environment.

Transmission Control Protocol (TCP): A connection-oriented network protocol that provides reliable delivery of packets over a network.

Transport Layer (OSI model): Layer 4 of the OSI model. *See also* Open Systems Interconnection (OSI) model.

Transport Layer (TCP/IP model): Layer 3 of the TCP/IP model. *See also* TCP/IP model.

Transport Layer Security (TLS): An OSI Layer 4 (Transport) protocol that provides session-based encryption and authentication for secure communication between clients and servers on the Internet.

transposition cipher: Ciphers that rearrange bits, characters, or character blocks in plaintext to produce ciphertext.

trap door: A feature within a program that performs an undocumented function (usually a security bypass, such as an elevation of privilege).

Trojan horse: A program that purports to perform a given function, but which actually performs some other (usually malicious) function. *See also* malware.

trusted computer system: A system that employs all necessary hardware and software assurance measures and meets the specified requirements for reliability and security.

Trusted Computer System Evaluation Criteria (TCSEC): Commonly known as the *Orange Book*. Formal systems evaluation criteria developed for the U.S. Department of Defense by the National Computer Security Center (NCSC) as part of the Rainbow Series.

Trusted Computing Base (TCB): The total combination of protection mechanisms within a computer system — including hardware, firmware, and software — that are responsible for enforcing a security policy.

Trusted Network Interpretation (TNI): Commonly known as the *Red Book* (of the Rainbow Series). Addresses confidentiality and integrity in trusted computer/communications network systems. *See also* Trusted Computer System Evaluation Criteria (TCSEC).

trusted path: A direct communications path between the user and the Trusted Computing Base (TCB) that doesn't require interaction with untrusted applications or operating system layers.

Trusted Platform Module (TPM): A hardware module in a computer that performs cryptographic functions.

trusted recovery: Safeguards to prevent the disclosure of information during the recovery of a system after a failure.

twinaxial cable: A network medium consisting of two solid wire cores that are surrounded by an insulation layer and a metal foil wrap.

twisted pair cable: A network medium consisting of four to eight twisted pairs of insulated conductors.

two-factor authentication: An authentication method that requires two ways of establishing identity.

unauthenticated scan: A vulnerability scan that does not log in to a device, system, or application during its search for exploitable vulnerabilities.

unicast: A type of network protocol whereby packets are sent from a source to a single destination node.

unified threat management (UTM): A security appliance that integrates various security features such as firewall, anti-malware, and intrusion prevention capabilities into a single platform.

uninterruptible power supply (UPS): A device that provides continuous electrical power, usually by storing excess capacity in one or more batteries.

unit test: A test performed on an individual source code module.

USA PATRIOT Act (Uniting [and] Strengthening America [by] Providing Appropriate Tools Required [to] Intercept [and] Obstruct Terrorism Act of 2001): A U.S. law that expands the authority of law enforcement agencies for the purpose of combating terrorism.

user: A person who has access to information and/or information systems.

user acceptance testing (UAT): Testing of systems and applications by end users so that they can verify correct functionality. Also, the environments where such testing takes place.

user and entity behavior analytics (UEBA): A process used to detect malicious activity and potential breaches or intrusions by creating a baseline of normal user and entity activity and analyzing anomalies.

User Datagram Protocol (UDP): A network protocol that doesn't guarantee packet delivery or the order of packet delivery over a network.

user entitlement: The data access privileges that are granted to an individual user.

user mode: A level of privilege, usually intended for ordinary users. *See also* Supervisor mode.

Vernam cipher: *See* one-time pad.

view: A logical operation that can be used to restrict access to specific information in a database, hide attributes, and restrict queries available to a user. Views are a type of constrained user interface that restricts access to specific functions by not allowing a user to request it.

violation analysis: The process of examining audit logs and other sources in order to discover inappropriate activities.

virtual desktop infrastructure (VDI): A desktop operating system running within a virtual machine (VM) on a physical host server.

virtual local area network (VLAN): A logical network that resides within a physical network.

virtual machine: An instantiation of an operating system running within a hypervisor.

virtual memory: A type of secondary memory addressing that uses both installed physical memory and available hard drive space to present a larger apparent memory space than actually exists to the central processing unit (CPU).

virtual private network (VPN): A private network used to communicate privately over public networks. VPNs typically utilize encryption and encapsulation to protect and simplify connectivity.

virtual reality (VR): A computer-generated three-dimensional (3D) image representation of an object or objects, which a user can interact with in a similar manner as real-world objects.

virtual tape library (VTL): A disk-based storage system that is used like magnetic tape storage for use in backup operations.

virtualization: The practice of running one or more separate, isolated operating system "guests" within a computer system.

virtualization (or VM) sprawl: The rapid creation of virtual machines without proper security and operations controls.

virus: A set of computer instructions whose purpose is to embed itself within another computer program in order to replicate itself. *See also* malware.

Visual Basic Script (VBScript): An Active Scripting language developed by Microsoft and modeled on Visual Basic.

Voice over Internet Protocol (VoIP): Telephony protocols that are designed to transport voice communications over TCP/IP networks.

VOMIT: Voice over Misconfigured Internet Telephone.

vulnerability: The absence or weakness of a safeguard in an asset, which makes a threat potentially more harmful or costly, more likely to occur, or likely to occur more frequently.

vulnerability assessment: The use of tools and techniques to identify vulnerabilities in an application, information system, facility, business process, or other object of study.

vulnerability management: The lifecycle process used to identify and remediate vulnerabilities in information systems.

vulnerability scan: The use of an automated tool or technique to identify vulnerabilities in a target system or network.

vulnerability scanning tool: A software program designed to scan a device, system, or application to identify exploitable vulnerabilities.

war dialing: A brute-force attack that uses a program to automatically dial a large block of phone numbers (such as an area code), searching for vulnerable modems or fax machines.

war driving: A brute-force attack that involves driving around, looking for vulnerable wireless networks.

warm site: An alternative computer facility that's readily available and equipped with electrical power, HVAC, and computers, but not fully configured. *See also* cold site, hot site, *and* HVAC.

waterfall: The software development process in which each phase is performed independently and in sequence.

watering hole attack: An attack on end-user browsers where malware is installed on a web server and downloaded to users' browsers.

web application firewall (WAF): A device used to protect a web server from web application attacks such as script injection and buffer overflow.

web content filter: A system or application that permits and blocks Internet access to websites based on a defined policy.

white-box testing: A security test in which the tester has complete knowledge of the system being tested.

whitelisting: A mechanism that explicitly permits access based on the presence of an item in a list.

Wi-Fi: A technology used for wireless local area networking with devices based on the IEEE 802.11 standards. *See also* Institute of Electrical and Electronics Engineers (IEEE).

WiFi Protected Access (WPA): A means of encrypting communications over 802.11 networks.

Wired Equivalent Privacy (WEP): A means of encrypting communications; specifically, 802.11/WiFi networks. WEP is obsolete.

Wireless Transport Layer Security (WTLS): A protocol that provides security services for the Wireless Application Protocol (WAP) commonly used for Internet connectivity by mobile devices.

work factor: The difficulty (in terms of time, effort, and resources) of breaking a cryptosystem.

worm: Malware that usually has the capability to replicate itself from computer to computer without the need for human intervention. *See also* malware.

X.25: The first wide-area, packet-switching network.

XML (Extensible Markup Language): A human- and machine-readable markup language.

Zigbee: A collection of high-level communication protocols for use in small, low-power personal area networks and smart home automation.

Index

American Society for Industrial Security (ASIS), 25, 30, 35

American Standard Code for Information Interchange (ASCII), 248

analog signaling, 277

analysis, 376, 386

analytic attack, 221

Annualized Loss Expectancy (ALE), 120, 466

Annualized Rate of Occurrence (ARO), 120, 466

anomaly-based endpoint protection, 293

anomaly-based IDS, 392

anti-malware, 411

antivirus software, 466

Anton Piller order, 385

applet, 466

application firewall, 467

Application Layer (Layer 7) (OSI Reference Model), 245–247, 467

Application Layer (TCP/IP Model), 279, 467

application penetration test, 363, 467

application programming interfaces (APIs), 317, 450, 467

application scan, 467

application software, 467

application state, 174

application virtualization, 309

application whitelisting, 293, 467

application-level gateway, 284–285

applications, 395

apprenticeship program, 140

archive, 220, 467

ARCnet, 264

area identifiers, 254

Arithmetic Logic Unit (ALU), 173

artificial intelligence (AI), 467

Asia-Pacific Network Information Centre (APNIC), 257

aspirating devices, 236

asset check-in/check-out log, 230

asset inventory, 394, 467

Asset Security domain
  about, 143
  classifying information, 143–146

determining data security controls, 151–153

determining ownership, 146–147

establishing handling requirements, 154

maintaining ownership, 146–147

protecting privacy, 148–149

retention, 150

supporting assets, 143–146

assets
  about, 117
  controlling physical and logical access to, 316–318
  defined, 467
  supporting, 143–146
  valuation of, 117–118, 129–130, 355, 467

Associate of (ISC)² certification, 33

assurance, 164, 166

asymmetric algorithm, 467

asymmetric algorithm cryptography. *See* asymmetric key cryptography

Asymmetric Digital Subscriber Line (ADSL), 267

asymmetric key cryptography
  about, 212–214
  Diffie-Hellman key exchange, 215, 476
  El Gamal, 215
  Elliptic Curve (EC), 216
  Merkle-Hellman (Trapdoor) Knapsack, 215–216
  RSA algorithm, 214–215

asymmetric key system, 467

asynchronous communication, 271

Asynchronous Transfer Mode (ATM), 268, 467

attack tree, 134

attacks, 221–222. *See also specific attacks*

attenuation, 275, 278

attestation, as a function of TPM, 181

attribute-based access control (ABAC), 352–353, 467

audit trail, 468

audits/auditing, 165, 377, 438, 444–445, 467

augmented reality (AR), 468

authenticated scans, 360, 468

authentication
  cryptography and, 196
  defined, 328, 468

integrating third-party identity services, 348

managing identification and authentication, 319–347

managing identity, 355–356

managing identity and access provisioning lifecycle, 355–356

preventing and mitigating access control attacks, 353–355

single sign-on (SSO), 319–327

identity fraud, in voice communication, 296

Identity-as-a-Service, 347–348, 483

ideological attacks, as a category of computer crime, 62

IETF, 258–259

illegal search and seizure, 382

implementation attack, 222

import/export controls, 74–75

inactivity timeouts, 344, 483

incident management, conducting, 407–409

indexed addressing, 178

indicators of compromise (IOCs), 483

indirect addressing, 178

indoctrination, to raise security awareness, 139

industrial control system (ICS), assessing and mitigating vulnerabilities in, 189–190, 317, 483

industrial espionage, as a category of computer crime, 60–61

inference, 484

inference channel, 484

inference engine, 484

information, 143–146, 316, 402

Information Assurance Support Environment (website), 170

information custodian, 484

Information Flow model, 162, 484

Information Lifecycle Management (ILM), 151–152

information owner, 484

Information Security Journal, 27

information security management system (ISMS), 484

Information Security Scholarship Program, 27

Information Systems Audit and Control Association (ISACA), 48, 437

Information Systems Security Architecture Professional (ISSAP), 33

Information Systems Security Engineering Professional (ISSEP), 34

Information Systems Security Management Professional (ISSMP), 34

Information Technology Act (2000) (India), 70

Information Technology Infrastructure Library (ITIL), 49–50, 407, 485

informative policies, 86

InfraGard (website), 30

Infrastructure as a Service (IaaS), 191, 483

inherent vulnerability, 201

initial cost, as an asset value element, 118

initialization vector (IV), 209

injection attacks, 449, 484

injuries, in disaster recovery (DR) plan, 418

input control, as a data integrity measure, 159

inquiry, as a control assessment technique, 127

inrush, 484

INSIGHTS (online magazine), 27

inspection, as a control assessment technique, 128

instant messaging (IM), 303

Institute of Electrical Engineers (IEEE), 484

Institute of Internal Auditors (IIA), 48

Institute of Management Accountants (IIMA), 48

insurance, 420

integrated product team, 439–440

Integrated Services Digital Network (ISDN), 268, 484

integrity, 52, 158–159, 196, 484

*-integrity property (star integrity property), 161

integrity verification procedures (IVP), 162

intellectual property, 72–74, 484

interface testing, 370–371

interfaces, types of, 277–278

interior walls, as a building design consideration, 227

Intermediate System to Intermediate System (IS-IS), 255

internal audit, 378

internal value, as an asset value element, 118

neural network, 489

next-generation firewalls (NGFWs), 288, 490

NIST Cyber Security Framework (CSF), 153

NIST SP800-37, 132

NIST SP800-53, 153

NIST SP800-171 Revision 1, 153

no write down (NWD), 160

nonce, 327

non-compete agreement, 490

non-disclosure agreement (NDA), 490

non-interference model, 162, 490

non-(ISC)2 certifications, 34–37

non-repudiation, 343, 490

non-technical/non-vendor certifications, 34–36

O

Oakley Key Exchange Protocol, 307

object, 180, 490

Object Linking and Embedding (OLE), 490

object reuse, 149, 163, 490

objectives, aligning security function to, 44–45, 490

observation, as a control assessment technique, 127

octets, 255–256

odd-parity bit, 208

omni-directional antennas, 272

one-time pad, 203, 490

one-time passwords, 335, 490

one-way function, 214, 218, 490

one-way hash function, 217

one-way hashing algorithm, 218

online business networking, 24

online orders, RPOs and, 104

online practice (website), 4, 12, 13

on-premises, 490

on-the-job training, 140

open message format, 490

open networkers, 24

open relay, 490

Open Shortest Path First (OSPF), 254

open source software, 447, 490

Open Study Group (website), 458

Open System authentication, 282

open systems, 182, 490

Open Systems Interconnection (OSI) Reference Model, 241–278, 491

Open Web Application Security Project (OWASP), 30, 369, 452, 491

OpenFAIR, 131

operating states, for CPUs, 174

operating system (OS), 179, 448, 491

operation, of software, 438–439

operational assurance requirements, 164

operational impact, risk management and, 124

operational requirements,, for investigations, 391

Operationally Critical Threat, Asset and Vulnerability Evaluation (OCTAVE), 131

Orange Book, 163–165, 491

organization, for exam, 457

organizational awareness, promoting, 110

organizational processes, 45–46

organizational value, as an asset value element, 118

orientation, to raise security awareness, 139

output control, as a data integrity measure, 159

Output Feedback (OFB) mode, 209, 491

outsourcing, 491

over-the-top (OTT) services, 296

ownership, determining and maintaining, 146–147, 491

P

packet sniffing, 354, 363, 491

packet-filtering firewall, 283–284, 491

packet-switched networks, 268–270, 491

pair programming, 368

pandemics, 418

parabolic antennas, 272

parallel test, of disaster recovery (DR) plan, 425–426

parity bit, 208

passive hubs, 278

passive IDS, 289

passphrases, 330–335, 491

prepared statement, 493

pre-purchased assets, 420

Presentation Layer (Layer 6) (OSI Reference Model), 247–248, 493

presentations, 139, 386

preservation of evidence, 386

Pretty Good Privacy (PGP), 300, 493

preventive controls, 125, 493

printed materials, to raise security awareness, 139

privacy, 75–76. See also specific privacy acts

Privacy and Electronic Communications Regulations of 2003 (U.K.), 70

Privacy Enhanced Mail (PEM), 246, 300, 493

privacy requirements compliance, 57–58

Private Branch Exchange (PBX), 295–296

private cloud computing, 191, 493

private key cryptography. See symmetric key cryptography

private network address, 493

privilege creep, 397, 493

privileged account management, 398–399

Privileged Attribute Certificates (PACs), 326–327

Privileged Attribute Server (PAS), 326–327

privileges, escalation of, 449, 493

problem state, 174

procedures, 85–87, 280, 493

Process for Attack Simulation & Threat Assessment (PASTA), 136

process isolation, 493

process management, as an operating system function, 179

process table, 494

product backlog, 435

professional ethics, 82, 83–85, 479

Programmable Read-Only Memory (PROM), 177

Project Management Institute (website), 35

Project Management Professional (PMP), 35

project plan. developing and documenting, 90–98

project scope, developing and documenting, 90–98

project teams, membership in, 90

promiscuous mode, 363, 494

proofing of identity, 344–346

*-property (star property), 160

protected computer, 64

Protected Extensible Authentication Protocol (PEAP), 494

protection domain, 177, 406, 494

protection of privacy, 345

protection rings, 183, 494

Protection Test Unit (PTU), 174

Protocol Data Unit (PDU), 251, 494

provisioning resources, 394–395

proximate causation, 494

proxy server, 284, 494

prudent man rule, 494

pseudo flaw, 494

public cloud computing, 191, 494

Public Company Accounting Oversight Board (PCAOB), 68

Public Company Accounting Reform and Investor Protection Act, 371

public key cryptography, 467, 494. See also asymmetric key cryptography

Public Key Infrastructure (PKI), 219–220, 494

Public Switched Telephone Network (PSTN), 266

public value, as an asset value element, 118

punishment, under criminal law, 53

punitive damages, under civil law, 54, 494

Purple Machine, 197

pursuit of excellence, 38–39

Q

qualification program, 140

qualitative asset value, 117

qualitative impact, of disasters, 98

qualitative risk analysis, 120–121, 494

quality of service, 415

Quality of Service (QoS), 494

quantitative asset value, 117

quantitative impact, of disasters, 98

quantitative risk analysis, 121–122, 495

quarantine, 495

question types, 18–19

quizzes, to measure effectiveness of security training, 141

R

U

W

wait state, 175

waivers, 11

walkthrough, of disaster recovery (DR) plan, 424

walls, 318

war, 416

war dialing, 361, 508

war driving, 362, 508

warm site, 97, 228, 413, 508

Warning icon, 4

water issues, 234

water protection, 96

water sprinkler systems, 236–237

waterfall model, 430–434, 508

watering hole attacks, 301, 508

wearables, 317

web application firewall (WAF), 285, 508

web communication, 300–302

web content filters, 290–291, 508

Web filtering, 410

web site security tools, 445

Web-based systems, assessing and mitigating vulnerabilities in, 193–194

websites. *See specific websites*

weighting, of questions in exam, 19

well-formed transaction, 162

wet-pipe system, 236

whaling, 298, 365

white-box testing, 508

whitelisting, 410, 508

wide area networks (WANs), 240–241, 266–271

Wi-Fi, 508

Wi-Fi Calling, 296

Wi-Fi networks, protecting, 281–282

Wi-Fi Protected Access (WPA/WPA2), 282, 508

Wired Equivalent Privacy (WEP), 281–282, 508

wired networks, protecting, 281

Wireless Access Points (APs), 272–273

wireless campus area network (WCAN), 243

wireless intrusion detection (WIDS), 392

wireless local area network (WLAN), 243, 265–266

wireless metropolitan area network (WMAN), 243

wireless network interface cards, 272

Wireless Networks For Dummies (Lewis and Davis), 266

wireless personal area network (WPAN), 242

Wireless Transport Layer Security (WTLS), 508

wireless wide area network (WWAN), 243

wiretaps, 382

wiring, as a building design consideration, 227

wiring closets, 229–230

work area security, 230

work factor, 222, 508

World Customs Organization (WCO), 72

World Intellectual Property Organization (WIPO), 72

World Trade Organization (WTO), 72

worm, 508

Write (W) access, 352

writing certification exam questions, 26

X

X (Execute) access, 352

X.21bis. ITU-T standard, 278

X25, 270, 508

Y

Yagi antennas, 272

Z

Zigbee, 508

About the Authors

Lawrence C. Miller, CISSP, has worked in information security and technology management for more than 20 years. He received his MBA from Indiana University and has earned numerous technical certifications throughout his career. He has previously worked in Vice President and Director level positions at several small to mid-sized companies in various industries. He served as a Chief Petty Officer in the U.S. Navy in various roles and is a veteran of Operations Desert Shield/Storm. He is the author of more than 130 other *For Dummies* Custom Edition books.

Peter H. Gregory, CISSP, CISM, CISA, CRISC, CCSK, CCISO, PCI-QSA, is the author of more than 40 books on security and technology, including *Solaris Security* (Prentice Hall), *Getting An Information Security Job For Dummies* (John Wiley & Sons, Inc.), *IT Disaster Recovery Planning For Dummies* (John Wiley & Sons, Inc.), and *CISA Certified Information Systems Auditor All-In-One Study Guide* (McGraw-Hill).

Peter is a career technologist and an executive security advisor at Optiv Security (www.optiv.com), the largest comprehensive pure-play cyber security solutions provider in North America. Prior to this, he held strategic security positions at Concur Technologies (www.concur.com) and in large wireless telecommunications organizations. He has also held development and operations positions in casino management systems, banking, government, nonprofit organizations, and academia since the late 1970s. Peter is the lead instructor and advisory board member for the University of Washington certificate program in information systems security and a graduate of the FBI Citizens' Academy.

Peter can be found at www.peterhgregory.com.

Dedication

From Lawrence C. Miller: To my wife, Michelle, and my sons, Eric and Ken.

From Peter H. Gregory: This one's for you, Mom.

Authors' Acknowledgments

Lawrence C. Miller would like to thank Amy Fandrei, Elizabeth Kuball, Peter Gregory, Peter T. Davis, and all the great people at Wiley.

Peter H. Gregory would like to thank Amy Fandrei, Acquisitions Editor at Wiley, for her guidance throughout this project. Thank you to Elizabeth Kuball for her help throughout this project. Subject matter expert Peter T. Davis showed much persistence that helped make the book much better. Thank you, Larry, for agreeing once again to coauthor this book. It's great as always to work with you on security books. Thank you, (ISC)², for your seal of approval — again, for this sixth edition.

There are many more people at Wiley and other organizations without whom this book could not be published and reach readers. I don't know who you are, but I know you are out there, and I am grateful for your dedication and hard work.

My contribution to this book would not have been possible without support from my wife, business manager and best friend, Rebekah Gregory. Thanks also to Carole Jelen, my literary agent, for guidance on this and other projects over the past 12 years.

Publisher's Acknowledgments

Acquisitions Editor: Amy Fandrei

Project Editor: Elizabeth Kuball

Copy Editor: Elizabeth Kuball

Technical Editor: Peter T. Davis

Production Editor: Magesh Elangovan

Cover Photos: © maxkabakov / iStockphoto

Take dummies with you everywhere you go!

Whether you are excited about e-books, want more from the web, must have your mobile apps, or are swept up in social media, dummies makes everything easier.

Find us online!

Leverage the power

Dummies is the global leader in the reference category and one of the most trusted and highly regarded brands in the world. No longer just focused on books, customers now have access to the dummies content they need in the format they want. Together we'll craft a solution that engages your customers, stands out from the competition, and helps you meet your goals.

Advertising & Sponsorships

Connect with an engaged audience on a powerful multimedia site, and position your message alongside expert how-to content. Dummies.com is a one-stop shop for free, online information and know-how curated by a team of experts.

- Targeted ads
- Video
- Email Marketing

- Microsites
- Sweepstakes sponsorship

20 MILLION PAGE VIEWS EVERY SINGLE MONTH

15 MILLION UNIQUE VISITORS PER MONTH

43% OF ALL VISITORS ACCESS THE SITE VIA THEIR MOBILE DEVICES

700,000 NEWSLETTER SUBSCRIPTIONS TO THE INBOXES OF

300,000 UNIQUE INDIVIDUALS EVERY WEEK

PERSONAL ENRICHMENT

     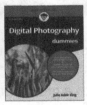

Staying Sharp	Facebook	Guitar	Investing	Beekeeping	Digital Photography
9781119187790	9781119179030	9781119293354	9781119293347	9781119310068	9781119235606
USA $26.00	USA $21.99	USA $24.99	USA $22.99	USA $22.99	USA $24.99
CAN $31.99	CAN $25.99	CAN $29.99	CAN $27.99	CAN $27.99	CAN $29.99
UK £19.99	UK £16.99	UK £17.99	UK £16.99	UK £16.99	UK £17.99

Meditation	Pregnancy	Samsung Galaxy S 7	iPhone	Crocheting	Nutrition
9781119251163	9781119235491	9781119279952	9781119283133	9781119287117	9781119130246
USA $24.99	USA $26.99	USA $24.99	USA $24.99	USA $24.99	USA $22.99
CAN $29.99	CAN $31.99	CAN $29.99	CAN $29.99	CAN $29.99	CAN $27.99
UK £17.99	UK £19.99	UK £17.99	UK £17.99	UK £16.99	UK £16.99

PROFESSIONAL DEVELOPMENT

Windows 10	AutoCAD	Excel 2016	QuickBooks 2017	macOS Sierra	LinkedIn	Windows 10
9781119311041	9781119255796	9781119293439	9781119281467	9781119280651	9781119251132	9781119310563
USA $24.99	USA $39.99	USA $26.99	USA $26.99	USA $29.99	USA $24.99	USA $34.00
CAN $29.99	CAN $47.99	CAN $31.99	CAN $31.99	CAN $35.99	CAN $29.99	CAN $41.99
UK £17.99	UK £27.99	UK £19.99	UK £19.99	UK £21.99	UK £17.99	UK £24.99

SharePoint 2016	Fundamental Analysis	Networking	Office 2016	Office 365	Salesforce.com	Coding
9781119181705	9781119263593	9781119257769	9781119293477	9781119265313	9781119239314	9781119293323
USA $29.99	USA $26.99	USA $29.99	USA $26.99	USA $24.99	USA $29.99	USA $29.99
CAN $35.99	CAN $31.99	CAN $35.99	CAN $31.99	CAN $29.99	CAN $35.99	CAN $35.99
UK £21.99	UK £19.99	UK £21.99	UK £19.99	UK £17.99	UK £21.99	UK £21.99

dummies.com

dummies
A Wiley Brand

Learning Made Easy

ACADEMIC

9781119293576
USA $19.99
CAN $23.99
UK £15.99

9781119293637
USA $19.99
CAN $23.99
UK £15.99

9781119293491
USA $19.99
CAN $23.99
UK £15.99

9781119293460
USA $19.99
CAN $23.99
UK £15.99

9781119293590
USA $19.99
CAN $23.99
UK £15.99

9781119215844
USA $26.99
CAN $31.99
UK £19.99

9781119293378
USA $22.99
CAN $27.99
UK £16.99

9781119293521
USA $19.99
CAN $23.99
UK £15.99

9781119239178
USA $18.99
CAN $22.99
UK £14.99

9781119263883
USA $26.99
CAN $31.99
UK £19.99

Available Everywhere Books Are Sold

dummies.com

Small books for big imaginations

GETTING STARTED WITH Coding
Get Creative with Code!

9781119177173
USA $9.99
CAN $9.99
UK £8.99

MODDING Minecraft™
Build Your Own Minecraft Mods!

9781119177272
USA $9.99
CAN $9.99
UK £8.99

MAKING YouTube® VIDEOS
Star in Your Own Video!

9781119177241
USA $9.99
CAN $9.99
UK £8.99

DESIGNING Digital Games
Create Games with Scratch!

9781119177210
USA $9.99
CAN $9.99
UK £8.99

GETTING STARTED WITH Raspberry Pi®
Program Your Raspberry Pi!

9781119262657
USA $9.99
CAN $9.99
UK £6.99

EXPERIMENTING WITH Science
Think, Test, and Learn!

9781119291336
USA $9.99
CAN $9.99
UK £6.99

CREATING Digital Animations
Animate Stories with Scratch!

9781119233527
USA $9.99
CAN $9.99
UK £6.99

GETTING STARTED WITH Engineering
Think Like an Engineer!

9781119291220
USA $9.99
CAN $9.99
UK £6.99

WRITING Computer Code
Learn the Language of Computers!

9781119177302
USA $9.99
CAN $9.99
UK £8.99

Unleash Their Creativity